Intermediaries, Interpreters, and Clerks

AFRICA AND THE DIASPORA
History, Politics, Culture

SERIES EDITORS

Thomas Spear
David Henige
Michael Schatzberg

Intermediaries, Interpreters, and Clerks

African Employees in the Making
of Colonial Africa

Edited by

Benjamin N. Lawrance,
Emily Lynn Osborn, and
Richard L. Roberts

THE UNIVERSITY OF WISCONSIN PRESS

The University of Wisconsin Press
1930 Monroe Street, 3rd Floor
Madison, Wisconsin 53711-2059
uwpress.wisc.edu

3 Henrietta Street, Covent Garden
London WC2E 8LU, United Kingdom
eurospanbookstore.com

Printed in the United States of America

Library of Congress Cataloging-in-Publication Data
   Intermediaries, interpreters, and clerks : African employees in
the making of colonial Africa / edited by Benjamin N. Lawrance,
Emily Lynn Osborn, and Richard L. Roberts.
      p.   cm. — (Africa and the diaspora)
      Includes bibliographical references and index.
      ISBN 0-299-21950-X (cloth: alk. paper)
      1. Africa—History—19th century.   2. Africa—History—1884–1960.
3. Europe—Colonies—Africa—Administration.   4. Europe—Colonies—
Africa—History—19th century.   5. Europe—Colonies—Africa—
History—20th century.   6. Colonial administrators—Africa—History.
7. Translators—Africa—History.   I. Lawrence, Benjamin Nicholas.
II. Osborn, Emily Lynn.   III. Roberts, Richard L., 1949-.   IV. Series.
      DT28.I57   2006
      324.6—dc22   2006008596

ISBN 978-0-299-21954-3 (pbk.: alk. paper)
ISBN 978-0-299-21953-6 (e-book)

Contents

The Maturing Phase of Colonial Rule, ca. 1920–1960

Afterword

Acknowledgments

Collaborative endeavors such as this volume emerge out of convergences of interests and institutions. Benjamin N. Lawrance, Emily Lynn Osborn, and Richard Roberts had been conducting research on the multiple meanings of the encounters between European colonialism and dynamic and changing African societies when we initially discussed the theme for the Eighth Stanford-Berkeley symposium on Law and Colonialism in Africa in 2002. Each of us had stumbled across archival traces of African intermediaries who had simultaneously served the colonial project while serving their own interests. We decided to make a call for papers on how African intermediaries contributed to the making of colonial legal institutions. The resulting conference, "Interpreters, Letter Writers, and Clerks: Meditating Law and Authority in Colonial Africa," featured papers that highlighted the wider roles of African intermediaries in the making of modern Africa. That theme became the focus of the current volume.

We wish to thank several of the original participants—Trevor Getz, James Hoover, Tim Lane, Moyisi Majeke, Louis Marquis, Tamba Mbayo, Arzoo Onsaloo, Ariana Killoran, and John Ademola Yakubu—whose papers do not appear in this volume, as well as Thomas McClendon and Roger Levine, who did not participate in the original symposium, but whose work on South Africa helps to flesh out the regional balance of this volume. We also wish to thank Stanford's Institute for International Studies, the dean of humanities and sciences, and the United States Department of Education's Title VI program support for the Joint Stanford-Berkeley National Resource Center for African Studies. The Institute for Scholarship in the Liberal Arts at the University of Notre Dame and the School of Humanities and Sciences at Stanford have also generously supported the production of this volume. We also offer special thanks to Adam Mehring and Barbara Wojhoski, who guided this project through production, and David Henige, Michael Schatzberg, and Tom Spear, whose rigorous intellectual guidance has greatly improved this volume and set high standards for their new series at the University of Wisconsin Press.

Intermediaries, Interpreters, and Clerks

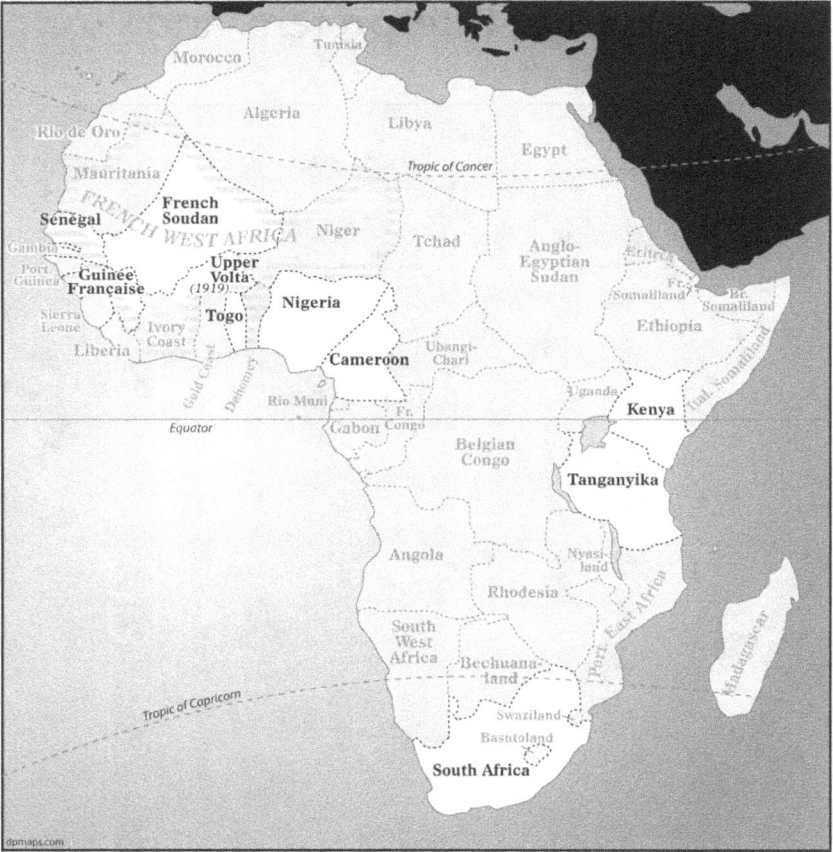

Map of Colonial Africa, ca. 1915

Introduction

African Intermediaries and the "Bargain"
of Collaboration

BENJAMIN N. LAWRANCE, EMILY LYNN
OSBORN, and RICHARD L. ROBERTS

In his autobiography Nelson Mandela explains that as a youth in South Africa his ambition was to become an interpreter or clerk. Although he was advised to study law, Mandela wrote, "I had my heart set on being an interpreter or a clerk in the Native Affairs Department. At that time, a career as a civil servant was a glittering prize for an African, the highest a black man could aspire to."[1] Among Mandela's predecessors in South Africa's politics of protest was Sol Plaatje, one of the founders of the South African Native National Congress, the precursor to the African National Congress. Plaatje spent years working as an interpreter in the frontier town of Kimberley in the 1890s. Plaatje was not only a court translator, but he also served as a cross-cultural broker. Among his many literary projects, Plaatje translated Shakespeare into Sethtswana and Tswana folktales and proverbs into English; he also produced an ethnography of the impact of the South African War on the Tswana.[2] In French West Africa in the early twentieth century, local populations referred to African employees of the colonial state as "white-blacks," a term that encapsulates their positions as representatives of

3

the white colonial state. Those Africans with the ability to mediate and bridge the gap between the colonizers and the colonized occupied important and sometimes powerful positions in colonial Africa. The goal of this volume is to examine the roles played by African employees in the making of colonial Africa

Africans in the lower ranks of the colonial bureaucracy often held positions that bestowed little official authority, but in practice the occupants of these positions functioned, somewhat paradoxically, as the hidden linchpins of colonial rule. African colonial employees bridged the linguistic and cultural gaps that separated European colonial officials from subject populations by managing the collection and distribution of information, labor, and funds. These intermediaries, who were almost without exception male, influenced colonial rule because they shaped the interactions of subject populations with European officials. African intermediaries did so as they translated, mediated, and recorded those interactions. In executing their duties as official representatives of the colonial state, these African employees consequently blurred colonial dichotomies of European and African, white and black, "civilized" and "uncivilized." At the same time, these men created key intersections of power, authority, and knowledge. Africans who rendered services to Europeans often strategically used their influence and authority to enhance their personal wealth, political power, and status. Although the roles of African employees in the construction and functioning of colonial states has been largely neglected in historical literature, an analysis of the conflicts, negotiations, opportunities, and constraints of their positions offers a fresh perspective on the nature of colonial rule.

Without exception the French, the British, the Belgians, the Portuguese, and the Germans relied on African colonial employees to help fulfill the day-to-day demands of administering their colonial empires. African interpreters, clerks, and secretaries proved indispensable to the colonial state, and Europeans' reliance on African employees complicated significantly the colonial project. The study of this cadre of employees engages a number of scholarly debates, including questions about the hegemony of colonial rule; collaboration and resistance; the invention of tradition; the production of knowledge and "expertise" in colonial settings; the role of language and education; and the relationship of colonialism to the production of differentiation by gender, race, status, and class.

In many ways African colonial employees acted as "silent informants," for colonial administrators often obscured the sources and routes of information on which they based official reports and assessments. Local people recognized that low-level employees served key roles in the operation of the colonial state, and evidence in the form of occasional scandals and periodic efforts to curtail malfeasance reveals that intermediaries often exerted influence in ways unanticipated by, ignored by, or unbeknown to Europeans. The competing pressures felt by Africans in colonial employment as well as the opportunities available to them because of their positions in colonial society illuminate the vernacular of colonial rule: the connotations and inflections that colonialism acquired in practice as it was negotiated by African elites, subject populations, and white officials and by the interpreters, clerks, and secretaries who mediated the encounters. The Africans who rendered crucial services to Europeans also acquired skills, knowledge, and situated authority with which they furthered their own strategies of accumulation.

Some Africans eventually filled senior appointments in the colonial administrations, but we are especially interested in the "junior clerks" of colonialism.[3] These Africans provided daily services central to the operation of colonies. Despite claims regarding the importance of native administration and "indirect rule" within British and also French colonial policy, the technical branches of colonial governments expanded throughout the era of colonialism and with them the numbers of Africans employed by the state. Africans eventually dominated the teaching profession in colonial Africa, and they became central to the technical services of the colonial state, such as the post and the telegraph, the railway, health services, forestry, mining, and so on. African dominance over the lower ranks of these technical divisions hints at the importance of examining changes in the structure of colonial rule and colonial bureaucracies. As the structure of the colonial state changed, so too did the opportunities for African intermediaries to accumulate wealth, political power, and status. The essays in this volume help to establish a chronology for interpreting the changing roles of African intermediaries in the colonial states of sub-Saharan Africa. Although the private sector counterparts of junior clerks also rendered similar services to European enterprises and missionary endeavors, we do not address these groups in this volume.[4]

Intermediaries and Colonialism

We recognize that Africans were employed in a wide range of service roles, including menial workers and skilled artisans, teachers and police, railway workers and "houseboys," forestry workers and nurses, but in this volume we focus on those Africans who served as interpreters and clerks, secretaries, and letter writers in administrative offices and courts. Numerous terms have been used to refer to Africans who worked in the employ of Europeans: "middle figures," "intermediaries," and "bureaucrats" are but three of them. In this introduction we refer to this cadre of employees as "African colonial employees" or "intermediaries" because these terms are laden with fewer negative connotations than other terms.[5]

African intermediaries might be described as collaborators, for they aided and abetted the expansion of the colonial state. Collaboration, in its simplest sense, means working together, and as such the term connotes a positive interaction. The term acquired its current pejorative character, however, partly as a consequence of World War II. Collaboration referred to the implicit or explicit act of cooperating with Nazi occupying forces in Europe. Moreover, as the field of African history emerged from anticolonial and nationalist struggles, it emphasized resistance to European imperialism. The term "collaboration" was contrasted with resistance and condemned as its antithesis.[6]

Focusing on intermediaries offers new insights into the old interpretative dichotomy of resistance and collaboration. A body of work produced in the 1960s and 1970s focused on African resistance to colonial rule, but few studies have examined the concept of collaboration. Notable exceptions include the work of Ronald Robinson and Shula Marks. Robinson alerted historians to the importance of collaboration for understanding colonial conquest and occupation. He argued that there could be no colonization without some forms of collaboration or implicit acceptance of colonialism. He noted that acts of collaboration could be passive or active and took place in administrative, commercial, educational, and ecclesiastical contexts. Furthermore, he described the "bargain of collaboration," in which collaborators exploited new opportunities to accumulate wealth, power, and prestige.[7] Marks explored what she described as varieties of dependence experienced by Africans working for the South African state. Marks, however, focused on the African chiefs and "intelligentsia" and left unexplored the rank and file of the colonial bureaucracy.[8]

More recently Colin Newbury has examined Robinson's "bargain of collaboration" between imperial societies and indigenous ones. Newbury sees "domestic bargains" appearing throughout the colonial world, in which a protective superior and an indigenous steward negotiated for "benefits of all kinds." Such domestic bargains were especially important in colonial contexts where sustained coercion was generally absent. "[T]he relationship between imperial powers and subordinate societies has always been a rich field for compromises in human interactions. In the long term, a degree of cooperation in the interests of colonial survival makes subordination bearable, if not agreeable."[9] Newbury describes the mutual dependency between imperial powers and indigenous rulers, but he overlooks the equally crucial roles of lower-level indigenous employees in the making of colonial rule. The social origins and cultural strategies of these employees influenced the shapes of the "domestic bargains" of colonialism.

This volume responds to the insights and challenges offered by Robinson, Marks, and Newbury and proposes an agenda for the social history of African intermediaries. Recognizing that African colonial employees were not simply lackeys of the colonial state, this collection of essays shows the importance of locating these figures within their respective social, economic, and political contexts. We are particularly interested in the changing meanings of the domestic bargains between Africans and the colonial state. As such this volume responds to a call made a decade ago by Frederick Cooper to overcome the binary of collaboration and resistance and to show that colonial rule was a complex process that cannot be explained through simplistic assumptions and identifications of "colonizer" and "colonized."[10] Instead, African intermediaries used the new opportunities created by colonial conquest and colonial rule to pursue their own agendas even as they served their employers. Studying intermediaries thus offers new insights into the old interpretative dichotomy of resistance and collaboration.

Colonial Hegemony

Any study of African colonial employees prompts a return to questions about the hegemony of the colonial state and its capacity to transform African peoples into colonial subjects. Historians, political scientists, anthropologists, and literary scholars have over several decades developed divergent analyses and interpretations of colonial rule. Most interpretations hinge on two overlapping sets of problems: Did the colonial state have the power to implement its policies consistently over time? And was colonial rule, especially native policy, coherent and coherently applied? These are linked questions, and both go to the heart of whether colonial states in Africa were strong or weak. The argument in favor of a strong state grew out of the relative ease of colonial conquest.

With a few celebrated exceptions, Europeans relatively easily won all
military contests with Africans. Success on the battlefield and superior
military might, however, did not mean that Africans accepted subsequent colonial authority or that colonial rule flowed seamlessly from
military might. Far from being hegemonic, the colonial state constantly
struggled with its own weaknesses and its contradictions. "In grappling
with these dilemmas," John Lonsdale and Bruce Berman write that in
Kenya, "the colonial state was obliged to intervene more directly in economic life than was characteristic of contemporary capitalist states."[11]

The history of the colonial state in Kenya in particular yields what
Berman has called the "two very different and apparently contradictory faces of the colonial state." On the one hand, there was the "weak"
colonial state: "the paternalistic mediator struggling to maintain a
precarious sovereignty over contending interests" and hobbled by inadequate resources and little coercive force. It had only a "facade" of
power. On the other hand, the "strong" colonial state continually expanded its bureaucratic apparatus and "intervened in ever-widening
areas of colonial political economy, directing change to serve the interests of metropolitan (or, in the case of Kenya, settler) capital, and containing and suppressing indigenous social forces." The colonial state,
Berman concludes, was a powerful instrument of political domination
and structural transformation, but one that constantly faced the "dialectic of contradictory forces that drove its development."[12]

Crawford Young has also examined the character of the African colonial state. If, as he argues, the state's performance up to World War II is
measured primarily by military challenges to its hegemony and its ability to secure local sources of revenue, then almost all colonial states in
Africa were "strong." They were so because they temporarily monopo-
lized the means of coercion and established few other expectations and
because Young measures challenges to hegemony in a narrowly formal
manner.[13] Mahmood Mamdani's study supports Young's argument but
focuses specifically on the decentralized, rural character of colonial hegemony. Mamdani uses twentieth-century South Africa to show that
with the backing of white officials, rural chiefs reigned with few checks
or constraints. These chiefs became "decentralized despots" and contributed to the creation of an authoritarian colonial regime that relied on
divisions of urban and rural, white and black.[14] Although both Young
and Mamdani offer important insights into the institutions and structures of colonial rule, their focus neglects informal challenges to empire.
Indeed, the work of James Scott and others who study resistance serves

as a reminder that the colonial state's control over Africans' lives was far from complete.[15] The state's ability to intervene significantly in the lives of its subjects varied temporally and spatially. As Jeffrey Herbst points out, the colonial state "broadcasted" its power—its ability to intervene significantly in the lives of its subjects—most effectively in capital cities and colonial centers of power; the power of the colonial state extended weakly, if at all, to the vast, rural hinterlands.[16]

Sara Berry and others characterize colonialism as a process prone to contradictions, fragilities, and deep structural weaknesses. Berry coined the term "hegemony on a shoestring," indicating that colonial administrators and planners did not arrive with a ready-made program but cobbled together their policies within the uneven parameters of grand ambitions and budgetary constraints.[17] Grand ambitions and budgetary constraints were central to the Lugardian model of indirect rule, which was originally applied to Uganda, elaborated in Nigeria, and eventually became the cornerstone of British colonial policy. Far from being a coherent and theoretically grounded model of enlightened native policy, the Dual Mandate has revealed itself to be a management scheme made up of a patchwork of shifting class alliances and failed efforts to contain costs and centralize authority in the governor's hands. It also harbored resentments against indigenous "modernizers."[18]

Anthony Kirk-Greene reminds us that although colonial states were militarily capable of exerting overpowering force in punctuated moments (but they were less able to sustain forceful military action beyond the short term), European provincial administration was actually a "thin white line." European colonial officials were few and far between in the vast rural backwaters of Africa's colonies. The "thin white line" was by necessity supplemented by a vast cohort of African intermediaries. "Without the manpower and machinery of the native administration or similar local government bodies, all the way from paramount chiefs, district headmen, and treasury staff to dispensers, foremen of works, and forestry assistants 'grade 4,' the colonial administrator could never have functioned or even survived in his job. It was the collaborative underpinning of the colonial administrator that enabled the district officer to become—and in appearance to remain—the squirarchal *roi de la brousse,* proud king of his castle and lone lord of all he surveyed, of the 'I-am-Sandi-who-sits-for-the-king-on-the-Great-River' breed."[19]

Without access to substantial and steady resources from the *métropole,* colonial administrators in Africa adapted local, African institutions to serve their purpose.[20] As a result, despite their different native policies, all colonial powers developed some form of indirect rule that responded to the need to construct a colonial administration that functioned "on the cheap." While indirect rule offered a way to delegate some of the responsibility for the maintenance of colonial rule onto African subjects directly, it also depended upon Africans employed directly by colonial states. All colonial states became dependent upon African intermediaries and employees.

Henri Brunschwig makes a point similar to that of Kirk-Greene in his study on colonial rule in French Africa when he notes that "colonization brought forth an abundant gaggle of voluntary collaborators. The Whites [colonial administrators], incapable of fending for themselves, have always and everywhere found agents: militia, police, boys, cooks, porters, etc., [who] constituted a proletariat recruited from among the less privileged groups in traditional societies."[21] As Heather Sharkey notes in her study of the Anglo-Egyptian Sudan, "colonialism was a day-to-day performance of power in which petty employees took part by presenting the face of the government to the general populace in their capacity as inspectors, collectors, law enforcers, teachers, and clerks."[22] The emphasis that Kirk-Greene, Brunschwig, Sharkey, and others place on the personnel of empire indicates that investigations into colonial hegemony must actually turn on the Africans who were employed in a variety of roles and on the nature of their "bargains" with colonial states.

Translation, Interpretation, and Power

African interpreters became indispensable to the operation of the colonial system. Benton argues that the "burden of translation was present in the least moments of the colonial encounter."[23] In colonial courtrooms, district offices, and health clinics, African colonial employees enabled communication, provided information, and oversaw the implementation—and reinterpretation—of colonial policies and processes. Interpreters were crucial to the functioning of the colonial administration because few Europeans learned African languages. With the exception of some British officials in Nigeria and Kenya, few European administrators remained in one posting long enough to develop sufficient linguistic and cultural familiarity to communicate independently with African colonial subjects.[24]

There were exceptions. A handful of British and French administrators did learn African languages, and several became leading scholars and "experts" of colonial Africa, such as Maurice Delafosse, Charles

Monteil, R. S. Rattray, H. R. Palmer, and Theophilus Shepstone, whose career Thomas McClendon explores in this volume.[25] But most colonial administrators did not learn local languages beyond a few command terms—speaking what Keletso Atkins refers to as "kitchen kaffir"—and they thus relied on interpreters.[26] Even when white district officers did learn local languages, ease of communication was not guaranteed.[27] As essays in this volume by Brett Shadle and Andreas Eckert show, even those British administrators who spoke Swahili in East Africa still depended on interpreters to maneuver the linguistic and cultural diversity of the regions in which they were posted.

All colonial administrators therefore relied to some extent on African interpreters. These interpreters provided colonial administrators with crucial services and became indispensable to the operation of the colonial system. And because colonial administrators did not understand African languages well enough, few checks operated on how interpreters translated and what they demanded. Abuses of power were common. Reliance on interpreters and local informants prompted administers to promote education, in particular for chiefs and sons of chiefs. European administrators viewed education as essential to eliminating additional layers of communication and establishing direct relations with chiefs and other colonial subjects.

African interpreters were a central part of the institutionalization of colonialism because they played a central role in transmitting and interpreting knowledge and power. Scholars of cultural encounters in contact zones have raised important issues about the power dynamics involved in translation. Translation in contact zones involved a form of unequal exchange, which was linked to the power relationship established.[28] A single European traveler, a missionary, or a European military leader were all dependent to a greater or lesser extent on their interpreters. However, the implications of translation were significantly different as were the potential rewards. Translating in contexts of asymmetries of power creates significant opportunity for mistranslation as well as for selective translation. Translation in colonial contexts was thus never an "innocent act."[29] In his monograph on the creation of a colonial lingua franca in the Belgian Congo, Johannes Fabian has demonstrated the inherent misunderstandings that shaped communication in colonial settings.[30] Much work has been done on translations of religious texts, especially by missionaries, and the consequent misunderstandings.[31] Our volume examines the role of intermediaries in the production of knowledge in colonial contexts.

Polyglossia was one skill common to all the intermediaries examined in this volume. Translation, interpretation, and reinterpretation all depend on a sophisticated knowledge of language and the capacity to "parse," to pursue William Worger's conceptualization.[32] All the individuals discussed in this volume were able to communicate in more than two languages: at least one European language (often several) and several (often many) African languages. But as linguists have often observed, it is not the number of languages but an individual's capacity to locate homology and analogy in the multivalent environment that defines the work of the interpreter.[33]

The dynamics of interpretation in colonial Africa changed over time and place. In French West Africa in 1856, Governor Faidherbe established the École d'Otages (School of Hostages) in Saint-Louis, Senegal. At the outset it was a school for hostages, mostly children and adolescents from African chiefly families sent to Saint-Louis according to the age-old practice of using relatives as pawns to guarantee a political or commercial transaction. Faidherbe's school transformed the "guarantee" into an opportunity to teach these children French language and "civilization." Faidherbe also deployed another strategy to enhance his ability to communicate with local Africans. He installed in his mansion a "beautiful Peul woman" to provide him with personal attention and intimate language training. The Saint-Louisian Catholic clergy were further scandalized when Faidherbe encouraged other French officers to do likewise.[34] Despite the precedent set by Faidherbe, throughout most of the colonial period, French colonial officials rarely took seriously the study of African languages, even after courses in several African languages were offered at the École Coloniale, the colonial training school in France. These language classes were shunned in part because the future administrators were never confident that they would be posted to the areas where the languages they learned were actually spoken.

While the colonial ministry did not reward linguistic dexterity on the part of its French administrators, it did seek to promote language learning among its colonial subjects. Faidherbe's School of Hostages closed in 1871 but reopened in 1894 with the more palatable (and welcoming) name of the School for Chiefs' Sons and Interpreters.[35] That school, as well as the primary school system more generally, reflected French efforts to promote the *mission civilisatrice* and the French language as the lingua franca of the colonies.[36] It was hoped that the dissemination of French language and culture, particularly among schoolboys and the sons of chiefs, would promote loyalty to the colonial

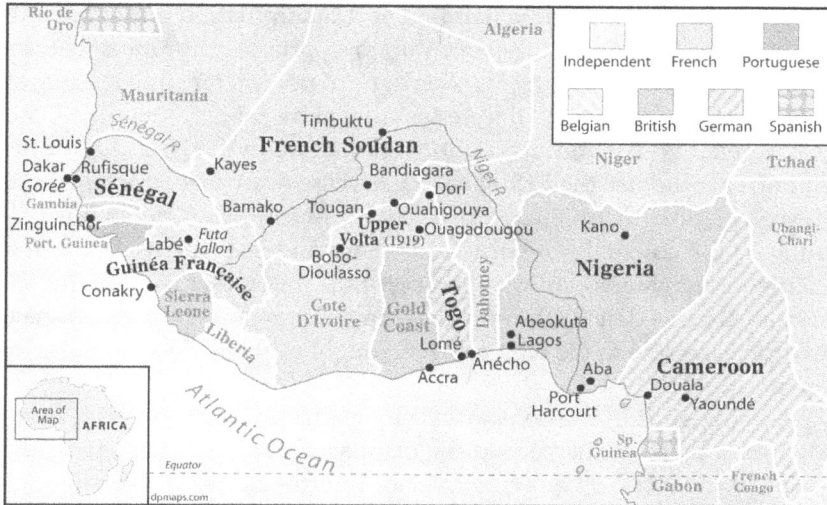

Map of West Africa, ca. 1910

project and facilitate direct communication between French officials and colonial subjects.

The early phase of colonial rule, from the era of conquest and the first generation of occupation through the 1920s, was a time when interpreters wielded enormous power. In the late nineteenth century the power of intermediaries often rested on their ability to cultivate or exploit a particular relationship with European officials. In the flux of conquest and its aftermath, African intermediaries working closely with European colonial officials (or appearing to) could develop or carve out positions of considerable authority. The "rules" of colonialism had not yet been set or developed; European "men on the spot" often developed colonial policies and procedures in response to local circumstances. As a result a trusted African intermediary could rise to positions of considerable authority, whether or not these positions carried with them official titles. A soldier might become an indispensable aid to a European administrator and be rewarded with an appointment as a chief; an African clerk might effectively manage an administrative post for months at a time in the absence of a European official.

As the bureaucracy of the colonial state solidified, however, the possibilities for Africans to rise to positions of authority declined. The positions held by Africans became more strictly codified: their duties, ranks, and salaries were regulated by the state. In this context intermediaries

came to rely on their understanding and manipulation of the bureaucracy, rather than on their relationship to a particular European patron.
A. E. Afigbo writes that the "golden age" of interpreters in Nigeria was
from 1914 to 1930, when "the clerk sitting at his table commanded and
was obeyed."[37] African men who were literate in the language of the
colonizer could use their skills to make a case or further a cause within
the colonial hierarchy, as described by Jean-Hervé Jézéquel in this volume. As the colonial state drafted its laws and policies, African intermediaries adjusted their roles and cultural strategies. Likewise, the assessors discussed by Ruth Ginio here similarly expose the way in which
African assessors in the native courts sought to shape the colonial state
from within.

Another shift in the context in which African intermediaries operated took place in the second major phase of colonial rule, from the
1930s to independence. The power of intermediaries during this period was conditioned in new ways as the result of increased primary
schooling in European languages. More Africans started to learn the
languages of the colonial rulers—and in some colonies European officials learned a local lingua franca (especially Hausa, Swahili, and Lingala). The emergence of more widely spoken administrative languages
changed but did not eliminate the influence of interpreters. Although
language barriers may have been eroded, intermediaries could still
exert considerable influence over who could access the colonial apparatus and interpret its rules and policies. Differences of class, religion,
status, and background continued to play an important part in deter-
mining who gained entry to and could negotiate within colonial corri-
dors of power. These forces help to explain the dynamics that shaped
the British investigation into the man-leopard murders in Nigeria as
described by David Pratten, the court case analyzed by Maurice Amutabi, and Shadle's discussion of court elders in Kenya.

The power of translation was greatest where the terms of reference
for European colonial officers were weakest. The language of the colonial courts may have been Arabic or the local language, but the court re-
corders usually recorded in a European language. While the testimony
was for the benefit of the plaintiffs, respondents, and native judges, the
text was produced for the colonial officers. Because litigants rarely
spoke European languages and Europeans speaking local languages
was rarer still, the lack of direct communication created nodes of power
used by interpreters. The barrier of direct communication also benefited the multilingual litigant. In our volume the Kenyan court dispute

examined by Amutabi provides the clearest support for this statement. Amutabi investigates a case that pitted two church leaders against each other. He argues that Lusuli, who was educated and spoke English and Swahili, had significant advantages in presenting his case over Estambale, who spoke neither English nor Swahili and whose occupation—other than as church leader—was that of hut repairer. But education alone did not give Lusuli advantage in the courts. Lusuli also had significant regional standing because of his service in the Kenyan African Rifles. Asituywa, the court's African translator and clerk, promoted Lusuli's case because he saw his own interests more closely aligned with Lusuli's and because he had been Lusuli's schoolmate. According to Amutabi, Asituywa was one of the wealthiest men in the region because he peddled his influence to shape court testimonies. In this case Asituywa actually mistranslated and distorted Estambale's testimony to sway the court's judgment.[38] Control over translation placed the African interpreter in the center of exchanges of information. As Shadle discusses in this chapter, Kurate, the long-serving president of a native tribunal in South Kavirondo, enhanced his income by demanding bribes as he translated testimony in the native courts. Kurate was initially dismissed for corruption and tried for accepting bribes, but he successfully appealed his sentence and returned to his post on the tribunal. These are examples of how interpreters benefited from the "bargain of collaboration" with the colonial state.

Amutabi's and Shadle's case studies also demonstrate that the process of translation was malleable and prone to manipulation, a perspective that is particularly important to consider when approaching the process known as the "invention of tradition." Terence Ranger gave this term to a process that involved both the colonial state and African elites. European colonial officials sought to collect and codify local traditions of rule in order to incorporate them into systems of indirect rule. These efforts created opportunities for local chiefs, elders, and elites to reinterpret, redefine, and enhance their "traditional" power and authority.[39] Martin Chanock and other scholars have documented how male elders in the colonial period leveraged "tradition" to increase their access to land and other resources and expand their control of women, slaves, subordinate men, and children.[40] More recent studies, including Thomas Spear, have exposed the "limits of invention" in colonial Africa.[41] Spear argues that other forces of change predating colonial rule and persisting afterward constrained the powers of chiefs and patterns of inventing tradition. Urbanization, religious conversion, and social and geographical mobility could all act as checks on the authority of chiefs and open new avenues to challenge both chiefly power and the colonial state.

As this discussion indicates, the debates surrounding the incorporation of chiefs into the colonial administration and the challenges to their authority have made us much more aware of the contingencies of colonial rule in Africa.[42] The attention paid to chiefs, however, has obscured the roles of other Africans in the shaping of colonial orders, in particular of the interpreters who translated local "traditions" and interpreted court proceedings. In his chapter, Shadle explores how the roles of "traditional elder" and "colonial clerk" melded together in Kenya in the 1940s. Shadle argues that the British were constantly searching for the "right kind of elder" to serve in colonial courts. He describes in particular the important shift in the late 1940s from a reliance on "traditional elders" to a program favoring the appointment of African "modernizers and progressives" to serve as magistrates in the African courts. By "professionalizing" the role of intermediaries, colonial officials hoped to overcome conservative views of chiefs and elders and cultivate a modernized, progressive class of court participants in order to reign in the rampant corruption. Despite improvements in education and literacy and the occasional anticorruption campaign, the British were unsuccessful in promoting transparency or in abolishing "abuses of power" in the native courts.

Professionalizing interpretation has a long history in Africa. In his research on colonial Senegal, David Robinson argues that the Muslim tribunals and the prominence of Islam at the very heart of France's Senegalese communes and later its colony "gave substance to the French claim of tolerance."[43] Saliou Mbaye's contribution in this volume examines several translators in qadi courts who played important roles in the early extension of French colonial control during the period when Arabic was still an official language of diplomacy in the region beyond the colony's borders and the official language of the Muslim tribunal. The lives of Mbaye's *hommes de confiance* are well preserved in the Archives Nationales du Sénégal. Some were marabouts, raised to the status of judges by colonial statutes. Others were related by blood to qadis and over time worked their way into the hierarchy of colonial authority. Mbaye's information complements Robinson's argument regarding the particular "paths of accommodation" that emerged between the Muslim elite and French colonial officials in the late nineteenth and early twentieth centuries.

Ruth Ginio's chapter explores the power of African assessors in the legal architecture of France's West Africa Federation. The 1903 decree creating a colonial legal system in French West Africa established a series of native courts that were to apply the relevant custom to disputes among African litigants. The decree assigned to African assessors the important role of "parsing" African grievances into forms intelligible to French colonial officials charged with overseeing the operation of the courts and hearing appeals from the lower native courts. Reliance on African assessors created an unanticipated paradox: on the one hand, the French were reluctant to delegate too much authority to African intermediaries, but on the other, their lack of knowledge of African languages and customs made them dependent on African assessors. Ginio exposes the failure of the French colonial judicial system to curtail the influence of African intermediaries, even after a major overhaul of the native courts in the 1920s. The shortage of European personnel capable of judging African disputes and the French insistence on charging Africans with "modernizing" their own customs continued to place African intermediaries at the center of the native court system.

While the primary focus of this volume is on employees of the colonial state who are African, we include two essays that, technically speaking, illuminate exceptions to this general theme. One focuses on an African "mediator" who worked within a missionary context, not within the formal structures of the colonial state; the other investigates a white interpreter in the employ of the colonial state. Both cases take place in South Africa and both challenge generalizations about who became interpreters and in what contexts they operated. We do not want to suggest that South Africa was somehow exceptional to the patterns we examine here. Indeed, the exceptions we address point strongly to general patterns about the importance of mediation to relations of knowledge and power.

In the first case Roger Levine examines the crucial role of Jan Tzatzoe, a Xhosa intermediary and interpreter who worked for Christian missionaries in the early nineteenth century. Levine shows that in the era preceding formal colonization of the region, white missionaries of the London Missionary Society station at Kat River relied wholly on Tzatzoe to maneuver through South Africa's spatial and religious frontier. Levine's chapter takes place almost a century earlier than the other chapters in this volume (with the exception of Mbaye's contribution on Senegalese interpreters). At the beginning of the nineteenth century, the

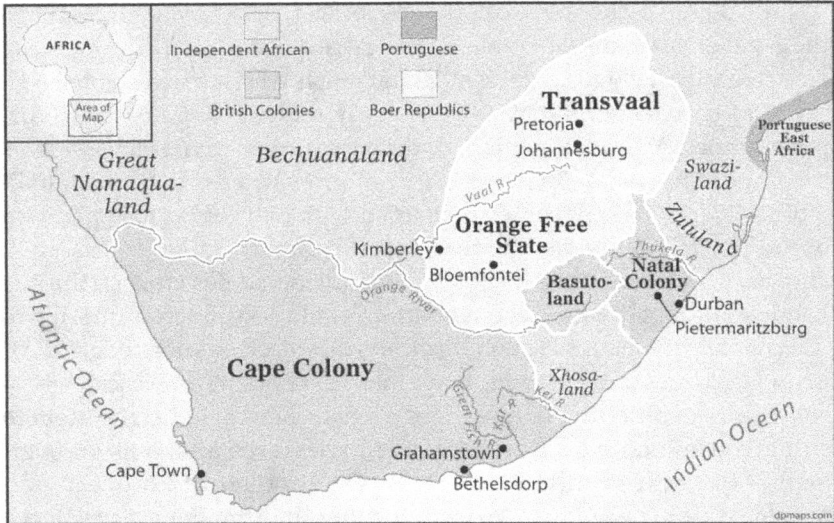

Map of South Africa, ca. 1870

Eastern Cape was rife with ethnic and religious tensions, not dissimilar to the Tswana frontier described by Jean and John Comaroff in their work on Christianity and conversion.[44] Tzatzoe's loyalties, beyond those to his immediate family, are hard to identify and even harder to explain. He worked for European missionaries and was to some extent committed to their cause, but he also funneled knowledge back to his Xhosa clan, which was engaged in fierce rivalries with other Xhosa leaders. While the missionaries could not manage without their interpreter, Tzatzoe himself moved easily back and forth between the missionary and Xhosa worlds. Levine's study thus highlights the importance of African intermediaries to European agendas in Africa well before the beginning of formal colonial rule.[45] Tzatzoe thereby signals a dynamic that figures centrally also in the later period of formal colonial rule: intermediaries straddled and moved constantly back and forth among different social and cultural worlds.

The second case that falls outside our focus on African interpreters is that of Theophilus Shepstone, a white official in the Natal who worked as an interpreter for the colonial state. Thom McClendon demonstrates in his chapter that by employing Shepstone as a translator, Natal's native administration placed white South Africans squarely at the center of the production of knowledge about Zulu society. Because a significant population of white settlers lived close to their African neighbors, they assumed a variety of intermediary positions in the colonial state that elsewhere in Africa were filled by black Africans. Even if white interpreters such as Shepstone were not expert at the services they provided, they nevertheless wielded great influence by virtue of their centrality to the interactions that took place between representatives of the colonial state and Zulu elites and commoners. Shepstone carefully crafted his linguistic knowledge to promote his view of Zulu society. He also cultivated a cadre of white interpreters and translators and imposed proficiency exams on them. In analyzing Shepstone's career, McClendon clearly demonstrates that Shepstone used his position as intermediary to promote his own very specific colonial vision. As we shall discuss in the next section, in this way Shepstone was not at all exceptional: African intermediaries often promoted their own goals even as they served their colonial employers.

Interpreters: Local Politics and the Production of Knowledge

Kirk-Greene begins his study of the size of the British colonial service in Africa by undermining the common notion that the district commissioner had an "iron rule" that formed the foundation of the "steel frame" of British colonial administration.[46] He demonstrates that the image of an iron rule was fictitious when considered in light of the number of European administrators, the size of their territory, and the number of their subjects. In a more recent study, Emily Lynn Osborn elaborates on this theme, in her consideration of colonial rule in Upper Guinea, in French Guinea. She shows that in the early colonial period, French colonial administrators were surrounded by a "circle of iron" formed of their complete dependency on interpreters and chiefs.[47] In her work on colonial rule in French West Africa, Denise Bouche likewise notes the dependence of European administrators on colonial employees, but she also emphasizes that the networks that surrounded European administrators could easily fracture. "[T]he power of the interpreter who controlled the district commandant and ruled in his name was large, but it was fragile. It rested on the commandant's confidence in his interpreter and could suddenly be lost, particularly at the moment of the transfer of personnel. . . . [The interpreter] risked being removed from office and imprisoned if he misjudged the complex intrigues that characterized the daily life of the *cercle*."[48]

The precarious yet powerful position of interpreters and clerks meant that a handful of African men exercised considerable influence over the implementation of policy and the production of knowledge in colonial Africa. Osborn's chapter on Boubou Penda, a former slave and interpreter, and Ernest Noirot, a French administrator, illuminates these processes during the early, formative phase of colonial rule. Noirot and Boubou worked together for over twenty years. As Noirot rose through the ranks, so too did Boubou accumulate power, status, and wealth. But in 1904, when a new governor arrived in French Guinea, Noirot and Boubou came under attack. The close working relationship that had been useful to the French state in the phase of conquest had become incompatible with the bureaucratic agendas of occupation. In the aftermath of this shift in administrative priorities, Noirot was exiled and Boubou imprisoned. Noirot and Boubou's downfall indicates a change in the context in which African colonial intermediaries worked. As conquest gave way to occupation, new, bureaucratic forms of rule replaced the expedient and often haphazard strategies that helped make possible colonial conquest and initial occupation of Africa.

Most of our information on intermediaries comes from official colonial records, including the occasional scandal. Not all our sources are European, however. As Ralph Austen explains in his chapter, we have a few, rare autobiographies written by African colonial employees. He examines two such autobiographies, both written by Francophone clerks: Amadou Hampâté Bâ and Jacques Kuoh Moukouri. Autobiographies are by their nature selective reproductions of past experiences, but Austen situates these two African clerks within the wider contexts of colonial employment and society. Both Hampâté Bâ and Kuoh Moukouri entered colonial employment in the 1920s as the power of interpreters began to wane; both rose to prominent positions with the late colonial administration and held important posts in the postcolonial period. Using their autobiographical writings, Austen examines the liminal positions of African colonial employees within the power dynamics of colonial offices. Indeed, Austen argues that the struggles for power within these offices was a microcosm of wider colonial struggles. These clerks, rather than seeking to destroy the structures in which they operated, instead tried to survive and to gain a degree of respectability within those structures. Among the tools available to African clerks was their control over the timing and flow of information. Austen also reminds us that Hampâté Bâ and Kuoh Moukouri produced their autobiographies late in their careers, when they had attained respect and privileges in their postcolonial positions. They may have repressed or forgotten the more onerous experiences of their colonial office days.

The reign of the interpreters persisted for much of the colonial era, but their power was progressively curtailed. The high point of their power coincided with the early phases of colonial conquest and the subsequent periods of establishing colonial rule. During this period, as Robert Delavignette describes it, "the interpreters kept the [commandant] turning in a narrow circle of intrigues," out of which he had no escape because he was dependent on them for information, for translation, for mediation, and often also for the basic necessities of daily life, such as food, labor, and sexual services.[49] This is exactly the role Levine's Tzatzoe played for a missionary family. While Tzatzoe did not appear to be engaged in the Wangrin-like patterns of self-aggrandizement (see the section on straddling the multiple worlds) using the new "resources" of the European missionary outpost, he clearly enhanced his own strategies for survival and accumulation by moving between the world of the mission and that of Xhosa political rivalries and intrigues. The period of dependency on African interpreters lasted until the mature colonial state imposed a degree of bureaucratic control over its interpreters and until basic literacy in European languages permeated outlying regions. By the interwar period the colonials expected to find Africans with some degree of facility in European languages. Even the most isolated villages now contained someone who had spent some time laboring in distant fields, mines, or towns. As late as 1939, Delavignette exhorted students of the École Coloniale, who were preparing for colonial service, to "get away from [t]his usual sedentary life. At his station, [the official] only meets certain natives—they are always the same one, and they belong to the colony [i.e., the colonized world] rather than to the country [i.e., the real, rural Africa]."[50] These natives of the "colony" always had instrumental interests in their interactions with the colonial administration.

While interpreting for the colonial administrator was the central task, an interpreter's command of European languages and knowledge of cognitive categories helped enhance his role as a cross-cultural broker. Translating not just words but concepts is the greatest challenge of interpretation. Jan Tzatzoe performed such interpretation for the London Missionary Society as it struggled to find a niche on the South African frontier. Tzatzoe's service included "parsing God." Worger notes that "language stood at the heart of the colonial encounter, mediating relations between Europeans and Africans."[51] But as Worger also observes, the meanings of words must also resonate with African concepts. Conceptualization made translation difficult; and it made interpretation essential for communication. Europeans could learn African languages, as McClendon discusses. Shepstone, who grew up in a mission station, used his skills to insert himself into the heart of the political reconstruction of the Zulu state. Few Europeans, however, managed that level of competence.

Typically in colonial Africa, it was Africans who learned European languages and learned to "parse" European concepts. In this volume Jézéquel describes a host of Western-educated Africans who came to play important roles in "parsing" African customs into forms intelligible to European colonial administrators. Jézéquel's interlocutors have a long and robust history in Africa. Mission-educated Africans were often quick to produce their own histories, not just in European languages but also in ways favorable to their particular interests. Samuel Johnson's posthumously published *History of the Yorubas* is one example.[52] In discussing colonial officials' abilities to understand local histories, Delavignette writes, "[T]here is no lack of documentation, some of it produced by Africans themselves . . . who were discovering their own country by methods we . . . taught them."[53] Indeed many African clerks drew on their scholarly training to shore up the colonial project even as they promoted their own interests.[54] Jézéquel details four Africans who used their cognitive and literary skills to promote their interests by producing local digests of customs or historical accounts. Some texts were published; others remained unpublished in local archives. But even in local archives, written reports exerted powerful influences over European administrators called on to adjudicate disputes and competing claims on chieftaincies. There is a growing literature from all parts of colonial Africa demonstrating how African clerks and teachers produced ethnographies and histories, many with a distinctively self-interested instrumentality.[55] As we discuss in the next section, many of our intermediaries straddled the intertwined and complex worlds of local African interests and European authorities.

Straddling the Multiple Worlds of Colonialism

An examination of African intermediaries provides a unique vantage point on the social worlds created by colonial rule. We have uncovered a rich historical vein of insight and detail into the colonial experience through our focus on African intermediaries. Indeed, all intermediaries controlled and shaped information and intelligence through their role as cross-cultural brokers. Knowing European languages or an African lingua franca, such as Kiswahili, Hausa, Lingala, or Arabic, was insufficient, however. Intermediaries needed to master European cultural and legal categories and to translate African experiences into terms that made sense to Europeans and vice versa. African intermediaries and interpreters thus lived in social worlds that straddled African and European universes. Many of the intermediaries and interpreters examined in this volume were *bricoleurs* in the Levi-Straussian tradition.[56] A *bricoleur* in the colonial context was a native who pieced together his (and only very rarely her) persona from an assemblage of precolonial, colonial, and European practices and traits. Some used their positions in colonial administrations to pursue precolonial patterns of accumulation and social status. Others invested themselves culturally, socially, and economically as modernizers. These intertwined African and European worlds of colonial Africa provided opportunities for and posed dangers to those who would navigate them.[57]

Our attention to these social worlds was originally drawn by the semi-fictitious character, Wangrin, who is the protagonist of Hampâté Bâ's novel *The Fortunes of Wangrin*.[58] Wangrin's adventures and intrigues expose the mutual dependency that emerged between European colonial administrators and African interpreters in the French Soudan. Hampâté Bâ calls Wangrin a "scoundrel," but this is a playful term. In *Fortunes* Wangrin uses his position as clerk within the colonial administration to insinuate himself into the center of intrigues, to make local French commandants completely dependent upon his services, and to enrich himself. Wangrin's career exposes the fragility of the interpreter's power especially during personnel handovers. Although Wangrin survives, he does so because he understands and manipulates both French colonial bureaucratic practices and African precolonial politics, which persisted into the early colonial era. Wangrin's power resides in his strategic position within circuits that connect the power and authority of the precolonial social order and that of the colonial social order, and he uses his cultural and linguistic knowledge to pursue his own goals.[59] Hampâté Bâ admires Wangrin's abilities to master the colonial situation and to exasperate his African and European enemies.

It is important to remember, however, that Wangrin was not born fully imbued with his powers, acquiring them rather only after exposure to European education, language, and ideas. The School for

Hostages taught Wangrin many of the tools with which he was later to
befuddle his "superior officers." Arguably of equal importance was the
on-the-job training, a form of self-education available only to those who
allowed themselves to adapt, to be molded, and to respond entrepre-
neurially to the changes wrought by colonial imposition and to the opportunities it created.

Jézéquel considers similar men whose lives were transformed by
their exposure to colonial education. His evidence comes from the experiences of teachers, boys from chiefly and commoner families, who
were put through the rigors of a French education and then thrust into
the role of educating Africans in French and in French ideas. The privileged experience of these men and the almost reverential esteem with
which they were held by most Africans gave them the capacity to carve
out for themselves, their families, and their clans unparalleled influence and wealth. These teachers' "bargains of collaboration" rested on
their use of Western education to shape local knowledge and to promote their own interests.

In this volume, Andreas Eckert focuses on the 1940s and 1950s, by
which time many British colonial officials in Tanganyika had learned
some Swahili, and with the exception of some isolated regions, Swahili
was widely spoken.[60] At this time interpreters were not quite as essential to the colonial state, but African intermediaries more generally
remained so. Eckert examines how Tanganyikan African bureaucrats
tried to position themselves to take advantage of the rapid postwar
professionalization of the African civil service by mobilizing to demand
better working conditions, salaries, pensions, and especially advancement. Advancement, however, could come in many forms. Some sought
to advance their own interests by producing local histories that focused
on the progressive aspects of their own societies. Eckert's intermediaries were modernizers, although they constantly grappled with what
he calls "intermediary ambivalence." These men were also the beneficiaries of the national independence movements of the 1950s and 1960s.
As elsewhere in postcolonial Africa, most senior administrators had
once been colonial employees.

In this volume, David Pratten and Benjamin Lawrance point to the
fact that intermediaries were socially mobile men who carefully crafted
their identities. Pratten considers the life of Usen Udo Usen, who was a
clerk in southeastern Nigeria and juggled the roles of modernizer and
respected community leader, moving carefully from lobbying and fund-
raising within a proto-nationalist political self-help group to serving in

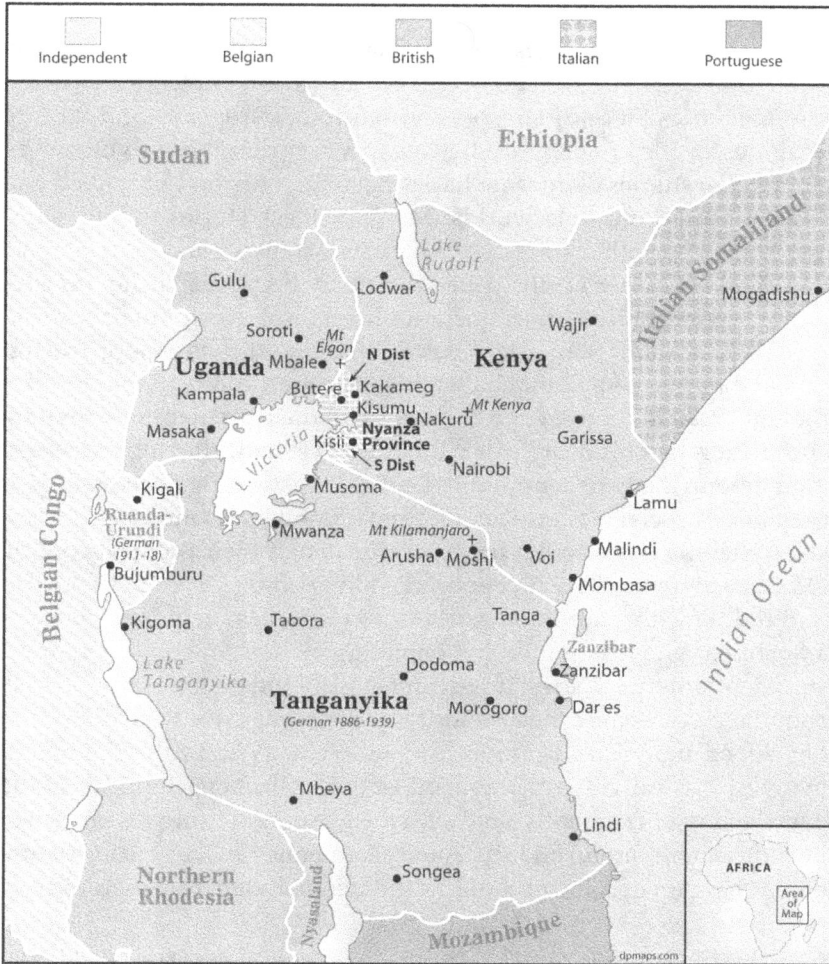

Map of East Africa, ca. 1940

an official capacity investigating a horrific series of ritualistic killings. On the way his allegiances shifted, and he also gained and lost allies. As Lawrance's chapter shows, the defeat of Germany in World War I and the British occupation of Togo afforded new economic opportunities to English-speakers from the neighboring Gold Coast. Robert A. Cole was one of these men. Fluent and literate in English, Cole was thus well positioned to navigate the complicated terrain of legal representation and official licensing introduced by the British.

Negotiating colonial and African social worlds was not easy nor was it without considerable risk. In his chapter Eckert includes a lengthy quote from former district officer J. C. Cairns, who noted that African intermediaries "face[d] stresses and tensions Europeans find hard to imagine, for they [were] torn between two worlds."[61] Our volume includes case studies of intermediaries detailing how they straddled and negotiated the multiple worlds. Many of these stories unfold sadly, and some end rather tragically. As Austen shows, Amadou Hampâté Bâ began his career for the colonial state by being dispatched to a remote, arid location as punishment for his refusal to continue his forced French education. Similarly Kuoh Moukouri's life is one of frustration at the glass ceiling that halted his education and hindered his promotion. Pratten's protagonist, Usen Udo, died prematurely, inviting speculation that his death was not natural. He had, after all, made enemies among the very community he was investigating. Jézéquel's self-proclaimed social modernizer, Ibrahima Bathily, was murdered by the chiefly family because his program threatened their political control. Osborn's antihero, Boubou Penda, died in prison.

Straddling the multiple worlds of colonialism required constant adjustment and adaptation to changing colonial practices. The most successful intermediaries, if we can measure their success by their accumulation of wealth, their seniority, or their longevity, were those who developed new skills at opportune moments. Within the lifetime of many of the individuals examined in this collection, the rules of the game changed frequently and without warning. Future research will include a more careful and sustained examination of the shifting nature of the "bargain of collaboration" as the colonial state itself matured.

Gender and Power in the World of the Intermediary

It is neither a coincidence nor an accident that men figure prominently in this volume. The protagonists of court cases analyzed by Amutabi and Shadle, the colonial employees examined by Ginio and Austen, and the advisors, teachers, and letter writers in Jézéquel's, Lawrance's, and Pratten's chapters are all men. Mbaye's contribution provides further evidence on how thoroughly male was the colonial enterprise. These examples reveal a point that is often made about colonial rule, namely, that it was essentially a male project, an undertaking in which European men employed, collaborated with, and confronted African men. We recognize the powerful role of female guides and intermediaries during the precolonial, early contact era, including the *signarés* of Saint-Louis and Gorée in Senegal and Eva, the Khoikhoi servant girl and guide of Jan van Reebeck in South Africa.[62] But few women served as official intermediaries and interpreters during the maturing phase of colonialism.

In colonial Africa the division between men and women was reinforced by policies and procedures and by the composition and organization of the colonial bureaucracy. Men, as farmers, laborers, employees, and chiefs, were viewed as key to the creation of a colonial order: male colonial subjects were held responsible for paying taxes and fulfilling labor requirements.[63] Male colonial subjects could occupy positions of authority, such as chieftaincies, and a small percentage of males attended colonial schools for boys, where they learned the language of the colonizer and other skills that the state deemed necessary to the creation of obedient male subjects and productive household heads. For almost all of the colonial era, only men could gain employment with the colonial state, where they worked as secretaries, clerks, and interpreters as well as household servants, cooks, and guards.[64]

Girls and women, on the other hand, did not develop direct ties to the colonial state, which tended to view women as dependents of men, as mothers, wives, and daughters. As a result, the burdens and responsibilities shouldered by women differed significantly from those of men, for women were deemed ineligible for the same opportunities made available to males for employment, education, and authority. In colonial schools girls were trained in the "domestic sciences," while boys were instructed on becoming future workers and household heads.[65] As adults African women were not usually required to pay taxes or fulfill requirements of forced labor, although in some colonies they were subjected to humiliating medical exams and procedures.[66] Moreover, when white colonial officials sought to codify "traditional" law, they relied on men as sources of knowledge and expertise; the resulting law codes tended to enhance the control of men over women.[67]

With limited access to the colonial state and few avenues for recourse, women consequently became particularly vulnerable to those men who benefited from the "bargain of collaboration." This process is demonstrated by Osborn's chapter, in which the interpreter Boubou Penda captures and rapes Satourou, a member of an elite family. In his attack on this noble African woman, Boubou not only forcibly possessed a woman against her will, but he made a powerful statement to local political leaders. Boubou's treatment of Satourou exposes the arbitrary violence to which women could be subjected by colonial officials, European or African.[68] Elsewhere scholars have documented how African women were forced into arranged marriages with European or African colonial officials, sometimes for reasons of political or financial expediency, other times as a measure of protection.[69] These patterns indicate that African women and their families were often severely constrained in the response they could make to colonial officials, white or black, who subverted or ignored African marital practices or sexual mores.

While violence sometimes configured the relations of colonial representatives and African women, it was not the only form that these relationships took. As Hampâté Bâ's novels and memoirs show, African women were sometimes able to exploit the desires of colonial officials, sexual or otherwise, to create unofficial positions of influence for themselves. For African colonial employees, winning the favor of the white commander's wife—whether she was African or European—could be key to developing a good working relationship with the commander himself.[70] African women began to enter colonial bureaucracies as clerks, secretaries, nurses, and teachers during the waning days of colonialism, when European powers made considerable effort both to expand the civil service and to Africanize it.

The ways in which women gained informal access to the colonial state merits further research, as does the effect of increased educational and employment opportunities for women in the post–World War II era. Nevertheless, in the overwhelming majority of cases, it was African men, not women, who could access the colonial state and influence its machinations. Indeed, African colonial employees exemplify and bring to life a point made by Gertrude Mianda, that "colonization improved some men's . . . positions by according them more privileges than women in political, judicial, economic and social domains."[71] By focusing on the role of African employees in the bureaucracy, this volume offers another perspective on the relationship of gender and colonial rule in Africa.

The authors of this volume not only examine the roles African intermediaries played but also probe the social and cultural spaces they inhabited. The roles Africans played and the spaces they inhabited changed over time in response to the bureaucratization of the colonial administration. While European dependence upon the skills of African translators lessened as European languages became more widely known, colonial officials continued to rely upon African clerks and inter-mediaries. Indeed, as the colonial state matured and sought to control Africa and Africans more fully, the dependence of European colonial officials on African intermediaries deepened. These processes of matu-ration and changing mandates were unevenly felt throughout the con-tinent and over time. Our contributors add to the study of the expan-sion of the African colonial state by developing a chronology of the roles and social spaces for African intermediaries.

While "middle figures" were certainly not new to Africa, the nature and organization of formal European colonial rule created a qualita-tively different organization and set of demands than that placed on their immediate predecessors. The essays in this collection concentrate both on the formative phase of colonialism (roughly 1870–1918), in which African intermediaries played crucial roles, enjoyed more auton-omy, and remade themselves with the intention of solidifying their status within the contexts of precolonial social orders, and on the pe-riod of the second colonial imposition, which has been dated variously from the interwar period to the post–World War II era (roughly 1921–52). This was a time of renewed colonial interest in African societies and in an elaboration of colonial development policies.

The expansion of the colonial state required the regularization of Africans in its employ. Africans continued to serve the colonial state as intermediaries, but many now filled the growing ranks of clerks as well as those of agricultural extension agents, customs officials, teachers, and so on. The routinization of their employment limited the scope of their activities and interactions with African subjects and thus rede-fined the space in which they lived. Many of these African intermedi-aries now aspired to urban, middle-class lives, and growing political pressure was placed on colonial states to regularize the pay and status of African bureaucrats, bringing them more in line with those of their European counterparts.[72] Lloyd Fallers described the gradual usurpa-tion by Western-educated young men of the lower-level judgeships among the Basoga, but this merely altered the social context of these new judges' "interestedness" in the outcomes of legal disputes.[73] Even well into the 1950s, native courts used interpreters, whose translations could be shaped by the pressures brought on them. The interest of the court translator was motivated by class or proto-class affinities or by self-aggrandizement that Europeans condemned as corruption.[74] But as the contributors to this volume show, these men can also be viewed as a window into the complex social worlds of colonial Africa.

There was, therefore, a significant difference in the lives of intermediaries who lived and worked during the early, formative phase of
colonialism following on the heels of conquest and those who worked
during the maturation of the colonial state. The second colonial imposition involved a significant routinization of colonial rule, the elaboration of colonial institutions, and the regularization of authority associated with the development of bureaucratic states. African clerks with
some degree of formal, Western education gradually eclipsed the intermediaries of the early formative stage of colonialism. Greater bureaucratization involved more sustained supervision over work and demanded more accountability. Periodic anticorruption campaigns hint
that self-policing bureaucratic institutions were not yet established. We
believe that this volume has opened up discussion on a rich, new approach to the study of how Africans contributed to the making of colonial Africa.

Notes

1. Mandela, *Long Walk to Freedom*, 38–39. This quote appears on page 45 of
the paperback edition.
2. See, for example, Shakespeare, *Dintshontsho tsa bo-Juiuse Kesara;* Plaatje,
Sechuana proverbs; Plaatje, *Native Life in South Africa.* For more detail, see Willan,
Sol Plaatje.
3. A tiny handful of Africans served in senior administrative positions in colonial Africa before World War II. More did so during the early phases of colonial rule, especially in British colonies, before the development of indirect policies. Institutionalized racism also contributed to the decline in the proportion of
senior Africans in colonial bureaucracies. The post–World War II period witnessed a dramatic enlargement of the place of Africans in middle and senior
positions. See Cell, "Colonial Rule."
4. Derrick, "'Native Clerk' in Colonial West Africa." The literature on
Africans in European missions is vast.
5. We have chosen not to use the terms "bureaucracy" and "bureaucrats"
for the period of colonial rule before the large-scale expansion of colonial institutions and administrative services in the late interwar period. With the expansion of these colonial institutions and the regularization of employment for
Africans, the bureaucratization of colonial administration proceeded apace.
See, for example, Berman, *Control and Crisis in Colonial Kenya.* Nancy Rose Hunt
terms these intermediaries "middle figures" in her study of how African employees of a Baptist medical mission in the Congo represented, mediated, and
produced knowledge and institutions. Hunt, *Colonial Lexicon,* 2, 7, 12, 23, 82.

Benton, *Law and Colonial Cultures,* uses the terms interlocutors and intermediaries, 16–17 and chap. 4. See also Heather J. Sharkey's study of the colonial bureaucracy in the Sudan; *Living with Colonialism.*

6. For example, see Isaacman and Isaacman, "Resistance and Collaboration," 57, for an assessment of the benefits of collaboration.

7. R. Robinson, "Non-European Foundations of European Imperialism."

8. Marks, *Ambiguities of Dependence in South Africa,* 45, refers to a "Christian African intelligentsia" as comprising "the more prosperous landowner and peasants as well as the clergy, clerks, interpreters, and teachers, who came to be among the [British] monarchy's most fervent supporters." See also Bill Nasson on Cape Colored supporters of the British colonial state, in "What They Fought As."

9. Newbury, *Patrons, Clients, and Empire,* 1–2. For a Southeast Asian comparison, see Trocki, "Political Structures," 83.

10. Cooper, "Conflict and Connection."

11. Berman and Lonsdale, "Coping with the Contradictions," 490.

12. Berman, *Control and Crisis in Colonial Kenya,* 424–25.

13. For Young civil society and international relations appear to be the main challenges to the autonomy of the colonial state. Young, *African Colonial State,* 95–133.

14. Mamdani, *Citizen and Subject.* Mamdani uses South African examples to demonstrate the parallels with other regions of sub-Saharan Africa.

15. Scott, *Weapons of the Weak* and *Domination and the Arts of Resistance;* Isaacman, *Cotton Is the Mother of Poverty.*

16. Herbst, *States and Power in Africa,* 79–81, 90–91.

17. Berry, *No Condition Is Permanent,* chap. 2.

18. See especially the study written by a former Nigerian administrator, I. F. Nicolson, *Administration of Nigeria.* See also Cell, "Colonial Rule," 239–43.

19. Kirk-Greene, "Thin White Line," 26, 41.

20. See especially Isaacman, *Mozambique.*

21. Brunschwig, *Noirs et Blancs,* 213.

22. Sharkey, *Living with Colonialism,* 138.

23. Benton, *Law and Colonial Cultures,* 16.

24. Alexandre, "Chiefs, *Commandants,* and Clerks." See the example of Samwiri Waiswa, who began as an interpreter and rose to become subcounty chief, in Fallers, *Law without Precedent,* 78–81.

25. Williams reflects on these relationships in *Gold Coast Diaries.*

26. Atkins, *The Moon Is Dead;* Jeater, "Rethinking the 'African Voice'"; Jeater, "Speaking like a Native."

27. See Smith, "Relationship between the British Political Officer to His Chief in Northern Nigeria."

28. Kartunnen, *Between Worlds.*

29. Alvarez and Vidal, *Translation, Power, Subversion.*

30. Fabian, *Language and Colonial Power.*
31. Raphael, *Contracting Colonialism;* Larson, *History and Memory.*
32. Worger, "Parsing God." To parse is to examine minutely words as parts of sentences and to work out the meanings of terms.
33. The literature of translations studies is vast. For matters pertaining to colonial contexts and polyglossia, see, for example, Franco, "Culture-Specific Items in Translation"; Alcaraz, "Translation and Pragmatics"; Niranjana, *Siting Translation;* D. Robinson, *Translation and Empire;* D. Robinson, *What Is Translation?;* Venuti, *Translator's Invisibility;* Venuti, *Scandals of Translation,* 67–87; Stam, *Subversive Pleasures.* See also B. N. Lawrance, "Most Obedient Servants"; B. N. Lawrance, "Bankoe v. Dome," 250.
34. Bouche, *Histoire de la colonisation française,* 2:134–35. These *mariages à la mode du pays* were a ubiquitous feature of French colonial society from the eighteenth century through the early decades of the twentieth century. See also White, *Children of the French Empire,* 10–12. On pawns in commercial transactions, see Lovejoy and Richardson, "Business of Slaving."
35. Bouche, *l'enseignement dans les territoires français.*
36. Conklin, *Mission to Civilize.*
37. Afigbo, *Warrant Chiefs,* 180.
38. See also Moore, "Individual Interests and Organizational Structures."
39. Ranger, "Invention of Tradition in Colonial Africa"; Ranger, "Invention of Tradition Revisited"; and Vail, *Creation of Tribalism.*
40. Chanock, *Law, Custom and Social Order.* See also Fuglestad, *History of Niger;* Olivier de Sardan, *Les sociétés Songhai-Zarma.*
41. Lentz and Nugent, *Ethnicity in Ghana;* Spear, "Neo-Traditionalism."
42. See, for example, Fields, *Revival and Rebellion.*
43. David Robinson, *Paths of Accommodation,* 80.
44. Comaroff and Comaroff, *Christianity, Colonialism, and Consciousness.* They pursue this line of discussion in *Dialectics of Modernity.*
45. The most famous West African example is the *signarés* of Gorée and Saint-Louis. See Brooks, "*Signarés* of Saint Louis and Gorée." See also Brooks, "Nhara of the Guinea-Bissau Region"; and Brooks, *Eurafricans in Western Africa.* For a general orientation, see also Curtin, *Cross-cultural Trade in World History.*
46. Kirk-Greene, "Thin White Line," 25.
47. Osborn, "Circle of Iron."
48. Bouche, *Historie de la colonisation française,* 136; editors' translation.
49. Delavignette, *Freedom and Authority,* 41.
50. Delavignette, *Freedom and Authority,* 41. Delavignette published *Les vrais chefs de l'empire* in Paris in 1939, but it was later subjected to German censorship. He published an uncensored version with some new material as *Service africain.*
51. Worger, "Parsing God," 417.
52. S. Johnson, *History of the Yorubas.*

53. Delavignette, *Freedom and Authority,* 39.

54. For one example of a colonial clerk who photographed ceremonies and authored documents pertaining to state amalgamation ceremonies in British Togoland, see Lawrance, "Bankoe v. Dome."

55. Monson, "Claims to History and the Politics of Memory." John Iliffe suggests that many authors of "valuable memoranda and reports" were hopeful they might be rewarded and raised up the colonial hierarchy. See his *Modern History of Tanganyika,* 357. See also D. W. Cohen, "'Case for the Basoga,'" 243–44, and Berry, *"Chiefs Know Their Boundaries."*

56. Lévi-Strauss, *La pensée sauvage,* 27.

57. See Roberts, "Case against Faama Mademba Sy."

58. The subtitle of the original French version, which is missing from the English translation, reveals the narrative thrust of Hampâté Bâ's novel: "The Trickeries of an African Interpreter" *(L'etrange destin de Wangrin; ou, Les roueries d'un interpréte africain).*

59. Laurent Fourchard, "Propriétaires et commerçants Africains," recently traced the ways in which a handful of interpreters invested considerable resources in the purchase of urban real estate, thus using their new knowledge of European property rights to buy into burgeoning colonial commercial districts.

60. This is in stark contrast to the interwar period when "colonization lost momentum." Iliffe observed that the Great Depression "shook British credibility in the eyes of education Africans. In 1931 promotion of African clerks was suspended as an economy measure." Iliffe, *Modern History of Tanganyika,* 356–57.

61. Cairns, *Bush and Boma,* 149, quoted by Eckert.

62. See note 45.

63. Fall, *Le travail forcé.*

64. See Lindsay and Miescher, *Men and Masculinities.*

65. See, for example, Summers, *Colonial Lessons;* and Schmidt, *Peasants, Traders, and Wives.*

66. Turrittin, "Colonial Midwives"; Jackson, "'When in the White Man's Town'"; and Hunt, *Colonial Lexicon.* For a revolt by women against taxation, see Lawrance, *"La Révolte des Femmes."*

67. See, especially, Chanock, *Law, Custom and Social Order;* Hay and Wright, *African Women and the Law;* and Mann and Roberts, *Law in Colonial Africa.*

68. The way in which these coerced relationships could come about is movingly recounted by Jeanne-Marie Kamboi-Ferrand in her description of her encounter with the colonial state in Upper Volta, and one French administrator in particular. Kamboi-Ferrand, "Souffre, gémis, mais marche!" See also White, *Children of the French Empire,* 28–31.

69. Owen White, *Children of the French Empire,* shows that the unions of French men and African women operated on the fringes of the colonial state but that they were nevertheless an enduring feature of colonial rule. European

officials, occupying "isolated" posts, often took local wives or concubines. The interest of these women being part of such relationships varied considerably; in certain parts of Africa these liaisons with "outsiders" were roundly condemned. The often violent treatment of an African woman by a colonial officer is detailed in Hampâté Bâ's novel *Wangrin,* when a French official kidnaps and keeps the wife of a local marabout.

70. See Hampâté Bâ, *Fortunes of Wangrin,* for Wangrin's experiences in this regard.

71. Mianda, "Colonialism, Education, and Gender Relations," 144.

72. Cooper, *Decolonization and African Society.*

73. Fallers, *Law without Precedent.*

74. Moore, *Social Facts and Fabrications.*

The Formative Period
of Colonial Rule,
ca. 1800–1920

An Interpreter Will Arise

Resurrecting Jan Tzatzoe's Diplomatic and Evangelical Contributions as a Cultural Intermediary on South Africa's Eastern Cape Frontier, 1816–1818

ROGER S. LEVINE

On November 18, 1816, from the banks of the Kat River, whose waters flowed through a fertile valley and whose higher ground ascended to a serrated crown of rocky crags, Joseph Williams—the first European missionary to cross the Great Fish River boundary separating the Cape Colony from its Xhosa neighbors with the intention of establishing a permanent missionary station among them—composed a panicked letter to the colonial authorities across the border. His situation was perilous. His mission station, sponsored by the London Missionary Society, stood in grave danger.[1] Williams's "every thought" was of a threat made by a powerful Xhosa chief, Ndlambe, to "come with his people and take all the cattle and murder us all."[2] All his hopes and prayers rested with a young Xhosa man named Jan Tzatzoe, who had embarked on a diplomatic mission to the nearby kraal of Ndlambe's nephew, Ngqika, to assess the extent of the threat and to gain diplomatic and military assistance.[3] On November 22, Tzatzoe could report that rumors of an imminent attack were untrue. Ndlambe had been understood to be enraged with the missionaries and the Xhosa residents of the station for "corrupting the mind" of Ngqika, but Ngqika himself had stressed to Tzatzoe that Ndlambe was, quite to the contrary, happy with the presence of the missionaries and their Word of God and that only distance prevented him from visiting the station.[4]

The dramatic episode described here reveals the precarious position of the incipient missionary institution on the roiling eastern frontier. While Williams tried to focus on his evangelical and ecclesiastical tasks, he increasingly found himself embroiled in the political and diplomatic conflict between the colony and the Xhosa chiefs living near the mission and the political conflict among the chiefs themselves. But in contrast to the story being fashioned for the voracious early nineteenth-century readers of evangelical periodicals such as the London Missionary Society's *Transactions*, Williams, upon embarking on the establishment of the mission, had not been set adrift in the African wilderness with God as his sole solace. When the seedlings in his garden— germinating from stock secreted away from Britain and stored in the dank holds of oceangoing ships—succumbed to the eastern Cape heat, he survived on food supplies bought with missionary society funds and transported from the colony by ox wagon.[5]

Most of all, Williams was not alone. His mission was also Jan Tzatzoe's mission; his journey, Tzatzoe's journey. Williams turned to Jan Tzatzoe for crucial aid with diplomatic and evangelical matters, and Tzatzoe in turn played a central role in the survival and work of the mission. In so doing Tzatzoe continued his lifelong attempt to establish a space for himself in the interstices between the colonial and the African worlds of the Cape frontier. Williams's story is just as much Jan Tzatzoe's story, and Tzatzoe's story has not yet been told.[6]

The early nineteenth century, which forms the setting for Tzatzoe's and Williams's story, was a volatile time in the history of South Africa, featuring a transition from Dutch to British colonial rule. Colonial armies had crushed the nomadic Khoisan pastoralists of the western Cape, and colonial officials from the Cape were beginning to extend their rule over African agriculturalists. This change was most explosive along the eastern Cape frontier, where relations between Africans and Europeans continued to evolve. Armed African resistance met colonial encroachment and its threats to African sovereignty and autonomy.

A case might easily be made that no other period or location in southern African history has enjoyed such extensive and repeated scrutiny from historians. This assertion holds especially true for the last two decades or so, which have witnessed a profusion of academic work.[7] In 1972, as part of this larger body of scholarship, Monica Wilson called for more attention to those people on this South African frontier (almost exclusively male) who participated in the translation of language, but who also "mediate[d] ideas, law, custom, symbolism . . . [who] listen[ed] as much as [they taught]." These were men who sought to "reconcile men, to achieve mutual understanding." In the end, Wilson concluded, they might be termed "cultural brokers."[8]

Jan Tzatzoe was precisely the type of person to whom Wilson was referring, but his life and work have received surprisingly little attention from historians.[9] Although this chapter draws on a longer and more complete accounting of Tzatzoe's life, its scope is limited to a particularly interesting period, 1816 to 1818. Tzatzoe had been educated by London Missionary Society missionaries, in particular, James Read, from around the age of fifteen in 1805 and had undergone a transformative spiritual experience when a revival swept the Bethelsdorp mission station, where he was learning Dutch and carpentry and wagon-repair skills in 1815. In 1816 he accompanied Joseph Williams and his wife, Elizabeth, to establish the first permanent mission station among the settled Xhosa polities of the frontier.[10]

Tzatzoe's diplomatic and evangelical contributions are best seen through an exposition of several key episodes in this brief but crucial period in his life and career on the eastern Cape frontier. My analysis focuses on Tzatzoe's diplomatic strategy and his central evangelical contributions, which lay in the area of translation. These illustrations of African agency can help to illuminate two major areas of historical inquiry that, while germane to southern African history, are important to the historiography of the frontier and comparative colonialism in general. The first relates to the political and diplomatic considerations that "middle figures" in a frontier setting face in attempting to mediate between competing interests insofar as they usually share parts of their identity with, and owe responsibilities to, at least two of these interests.[11] The second follows from the burgeoning and vital subfield of African history and, in particular, southern African history. This second area is variously identified as religious history, mission history, or simply the history of the "colonization of consciousness," to borrow a phrase from the two-part study *Of Revelation and Revolution,* which—along with many articles and monographs published similarly in the late 1980s and early 1990s—reinvigorated scholarly inquiry in this area.[12]

In many ways this body of work can be seen as one of the most fruit-ful offspring of the "linguistic turn" in the field. Recent articles by Paul Landau, Derek Peterson, and William Worger open up the space for further examination of the critical period in the colonial encounter when indigenous words and ideas were appropriated by Europeans in the service of disseminating (or imposing) their own religious world-view.[13] The new scholarship argues for renewed attention to African participation in the process. A microhistorical approach to the story of Jan Tzatzoe and Joseph Williams offers a unique entrée into the shared encounter.[14] Jan Tzatzoe's case is in many ways exceptional because of his close and personal ties to various London Missionary Society mis-sionaries, whose letters and documents have survived; it is, however, perhaps most exceptional in the degree to which it allows for such an examination, and therefore, it might be illustrative of the many other Africans who performed similar roles but whose contribution is harder to recover.

A Triangulating Diplomatic Strategy

In the early nineteenth century, missionaries such as Joseph Williams began to establish themselves among the independent African polities beyond the colonial boundaries of South Africa. In so doing they sub-mitted themselves to the political realities of the Africans among whom they settled. Inevitably the missionaries also came to be seen as repre-sentatives of the colony. Many relied on the threat of colonial force to safeguard themselves and their followers, while still making active at-tempts to mediate the relationship between Africans and Europeans and to ensure some African political access to the highest levels of Brit-ish government. But one primary source of tension was that many were also put to work by those colonial officials who had been charged with surveillance of the frontier and other diplomatic tasks.

Tzatzoe's career as an intermediary on the frontier and as a represen-tative of the Kat River mission fit into this emerging paradigm. Unlike many other African adherents of the early missions, his status as the son of a minor Xhosa chief enhanced his diplomatic capacity. One cru-cial consideration was that Tzatzoe's Ntinde subgroup did not owe its primary allegiance to either of the two major, and competing, group-ings, in the region, respectively headed by Ndlambe and Ngqika.[15] But Tzatzoe's father was a relatively poor man, whose people numbered at most around two thousand, and who could only provide three head of cattle to his son. The amount was a grave disappointment to the Williamses, who had expected that Tzatzoe's father would support the mission to a far greater degree with the most prestigious and visible symbol of wealth and power in Xhosaland.[16]

Besides the mission's powerlessness as reflected by its extreme poverty in cattle, Williams quickly realized that the threats to his mission derived not from the resistance of the Xhosa to the disconcerting power of his teachings but from the ongoing strife between the Xhosa chiefdoms that preceded his arrival in their midst. When Williams sought to protect his institution, he turned to Tzatzoe to mediate between himself and the chiefs, and he did so with complete trust. Rather than accompanying the young interpreter, he sent him off alone, when his life and that of his wife hung in the balance.

On these diplomatic journeys, Tzatzoe's status as a member of the Xhosa royal lineage likely gained him an easier passage into the chiefs' councils, but once there he had to rely on his oratorical skill and reasoning ability to present to a skeptical audience the challenging proposition of allowing the colonial intrusion in the form of the mission. Tzatzoe developed a triangulating strategy to negotiate among the competing agendas of Williams and his desire to build the institution and convert the local inhabitants, the colonial government and its continual demands on the mission, and his own interests in maintaining and perhaps expanding his own political status and security. Triangulation meant setting himself apart from each of the agendas and yet occupying their nexus. As we will see, if any one agenda threatened to overrun his intermediary position, he sprang into action to redistance and recenter himself.

The difficulty of their new situation was apparent from the first day the party arrived at the location of their encampment on the banks of the Kat River, on July 15, 1816. The site was about fifteen miles from Ngqika's main kraal but relatively isolated from any of the other Xhosa settlements.[17] Williams was surprised, therefore, upon their arrival, to find a group of Xhosa men from a nearby kraal who sat waiting for them on the riverbank. The men crowded around, asking for food and beads in a "very pressing" manner, but their main object was to complain that a mounted party of Boers had come a few days before and ridden off with thirty head of their cattle. Williams's indignant response to the situation is clear from his journal. He had not traveled to Xhosaland to adjudicate property disputes. He in turn questioned the men. Did they know of the "existence of their never dying souls?" Were they consequently aware of the "necessities" to which they must attend for their souls' preservation throughout eternity?[18]

If Williams had expected the local Xhosa to flock to him to hear the Word of God, he experienced a rude awakening. The Xhosa men knew that the Williams mission was the first permanent post to be established with the permission of the Xhosa chiefs and that it brought with it the displaced power of the colonial authorities. Whether the local men were appealing to Williams or to Tzatzoe, or to both, the first encounter of the party with the inhabitants of the area where they would be building their own homesteads and kraals reads like a routine request handled by all the Xhosa chiefs as they held councils and fulfilled their primary obligation to those commoners who settled on lands under their control—the adjudication of property disputes, in particular involving thefts of cattle.[19]

Before they had the time to unpack their ox wagons or to begin building a structure for worship, both Williams and Jan Tzatzoe were confronted with the principal, powerful, and at times paralyzing predicament that would underlie their lives in Xhosaland, constrain their actions, and ultimately undermine their missionary work. However much they might try to fulfill the role of messengers of God's word, sent by a higher power, or at least by a more enlightened segment of colonial society than the government itself, their presence in Xhosaland and the actions and decisions they took and could not take would be viewed by the people among whom they settled through the people's own understanding of the power and potential of the chiefs to whom they paid allegiance but whose hold over them was always tenuous.

Tzatzoe surely recognized this position into which he and Williams had been placed, and whether he took an active role himself in such disputes or convinced Williams to do so, it is clear that Williams came to understand his new, and unwelcome, role and did his best to fulfill the mission's obligations in this sphere. Writing to a colonial official in November 1816, Williams conveyed the complaint of a minor Xhosa chief, Jan Luza, against a Boer named Philip Opperman for taking thirty head of cattle from his kraals. "This is now the third time of application to ask if they can get no recompense," he pleaded with Major George Fraser, "they plague me for an answer."[20]

But as much as Williams was distracted from his spiritual work by the appeals of the Xhosa among whom he now lived, the colonial government that granted permission for the mission proved even more troublesome. The colonial government wanted a nation of peace-loving

Xhosa people. A nation where each individual was beholden to a chief, who was ultimately responsible for his subjects' actions. A nation whose individuals did not cross colonial boundaries into land that was until recently their own to hunt and graze cattle upon, who did not attempt to recover cattle stolen by colonialists but instead sought restitution through an enlightened colonial government, who did not engage in cattle raids of their own. A compliant and quiescent nation that would trade ivory and corn and forest products for British manufactured goods. Only "measures, firm yet tempered by forbearance & humanity," would enable the Xhosa to "understand the principles upon which civilized nations act, and teach them the necessity of abandoning that system of plunder which up to this period is so distressing to the Inhabitants of the Frontiers," concluded the colonial secretary, Colonel Christopher Bird, in a letter to a prominent frontier administrator.[21]

Being associated with the mission meant that Jan Tzatzoe was also tarred with the brush of colonial demands. It was up to him to mediate between the demands placed on Williams and thereby on Williams's work at the mission and the continued political goodwill of the local Xhosa. In any event Williams was evasive at best in his response to the colonial officials. It was "with pleasure," he wrote to Captain Fraser, the appointed colonial liaison on the frontier, that he would comply with the governor's request to provide information "respecting such Robberies as [were] committed by the Kaffers," but it was "very unlikely that their misdeeds should come to my knowledge."[22]

The mission, enjoying only the nominal support of the chiefs, struggled. Attendance gradually dwindled, and a series of diplomatic disasters left the institution by the middle of April 1818 not only poor and powerless but also in grave danger. It is in his diplomatic maneuvering during the station's last days that Tzatzoe's triangulating strategy is most easily observed. The decline started in April 1817, when Governor Somerset convened a grand summit meeting between himself and the frontier chiefs on the banks of the Kat River. The event allowed a considerable display of military might by the governor and his army, and Ngqika, fearing for his life, had to be cajoled into attending by repeated reassurances from Jan Tzatzoe.[23] Contrary to his fears the occasion was marked by a ceremony in which the colonial administration (despite the chief's best attempts to abrogate the position and deny his power to comply with its demands) enshrined Ngqika as the paramount chief of the Xhosa west of the Kei, guaranteeing him the full military support of the colony in his new role, and appointed his uncle, Ndlambe, who lived closer to the boundary, as a subsidiary figure.[24] Besides serving as a mediator between the government and the chiefs in this case, Tzatzoe was asked to provide lists of whose people belonged to which chief.[25]

The creation of a distinct hierarchy from among the scattered and ever shifting political allegiances of the Xhosa had been a long-term goal of the colonial administrators, and Tzatzoe was at the center of this attempt to extend colonial power and hegemony.[26] Yet Tzatzoe was quick to note, when he recalled his role in the conference, that he had been seated with the other Xhosa chiefs and not on the colonial side, and that the Governor had forced Ngqika into acknowledging his new status as "head over all the chiefs in [Xhosa]land" by an overwhelming display of military might.

The only result of the appointment of Ngqika was to further inflame tensions on the frontier and divide Xhosa allegiances into two camps. In fact Ndlambe had repeatedly attempted to make his own peace with the colony. But despite Ndlambe's strident denials of his peoples' culpability, Somerset chose to mount a punitive campaign against him with the intention of confiscating thousands of head of cattle.[27]

Word of a gathering colonial army reached Ngqika while he was visiting with the Williamses and Jan Tzatzoe at the Kat River. Ngqika was worried, indeed. He quickly received reassurance for his worries about the colonial commando from Jan Tzatzoe, who arrived at his kraals soon after the chief returned home to disclose the contents of a letter written to Ngqika by Major Fraser and conveyed via Williams. Tzatzoe explained that Fraser, head of the impending commando, had made it clear that he was after Ndlambe's cattle and not Ngqika's.[28]

In late January 1818, Fraser led a party of 300 British infantrymen and 150 mounted Boers into Xhosaland but was in turn confronted by Ndlambe with two thousand warriors.[29] Attempting to seize some cattle, the colonial force found itself surrounded on three sides by Ndlambe's men and retreated. Still looking for booty, the commando ransacked the surrounding countryside, attacking indiscriminately, killing Xhosa men, women, and children, and seizing cattle from both Botomane's and Ngqika's people. Jan Tzatzoe, cutting wood near the Kat River station, could hear the echo of gunfire as it consumed the valley.[30]

A shocked and exasperated Ngqika immediately sent envoys to the missionaries, accusing the missionaries of "betraying" him "into the hands of these people." Williams and Tzatzoe could only reply that they did not know what had happened but that they had told Ngqika exactly what Fraser's letter had said.[31]

In the aftermath of the raid, the mission was left deeply damaged. Jan Tzatzoe, understanding that his triangulated position was under threat by his apparent betrayal of the Xhosa royalty, undertook a stunning personal diplomatic mission to Grahamstown to visit Major Fraser. Fraser had not responded to Williams's correspondence and was in the delicate position of denying any wrongdoing in the conduct of his commando to an official colonial office enquiry and, instead, was arguing for a case of mistaken identity based on the fact that at least half of the chiefs from whom his commando had been accused of taking cattle were not identified as being under Ngqika's control on Tzatzoe's list.[32]

The trip to Fraser further demonstrates Tzatzoe's reach as a diplomat and his importance to the mission as a mediating figure. He undertook it because he felt that the government was ignoring Williams' entreaties and because the colonial officials did not appreciate the damage they had done to diplomatic relations on the frontier. The undertaking also speaks to Tzatzoe's sense of himself as an important player in the diplomatic arena and to the need he felt on a personal level to keep all sides content in his impartiality. Tzatzoe began by addressing Fraser:

How is this, Major Fraser? You sent a letter to Ngqika to say, that you were not going to attack him; that the object of your commando was to attack Ndlambe; how is it that you have broken your word and attacked Ngqika's people?

It would have been much better had you yourself gone to Ngqika and told him this; you have ruined us; Ngqika will never put any confidence in us.

Fraser replied: "Were those Ngqika's people that I attacked?"

You knew very well that those people belonged to Ngqika; you were present when the governor had a conference with Ngqika on the Kat River; if the impression on your mind was that those people belonged to Ndlambe, you would not have gone through Trumpeter's Drift, but you would have come by Brun's Drift.

According to Tzatzoe's recollection of the meeting, a chastened Fraser made no effort to reply.[33] Jan Tzatzoe acted decisively on behalf of himself and the mission when he confronted Fraser in early 1818, but in a continuation of his triangulating strategy, he also appeared to be currying favor with Ngqika and trying to ameliorate the diplomatic damage resulting from colonial double-dealing.

Evangelism and Translation

At the Kat River mission, Jan Tzatzoe found himself charged with several key tasks. While his diplomatic skills ensured that the mission remained standing, he worked at increasing the size of the mission, aiding the missionaries in their search for converts, and spreading the word himself.[34] Furthermore, Tzatzoe served as a translator and interpreter for Williams in ways greatly exceeding a narrow understanding of these tasks as mere transmission of one language into another. Tzatzoe was a guide to the meanings inherent in the conversations, the actions, and even the appearances of the African people among whom they had settled.

In the work of evangelizing, Williams and Tzatzoe chose to confront those Xhosa men and women who claimed the mantle of spiritual power, of recourse to unseen affective and effective metaphysical forces that could influence events in daily life. In so doing Williams and Tzatzoe called into question both the chiefs' and their peoples' reliance on and belief in a convergence of understandings that the Europeans termed witchcraft and in particular their recourse to people identified by varying contemporaneous European names as prophets or doctors and later as witch doctors, mediums, healers, and seers.[35]

Tzatzoe's work as an evangelist and interpreter revolved around the question of whether he could transmit the strength of the new spiritual power that he and Williams represented and do so in terms that were accessible to the local people. The daily work of evangelizing required Jan Tzatzoe to make his own case for the power of the transformations wrought by the God to whom he prayed, and it required him to translate the words Williams spoke to potential converts when seeking to convince them of the efficacy and potential of the spiritual power of which he claimed to be a vessel. Their task was complicated by the fact that they had to compete with people such as the syncretizing Xhosa leader Makana, who had spent time in the colony and who claimed to exercise the power of the ancestors along with the power of the Christian God and his son, thereby challenging the missionary's access to that power.[36]

Although the historical record does not contain verbatim examples of Tzatzoe's preaching, it does reveal the words and concepts that Williams asked him to translate. It is clear that in so doing Tzatzoe had to move beyond literal translations. For example, during a conversation between Williams and Ngqika, Tzatzoe translated Williams's description of the Devil as one of God's chief servants into one of God's chief soldiers—revealing Tzatzoe's concern that the Xhosa term for servant would reflect too servile a meaning and would not convey the distinguished and important work of an angel.[37]

As Williams and Tzatzoe confronted chiefs directly with regard to their reliance on doctors and prophets and engaged with the doctors themselves, Tzatzoe was at the center of the conversations, and the encounters reveal the intellectual steps he took in attempting to convey the central tenets of the belief system that he and Williams were championing into language and concepts that his Xhosa audience could comprehend.[38] The exemplary nature of Tzatzoe's work with regard to other African intermediaries is underscored by recent scholarly inquiry. William Worger has called attention to the importance of language in the colonial encounter, namely, as the "key to the translation, exchange and transmittal of ideas."[39] In analyzing the ways that missionaries and Africans (mis)communicated about ideas of God in the early to mid-nineteenth century, Worger valuably points to the central importance of metaphor in African languages and the degree to which missionaries failed to understand that the words they chose would be understood metaphorically. As we will soon see, Tzatzoe exemplified African involvement in the creation of language on the frontier and did so in ways suggesting he was keenly aware of the metaphorical reach of the language into which he was translating. In this regard Tzatzoe and African intermediaries like him might be viewed as the vanguard of an African intellectual tradition born in the colonial encounter.[40]

Christ as Prophet

During their time at the Kat River, Jan Tzatzoe and Williams were involved in several witchcraft allegations and investigations, and Williams used these encounters as opportunities to challenge local understandings of access to and management of spiritual power. The most significant incident occurred when the head of a nearby kraal who had fallen ill invited Williams, with Tzatzoe as his translator, to witness a smelling-out dance ceremony. A prophet had determined that the kraal head was suffering from the long-distance effects of poison created by an evildoer who had mixed some of the muddy ground on which the leader had urinated while hunting with the blood of his brother, who had been injured during the same hunting trip.

The prophet led about 150 warriors, who had assembled at their leader's kraal, into a neighboring valley. There, with triumphant gestures, she uncovered a calf's foot bound tightly with the bark of a tree, inside of which was located the poisonous mud. She emptied the foot onto the ground, making a point not to touch it.

Williams appealed to the leader of the kraal, who was still on his sickbed, for permission to address the gathering. He started by urging them to be content that the poison has been thrown away and to stop talking about who the poisoner might be. He then addressed them with the following words: "All the poison is not yet found but the great Prophet Christ is on his way to find it woe the man who has it hid when he cometh."[41]

Williams' journal does not indicate, as it does for the soldier/servant equivalency mentioned earlier, whether it was Tzatzoe himself who chose to translate the concept of Christ with the Xhosa term for prophet. Did Williams ask Tzatzoe to translate the English term "prophet"? Or did Tzatzoe suggest the Xhosa term for prophet as a direct translation of Christ? The important point is that the men acted in concert, that Williams relied on Tzatzoe, and that Tzatzoe was acting based on his personal conversion experience at Bethelsdorp. It is doubtful that Tzatzoe would have employed a straight translation of Williams's word, "prophet," if it inaccurately portrayed the concept that Williams and he were attempting to convey and to which I return in the next paragraph. What we do not know, however, is the exact Xhosa word that Tzatzoe employed. It would not be until the late 1820s that Tzatzoe would have his chance to contribute to the fixing of words to paper, a story transcending the scope of this essay.[42]

Williams's and Tzatzoe's choice of the Xhosa word for "prophet" to represent the concept of Christ, especially during a conversation in which the evangelists were discussing claims to spiritual authority, was a momentous and revelatory choice.[43] Williams and Tzatzoe understood that how a word, especially in translation, is received and made sense of by the person to whom it is directed is more important than its meaning within the language of origin.[44] Ultimately it shows that Williams and Tzatzoe were hoping that the Xhosa would appreciate the word on both a literal and a symbolic level.[45]

This was a remarkable feat of translation by an Englishman accused of illiteracy by his peers and by a young Xhosa man with a nominal formal education, and it fits neatly with the biblical narrative of the Last Judgment. Calling Christ a prophet portrayed him as a force that would continue the work of seeking out and destroying evildoers and the fomenters of misery. But this prophet was promised in an unseen fashion, and it is unclear how many of the Xhosa listeners would have understood that his arrival as an incarnate figure was not imminent.

Understood on this literal level, the concept conveyed by portraying God as a prophet who could find the cause of people's ailments and seek out evildoers had unintended and insidious consequences. Tzatzoe and Williams ultimately wished to expand on the simplified equivalence between Christ and a prophet, to use the term "prophet" metaphorically. They wanted the audience to appreciate the novelty of the truths they were sharing with them and to recognize the transformation in beliefs and practices that had to follow from a proper understanding of God and Christ. Instead, the people, their path eased by the language employed by Tzatzoe and Williams, merged the new Christian notions with their prior understandings and to Williams' mind did so in decidedly illogical, irreligious, and unorthodox ways.[46]

Jan Tzatzoe and Williams were among the first missionaries to spread the Word in Xhosaland, and theirs were some of the first attempts to translate scriptural messages into language that burrowed into Xhosa understandings of spiritual power and of the unfolding and investigation of misfortune. This approach led to difficulties and relied on a metaphorical understanding that the terms may have lacked. But the approach also led to an embracing of Christian thought. Subsequent missionaries were far less likely to use this approach. Instead, they invented new Xhosa terms or incorporated words with foreign roots. But it must also be noted that they had far less success in encouraging Xhosa conversion or even in securing residents for their mission stations.[47] The Kat River station, by comparison, bequeathed to future missionary institutions in Xhosaland the majority of their Christian adherents, including one man in particular, Ntsikana, who was remembered as the first great Xhosa Christian spiritual leader and composer of many of the Xhosa hymns that filled the air of future mission stations.[48] These hymns drew on an ameliorative flowering of metaphor for God and Jesus Christ that built on but surpassed Williams's and Tzatzoe's great Prophet.

Tzatzoe and Williams's efforts might serve as one of the earliest examples of the hybrid nature of the intellectual and linguistic innovations that attended the dramatic spread of Christianity throughout Africa, which flourished only when it escaped the control and surveillance of the formal mission churches. I do not think it a coincidence that this approach was attempted at the Kat River long before its time, during a period when it appears that there was a true partnership between an English missionary and his African assistant.

In the early months of his mission to the Xhosa, Joseph Williams wrote sparsely, if at all, of the young Xhosa chief who had accompanied his family into Xhosaland. By 1818, when Tzatzoe and his Khoi companions abandoned Williams under a renewed diplomatic threat, Williams's respect for Tzatzoe's contribution to the work of the mission was evident: "All the people who came with me from Bethelsdorp are now on the point to return . . . *this would have been no loss had Jan Tzatzoe not been prevailed upon to leave me also this is to me a great loss as there is not an individual to whom I could speak with any satisfaction besides him nor have I now any suitable interpreter*" (my italics).[49]

Jan Tzatzoe had become the critical figure at the mission station on the colonial frontier, the figure through whom the missionary spoke in both his diplomatic and evangelizing conversations. Tzatzoe's role was to make Williams understood, to give flight to his words. He also appeared to care deeply about spreading his own understanding of the Word of God and about relating the transformation it had wrought within him. Tzatzoe's work was to fit both his own and Williams's understanding into the vocabulary of his childhood, and, in part, to try to defend the actions of the men who had given him this great gift but who seemed to contradict its utterances with every cattle rustling commando and diplomatic sword swipe.

The life and work of Jan Tzatzoe at the Kat River are a compelling example of the intensive but hitherto underrecognized role of Africans in actively shaping the colonial encounter. His contributions also illustrate various aspects of the historiography of intermediaries and interpreters, the "cultural brokers" in Monica Wilson's words, on the colonial African frontier.

Certainly Tzatzoe played a critical role in ensuring the diplomatic survival of the institution in whose evangelizing mission he had a heartfelt stake. Yet, we have also seen how an African intermediary like him needed to adopt a triangulating strategy when dealing with the major forces that influenced his political and diplomatic moves. He needed to maintain the respect of the African rulers in the area, heed the interests of the mission itself, accede to requests for information and assistance from the colonial government, and keep an eye out for his own potential political and economic development. Tzatzoe kept his balance by moving into the nexus of the competing influences—if one wind blew too strongly, he let it blow him just far enough so that its strength was counteracted by another. This triangulating position was only possible in a frontier setting where colonial influence and hegemony had not become overbearing, but Tzatzoe's strategy might comfortably explain the actions of many other Africans who flourished in similar settings but whose lives are not so easily recoverable from the historical record.

Tzatzoe as a "cultural broker" served mainly in the capacity of interpreter and translator for Williams in both his diplomatic and evangelizing conversations with Africans. I have tried to stress Tzatzoe's fundamental role in the process of translation to illustrate the role of African agency in the "colonization of consciousness." Renewed attention to language and the exact nature of the individual words being translated reveals that Williams and Tzatzoe shared a successful partnership in attempting to convey the central concepts of Christianity, but that the act of translation, in which Tzatzoe and many other Africans such as him played the key role, brought as many potential difficulties as possibilities based on the ways that the translated words were understood.

Despite Jan Tzatzoe's important contributions to the Kat River mission, history has remembered him, if at all, only as Williams' "native assistant." In attempting to resurrect his legacy, I have stressed his service to the mission as a diplomat and translator and his personal contributions to the dispersion of the gospel into the consciousness of the Xhosa. But the racial dynamics of the frontier were such that it would be half a century before the London Missionary Society would ordain a Xhosa minister and missionary, Tiyo Soga.

Tzatzoe himself would continue his career as an evangelist on the frontier, helping in the late 1820s to translate large sections of the scripture for the Reverends Brownlee and Kayser. Gradually, though, his identity as the son of a Xhosa chief and leader of the Ntinde people would begin to trump his work with the missionaries. He would travel as a guest of the London Missionary Society to Great Britain in 1836 to evangelize and raise funds for the African missions, but on his return the secular concerns of his people would destroy his devotion to the church, and he would be accused (with some merit) by colonial settlers of fighting against them in the frontier war of 1846–47. Did Tzatzoe's life in fact reach a fork on the banks of the Kat River?

After the sudden death of Joseph Williams in the last months of 1818, Tzatzoe led a party back to the Kat River to rescue Elizabeth Williams and her two infant children. Elizabeth was distraught at the abandonment of the institution and implored Barker to appoint another missionary. One was not forthcoming. On hearing the news, did Tzatzoe, the young Xhosa chief, ask himself or, indeed, the English missionaries he accompanied, why he was not qualified to guide the people of the

Kat River in their commitment to Christianity? Why could he not be the man to assume the mantle of the mission?

Notes

I would like to thank Richard Roberts, Emily Osborn, Benjamin Lawrance, and the anonymous reviewers of this volume for their comments on this chapter. The research on which it is based was funded in part by the U.S. Fulbright Commission, the Giles Whiting Foundation, and various bodies at Yale University.

1. The mission station was continually beset with reports of great disaffection among the local Xhosa. Tzatzoe repeatedly traveled the arduous fifteen miles to Ngqika's kraals. For example, in September 1816 he assured the chief that the rumor being circulated claiming that the mission was being established in Xhosaland in order to "betray" the Xhosa "into the hands of the English [was] false" and based on the provocation of frontier Afrikaaners chafing under British rule. Council of World Missions (hereafter LMS), London, SA Incoming, box 6, folder 3, D, Williams to London Missionary Society, June 15, 1816, to August 7, 1817, unpaginated.

2. Cape Archives (hereafter KAB), Cape Town, R.S.A., Colonial Office, CO 2603, Williams to Fraser, Kat River, November 18, 1816.

3. For a description of the early days of the mission, see Holt, *Joseph Williams*, 40–44.

4. KAB, CO 2603, Williams to Fraser Kat River (November) 22, 1816, original just has 22nd.

5. Holt, *Joseph Williams*, 43.

6. I have been able to find only two pieces on Tzatzoe. Crafford, "Jan Tshatshu"; and Jonas, "Jan Tshatshu and the Eastern Cape Mission." Both accounts are drawn from secondary sources.

7. For a brief selection of the best of the more recent work with particular relevance to the interaction of the Xhosa and the British, see Crais, *White Supremacy and Black Resistance*; Crais, *Politics of Evil*; Elbourne, *Blood Ground*; Keegan, *Colonial South Africa*; Lester, *Imperial Networks*; Mostert, *Frontiers*; Peires, *Dead Will Arise*; and Peires, *House of Phalo*.

8. M. Wilson, *Interpreters*, 17–20.

9. In the histories of the period cited in note 7, Tzatzoe is mentioned most in Mostert, *Frontiers*, and in passing in Elbourne, *Blood Ground*.

10. I examine Tzatzoe's fascinating life, including his experiences at Bethelsdorp, his work as a translator for three missionaries, his journey to Great Britain in 1836, the increasing tension that developed over his responsibilities as a chief in the 1840s, and his "betrayal" of the British during the war of 1846–47 in my dissertation, "Sable Son of Africa."

11. See Emily Osborn's comprehensive discussion of the literature surrounding "middle figures" in "Circle of Iron," 33–34.

12. For outstanding examples, see Comaroff and Comaroff, *Christianity, Colonialism, and Consciousness in South Africa;* Comaroff and Comaroff, *Dialectics of Modernity on a South African Frontier;* Landau, *Realm of the Word;* Sanneh, *Translating the Message.* For a good introduction to the more recent work, see Peterson and Allman, "Introduction."

13. Landau, "'Religion' and Christian Conversion in African History"; D. Peterson, "Translating the Word"; Worger, "Parsing God."

14. In adopting a microhistorical tact, I refer to particularly effective microhistories (with a firm scholarly basis) in African history in recent years, including Harms, *Diligent;* Thornton, *Kongolese Saint Anthony;* Van Onselen, *Seed Is Mine.*

15. Anthropologists and historians have debated for years over what to call the small Xhosa polities that were known as "tribes" at the time. Each group's members could usually claim descent from a chief or a chief's ancestor. These designations were ever shifting. Perhaps it would be best to follow a Xhosa intellectual, John Henderson Soga, who, possibly in deference to his Scottish heritage, employs the term "clan." Soga, *Ama-Xosa.*

16. LMS, SA Incoming, box 6, folder 3, D, Williams to LMS, June 15, 1816, to August 7, 1817, unpaginated.

17. Holt, *Joseph Williams,* 42.

18. LMS, SA Incoming, box 6, folder 3, D, Williams to LMS, June 15, 1816, to August 7, 1817, unpaginated.

19. Peires, *House of Phalo;* Stapleton, *Maqoma.*

20. KAB, CO 2603, Williams to Fraser, Kat River, November 13, 1816.

21. KAB, CO 4838, Bird to Stockenstrom, July 2, 1816.

22. KAB, CO 2607, Williams to Fraser, October 7, 1816. The reason Williams was unlikely to hear of raids across the boundary, he admitted in a letter to the LMS, is that he made it a "point of [his] object to expose the evil of such conduct and also to condemn it." LMS, SA Incoming, box 6, folder 3, D, Williams to LMS, June 15, 1816, to August 7, 1817, unpaginated.

23. LMS, SA Incoming, box 6, folder 3, D, Williams to LMS, June 15, 1816, to August 7, 1817, unpaginated.

24. LMS, SA Incoming, box 6, folder 3, D, Williams to LMS, June 15, 1816, to August 7, 1817, unpaginated.

25. KAB, CO 4840, Bird to Williams, at Kat River, Colonial office, September 8, 1818.

26. This formalizing of allegiances can be seen as one of the first steps toward indirect rule, and it anticipated the type of colonial control that would be imposed in the region beginning with the ill-fated Queen Adelaide's Province; see Lester, *Imperial Networks,* 78–105.

27. Peires, *House of Phalo,* 61.

28. LMS, SA Incoming, box 7, folder 4, C, Williams to Burder, Kat River, April 14, 1818.

29. Stapleton, *Maqoma*, 27.

30. Great Britain, House of Commons, "Report from the Select Committee on Aborigines (British Settlements)," (London, 1836–37; Cape Town: C. Struik, 1966), 563–70.

31. For diplomatic background, see Mostert, *Frontiers*, 457–61; and "Report from the Select Committee on Aborigines," 569. Stapleton, *Maqoma*, 27, relies on the *Cape Frontier Gazette* and gets the assignation wrong.

32. In fact the cattle were restored to Ngqika and his followers when the government realized a mistake had been made.

33. "Report from the Select Committee on Aborigines," 569–70. Despite an extensive search, I could find no record in the archive in which Fraser discussed this meeting.

34. Because he knew very little Dutch and no Xhosa, Williams let Tzatzoe address the many groups they encountered around the mission station. The mission also held to a strict schedule of worship. Sunday was devoted to day-long prayer. There were five meetings: the first after sunrise, the second at nine o'clock to go over Sunday School subject matter, the third at eleven to "dispense the word of eternal life and after the same form as [was] common among dissenters," the fourth in the afternoon similar to the third, and a fifth in the evening, when Jan Tzatzoe climbed the dais and addressed the people "either from a single text or a large portion of the word." LMS, SA Incoming, box 6, folder 3, D, Williams to LMS, June 15, 1816, to August 7, 1817, unpaginated.

35. There is an extensive literature on witchcraft, particularly in Africa, and the terminology involved resembles a minefield. I have chosen to use the nineteenth-century terms "doctor" or "prophet" interchangeably as the missionaries apparently did to describe people who variously fulfilled the roles of rainmakers, healers, shamans, oracle priests, and so on. For a fresh and well-argued approach to the subject or witchcraft in Africa, see Geschiere, *Modernity of Witchcraft*.

36. For more on Makana, or Nxele, or Links as he was known at the time, see Peires, *House of Phalo*, and Hodgson, "Study of the Xhosa Prophet Nxele."

37. The incident is described by Williams in LMS, SA Incoming, box 6, folder 3, D, Williams to LMS, June 15, 1816, to August 7, 1817, unpaginated. It is one of unfortunately few cases of translation where Williams notes both his own choice of words and Tzatzoe's translation.

38. In the interests of conserving space, I have omitted the description of the meeting of Ngqika, Makana, and Williams at the Kat River. Tzatzoe and Williams confronted the chiefs directly on the issue of the widespread drought in Xhosaland and blamed them for the lack of rain (the provision of which was the prophets' main function) because of personal immorality and the torturing

of witchcraft suspects. By implication the Christian God would be able to do better. See Levine, "Sable Son of Africa."

39. Worger, "Parsing God," 419.

40. I am indebted to Paul Landau for this formulation.

41. The encounter at the kraal and dialogue are from LMS, SA Incoming, box 6, folder 3, D, Williams to LMS, June 15, 1816, to August 7, 1817, unpaginated.

42. See Levine, "Sable Son of Africa." Tzatzoe worked with the missionaries Brownlee and Kayser in an extremely collaborative fashion to translate large chunks of scripture and developed a notion of Christ as healer in doing so.

43. Given the evidence I present in the discussion of this incident in "Sable Son of Africa," it is evident that this was not the first time that the duo employed this concept.

44. Walter Benjamin makes this point when discussing translation. "The task of the translator consists in finding that intended effect upon the language into which he is translating which produces in it the echo of the original." He concludes his meditation by discussing how scripture like all great texts contains its "translation between the lines." Benjamin, "Task of the Translator," 76–82.

45. I follow here in part Worger's provocative work on the words assigned to "God" in the colonial encounter and his argument that during the process of translation, the missionaries' (and I suggest native assistants') choice of these words either took into account or was forced to interact with the outstanding degree to which African languages rely on metaphor. Worger, "Parsing," 419–20. But I differ from Worger in that I think Tzatzoe consciously chose the term with the most literal connection to the concept of Christ, one that relied the least on the listener making any metaphorical leaps.

46. For example, adherents of the mission began to use the language of prophets and witchcraft to describe their relationship with Christ. He would "smell out" their evil in the form of sin and cleanse them. Contrary to Worger, they appear to have thought of Christ literally as an incarnate prophet. Please refer to the far more extensive discussion in Levine, "Sable Son of Africa."

47. Peires, *House of Phalo;* and Peires, *Dead Will Arise.* It seems to me that Africans, when they translated or incorporated European religious terms, often relied on metaphor, as Worger suggests. But as other historians, Landau in particular, have pointed out, when missionaries invented African words or relied on their own translations, their figures of speech were most often taken literally (and, often, literally as nonsense).

48. Regarding the legacy of the Kat River station, see "Report from the Select Committee on Aborigines," 572. Regarding Ntsikana, see Hodgson, *Ntsikana's Great Hymn.*

49. LMS, SA Incoming, box 7, folder 4, C, Williams to Burder, Kat River, April 14, 1818.

Interpreting Colonial Power in French Guinea

The Boubou Penda–Ernest Noirot Affair of 1905

EMILY LYNN OSBORN

In an article published in 1922, a high-ranking French colonial official, Camille Guy, wrote about the challenges that African colonial employees presented to French administrators. He noted that administrators find themselves "at the mercy" of their interpreters "who abuse the situation, betray the administrator and sell themselves to the highest offer." Speaking from personal experience, Guy counseled his French officials to "learn the language of the country that they govern." Guy went on to describe an investigation he conducted in which he would have committed a "monstrous" miscarriage of justice "due to [his] interpreter, who falsified the depositions of witnesses." Guy rectified the situation, however, when his "domestic" told him of the "betrayal of the interpreter."[1] As it turned out, the household help proved more credible than the interpreter, and the information he provided changed the outcome of the case.

The processes of mediation to which Guy refers has been discussed by other participants and observers of colonial rule: in the memoirs and fiction of Amadou Hampâté Bâ, the novels of Chinua Achebe and Amadou Kouroumah, as well as the historical analyses made by Pierre

Alexandre, Henri Brunschwig, and the contributors to this volume.[2] These writings all expose a persistent feature of colonial rule, one that this essay also confirms: the proximity, access, and interpretive skills of African intermediaries played a critical role in shaping the meanings and nuances that colonialism acquired in practice.

In 1905 a scandal broke in the French West African colony of French Guinea that sheds light on the powerful but obscured position occupied by African employees. The case involved a French colonial official, Ernest Noirot, and his interpreter, Boubou Penda. The pair worked side by side for almost twenty years. But in 1905 Noirot and Boubou came under investigation for their alleged involvement in a variety of crimes including extortion and "abuse of power."[3] Despite considerable pressure, Boubou and Noirot denied the charges leveled at them, and each refused to implicate the other. The scandal took a heavy toll on Noirot's career and ultimately cost Boubou his life.

The loyalty of Boubou and Noirot to each other may have been unusual, as was the degree of Boubou's influence within the colony of French Guinea. But Boubou's life and career provide a vivid illustration of the power and influence that African employees could derive from their affiliation with the colonial state, while also revealing how intermediaries could shape colonial politics. This case shows that although colonialism imposed an alien grid of governance on African peoples and institutions, Africans made inroads into the apparatus of rule and shaped its operation. Colonial rule, in other words, was not a top-down, unidirectional event but a complex process shaped by uneven power relations, strategic bargains, and competing interests.

Noirot and Boubou in Senegal

From the vantage point of dedicated French imperialists, Ernest Noirot participated in the most dramatic period of French colonial expansion. Born in 1851, Noirot served in the military as a young man. In 1881 he joined a small French-sponsored diplomatic expedition to the Futa Jallon in present-day Guinea (Conakry). The purpose of the trip was to promote French commercial interests and weaken the well-established commercial networks that linked the region to the British port city of Freetown, Sierra Leone.[4] That mission shows that the French initially relied on informal diplomacy to expand their influence in the interior of West Africa. This strategy changed and became more muscular in the late 1880s, when the French launched a series of military campaigns through present-day Senegal, Mali, Upper Guinea, and northern Côte d'Ivoire.

The state that Noirot visited in the early 1880s, the Futa Jallon, or Futa, was an Islamic theocracy that had been founded in the early eighteenth century. Most inhabitants of the Futa are members of the Fulbe, or Peul, ethnic group, and they are speakers of FuFulbe, or Pulaar. The leader of the Futa was the *almamy*, and the holder of this office overlooked a series of lesser chieftaincies resident in nine *diwal*, or provinces. But as Noirot learned during his visit, the Futa's leadership structure featured a distinctive twist. Two ruling families, or houses, alternated holding the highest office in the land, the *almamymate*, every two years. The families, the Soriya and the Alfaya, were ancient rivals. This system of power sharing reflected a truce that had been brokered between the houses, probably in the 1840s.[5]

The Futa made a deep impression on Noirot. After returning to France in 1882, Noirot completed a lively book about his visit, and in 1886 he secured a permanent position working for the colonial state as a third-class commander.[6] Initially posted to Dagana, Senegal, Noirot was then transferred to Sine Saloum, where, as historian Martin Klein notes, he demonstrated energy, passion, and a tendency to produce long memos.[7]

It was while in either Dagana or Sine Saloum that Noirot first met and employed Boubou Penda. Boubou was initially hired as a "boy," or house servant, but he soon became involved in Noirot's official duties. An 1889 treaty drawn up by Noirot with various chiefs from Sine Saloum bears Boubou's uncertain signature (see figure 1).[8] But the documentary record offers few details about Boubou's youth and little explanation for why he came to work for Noirot. While Noirot always insisted that Boubou was of noble birth, almost everyone else believed that Boubou was, as one of his later adversaries put it, of "base extraction."[9] Broader patterns of colonial recruitment and employment offer further indication that Boubou was probably of low social status. The French faced considerable difficulties in finding African men to work for them; usually the only ones willing to do so were slaves, former slaves, or descendents of slaves.[10] Boubou's humble social origins make the interpreter's later ascent to a position of power and influence all the more stunning and, for many of the African elites with whom he came into contact, problematic and offensive.

The period that Boubou and Noirot spent in Sine Saloum, Senegal, proved significant in the careers of both men. Noirot impressed his

1889 Treaty, Sine Saloum, Senegal. The first time that Boubou Penda enters the documentary record. Boubou's signature is on the upper right, while Noirot's is on the lower left. (from Ernest Noirot's personal papers)

superiors enough to earn a significant promotion in 1897. Boubou, meanwhile, seems to have established himself as Noirot's indispensable and trusted aide.

While Noirot and Boubou solidified their working relationship in Senegal, political tensions intensified to the south in the Futa Jallon, the region Noirot had visited on his first trip to West Africa. The Futa had maintained its status as an independent, sovereign state, but its leaders felt the squeeze of French territorial aspirations from three sides: from the western Soudan to the east (the interior savanna region of West Africa), the Casamance to the north, and the French port of Conakry to the west. These external pressures mounted at a time when internal conflicts threatened to fracture the Futa from within. A member of the Soriya clan had refused to give up his position as *almamy* after his allotted two-year term. In 1896 the dispute between the Soriya family and the Alfaya family over the *almamymate* threatened the political stability of the region.

In a decision that proved critical to the future of the Futa, Oumarou Bademba, of the Alfaya family, turned to the French for support in his quest to reclaim the *almamy*'s turban.[11] French officials agreed to help on the condition that they could build a French post in the region. When a small French force marched into the region in late 1896, the opposition to Bademba dissolved. Bademba was then installed in Timbo, the capital, as *almamy*, and the French declared the region a French protectorate.[12]

In occupying the Futa, the French established what was, in effect, a system of indirect rule. The French resident in Timbo was responsible for the "oversight" of the *almamy* and for French district commanders who were to be attached to the lesser chiefs in each of the Futa's *diwal*. The man charged with establishing French rule in the Futa was Ernest Noirot, who was appointed the first French resident of the Futa Jallon. In 1897 Noirot arrived in Timbo accompanied by his servant-turned-interpreter, Boubou Penda.

The Official Record, 1897–1900

Noirot worked quickly to make himself a significant power broker in the Futa by leveraging the region's fierce rivalries into a foundation for French rule. Using diplomacy, coercion, and intimidation, Noirot forged coalitions with individuals and factions he thought to be sympathetic— or vulnerable—to French interests. Soon after his arrival, Noirot took aim at the highest position in the land, the *almamy*. When Noirot arrived in the Futa, he was met by Almamy Bademba, whom the French had helped install. In 1898 Noirot decided to invoke the rule that the position of *almamy* should rotate every two years between the Alfaya family and the Soriya family. In a meeting that brought together the Futa's notables, Noirot successfully championed a weak and probably ineligible candidate from the Soriya clan, Baba Alimou. By engineering the appointment of Alimou, Noirot seems to have thought that an *almamy* of questionable legitimacy who owed his position to the French would be more malleable to colonial demands. To help reinforce the new *almamy*'s authority, Noirot put a small military regiment of ten

African men in French uniforms at Alimou's disposal.[13] But neither French endorsement nor a colonial militia altered the general opinion in the Futa that Almamy Alimou was a usurper and a fraud.[14]

Having destabilized the *almamymate,* Noirot further manipulated the Futa's ruling structures through his relationship with another prominent leader, Alfa Yaya. Alfa Yaya was the chief of the *diwal* of Labé, the economic capital of the Futa and the region's most important commercial hub. For years Alfa Yaya had tried to extricate himself from the strict ruling hierarchy that subordinated his chieftaincy and the *diwal* of Labé to the *almamy* in Timbo.[15] In Alfa Yaya's agitations against the authority of the *almamy,* Noirot saw an opportunity to win an ally and weaken a potential foe. Noirot elevated the status of the Labé chieftaincy and bequeathed Alfa Yaya with the utterly invented title "King of Labé." By allowing Alfa Yaya to operate under his direct supervision, Noirot took Labé out of the traditional ruling structure and deprived the *almamy* of oversight of the Futa's most important provinces.[16]

On the surface Noirot's efforts to establish the French presence in the Futa paralleled the "divide and rule" strategies used at the time by other French colonial officials throughout West Africa. But a careful reading of evidence from 1897 to 1900, the period during which Noirot served as French resident, reveals that a more complex set of power relations operated below the surface of official reports and formal mandates.

Boubou in the Futa Jallon

The man who always stood by Noirot's side and joined in all official negotiations was Boubou Penda. Noirot publicly described Boubou as his "man of confidence" and as "my son," and he frequently reminded French and African audiences alike that "the words of Boubou" were his own. Noirot made it clear that he expected Boubou's orders and declarations to be respected just as if they had been issued from the resident himself.[17] One French official, Hubert, later testified that "the confidence shown by Noirot for Boubou was . . . notorious. Everyone, Europeans and natives, knew it." Hubert explained that when he first arrived in the Futa, "everyone" warned him about Boubou. He was told: "'Noirot is a brave man, unfortunately at his side is his interpreter, Boubou Penda, and if you are not in the good graces of Boubou, Noirot will not tolerate you. . . . [A person] who wants to get along well with one must get along with the other.'"[18] Hubert's observations are confirmed by three incidents that involved Boubou Penda. They show that Boubou carried the mantle of French authority with considerable effect on local populations.

COLONIAL *TIRAILLEURS*

One day in December 1898, a group of about twenty *tirailleurs,* or African soldiers in the French military, harassed Boubou on the roadside as he passed by on horseback on his way to see the *almamy*. The *tirailleurs* were angry because Boubou had told Noirot that they had stolen some alcohol. Boubou managed to escape their threats and insults, but he subsequently reported the incident to Noirot.[19]

This initial event alone offers a number of indications of Boubou's primacy in the Futa. First, the *tirailleurs* were angry because Boubou had reported them for theft. Boubou's allegations had been proof enough for Noirot, who had then disciplined the soldiers. Second, when the *tirailleurs* confronted Boubou, he was riding horseback to see Almamy Baba Alimou. Expensive to acquire and maintain, horses in the Futa were typically owned and ridden only by wealthy elites. The symbolic significance of an affiliate of the French state and a man of putative slave descent riding a horse would not have been lost on the population of the Futa. Finally, that Noirot's interpreter was on his way to see the *almamy*, whether for official reasons or not, demonstrates that Boubou was a figure of importance in the region.

The hostilities between the *tirailleurs* and Boubou did not stop with this initial confrontation. A day later, the *tirailleurs* attacked Boubou again, this time at the colonial post. Noirot saw the assault, and he rushed to his interpreter's side, throwing himself in the middle of the scuffle. Bystanders broke up the altercation, but not before Boubou and Noirot received minor injuries.[20]

Noirot's willingness to intercede in defense of his interpreter created a minor furor among the Futa's European community. It was unseemly for the French Resident to brawl in the courtyard of the colonial post. Furthermore, Noirot's display was probably troubling because it crossed racial lines and undermined the hegemony of whiteness in the French colonial state. A small committee of French officials was subsequently assembled to investigate the matter and collect testimonies from eyewitnesses and community members. The story of one of the men interviewed provides the second notable illustration of Boubou's interpretation and use of French authority.

A LOCAL BLACKSMITH

Ousmane Sissoko, a blacksmith and jeweler, told the committee that he had suffered at Boubou's hands. Sissoko explained that one day he sent his brother to the market to sell some rings. The brother returned quickly, reporting that Boubou had stopped him, taken his rings, and then beaten him. Sissoko then went to the market and confronted Boubou, who explained: "He's a Bambara and I mock all Bambaras."[21] To reiterate his disdain for this ethnic group, Boubou then hit Sissoko. A day later Boubou gave Sissoko a franc, but Sissoko did not know if it was intended as payment for the ring or for other, still uncompensated work he had done for the interpreter.[22] This episode shows the latitude that Boubou enjoyed in the Futa: Boubou could act with violent whimsy and pay at will for goods and services rendered.

Sissoko's deposition apparently caused little concern, and ultimately little came of the inquiry into Boubou and Noirot. But it was not the last time that news of Boubou's actions traveled official channels of communication.

A FRENCH COLONIAL ADMINISTRATOR

In 1899 Rauch, a French official posted to the Futa, wrote to Noirot about Boubou. Rauch related that while visiting a neighboring village, one of the local chiefs presented him with a letter that Boubou had delivered. The letter contained an order, written allegedly by Noirot, for the chief and his village to give a certain number of goats to Boubou. Upon reading the order, Rauch knew something was amiss. As he wrote to Noirot, "I understood immediately . . . it [the letter] was not from you. . . . [Y]ou would never have given such an order."

Rauch explained that he questioned Boubou about the letter, but the interpreter insisted on its legitimacy. Then, complained Rauch, Boubou "allowed himself, even though he does not know me well, to give me the order to enforce his illegal request."[23] Offended by this African interpreter, who clearly was used to getting his way, Rauch warned Noirot, "[Y]our interpreter used your name to try to commit an abuse of authority, an illegal act that I would even qualify as theft."

Throughout the letter, Rauch made clear his assumption of Noirot's ignorance of Boubou's actions. But Rauch's attempt to alert Noirot quietly and diplomatically did not produce the intended result; Noirot was not in the least convinced of Boubou's guilt. On the contrary,

Rauch's accusations enraged Noirot, and he publicized widely his dissatisfaction. According to one French observer, Noirot told Rauch "'that
Boubou was a bureaucrat with the same title as him and that he had
to show him respect and not attack his reputation.'" According to this
observer, Rauch was "extremely affected by this unjust reprimand."
Moreover, everyone knew from that day forward that Noirot regarded
Rauch with "an implacable hatred that even death would not dilute."[24]

This incident, like the others, reveals the sometimes painful lesson
that local residents, elites, and French officials learned about the politics
of colonial rule in the Futa. Boubou had to be treated as an extension of
Noirot himself. Boubou was, in effect, the second-in-command of the
French colonial state in the Futa.

Beyond the Futa

In 1900 Noirot was promoted again, this time to Conakry, where he became the director of Native Affairs, the most important position in the
colony after the governor. As director of Native Affairs, Noirot oversaw
the commanders who were posted to districts throughout the colony.
Noirot also continued to rely on his interpreter, Boubou Penda, who
also moved to Conakry in 1900 and joined the Department of Native
Affairs.[25] In 1902 Boubou was promoted from fourth-class to third-class
interpreter, becoming one of the better paid African employees in the
colony.[26] Boubou and Noirot did not simply work together, however.
In 1900, Boubou accompanied Noirot on their second trip together to
France (they had visited France for the first time in 1897).[27] And in 1903
each applied for and received neighboring land concessions in Ca-
mayenne, on the outskirts of Conakry.[28]

Noirot and Boubou's close personal and professional relationship
may not have been as extraordinary as it might appear in retrospect. At
the turn of the century, Conakry was a boom town built on the trade in
wild rubber. It was home to a small, tightly knit group of French administrators and businessmen who considered themselves resourceful and
fiercely independent advocates of French civilization and commerce.[29]
This entrepreneurial spirit reflected the particular context of the early
colonial occupation of Guinea. With few financial, military, and personnel resources, Guinea's first generation of French administrators relied
on what they could acquire, manipulate, and manage locally. In this setting Noirot's willingness to use whatever means available, including
the skills of his interpreter, to promote French rule reflected the modus

operandi of colonial Guinea. Noirot's relationship to Boubou may have stretched the bounds of acceptability, but it was probably viewed more as an eccentricity than as a problem.

Until 1905 Noirot's resourcefulness and flexibility were consistently praised by his superiors. In a 1902 personnel report, Guinea's governor described Noirot as zealous and devoted, a man of "brilliant" achievements.[30] In Dakar, however, the governor general's reaction to Noirot's review was less enthusiastic. While the governor general agreed that Noirot had given "excellent service" to the colony, "his sympathies for the Peul population render him sometimes unjust with regards to the other populations of Guinea." The governor general further warned that Noirot's ties to prominent chiefs in the Futa compromised official French policy.[31] The governor general's assessment of Noirot was but a small indication of changes that were taking place in the colonial governance of French West Africa.

Changing Colonial Prerogatives

In 1905 the approach to colonial rule that had helped give form to colonial Guinea came under fire from two arenas, from the governor general in Dakar and from the population and leadership of the Futa. These pressures transformed Guinea's colonial situation and the paradigm in which Noirot and Boubou lived and worked.

Administratively the roots of change came out of the governor general's attempt to systematize the administration of the West African colonies. In 1895 the governor general of French West Africa arranged France's West African colonies into a federation to centralize policy and finances. For several years little attempt was made to impose policies on or collect revenues from the federation. That changed in 1902 with a new governor general who sought to implement procedural uniformity througout French West Africa. These efforts, however, were not well received by "old Guinea hands," who resented sending taxes to Dakar and who had no interest in enforcing laws that had been generated elsewhere. Whenever possible Guinea's French officials simply ignored the decrees and directives issued from Dakar.

Guinea's recalcitrance did not sit well with Dakar. The governor general sent an inspector to investigate the colony's affairs in 1904. The inspector concluded that Guinea needed a more "formal" administration, "less paternal, less influenced by the demands of commerce, and which [would] have more direct action on the natives."[32] Soon thereafter a new governor, Governor Frézouls, arrived in Guinea. For the first time Guinea was to be governed by someone who had no ties to or previous experience in the colony. The change was significant. Noirot's generation of colonial administrators—flexible, versatile, and able to "make do" with limited resources—often spent their whole career in one place. Members of the second generation of administrators embarked on a very different career path. They were attuned to bureaucratic principles of governance, possibly having been trained in the newly formed École Coloniale in Paris, and were unlikely to develop enduring relationships in any one colony. The new arrivals tended to view the tactics of the first generation of colonizers with mild alarm, seeing them as too irregular, arbitrary, and personal.

From the outset Governor Frézouls made it clear that he wanted to wrest control of the colony from entrenched French interests. Not surprisingly Frézouls's efforts to "clean house" met with great hostility. One group of residents claimed that the new governor was "filling the colony with a terrible terror."[33] Another official asserted that Frézouls "undertook hasty reforms without knowing the country" and that he thereby immersed the country "in fire and in blood."[34] Frézouls coolly dismissed the reactions of Guinea's old guard, explaining that they were the predictable result of "a period of inevitable transformation."[35]

Frézouls also took a dim view of the man who occupied the number two spot in the colony. Frézouls commented that Noirot "possesse[d] no administrative understanding" and that he would never have a place in an "organized colony." Furthermore, Noirot "identifie[d] with the natives, whose usages and tendencies he [had] adopt[ed]." Frézouls expressed particular concern about Noirot's reliance on Boubou, noting that Noirot's actions were "nothing but the reflection of Boubou Penda, his interpreter and friend."[36] To demonstrate Boubou's influence, Frézouls had only to quote a letter that Noirot had sent him the previous year. Noirot had written: "For 19 years, Boubou Penda has lived in the most absolute intimacy with me. His affection toward me blends with his interests."[37]

Meanwhile, another critique of Guinea's colonial order came out of the Futa, in the form of a general exodus out of the region.[38] Whole villages were leaving for neighboring British territories, abandoning their fields and taking their herds. Areas around Timbo, the capital, had emptied completely. Moreover, the militia of ten men that Noirot had organized years before to prop up Almamy Baba Alimou was running roughshod through the countryside. On learning of these agitations,

Frézouls decided to take action, but the way in which he did so gives some indication of his precarious position atop the administrative hierarchy. Frézouls apparently felt that it was impossible to investigate the unrest in the Futa with the old guard, including Noirot and his interpreter, in the vicinity.

Frézouls first sought to remove Noirot from the colony. In January 1905 Frézouls demoted Noirot and ordered him to carry out an extended mission to the Upper Niger and the Liberian border.[39] Noirot initially resisted the assignment, claiming that the mission was not necessary and that, quite implausibly, he did not understand his orders. The real reason that Noirot stalled, however, was because he had learned that Boubou was in danger and that it would be wise to "distance Boubou from Conakry."[40] Noirot arranged for Boubou to be secreted out of Guinea and back to Senegal. On March 22, 1905, after a stern letter from Frézouls, Noirot could no longer defy his superior, and he headed to the interior, leaving Guinea behind.[41]

With Noirot gone and Boubou missing, two major impediments to colonial reform in French Guinea had been removed. But at least two remained. The first was Hubert, Noirot's replacement as French Resident of the Futa, and the second was Alfa Yaya, chief of Labé, longtime ally of Noirot's, and one of the most powerful men in the Futa. Hubert garnered suspicion because his alliances lay clearly with the first generation of French administrators and, moreover, his administrative skills seemed lacking, a point that a later investigation clearly confirmed. Hubert's exit was easily arranged, for he left the colony voluntarily to take his vacation to France. On his arrival there, Hubert learned that he had been formally suspended from the colonial service. Removing Alfa Yaya proved somewhat trickier, but Frézouls resolved the challenge by inviting Alfa Yaya to visit Conakry. Expecting to be received with accolades and honors by the new governor, Alfa Yaya arrived in the capital with great fanfare. He was promptly arrested and deported to Dahomey.[42]

Having eliminated these major powerbrokers, Frézouls sent a team of colonial inspectors to the Futa to investigate the causes of the region's unrest. The immediate focus was Hubert, Resident of the Futa, a feeble administrator who, it turned out, had a prodigious capacity for excess and abuse. It is somewhat ironic that Hubert is on record for noting with great derision that Boubou and Noirot allegedly ate together "at the same table."[43] Hubert himself did not in any way live according to the racial code and definition of "proper" colonial behavior that this remark implies. He had married five Peul wives, two of whom were twins, a fact that particularly horrified local populations. Hubert frequently went on tours through the countryside, accompanied by an enormous retinue, and he also required both French and African officials to fund public ceremonies held to celebrate the birth of his children.[44] The investigative team discovered that Hubert's grandeur, the cost of which was borne by the elites and commoners of the Futa, was a primary cause for discontent and the depopulation of the Futa.

The colonial inspection teams did not, however, confine their focus to Hubert. Hubert's actions generated questions about his predecessors in the Futa, in particular Noirot and Boubou.[45]

Boubou Penda in the Spotlight

While previous events serve as indicators to Boubou's influence in the Futa, the investigation of 1905 fleshes out that picture. The investigation revealed that Boubou's personal enemies and allies helped to shape the foundations of French colonial rule in the region. Witnesses explained, for example, that the real reason that Bademba had been pushed out of the position of *almamy* had nothing to do with ideology or respect for the traditions of political power in the region, as Noirot claimed. Bademba was ousted because of a conflict he had with Boubou over a woman. Bademba testified that when Noirot and Boubou arrived in the Futa, he gave Boubou many gifts, including money and a woman, Talla. Boubou married Talla and had children with her.[46] But Bademba soon learned that Boubou had eyes for another woman, Satourou. As Bademba explained, "One evening, Boubou Penda . . . came to my house to ask me to give him a princess named Satourou in marriage. . . . Boubou sought to marry this woman because she was rich and she possessed a number of herds and slaves. I refused because Satourou was already engaged to my son . . . and because Satourou herself would not consent to marry a man of base extraction such as Boubou. The next morning, Boubou returned. . . . I gave him the same response and added, moreover, that I had already given him a wife, name Talla, whom he still has with him and with whom he has since had three children. Boubou came back again in the evening with the same motive."[47] Bademba continued to refuse Boubou. Angry, Boubou warned the *almamy*: "'A man who has no fingers cannot milk a cow, but he can upset the calabash that contains the milk. It is like that I will have you deposed and chase you from the country. You will live in the bush like a monkey.'"[48]

Boubou Penda and his wife, perhaps Talla (from Famechon, *Notice sur la Guinée française*)

Satourou did marry Bademba's son as planned, but the new groom took the precaution of paying Boubou three hundred francs to stay away. Boubou took the money, but "this did not stop [him] from taking [Satourou] by force and returning her only after he had served himself of her for four days at the [French] post."[49] This episode is indeed telling, for Boubou was so assured of his position—and the protection that came with being Noirot's favored associate—that he could kidnap and rape a noble woman without fear of punishment. Even the *almamy* himself could do nothing when the author of such gross violations was Boubou.

Bademba believed that his refusal to turn Satourou over to Boubou polluted his relationship with Noirot. According to Bademba, Boubou used his influence over Noirot to turn the French resident against him and toward Baba Alimou. Recalling how Boubou warned him that he would "live in the bush like a monkey," Bademba reflected, "this is, in effect, what has happened to me."[50]

This episode is but one of the many ways in which Boubou molded colonial rule in the Futa. Gaining an audience, a favorable judgment, or a coveted position required plying Boubou with gifts and attention. Baba Alimou, for example, enumerated the gifts he had given Boubou to help promote his unlikely but ultimately successful bid to become *almamy*. Moreover, as the people of the Futa discovered, Boubou's mere proximity could be costly; Boubou demanded that villagers and elites pay their respects in slaves, women, cattle, goats, sheep, grain, cloth, gold, and cash.[51]

One of Boubou's African colleagues in the colonial service, Alioune Salifou, described the wealth that Boubou thus accumulated. Salifou, who also worked as an interpreter in the late 1890s, once witnessed Boubou count "his treasure," which consisted of two sacks filled with gold dust and gold pieces. Salifou noted that Boubou's also owned many slaves, who farmed and looked after his herds of goats and sheep. As Salifou pointed out, Boubou's salary of thirty francs per month could not account for such wealth.[52]

It is difficult to ascertain the degree to which Noirot was aware of or party to Boubou's actions. Did Noirot profit from Boubou's demands on local populations? Did Noirot order these excesses? Or was Noirot ignorant of Boubou's greed and brutality? The views of witnesses, French and African, diverged considerably on these points. But Boubou and Noirot nevertheless expose a whole new set of causalities, possibilities, and relationships to explain shifts in colonial policy in French

Guinea at the turn of the century. Boubou could influence and filter information to Noirot. The interpreter could and did act with violent cruelty and never felt threatened by recourse or recriminations. Boubou very clearly mattered to colonial rule in the Futa Jallon, and in the mind of local elites and local commoners, he mattered very much.

The Aftermath

Eight months after he left Guinea on his mission, Noirot returned, exhausted and sick, to a very different colony, one that no longer tolerated close working relationships of African and French colonial employees. That became evident by news that Noirot received on the day he arrived in Conakry, when he learned that the man with whom he had worked closely for twenty years had died in prison. "My poor Boubou, succumbed to his miseries, had been buried the previous day."[53]

Before leaving Guinea, Noirot had done his best to protect Boubou by arranging for him to go to Senegal. But Boubou was located there and sent back to Conakry, where he was imprisoned and interrogated. Although he suffered from neglect and a lack of food, Boubou steadfastly refused to testify against his long-time employer and companion. Boubou eventually succumbed to illness. Noirot was not allowed, however, to stay in Guinea to mourn his loss; he was suspended from the colonial service and sent to France.

Ultimately, the investigation into Hubert, Noirot, and Boubou fizzled. The affair received coverage in the French press in 1906, usually to the detriment of Governor Frézouls, the man who had tried to reform Guinea's colonial administration. Although Frézouls ultimately managed to disassemble the colonial machine he had found in Guinea, his superiors proved unable to withstand the negative publicity that those actions produced. Having served just two years as governor of Guinea, Frézouls was removed from office and sent back to France.[54]

Noirot proved more resilient. In 1908 the ever-persistent Noirot was reappointed to the colonial service in Sénégal, where he earned a letter of commendation.[55] Soon thereafter, he retired and moved back to his hometown in France, where he died in 1913.

To the end Noirot refused to implicate Boubou or even to concede that Boubou had been anything but a faithful servant loyal to France. In a 1906 statement Noirot contended, "[I]f I have rendered service to French colonization, I consider that the collaboration of Boubou was a large part of it."[56] In another interview during his suspension, Noirot asserted, "[Boubou] was a proud man, with a beautiful character. It is because of his devotion not only to myself but to the interests that I was defending, that I was able to obtain the results that I did in Futa."[57] Even after Noirot was reinstated into the colonial service, he continued to write letters to the colonial ministry decrying Boubou's wrongful death.[58]

In 1905, as Boubou's death and Noirot's exile demonstrate, the terms of colonial rule in Guinea changed. The personalized methods of rule that were the cornerstone of the first generation of French officials, such as Noirot, came under fire from a younger generation who held different views of the colonial project and of African colonial employees. The new arrivals did not see African colonial employees as resources who could be trusted and relied on, as Noirot did Boubou. They viewed them as threats to the racial and administrative hierarchies of the colonial state. New rules and policies of the French state made it impossible for a French official and an African employee to work together for as long and as closely as did Noirot and Boubou. But it would be a mistake to think that regular transfers of French officials and rigid bureaucratic procedures meant that influence of intermediaries evaporated. As Camille Guy's concerns discussed at the beginning of this essay show, African colonial employees continued to complicate significantly colonial agendas.

It is well known that European colonial rule was a highly arbitrary and coercive system of rule. But Boubou demonstrates that the brutality and violence of colonialism could be appropriated and controlled by people overlooked and ignored by the upper reaches of the colonial hierarchy. Boubou's power in the Futa derived from his employment within the French state and from the confidence he enjoyed as Noirot's trusted aid and advisor. Boubou helped determine both the allies and the enemies of the French. He was recognized by local populations as a key figure in the colonial hierarchy; as gatekeeper and translator, Boubou effectively managed the interaction of local populations with his superior and thus with the colonial state. Boubou's particular position in the Futa, however, cannot be understood simply as the result of colonial affiliation. Boubou's influence was widely and begrudgingly recognized by elites, commoners, and French officials. But Boubou was also heartily despised, because he made claims to privileges that defied the Futa's cultural conventions and flaunted its social hierarchies. He, a man of putative slave descent, intervened in the political intrigues of the Futa's elites and demanded noble women—even forcibly possessing one on at least one occasion. Understanding the significance of Boubou's role in the Futa therefore requires looking beyond the confines of the colonial state and recognizing the nuances and implications of his actions in the context of local norms and practices. This analysis shows how Boubou—despite his social status and relatively low rank within the colonial hierarchy—became an important representative of the colonial state and powerful interpreter of French rule in French Guinea.

Notes

1. C. Guy, "La langue française," 42.This and all translations in this chapter are the author's.

2. Amadou Hampâté Bâ, *Oui mon commandant!;* Hampâté Bâ, *L'étrange destin de Wangrin;* in English: Hampâté Bâ, *Fortunes of Wangrin*. Achebe, *No Longer at Ease;* Kourouma, *Monnè;* in English: Kourouma, *Monnew;* Alexandre, "Chiefs, Commandants and Clerks"; Brunschwig, *Noirs et Blancs.*

3. Boubou is referred to by his first name; Penda is likely the name of his mother and not a family name.

4. I. Barry, *Le Fuuta-Jaloo,* 1:114–19.

5. It is often asserted that the truce dates from the late eighteenth century, but according to Jean Suret-Canale it was probably of a more recent vintage. Suret-Canale, "Fouta-Djalon Chieftaincy," 81. For the conquest and colonization of the Futa Jallon, see I. Barry, *Le Fuuta-Jaloo;* B. Barry, *Bokar Biro;* Diallo, *Alfa Yaya;* McGowan, "Fula Resistance to French Expansion."

6. Noirot, *À travers le Fouta-Diallon.*

7. Klein, "Rule of Law." See also Debien, "Papiers Ernest Noirot," 676.

8. Sine Saloum Treaty, 1889, Personal Papers of Ernest Noirot, 1881–1909, Hoover Institution, Stanford, Calif.

9. Testimony of Oumarou Bademba, "Affaire Hubert Noirot," Archives Nationales de la Guinée, Conakry, Guinée (hereafter ANG) 2 D 115. (Much of this essay draws on this report.) Noirot frequently claimed that Penda was an aristocrat. Noirot, June 2, 1911, Fonds Ministeriels, Series Géographiques, Centre d'Archives d'Outre Mer, Aix-en-Provence, France (hereafter CAOM) AOF/ XVIII/1–4.

10. On recruitment, slavery, and French colonial rule, see Klein, *The End of Slavery;* Echenberg, *Colonial Conscripts,* 7–19.

11. For more details on these complex disputes, see Suret-Canale, "Fouta-Djalon Chieftancy," 82–84; B. Barry, *Bokar Biro,* 72–73, 84–85.

12. When his loyalty later came into question, Bademba reminded colonial officials how he had "called on all the notables of the Fouta" to recognize

French authority at his coronation. Deposition of l'Almamy Oumarou Bademba, May 29, 1905, "Affaire," ANG 2 D 115.

13. There is some dispute as to when the French state stopped paying the salaries of the militia. See deposition of Amadou Djawendé, June 2, 1905; Extract of deposition of Baba Alimou, Almamy of Timbo, June 2, 1905; Translation of letter from Baba Alimou, Almamy of Timbo, and elders, n.d. (probably January 1905); Deposition of Maillet, June 10, 1905. All depositions in "Affaire," ANG 2 D 115.

14. Letter from Frézouls to Gouvernor-général, July 10, 1905, "Affaire," ANG 2 D 115.

15. B. Barry, *Bokar Biro*, 73.

16. Suret-Canale, "Fouta-Djalon Chieftancy," 84–86.

17. Deposition of Pierre Francon, May 22, 1905, "Affaire," ANG 2 D 115.

18. Deposition of Georges Hubert, Administrateur adjoint de 2ième classe, 1906. Noirot, Dossier Personnel, CAOM FM/EE/II/1160/1.

19. Official telegram to governor in Conakry, no. 876, December 25, 1898, CAOM FM/SG/GIN/IV/6B.

20. CAOM FM/SG/GIN/IV/6B.

21. Declaration of Ousmane Sissoko, blacksmith in Timbo, CAOM FM/SG/GIN/IV/6B. Bambara is an ethnic group. Among the Bambara, as with other West African ethnic groups, lineage determines who works in certain artisan professions, such as blacksmithing. See David C. Conrad and Barbara E. Frank, *Status and Identity in West Africa*.

22. CAOM FM/SG/GIN/IV/6B.

23. Rauch, Native Affairs clerk to administrator of Futa Jallon à Timbo [Noirot], September 15, 1899. Noirot, Dossier Personnel, CAOM FM/EE/II/1160/1.

24. Deposition of M. Francon, May 22, 1905, pp. 292–93, in "Affaire," ANG 2 D 115.

25. Penda may have worked briefly in Senegal in 1900–1901 with Governor-General Ballay (previously the governor of Guinea). "Verbal d'interrogatoire de M. Noirot," Rheinhart, Inspecteur du 1ière classe des colonies, August 24, 1906. Noirot, Dossier Personnel, CAOM FM/EE/II/1160/1.

26. In Guinea there were very few first- or second-class interpreters at this time; most were third- or fourth-class. Boubou earned the relatively hefty annual salary of Fr 1320. "Nominations et Mutations," 6 (June 1, 1901), *Journal Officiel de la Guinée Française* (hereafter *JOGF*).

27. "Verbal d'interrogatoire de M. Noirot," Rheinhart, Inspecteur du 1ière classe. Noirot, Dossier Personnel, CAOM FM/EE/II/1160/1.

28. "Décision par laquelle une concession provisoire est accordée à M. Noirot;" and "Décision . . . à M. Boubou Penda." 27 (February 1, 1903), *JOGF*. The pair also participated in activities important to French Guinea's colonial community: both contributed to the campaign to construct a monument to Guinea's first governor, Governor Ballay. Noirot contributed one hundred francs and

Penda twenty-five to help pay for the construction of a statue that still stands in Bolbinet, Conakry. "Souscription pour le monument Ballay," 16 (April 1, 1902) *JOGF.*

29. On Conakry's growth and the rubber trade, see Arcin, *Histoire,* 591; Goerg, *Commerce et colonisation,* 337–58; Goerg, *Pouvoir colonial, municipalités et espaces urbains;* Osborn, "'Rubber Fever.'"

30. Notes of lieutenant governor, French Guinea, Bulletin individuel de notes, 1902, Noirot, Dossier Personnel, CAOM FM/EE/II/1160/1.

31. Response of the governor-general, 1902, Noirot, Dossier Personnel, CAOM FM/EE/II/1160/1.

32. Arcin, *Histoire,* 715.

33. Letter signed "Un groupe d'habitants," March 26, 1906, CAOM FM/SG/AOF/XVIII/2bis.

34. Arcin, *Histoire,* 717.

35. Governor Frézouls to governor-general, "Rapport trimèstriel," July 11, 1905, ANS 2G5-1.

36. Personnel Report 1905, Noirot, Dossier Personnel, CAOM FM/EE/II/1160/1.

37. Letter from M. Noirot to Gouverneur, November 1904 in Personnel Report 1905, Noirot, Dossier Personnel, CAOM FM/EE/II/1160/1.

38. Letter from Frézouls to Gouvernor-général, July 10, 1905, "Affaire," ANG 2 D 115.

39. Letter from Noirot to Minister of Colonies, June 2, 1911, CAOM FM/SG/AOF/XVIII/1-4.

40. "Verbal d'interrogatoire de M. Noirot," Rheinhart, Inspecteur du 1ière classe, Noirot, Dossier Personnel, CAOM FM/EE/II/1160/1. The story that Noirot recounted then is remarkably consistent with his narrative written five years later. Letter from Noirot to Minister of Colonies, June 2, 1911, CAOM FM/SG/AOF/XVIII/1-4.

41. Correspondence, Frezouls to Noirot, 1905. Noirot's 1911 letter also indicates that Noirot "received word" of Boubou's imminent danger. Letter from Noirot to Minister of Colonies, 2 June 1911, CAOM FM/SG/AOF/XVIII/1-4.

42. Considerable debate took place over Alfa Yaya's alleged culpability. It is clear, however, that from the outset Alfa Yaya played a crucial role in the French annexation of the Futa and that he was a close ally of Noirot. See Créspin, "Alfa Yaya et M. Frézouls"; Fillot, "Affaires de Guinée"; Arcin, *Histoire,* 682.

43. Deposition of Georges Hubert, Administrateur adjoint de 2ième classe, 1906, Noirot, Dossier Personnel, CAOM FM/EE/II/1160/1.

44. Deposition of Alioune Salifou, June 1, 1905, "Affaire Hubert Noirot"; Depositions of Bedemba Abdoulaye et al., June 6, 1905; Deposition of Soryba Camara, June 7, 1905, all in "Affaire," ANG 2 D 115. Deposition of Georges Hubert, Administrateur adjoint de 2ième classe, 1906, Noirot, Dossier Personnel, CAOM FM/EE/II/1160/1.

45. Report by Mr. Guyho, "Question Special," Cercle de Labé, Mission Saurin, 1908, CAOM FM/Contr//908.

46. Deposition of Oumarou Bademba, May 29, 1905, "Affaire," ANG 2 D 115.

47. Bademba, in "Affaire," ANG 2 D 115.

48. Bademba, in "Affaire," ANG 2 D 115.

49. Bademba, in "Affaire," ANG 2 D 115.

50. Bademba, in "Affaire," ANG 2 D 115.

51. Bademba, in "Affaire," ANG 2 D 115.

52. Deposition of Alioune Salifou, June 1, 1905, "Affaire," ANG 2 D 115.

53. Correspondence, Noirot, Personal Papers, Hoover Institution Archives, Stanford University.

54. Frézouls came under attack for the way he handled the investigation and—in another intriguing twist—for his reliance on Alioune Salifou. Salifou, the interpreter who had served in the Futa under Noirot (and Boubou), had translated the testimonies collected during the investigations into Hubert and Noirot. It was pointed out that Salifou was not an impartial observer but a man whose own ambitions had been frustrated by Boubou and Noirot. CAOM FM/EE/II/1160/1; CAOM Dossier Personnel, Frézouls; Guinée Française, Affaires diverses, ANS 7 G 61.

55. Decree of March 2, 1907, Ministry of Colonies to governor-general, Paris, March 19, 1907. M. Noirot earned a *letter de felicitations,* July 15, 1909, for action he took in Senegal against. Fode Souleymane Bayaga, Noirot, Personal Papers.

56. "Verbal d'interrogatoire de M. Noirot," Rheinhart, Inspecteur du 1ière classe des colonies, August 24, 1906, Noirot, Dossier Personnel, CAOM FM/EE/II/1160/1.

57. CAOM FM/EE/II/1160/1.

58. Letters from Noirot to Ministry of Colonies, 1909 and 1911, Noirot, Personal Papers, Hoover.

Interpretation and Interpolation

Shepstone as Native Interpreter

THOMAS MCCLENDON

While I was conducting oral research in rural KwaZulu-Natal, South Africa, in the early 1990s, one of the interpreters I worked with was a young white man named Rauri Alcock. The suitability of this choice was driven home when Sifiso Ndlovu, an African postgraduate student who translated my interview tapes, found himself puzzled by some of the locutions employed by my elderly African informants and exclaimed at Alcock's skill. Alcock had grown up among African peasants who were clients and neighbors of his parents' rural development project on the Thukela River valley border between the then province of Natal and the then homeland of KwaZulu. In that environment his immediate family and a handful of white neighbors—none closer than a half a mile away—were the only first-language English speakers nearby until he went to boarding school. Not surprisingly, Rauri—known to Africans as Makhonya—grew up equally conversant in English and isiZulu, both linguistically and culturally. Ndlovu, on the other hand, had come of age in the black townships of South Africa's industrial heartland. Both Ndlovu and Alcock were speakers of English and isiZulu, but the range of their literary and oral knowledge of the languages varied considerably. Ndlovu was an urban intellectual; Alcock, though also strikingly intelligent and articulate, was then a barefoot country boy with no university education and minimal experience of city life. These differences were reflected in the scope of their linguistic skills.

Alcock fits into a long tradition of whites working as interpreters of indigenous languages and cultures in southern Africa. Africans, of course, served as interpreters in a variety of situations, from the days of Van Riebeeck's servant Eva onward.[1] Additionally, some of South Africa's best-known nationalist leaders of the twentieth century either served as or aspired to positions as official interpreters. For instance, Sol Plaatje, one of the founders of the African National Congress, used his mission education to become a court interpreter in the Northern Cape Colony town of Mafeking before going on to a career as a journalist and politician.[2] Nelson Mandela, born two generations later in the Eastern Cape and also educated in mission schools, had an early ambition to become an interpreter, displaced by his later training as a lawyer. As Mandela recalls in his autobiography, "A career as a civil servant was a glittering prize for an African, the highest that a black man could aspire to. In the rural areas, an interpreter in the magistrate's office was considered second only in importance to the magistrate himself."[3] By the time Mandela was at the university, during World War II, such an ambition was realizable, at least in the Cape Province, which had a longer tradition of Western education for Africans and a somewhat more liberal tradition with respect to opportunities for African professionals in comparison to other parts of South Africa. Before the 1940s, though, such opportunities do not appear to have obtained for Africans in Natal. Natal's white governments appear to have preferred white interpreters; before World War II Africans are almost never mentioned in government records in the capacity of official interpreters.

Why this is so relates to special features of the history of colonial Natal (subsumed within contemporary KwaZulu-Natal) and of the larger region that united as South Africa in 1910. South Africa's colonial and settler-dominated history is both like and unlike the histories of other parts of colonial Africa; within South Africa, Natal has its own peculiarities. The two main aspects of South African history that most clearly set it apart are the early colonial presence and the large number of white settlers attracted by a temperate climate, opportunities for accumulation, and pursuit of the civilizing mission in its various guises. White settlers in southern Africa were therefore available to fill a variety of official positions that were of necessity filled by indigenous people in tropical colonies. In addition, settlers asserted their right to fill such positions as a benefit accruing from the naturalization of racial hierarchies that grew alongside Western expansion and domination. Natal came into being as a colonial offshoot of the Cape Colony in the 1840s. During that decade and the following one, imperial policy remained in flux as expansionists began to gain ground on fiscally cautious officials and committed humanitarians, with all points of view forming and changing against the backdrop of African political and economic interaction with the northeastward thrust of white settlers, missionaries, and officials.[4] In contrast to the strength of the humanitarian lobby in the early decades of the nineteenth century in the Cape, the political climate in colonial Natal was quickly dominated by a more assertive and reactionary settler presence, perhaps partly because of its relatively small size in relation to the indigenous population. Natal consistently placed more legal and social barriers in the way of African equality than was the case in its sibling colony to the southwest. For instance, although enfranchised Africans were numerous enough to have a significant effect on politics in the Cape, Natal permitted the vote to only a handful of Africans before national legislation expunged this right in the 1930s. These factors help to explain the domination of whites in official employment as interpreters. The relative silence of the colonial archive concerning African interpreters may, of course, reflect official disdain for such employees rather than their literal nonexistence, a point I will take up later.

Somsewu: The White Native Interpreter

The interpreter and intermediary who is the main subject of this chapter is a white man aptly remembered by two names (not unlike Rauri/ Makhonya): Sir Theophilus Shepstone, known to Africans as Somsewu.[5] Although Shepstone was the main official responsible for Africans in colonial Natal for over thirty years, his main role from youth to old age was that of an interpreter. Shepstone, though born in England, was raised by Wesleyan missionary parents in a series of mission stations in the Xhosa-speaking areas east of the Cape's colonial frontier. The experience apparently equipped him well for a lifetime spent as a politically attuned interpreter of languages and cultures. In 1831, when Shepstone was fifteen, his parents sent him to live with missionary William Boyce for a period of two years. Boyce was to bring young Shepstone's education above the level that could be offered by his stonemason father, while the boy was to assist Boyce in translating hymns and portions of the Bible into "Caffre."[6] A dozen years later, Boyce still contended that the Wesleyans had an edge over the Glasgow Missionary Society because of the superiority of Shepstone's translations, since the latter had "spoken Kaffer from childhood."[7]

From this beginning young Shepstone was launched into a career as a linguistic and cultural interpreter, carrying with him a set of skills that soon included exercising governmental authority over indigenous communities as a colonial officer. He served in the British military under Colonel (later Sir) Harry Smith during the Anglo-Xhosa war of 1834–35, and at the conclusion of that war was appointed "Kafir Interpreter and clerk" in Grahamstown, in the Eastern Cape Colony.[8] This service led to Shepstone's appointment in 1839 as Resident Agent at Fort Peddie, a frontier post he retained for the next seven years. There he was responsible for a community of several thousand Mfengu as well as the followers of Xhosa chiefs Phato and Kama.[9] This period ended badly, with strong suspicion that Phato was attempting to assassinate Shepstone after the latter distributed Kama's abandoned land to Mfengu rather than to followers of Kama's brother Phato. Even this incident burnished rather than harmed Shepstone's reputation, as his avoidance of an assassination attempt (which succeeded instead in killing a neophyte missionary) was attributed by colonial observers to Shepstone's superior insight into the "native mind."[10]

By late 1845, at the age of twenty-eight, Shepstone had already spent eleven years in official service as an interpreter and government official ruling over indigenous communities. This service—along with his urgent need to skip town—earned him appointment as "Diplomatic Agent with the native Tribes in the Natal Settlement," Britain's newly annexed colony sandwiched between Xhosaland and the Zulu kingdom.[11] Here he was responsible for a collection of indigenous communities, soon to grow to one hundred thousand people according to colonial estimates.[12] What language or languages did these peoples speak? Just as whites referred to the peoples of the Eastern Cape as "kafirs," "kaffirs," or "kaffres," and Shepstone was praised for having "spoken Kaffer" from childhood, the indigenous peoples of Natal were often referred to in the early colonial period as "Natal kaffirs." Indeed, the 1853–53 Natal Native Affairs Commission was popularly known among whites as the "Kaffir Commission."[13] Interpreters appointed by Shepstone to the colonial courts were denominated "Kafir Interpreters" (in context clearly referring to whites who spoke "kafir" rather than to Africans who were interpreters).[14] The colonizers did not consider the language(s) of Natal to be identical to those of the Eastern Cape and Xhosa lands, but they did see them as closely related.[15] One applicant for appointment as an interpreter in a Natal court in 1852 gave as one qualification that he had lived in the Eastern Cape and traded from there into "Kaffir Land" (Xhosaland), referring to the language spoken in those areas as the "Old Frontier dialect." He said that he had subsequently become well acquainted with the dialect spoken in Natal.[16] Thus, the colonists correctly perceived a linguistic continuum up and down the coast. Whenever it was to his advantage, however, Shepstone was keen to exploit the linguistic edge he was believed to possess through talent and experience. In the course of a memorandum arguing for reopening a capital case he thought wrongly decided, Shepstone emphasized instead the local variations of dialect even within Natal: "There are numerous dialectic differences in the languages used among the tribes of this District [Natal], a misapprehension of one of these local or tribal expressions would of course be perpetuated throughout the trial supposing the same Interpreter to be engaged, and an error, serious or otherwise according to circumstances, would result."[17] Only a subtle and practiced set of skills, such as his own, would do. Thus, although experience in the Eastern Cape could enable a colonist to learn the Natal version of "Kafir" more quickly, only long study and some innate talent could produce the subtle fluency of native speakers and skilled interpreters like Shepstone.

Interpretation was at the heart of Shepstone's position and of the native administration empire he built over the succeeding decades. The tasks entrusted to the Diplomatic Agent combined executive and judicial functions. Given the situation of alien Anglophone rule imposed on a large Zulu-speaking indigenous population, a scattering of Dutch speakers, and a growing English-speaking settler presence, these functions necessarily entailed regular translation of trials, complaints, speeches, and documents. As a fluently bilingual official, Shepstone was able to conduct proceedings in local dialects and record the proceedings in English. Men who served under him in native administration did not necessarily possess these abilities, though Shepstone was convinced that it was essential that they should. In the 1847 report of the Locations Commission, for instance, Shepstone and his fellow commissioners argued that the locations (native reserves) should be ruled by a white "superintendent" whose powers, the commissioners believed, would eventually overshadow those of subordinate chiefs. This system aimed for rapid transformation of indigenous subjects under relatively close governmental and spiritual supervision. The Natal commissioners insisted that "he in particular [the superintendent] and all under him should be conversant with the language of the Natives," going on to add that they realized high salaries would need to be paid to secure officials with this and other important qualifications. The report of the Locations Commission was shelved due to the high costs of the relatively direct style of rule proposed by it, but the more indirect "Shepstone system" that emerged in the 1850s continued to depend on interpretation, with Shepstone's own interpretive abilities at the center.[18]

The Shepstone system, the putative model for indirect rule systems throughout colonial Africa, was initially a rather basic system dependent on the recognition of a series of hierarchical relationships.[19] At the apex was the lieutenant governor, styled for this purpose as "supreme chief." In bureaucratic-political reality, that responsibility was carried out by Shepstone, who issued directives to and sought taxes and corvée and military levees from recognized and newly appointed chiefs. In the early 1850s, Natal's lieutenant governor Benjamin Pine appointed several rural magistrates whose jurisdiction extended over both white and black residents in their magistracies, including those in the locations. Like the chiefs over whom they were placed (but at a greater remove than proposed by the Locations Commission, since they also were responsible for governance of white settlers), magistrates possessed both administrative and judicial authority but were assisted only by the apparent power vested in their office and skeletal staffs of African police and messengers. Shepstone was unhappy with the quality of the magistrates appointed by Pine, as some of them proved to be brutal abusers of power and most lacked the necessary linguistic skills for the job. To remedy the latter deficiency, the government undertook to provide magistrates with their own interpreters.[20] At the same time, the government occasionally appointed interpreters (of language and custom) to assist other officials. In nearly all recorded instances, the interpreters were white men.[21] Shepstone saw this instance of racial privilege as a matter of bureaucratic necessity, arguing that "native" interpreters were inevitably seen as corrupt by Africans, as he argued in the following communication: "[E]very magistrate who is unable to speak the language fluently should be provided with an [sic] European interpreter. Native interpreters are without exception liable to the imputation of being corrupt, and in many instances to my knowledge upon very sufficient grounds. Well knowing their own weakness in this respect the natives usually look upon interpreters from among themselves with the utmost distrust, and I have frequently heard them lamenting that white interpreters were not generally employed." Shepstone went on in this letter to praise a magistrate's interpreter named A. Asborne as a white interpreter who, by contrast with African interpreters, was well respected by Africans.[22]

The puzzle this letter raises, of course, is that it suggests there were in fact some African interpreters employed, whereas they appear at best rarely in the official records until the 1940s. Does the near-absence of discussion of African interpreters mean that they were extremely thin on the ground, or is it merely a case of official silence?[23] This question, of course, is difficult to answer. Shepstone's discussion of the corruptibility of native interpreters suggests that Africans were in fact so employed; the rarity of their being named in official records suggests either official disdain for these employees or perhaps a nonchalance born of their commonality. African police and messengers, also integral to the court and administrative systems, also rarely appear by name, though they are more commonly mentioned at least by category.

The one exception I have found for the early colonial period, where an African interpreter appears by name in the colonial archive, suggests there were indeed at least some African complaints about the corruption of African interpreters. In 1862 a man named Umlenze, apparently the losing party in a legal case before the magistrate of the Lower Umkomanzi district, complained to Shepstone that the magistrate, "through not knowing the Native Language, was led to believe one-sided statements by the Interpreter and Policemen who were influenced by bribes."[24] The interpreter in question was apparently a man named Nyoniwesiwa, a relative of the policemen. Of course, there is no way to know whether Umlenze's complaint was valid or if it was merely a fiction designed to bolster his own weak case. But it is clear that such a claim might well be believed by colonial officials, especially in an instance where kinship between two minor officials might suggest a commonality of interest in opposition to the losing party. Complaints like this one could help to reinforce a degree of colonial terror at being abroad in the land of the Other, whose language and motivations only some of the colonial officials and settlers knew well.[25] Even interpreters could not necessarily be trusted, as those who were not intimately familiar with the language(s) and culture(s) of the region in the way that Shepstone was could not be sure of the interpreter's loyalty and hence accuracy. Maurice Amutabi's chapter in this volume suggests that these fears were not without foundation; interpreters were not machines but human beings embedded in complex social relations.

In a broader sense the relative archival silence about African interpreters indirectly confirms the colonial prejudice that only whites could be
"official" interpreters; Africans were those with whom one made do if
necessary. However, the implicit claim that only African interpreters
were subject to corruption was belied by an 1856 directive—specifically
stated to be in response to recent disclosures—that "all interpreters in
the employ of the Government" were prohibited from "receiving any
fees or presents from natives or others connected with any case."[26] The
nature of official colonial language suggests that if the directive had
been meant only to refer to African interpreters, then the phrase "native
interpreters" would have been used. Certainly white interpreters, as
relatively low-paid colonial employees, would have been subject to
some of the financial pressures that might beset African employees,
though, of course, they were unlikely to face conflicts related to kinship
or political affiliation. On the whole Umlenze's complaint about Nyoniwesiwa supported Shepstone's sense that only white court interpreters
could adequately protect the integrity of colonial rule.

The effort to appoint official white interpreters for the magistrates
dragged on through the mid-1850s. Assistant Resident Magistrate J. P.
Steele of Inanda, for instance, began clamoring for an interpreter in the
middle of 1852. A year later he was forced to refer a case to Shepstone to
determine whether it required the services of the Crown Prosecutor. As
he complained, "I have no *Interpreter*," and "cannot trust my own
knowledge of the Language."[27] By the late 1850s the colony was on
firmer financial footing and had a growing population of settlers, at
least a few of whom were proficient in the local language. Shepstone
was therefore able to periodically examine and appoint white interpreters to the court system, allowing a certain degree of on-the-job training:
"I have examined Mr. John Eustace Tannin as to his capability for a
Kafir Interpreter, and I have found him tolerably sufficient in all ordinary conversation but somewhat deficient in his knowledge of Judicial
terms. I consider however that the latter can only be acquired by being
sometime engaged in the interpretation of Native Law."[28] By the mid-
1860s Shepstone had systematized his ranking of interpreters and was
awarding certificates of "first class" or "second class" to passing applicants.[29] Despite this systematization of ranking, there is no evidence
that the exam itself was systematic or regulated by anything other than
Shepstone's own sense of an applicant's abilities. One imagines an
eager but perhaps timid young man approaching the intimidating authority figure suggested by Shepstone's official portraits. Shepstone's

brief notes of these exams suggest that he would engage the applicant in isiZulu conversation on a variety of topics, including vocabulary that Shepstone's experience told him might well arise in judicial matters. The applicant would then be judged according to the accuracy and fluency of his responses.

Interpretation, Interpolation, and Cultural Knowledge

Through this period Shepstone himself remained the chief interpreter, in every sense, of African affairs to colonial officialdom. Jeff Guy has argued that Shepstone circulated simultaneously in the oral world of Africans and in the literate world of the colonial state, with his own words providing one of the few consistent links between the two.[30] His location at the meeting of two linguistic and cultural communities gave him enormous power, and he was never shy about using his powers of interpretation to advance his own position. One such instance was Shepstone's extensive commentary on a mid-1850s murder case that he believed to have reached an unjust conclusion, resulting in the capital conviction of four defendants. For reasons that are not clear in the archival record, Shepstone and the prosecutor conducted a joint inquiry after the conclusion of the case, essentially rehashing the facts and the trial itself. Their disagreement was in the end so intense that the two men issued separate reports. Shepstone's report is twenty-five pages in length and contains a wealth of commentary on the problems of inter-pretation in multiple senses.[31]

The case concerned the murder of a leading man of "Dumisa's people," Unopapa. When the body of this fit middle-aged man was dis-covered in the veld not far from his homestead, his wives and rela-tions, along with the authorities, presumed that he had been murdered. Four "Quabi" (Qwabe) men living among Dumisa's followers, who had had a dispute with the deceased, were found guilty of murdering him. Shepstone's memorandum was essentially a brief arguing that the men were wrongly convicted. The first part of his argument rested on a ques-tion of linguistic interpretation, revolving around the connotation of the first-person plural pronoun. The prosecutor, Mr. Shuter, had taken the defendants' use of the pronoun, as in "we heard x at time y," to refer to their own personal knowledge. Shepstone argued, however, that the defendants were instead using the pronoun to refer to knowledge col-lectively attained by the Qwabe community to which the defendants were attached. Proper linguistic interpretation, Shepstone implicitly contended, depended on a deeply informed background in general matters of culture and specific matters of ethnography. The strong tone of this argument becomes apparent when one realizes that Shepstone was in effect criticizing translations offered by Henry Francis Fynn, a colonial magistrate whose presence in the region predated the colonial era, going back to the 1820s. Fynn was one of a handful of whites in Natal who could claim a broad knowledge of African affairs on a par with Shepstone's.[32]

Getting beyond this matter of linguistic interpretation, Shepstone in the last half of the memorandum discussed the facts of the case, again making a number of arguments based on cultural knowledge, while also drawing on Western scientific knowledge to advance his case for the innocence of the defendants. The case turned (not unlike the 1995 murder trial of O. J. Simpson) on the timing and significance of dogs barking at Unopapa's homestead at about the time he collapsed (or was struck down) a short distance away. To establish his version of events, Shepstone constructed a sort of thick description of the testimony, including observations such as the following: "Everyone acquainted with the South African Tribes is aware that cattle are invariably brought home *before dark*." Later in the document he observed: "The natives generally attribute all sudden death and many ordinary ones to some extraneous cause such as violence or witchcraft, and on this occasion we find that as soon as the death of Unopapa became known the belief that he had been 'killed' took firm possession of their minds, and their examinations and investigations were all directed to the enquiry." Shepstone contended, however, that the death was not the result of murder, and he turned to Western science to drive home his point. The witnesses had concluded that the death was the result of an assault because when they moved the body the head hung loose, as if the neck had been broken. Anticipating a scientific point emphasized by James McClure in one of his Natal-based mystery novels, Shepstone argued that the neck hung loose because, the body having been discovered twenty-four hours after death and not touched until the following morning, rigor mortis had dissipated.[33] He cited the evidence of Dr. Holland, the district surgeon, that "'the muscular rigidity which usually follows death would have gone off, and the head, unless supported, would fall about as described by the witnesses.'"

But Shepstone did not stop there in his multivalent interpretation of the evidence. The penultimate arrow in his quiver (as American lawyers like to say) was an argument that depended on knowledge of local flora. Some witnesses, including Gungweni, had concluded that the deceased had died violently because "the mark of the trampled down grass was larger than could be made by one body." Here, Shepstone turned to evidence provided to the commission, combined with his own knowledge of language and flora. Though the word used by witnesses in court had been alternately translated as "grass" or "reed," (again pointing to the confusion that could arise from poor interpretation), the commission called for a specimen to be brought in and found that it was a "peculiarly soft . . . grass, found only in marshy damp places." He went on to note that this type of grass was "easily blown down by the wind." As a result a body rolling over once would depress an area six feet wide, Shepstone claimed. Finally, Shepstone argued that the failure to produce this kind of evidence in court resulted from a lack of understanding on the part of the defendants of the roles of various players in the colonial legal system as well as a failure of communication between them and their lawyer. As Shepstone reiterated, "[T]he Counsel, to be effective, must know [his clients'] language."[34]

I have discussed this source at length because it captures succinctly the variety of intermediary and interpretive roles that Shepstone occupied in Natal. Most prominently, as Secretary of Native Affairs (from the early 1850s, when this title succeeded that of Diplomatic Agent), Shepstone was effectively "supreme chief" over the array of chiefs appointed by him in Natal.[35] The Shepstone system allowed whites, including Shepstone himself, to imagine that he headed a hierarchy of African chiefs and homestead heads, whom he could bend to his will. At the same time, Africans treated Shepstone as a chief in the sense that he was expected to be their benefactor and protector. For instance, when Africans were dissatisfied with the often brutal and inept methods of the magistrates, they came to Shepstone to complain and to demand that he remain their "chief."[36] In that sense, though hierarchically superior to both parties, Shepstone was positioned as an intermediary between chiefs and magistrates, interpreting the actions and words of one to the other.

In a broader sense Shepstone occupied a middle position in his ongoing role as an embattled official with primary responsibility for a key aspect of the colonial state. Very soon after taking office in the late 1840s, Shepstone found himself at odds with the interests of the settler community, whose members resented his plans for relatively large and relatively developed reserves, while being suspicious of the unilateral control he exercised over native administration. The Native Affairs

Commission of 1852–53 expressed the interests of such settlers, in opposition to the aborted plans of the Locations Commission. Even before
this the premature death of the first lieutenant governor, Martin West,
who had been Shepstone's ally, led to efforts by the incoming lieutenant
governor, Pine, to undermine Shepstone's authority.[37] This kind of tension remained a hallmark of Shepstone's career. On the one hand, he
was lauded as a skillful administrator whose expertise had helped to
prevent the kinds of disturbances that plagued the Eastern Cape frontier. On the other hand, his penchant for secrecy and autocratic methods cultivated resentment; settler hostility to the relative autonomy of
Africans in the colony was often directed toward him.

However, Shepstone portrayed himself, and was credited by other
whites, as a linguistic and cultural expert with respect to indigenous
communities, as we have seen. Likewise, his ability to play the part of
an African patriarch in terms of oratory and projection of power enabled him to effectively conjure an image among Africans as, to some
degree, their protector against otherwise unbridled white interests. That
this was so is shown most clearly by the outrage expressed by Africans
when, as they saw it, Shepstone turned against them in favor of his
"white cousins." This moment came in 1869, more than two decades
after Shepstone had come first come to Natal, when he introduced new
regulations governing marriage. The regulations were designed to simultaneously raise revenue and regulate marriage in a way that was
harmful to the interests of elder patriarchs, since it effectively taxed po-
lygyny by imposing steep fees for the registration of each marriage.[38] In
addition the regulations imposed limitations on the amount of bridewealth to be exchanged, effectively capping amounts that fathers could
hope to receive in exchange for their daughters. The colonial state,
highly dependent on revenue raised from its African subjects during
the early decades of colonial rule, hoped to raise significant revenue
while also placating younger men who would now have a greater
chance of entering into a first marriage. Finally, in response to the concerns of missionaries and other reformers about young women being
forced into marriages with senior men, weddings were now to be conducted before an "official witness," who was charged with ensuring
that young brides were voluntary participants.

While touring the countryside to explain and promote these provi-
sions, Shepstone encountered significant opposition from chiefs and
other senior men whose interests were severely threatened by the new
law. In one instance Shepstone recorded some quite harsh words

spoken by his African interlocutors in response to his presentation. The men argued passionately that they not only were displeased by the new regulations but also felt betrayed by someone they had until then trusted. "We claim you and your powers . . . but you have gone over entirely to your [white] cousins. . . . You should protect us instead of betraying us." The speaker went on to argue, with a dramatic metaphorical flourish, "You open your hand, you draw us to your middle finger, then gently on to your palm. The rise is but small over the heel of your hand and along your arm to your elbow it is pleasant, and then you squeeze us between your arm and your body and we die."[39] From the point of view of these leading African men, a former protector against the unbridled greed of white settlers, who had formerly extended his hand in friendship, had now become a slithery and dangerous python, whose embrace was deadly rather than protective.

As the marriage-regulation incident shows, there was a significant difference between colonist interpreters and indigenous interpreters. The former, no matter their linguistic skill and no matter their relative sympathy for colonized communities, had worldviews and interests that aligned closely with those of other settlers. Although Shepstone was raised in African communities, his family nevertheless constituted a white Christian colonial island in those communities. Despite use of an African name and a flair for flourishes such as having a "snuffbox bearer" in the style of an African chief, Shepstone remained firm in his white identity.[40] As far as the record indicates, he did not have African wives or children, unlike some of the late precolonial white adventurers in the region. Shepstone remained firmly convinced of the superiority of white civilization. With advancing age, parallel to the expansion of colonial interests in southern Africa, his actions were increasingly those of a grand imperialist. Four years after the introduction of the marriage regulations (parts of which had to be rescinded in the face of continued African opposition), Shepstone crushed and humiliated a powerful chief and rainmaker, Langalibalele, over the latter's refusal to submit to Shepstone's authority. Although the incident in some ways triggered a colonial loss of confidence in Shepstone's secretive and autocratic methods, it marked his decisive tilt against African communities retaining any independent power. By the end of the decade, Shepstone helped to precipitate the crisis that led to the Anglo-Zulu war from his new position as British administrator of an annexed Transvaal (home of the Boer South African Republic). Back in Natal in the aftermath of that war, Shepstone was officially retired but remained highly influential behind the scenes. He continued to use his influence to undermine the Zulu royal house, in opposition to his former friend Anglican Bishop John Colenso, who had broken with him over the Langalibalele affair.[41] In contrast to Shepstone, Colenso and his family, who from their position as missionary Christians had also become key cultural and linguistic interpreters and intermediaries in the colonial milieu, remained active protectors of what they saw as African interests. By the 1870s Shepstone was a more open advocate of imperial expansion and control. Nevertheless, he continued to serve an interpretive role, always in a sense standing between white and African communities.

In an incident intricately analyzed by Carolyn Hamilton, one of Shepstone's most intriguing interpretive acts was his role at the coronation of Cetshwayo as Zulu monarch in 1873, just after the events surrounding the crushing of Langalibalele and six years before the British invasion of the Zulu kingdom.[42] There, for reasons related to dynastic disputes within the Zulu royal house and to that kingdom's relatively dependent status with reference to the British empire, Cetshwayo called on Shepstone to appear "as Shaka" (the Zulu founding king, Cetshwayo's uncle) during a phase of the coronation ceremonies. Shepstone's report of this event, not surprisingly, portrays his own role in the most grandiose possible terms. He also tried to use his appearance to inflate both his own role and British power in the Zulu kingdom, purporting to lay down a series of "laws" that the kingdom must adhere to. Zulu failure to adhere satisfactorily to these laws then figured strongly among the pretexts for the subsequent British invasion of Zululand. While officials and settlers in neighboring Natal were content to swallow Shepstone's interpretation of these events, Zulu royal participants had their own reasons for including Shepstone (in a very ambiguous manner) in the ceremonies, and as Hamilton shows, they continued to develop their own discourse of the event independently of Shepstone's brief physical intervention.

Official interpreters have considerable power to shape, whether intentionally or otherwise, the meanings that auditors attach to the words of those whose language they do not speak. Their ability to use such power arbitrarily or corruptly, however, is limited by the need to be relatively consistent and the possibility that other auditors or later critics may question their initial interpretation. Shepstone was an unusually important and powerful interpreter for a number of reasons. In the context of a book on intermediaries in colonial Africa, he is unusual by virtue of his whiteness. As we have seen, however, white interpreters were the hegemonic and perhaps numeric norm in official contexts in this particular phase and space of colonial history. Shepstone, of course, went well beyond the role of an interpreter of language. Building on his skills and early positions in language interpretation, Shepstone became a colonial officer and then the supreme colonial official over Africans in Natal. In that position he combined his linguistic abilities with his official position and rhetorical skills to shape the broader interpretive landscape. He interpreted white intentions and actions to African leaders, and African intentions and actions to white officialdom and settlers, always with an eye to his own advantage. In so doing he continually drew on his intermediary position, calling attention to his knowledge of indigenous norms while situating himself as a modern man of Western civilization. As senior African men saw with the promulgation of the marriage regulations in 1869, it was to the colonial community that this interpreter's loyalties remained attached. Shepstone's ultimate loyalty, though, was to himself and his view of how the civilizing mission should be carried out. His interpretations, at all levels, were self-conscious actions in pursuit of his own colonial vision.

Notes

The research for this chapter was supported by a National Endowment for the Humanities Summer Stipend, a United Methodist Board of Higher Education Fellowship, and Southwestern University's Brown Fellowship and Cullen Faculty Development grants. My thanks to the editors of this volume for their helpful comments.

1. Elphick and Shell, "Intergroup Relations," 186–87.
2. Willan, *Sol Plaatje*, 54–76.
3. Mandela, *Long Walk to Freedom*, 45.
4. See McClendon, "Man Who Would Be *Inkosi*."
5. The term has been variously translated as "father of whiteness," "white father," and other phrases. Its meaning seems to have been fluid over Shepstone's lifetime, as it was a praise name he earned in his youth. McClendon, "Man Who Would Be *Inkosi*;" J. Guy, *View across the River*, 37; Gordon, *Shepstone*, 100 n50.
6. "Extracts from Mr. Boyce's Journal," *Methodist Missionary Notices* 6, no. 201 (September 1832): 133. Boyce believed that it was well-nigh impossible for an adult to acquire "a perfect knowledge of the Caffre language," although the abilities of the locally raised Shepstone boy were "invaluable." "Kaffir,"

originating from an Arabic word for infidel and widely used in the nineteenth century to denote Africans on the east coast of South Africa, is today a vile term of abuse, roughly equivalent to "nigger."

7. Methodist Missionary Society (hereafter MMS) records 305, 1846–47, no. 112, W. B. Boyce to Rev. G. Brown, December 3, 1844.

8. Regarding Shepstone's military service see Gordon, *Shepstone*, 86–87. His appointment as interpreter can be found in Pietermaritzburg Archives Repository (hereafter PAR), Shepstone Papers 1/1/7/3, vol. 13, John Bell to T. Shepstone, February 26, 1836.

9. Public Record Office (hereafter PRO), Colonial Office (hereafter CO) 48/200, 140, Governor G. T. Napier to T. Shepstone, March 20, 1839; *Graham's Town Journal*, April 4, 1839, quoted in Gordon, *Shepstone*, 103n1.

10. See "The Murder of the Missionary Scholtz," *Graham's Town Journal*, December 11, 1845.

11. PAR, Shepstone Papers 1/1/7/3, P. Maitland to Col. Hare, Lt. Governor, October 30, 1845. The Grahamstown newspaper had referred to Shepstone as "diplomatic agent" in his previous post.

12. PAR, Secretary of Native Affairs (hereafter SNA) 1/8/1, Report of the Locations Commission, n.d. (circa 1847).

13. PAR, SNA 2/1/1–3, Natal Native Commission, 1852–53.

14. See, for example, PAR, SNA 1/7/2, Memorandum of T. Shepstone, December 22, 1855.

15. Linguists now agree; they classify isiXhosa and isiZulu as Nguni languages, belonging to the Bantu group. Speakers of the two languages say that they are mutually intelligible. The dialects of the KwaZulu-Natal region were eventually standardized, through the efforts of missionaries, as isiZulu. By the early twentieth century, Zulu-speakers from Natal as well as those from the former Zulu kingdom began to identify themselves as Zulus.

16. PAR, SNA 1/1/4, T. Mitchley to T. Shepstone, March 2, 1852. His added note that he spoke Dutch testifies to some of the linguistic complexity of this colony, whose first white settlers, fifteen years earlier, were Dutch-speaking emigrants from the Cape Colony.

17. PAR, SNA 1/8/5, T. Shepstone to the Colonial Secretary, April 23, 1855.

18. For the demise of the Locations Commission report and rise of the Shepstone system, see McClendon, "Man Who Would Be *Inkosi*"; Etherington, "'Shepstone System.'"

19. Lambert, *Betrayed Trust*; Etherington, "'Shepstone system.'" For an argument that this system provided the model for subsequent systems of indirect rule, see Mamdani, *Citizen and Subject*.

20. PAR, SNA 1/3/1, Letter to T. Shepstone, July 1, 1850; SNA 1/7/2, Memorandum of T. Shepstone, November 11, 1852.

21. See, for example, PAR, SNA 1/8/5, S. B. Gordon to Crown Prosecutor, December 3, 1851.

22. PAR, SNA 1/8/2, T. Shepstone to Acting Secretary to Government, July 21, 1852.

23. Moore and Roberts, "Listening for Silences."

24. PAR, SNA 1/6/1, Statement of Umlenze, July 10, 1862.

25. White ignorance and distrust of blacks persists in present-day KwaZulu-Natal, often with deadly consequences. See Steinberg, *Midlands.*

26. PAR, SNA 1/8/6, T. Shepstone Circular to Resident Magistrates, January 25, 1856.

27. PAR, SNA 1/3/2, J. P. Steele to T. Shepstone, June 25, 1853 (emphasis in original).

28. PAR, SNA 1/7/2, Memorandum of T. Shepstone, December 22, 1855.

29. PAR, SNA 1/7/5, Memorandum of T. Shepstone, February 7, 1866.

30. J. Guy, *View across the River,* 34–38.

31. PAR, SNA 1/8/5, T. Shepstone to the Colonial Secretary, April 23, 1855.

32. For Fynn, see Hamilton, *Terrific Majesty,* 37–47.

33. McClure, *Snake.*

34. There is no further discussion of the case in the archives, so we do not know if Shepstone's arguments were accepted.

35. Formally the lieutenant governor was supreme chief, but effectively that role was carried out by Shepstone. Etherington, "'Shepstone System.'"

36. See, for example, PAR, SNA 1/7/1, Statement of Umbokwana messenger from Nodada, July 26, 1851.

37. McClendon, "Man Who Would Be *Inkosi*"; Welsh, *Roots of Segregation.*

38. McClendon, "Coercion and Conversation."

39. PAR, SNA 1/7/8, Memorandum, September 2, 1869.

40. McClendon, "Man Who Would Be *Inkosi.*"

41. J. Guy, *The View across the River.*

42. Hamilton, *Terrific Majesty,* 88–111.

Petitioners, "Bush Lawyers," and Letter Writers

Court Access in British-Occupied Lomé, 1914–1920

BENJAMIN N. LAWRANCE

On May 22, 1918, Lomé's Chief Political Officer, A. R. Holliday, took the unusual step of rescinding and demanding the surrender of the letter-writing license of one Lomé merchant, a certain Robert A. Cole. According to the testimonies of Cole and Holliday, Cole had acted as a letter writer for a group of disgruntled subjects of Chief Abraham of Amoutivé, a village adjoining Lomé, who insisted that they had destooled the said chief. Cole was allegedly a party to the plot to destool Chief Abraham and had aided and abetted the plotters by preparing letters that questioned the authority of the "traditional ruler of the Amoutivé people." Cole was described as a "troublesome man" who had received several warnings about coming frequently to court and "encourag[ing] people to reopen matters that ha[d] been settled." In his defense he countered that he was "only a letter writer" and that over the past four years he had written 1,072 letters, all in good faith.[1]

This brief but tense exchange sheds important light on the role of the public letter writer in the administration of British-occupied Lomé. On

94

the one hand, the letter writer, although not employed by the state, was in the position of acting as a go-between amid litigating parties and was charged with the task of conveying a legal matter to colonial authorities. Because letter writers functioned as intermediaries, albeit in a capacity different from that of interpreters and clerks and with different constituencies, they sparked concerns on part of colonial officials. On the other hand, the writer was frequently a partisan individual, one who charged a fee for services, and one whose legal authority as a middle figure rested completely in the hands of the colonial state, which at once could strip him of his profession and render inadmissible any letter or petition in an ad hoc manner reminiscent of *la loi bureaucratique.*[2] Thus, anxiety about the roles of letter writers speaks broadly to colonial concerns about interpreters and clerks, as they occupy similarly ambiguous nexuses of power and authority.

Among the most surprising changes instituted by the British occupation of Lomé at the onset of World War I was the decision to regulate letter writers via the creation of a licensing system. Although a system of regulation itself is not particularly unusual, its invocation at this juncture, after the brief but violent conquest of German Togoland, sits uneasily with developments elsewhere in the British colonial empire, making it worthy of further investigation. The role of public letter writers (in French colonies and mandates the term *écrivains publics* is equivalent), sometimes disparagingly referred to as "bush lawyers," is a central component of the social history of access to the colonial court system.

Letter writing for hire operated as a mechanism whereby all colonial subjects—educated or illiterate—could have their grievances brought to the attention of appropriate legal authorities or to senior administrators in an act of supplication. The letter writers, like the court interpreters and the chiefly linguists, functioned as intermediaries in a multivalent legal environment: they negotiated access to the judicial tribunal; they framed and reframed the language of the plaintiff's case; they conveyed information between the chief, colonial officers, and a rural community; and they collected a fee for their services. To the African litigant they represented an avenue to legal review of justifiable expense. To the colonial, official letter writers both facilitated and obfuscated judicial process. For the vast preliterate African majority, they were crucial to the court system, because written documents were far more likely to stimulate a civil or criminal proceeding. Letter writers were indispensable to the evolving legal apparatus but were frequently viewed as profiteers of personal misfortune, charlatans, and busybodies.

My purpose here is severalfold. On an empirical level I provide new data about the operation of the colonial court system in British-occupied "Lomé and Lomeland," the brief 1914–20 interregnum about which there exists almost no historical writing.[3] In so doing, I aim to answer a central guiding question, namely, why regulate letter writing during a period when administrative resources and personnel were at a premium? Second, on a conceptual level I interpret the importance of letter writing as an avenue of legal review, as an integral component of the drive to provide a statutory legal basis to colonial rule, and contextualize the Lomé experience with developments in neighboring territories. Finally, building on this explanation, I anticipate the development of petitioning by indigenous subjects to the League of Nations in Geneva as a logical step in an increasingly literate and bureaucratized colonial milieu.

Colonial Traditions of Legal Review

When the British initiated letter-writing licenses soon after their arrival in 1914, the decision was calculated to both enhance and hinder the legal capacity of Lomé's population. Letter writing within the British empire—interpreted at its broadest as the ability to compose complaints, defense statements, petitions, affidavits, summons, and statutory declarations, all with legal standing—was the activation of a broad privilege of all British imperial subjects instituted by Queen Victoria, that of the right to appeal directly to the monarch. Letter writing as a vehicle of access to the courts was important too in French colonies. And in the twilight years of Germany's empire, the flourish of petitioning against various grievances indicates that imperial subjects had also taken steps to assert their "right" to this mechanism of direct legal redress.[4]

In various ways in each of these empires, legal apparatuses came into being during the formative years of colonial rule to engage the colonized in the colonial project. Legal redress and the validation of the statutory authority "on the ground" demanded that subjects have a means whereby they could aspire to justice. David Groff interprets the involvement of Africans in the creation and application of the colonial law as a dynamic narrative of collaboration.[5] The establishment of some reasonable facsimile to the rule of law was both an ideological and a practical imperative. Metropolitan pressures, League of Nations' scrutiny, and criticism from local African intelligentsia necessitated legal reform. From a practical angle the rule of law facilitated colonial commerce, promoted capitalism, and provided external legitimacy.

Accommodating the conflicting interests of colonial governments, local elites, and rival indigenous communities was a joint effort. Martin Chanock demonstrated that the creation of laws, procedures, and "traditions," some invented specifically to counter social change wrought by colonization, resulted in new spheres of legal authority for chiefs separating customary law from process.[6] The arbitrariness of legal systems and the opportunities that arose for collaboration both reduced African resistance and created stable, working, collaborative mechanisms. Because direct access to the courts was a fundamental component of colonial legal systems, there arose new opportunities for self-advancement by ambitious Africans. Groff's story about the life of the Kwame Kangah represents one such lesson in both the opportunities and the constraints of collaboration. Groff explains that the relationship between Kangah and the local French authorities was marked more by "inegalitarian patterns of exchange" and "reciprocity" than "clear-cut domination."[7] Kangah's middle role also allowed him to accrue substantial personal wealth in a manner not unlike that of Amadou Hampâté Bâ's Wangrin.[8] Groff describes Kangah's court victory against a chiefly rival and French officials and the restitution of his wealth and privilege as a highly qualified "victory for the principle of the rule of law."[9] The resolution was a messy one in which the regular court had played no significant part. The actions of Kangah demonstrated that the French colonial justice system was incapable both of impartial judgment and of resolving its own internal contradictions. That notwithstanding, l'affaire Kanga also indicates a commitment to elements of la mission civilisatrice, such as the principle that one's personal property could not be seized without both a criminal conviction and an additional hearing with respect to the seizure.[10] Although Kangah's behavior was intolerable from the point of view of administrators, French respect for the law of property trumped this.

Richard Roberts finds a parallel case privileging property law in early twentieth-century Dakar.[11] The long struggle between French administrators, magistrates, and Senegalese over the extension of legal and electoral rights to the inhabitants of the four communes enabled Africans, such as the dyer of cloth, Mariem Seck, to bring civil cases for property disputes before French courts. Because the French civil code and civil procedures were inseparable in practice, and because the civil law tradition has a bias toward written forms, the role of intermediaries in preparing texts formed a fundamental step in the path to court access.[12] Roberts reads texts as testimony of the social action of and social structures enveloping African voices. Not only were the texts shaped by several stages of the civil hearings and translation, but *huissiers de justice* (bailiffs) or *écrivains publics*, to whom they turned "to ensure that they conformed properly to the narrative formula," may also have been influenced by the proceedings.[13]

In British colonies litigants drew on the deeper colonial tradition of petitioning to take disputes to courts "to achieve ends meaningful to them within the context of their social practices."[14] Petitions became popular in early nineteenth-century Britain as a vehicle for agitating for reform, and soon spread to the colonies.[15] In the Gold Coast Colony, Ordinance 12 of 1877 governed the content of and mechanism for "Petitions of Right."[16] But these early petitions with their formulaic and memorializing overtones remain a neglected source of African agency in the colonial encounter. K. O. Akurang-Parry, however, has turned afresh to these documents and narrated the attempts by various Gold Coast elites to seek compensation or redress as the full social and economic impact of the abolition of domestic slavery and pawnship swept the territory.[17] John Kwadwo Osei-Tutu also demonstrates how different classes of people in the Gold Coast challenged colonial authority by making "radical, albeit informed, demands."[18] Over time the number of petitions seeking redress escalated enormously, and the status of the authors of the letters transitioned from quasi-legal to legal.

Petitions and legal briefs are very different political acts ushering toward civil litigation. For the moment, however, it is sufficient to state that regulation of the letter writers' status is indicative of the growth of importance of the courts in the lives of the mass of African subjects.[19] As literacy spread and as the burgeoning property-owning African merchant class began flexing its legal muscles, colonial courts increasingly received written testimonies, complaints, and allegations. Furthermore, as colonial officers increasingly referred to these letter writers as "troublemakers and political parvenus" representing their self-interest more than the views of indigenous rulers, Africans turned to their allies in the local press to deliver further condemnation of colonial practices in a manner that seems identical to the tactics employed by anticolonial protesters in German Togo.[20]

In 1900 in Southern Nigeria, letter writing became an officially recognized trade, governed by the Illiterates' Protection Ordinance. Framed not so much to "regularize" letter writing (i.e., in the sense of formulaic standards) as to protect nonliterate litigants from exploitation, the ordinance prescribed a rate of remuneration of ten krobo (about one shilling) per one hundred words. By 1905 letter writers were further controlled by a requirement that they have a nontransferable license, obtained for the fee of one naira (about two shillings). The holder was expected to produce it on demand at the request of any official. Omoniyi Adewoye interprets this as a means whereby colonial officers could "check irregularities and perhaps . . . set up a standard of admission to the profession."[21] This new system of regulation, however, soon led to serious abuses. As with the "warrant chiefs" of Igboland, the licenses gave letter writers an official recognition of which the unscrupulous could take advantage. Some added many forms of legal transactions to their activities for hire, many charged excessive fees, and the most educated acquired legal textbooks from Britain, giving rise to the derogatory term "bush lawyers."

The British began regulating letter writing in the Gold Coast via the similarly framed Illiterates Protection Ordinance.[22] Ordinance 166 of July 1, 1912, provided for annual licenses at a fee of five shillings and simultaneously banned letter writing for profit or the representation of illiterates unless the writer or representative was licensed. Other clauses specified the responsibilities of the writer, including that he must clearly read over and explain what he had written; cause the illiterate to write his signature or mark; write his own full name and address; and state the amount charged for the service. The licensee was permitted to charge no more than one shilling per one hundred words. Any contravention of this could be punished by a fine of five pounds or one month of hard labor and forfeiture of the license. The ordinance also provided for the local administration of the licenses via the local district commissioner.

When the British took possession of Lomé, Proclamations 1 and 6 (a) of September 13, 1914, provided for the extension of Gold Coast Colony law governing access to the courts to the occupied territory. By implication the laws governing letter writing and illiterates were also extended to Lomé. Adewoye considers some form of regulation better than none, and evidently the new British regime felt similarly. Whereas elsewhere in the empire, letter writers were acting with increasing freedom, in Lomé in 1914 a form of regulation new to the local community was created that was to have serious impact on access to the colonial courts.

It is with this context and background in mind that I propose to examine the new dimensions of regulation imposed in British-occupied Lomé. Why was it that the new British officers pushed court access toward regulation when elsewhere deregulation was gaining favor? How prevalent was illiteracy in Lomé such that the role of letter writers could become so significant? How did letter writers operate in Lomé? What sort of cases did letter writers bring to court, and what do we know of the outcome of these cases? What financial, social, cultural, and political impact did regulation have on local access to the courts? To what extent was the climate of war and provision for the war effort a factor in this decision? What other significant administrative changes did the British enact, and how did letter writers themselves react to the regulation? What were the long-term consequences of the privileging of the letter-writing "profession"? And what more do we know of the actions of Robert A. Cole?

Lomé: From *Schutzgebiet* to Military Occupation

The conquest and partition and reconquest and repartition of Togoland over a period of forty years provide a window into the interaction between Africans and Europeans during the formative years of colonial rule. Various clans of Ewe speakers sparsely settled much of what is today the coastline of the Republic of Togo several centuries prior to the establishment of formal German rule in 1884.[23] After just over ten years with Zebe as the base for German administration, the capital shifted in 1897 to Lomé, a small beachfront settlement that had risen to prominence as a site of cross-border smuggling.[24] Thus, with the exception of a seminomadic market community that straddled the border, the new city was a carefully planned colonial capital and the pride of the German colonial lobby in Berlin.

German Lomé lay at the junction of road, rail, and sea transportation between Europe and the colonial hinterland. Three railways branched to Kpalimé, Atakpamé, and Aného, often referred to as the cocoa, cotton, and copra lines, respectively, because of the raw materials they funneled to Europe. The city fanned out in a semicircle and was divided into European, commercial, and African quarters. In due course chiefly families from the neighboring village of Bè as well as Ewe outsiders from beyond the Bè region, such as the commercial elites from Keta, Denu, Anlogã, and Aného who purchased land and settled within its boundaries, were incorporated into the native administration with all the concomitant invented traditions, hierarchies, and authorities. As well as being the commercial center, with many factories located on the beachfront, Lomé was also the center of several sects of the rapidly growing Christian religion as well as the European education system.[25] On the eve of World War I, German Lomé was at the height of its influence along the coast. Increasing numbers of Africans purchased freeholds in the capital, and many of the established families from Ewe commercial centers, such as Keta and Aného, relocated their social as well as their commercial operations to Lomé.

Acting governor Hans-Georg von Doering had many plans for the *Musterkolonie* in 1914.[26] With the outbreak of hostilities in Europe, however, all plans were put on hold. Von Doering tried vainly to arrange a neutrality agreement with his counterparts in Accra and Cotonou, but on August 6, 1914, Captain Barker began the British-led invasion of the capital. After several violent battles the German regime surrendered on August 26, 1914, in the first allied victory of World War I. Yves Marguerat has described Lomé as an unconventional colonial city, a product of "African civil society" in which poor lived alongside rich and where political and commercial power lay unusually in the hands of African entrepreneurs.[27] Far from static it was a dynamic and changing urban center. At the same time, German colonialists, lacking the means to develop the city as they desired, tightened their grip on the economic life of Lomé, with the goal of eliminating African competition with German firms. Legal maneuvers and discriminatory tactics slowly strangled the independent activities of the founders of the town, allowing them only the capacity to act as clerks or shop owners in Lomé, or purchasing agents for the less important products of the interior of the land.[28] The status of Africans in social and economic affairs was generally inferior to that in neighboring French and British colonies.[29] Although the economic conditions of the German colony, which gave rise to a preponderance of Africans in clerkship positions, and their evolution under British rule are relevant to the narrative, it is important also to consider the status of the courts and judicial activity during German rule.

Tribunal activity and litigation in the southern Ewe-speaking territories remains a largely unexplored and undocumented aspect of German colonial rule. According to Arthur Knoll, Governor Jesko von Puttkamer (1889–94) wanted the Ewe to "continue to transact as much of their own legal work as possible."[30] When chiefs became bureaucrats, the local government representative defined their legal competencies.[31] For example, in the *Bezirk* (district) of Misahöhe, the village chief's court consisted of the chief and four associates, each of whom could vote. The court was competent in civil matters only and could levy fines up to thirty marks. Defendants dissatisfied with the village chief's decision could appeal to the superior chief and ultimately to the *Bezirksamtsmann* (German district officer). Chiefs "reimbursed" themselves through collection of 10 percent of the value of an award.[32] As a result of this practice and other attitudes, individual district officers soon evolved their own corpus of law known as the *Bezirksleiterrecht*, a pastiche of German criminal law and local cultural legal tradition subordinated to the statutory authority of the chancellor. Counterintuitively Knoll considered this ad hoc civil and criminal procedure effective to some degree because district officers reported increases in the amount of legal business transacted in their courts.

Tribunal records from this period exist in the Lomé archives, but they have yet to be examined in depth. These regional law collections, the *Bezirksleiterrecht*, were contradictory and lacked uniformity, prompting Governor Graf von Zech (1903–10) to support a process of standardization. This failed to materialize, however, because his tenure ended, his successor was unsympathetic, and the war interrupted completion. Native tribunals dealt exclusively with civil cases, and criminal courts were under the direct control of Europeans. Thus control over the civil courts was part and parcel of the German approach to the Ewe chieftaincy. Ex post facto observations by British, French, and local Ewe people generally concur that the Germans opposed the amalgamation of Ewe chieftaincies, *dukowo,* or divisions, and disassembled those, such as Buem, that seemed strong enough to oppose German political authority.[33] The capacity to hold native tribunals was awarded to the respective chiefs of Ewe *dukowo* when their size posed no threat to the local German *Bezirksamtsmann.*[34]

In Lomé, however, judicial authority rested almost exclusively on German shoulders. Because the city was "new" and chiefly authorities were "imported" from neighboring towns and villages, the judicial system could not fall under the purview of any individual Ewe chief. In urban colonial courts German officers judged civil and criminal cases, while local residents acted as court interpreters, clerks, and reporters. On the rare occasion when African plaintiffs had any success in a civil or criminal matter in German-ruled Lomé or other larger towns, an individual or group had to secure the services of an eloquent and trustworthy letter writer. One such case was that of the d'Almeida family versus the German merchant Martin Paul.[35] But such instances were exceptional.[36] When British-led forces began their occupation of the city, they found numerous local individuals, many fluent in English, who were familiar with court procedure, anxious to continue in their capacity as clerks, and keen to reassert their economic control over the city. Moreover, the last few years of German rule, characterized by interference with the chiefly authorities, manipulation of contracts and financial agreements in the city, and especially by micromanagement of social customs and morality, meant that there was no shortage of civil disputes awaiting a judicial hearing.

Letter Writing in British Lomé

The British began regulating professional letter writers almost immediately after they assumed control of the administration of Lomé. The city itself was governable under emergency wartime legislation, and all measures taken during the occupation were of a quasi-constitutional and temporary nature. As far as the local population was concerned, the most significant administrative change was surely the suspension of direct taxation, a means of harmonization with the fiscal regime of the Gold Coast.[37] But court access and judicial review had equal standing with revenue in the system of indirect rule taking shape throughout the British West African colonies. Indeed, these two components of colonial administration were mutually informing and interdependent. When one examines court records from British Lomé, it is important to remember that chiefly native tribunals extracted fees for procedures and fines that in turn provided the financial reserves for local administration, in much the same way as the small letter licensing fees partly contributed to underwriting the cost of civil tribunals in the capital.

The questions then arise, why did the British privilege civil court access to those who had first paid the services of a letter writer, and why at this particular historical juncture?[38] From the evidence it would seem that, besides the small revenue accrued from the licenses themselves, three concerns were paramount during a period of wartime exigency. First, by providing for letter writers who could frame demands for judicial review, the government placed an impediment in the path of those who would bypass the authority of the local chiefly tribunals existing outside Lomé, for which no written or formal procedures were necessary. It thus ensured that the majority of local justice was administered outside the capital, at the local level, and with minimal cost. Second, the British were determined to stem the flow of cases to higher courts, because they desired that no verdicts decided during the German rule be revisited.[39] Third, the British decided that all cases relating to chiefly disputes, land conflicts, and related matters that pertained to traditional chiefly authority and civil procedure await the creation of a postwar formal and legitimate statutory authority for the former German territory.[40] Indeed Cole's appeal to his suspension included the following statement in his defense: "[A]nd if I had known that the people were told not to bring the question of destoolment till after the war, I would not have condescended to write for them."[41] Furthermore, when compared with the contemporaneous trend toward deregulation in Southern Nigeria, it must be remembered that the British had little documentary or statistical evidence of Lomé illiteracy and urban inequalities—the main factors leading to the introduction of licensing in Nigeria and the Gold Coast—and thus wartime constraints seem to have overridden all other concerns.

Male professionals in Lomé began applying for letter-writing licenses in late 1914. Although the exact number of licenses granted remains unclear, at least fifteen applications exist from various men, most of whom were likely Lomé residents at some point prior to the war. They addressed themselves directly to the District Political Officer and enclosed a fee of one shilling for the annual license; the number of fifteen or so sits comfortably with the figures given by Adewoye for the various provinces and large cities of Southern Nigeria.[42] No copies of the licenses themselves exist, but Cole's narrative and information furnished by Adewoye suggest it was a small card or piece of paper bearing the name of the licensee as well as the signature of the political officer granting the license.

Letter writers did not only write legal briefs to gain access to the courts. Besides related legal documents, such as wills and testaments, documents granting the power of attorney, and so forth, they also wrote personal correspondence, completed applications and financial forms, assisted with the creation of bank accounts, and any number of the plethora of tasks and expectations ushered in by a colonial order operating on the presumption of literacy and numeracy. The growth of letter writing as a profession is thus a lens through which one can assess the historical significance of preliteracy during the colonial period. Once the individual was licensed, he was free to set up shop where he pleased. And, as anyone visiting any part of Africa, India, Iran, or any number of other countries can attest, individuals usually establish themselves outside the law courts, the post office, or administrative centers. More recently youth congregate outside the new cybercafés in Togo and elsewhere to type e-mail for a fee.

Just who became a letter writer is itself a fascinating question. Colonial officials noted that several writers in parts of Nigeria came from as far afield as Sierra Leone and the Gold Coast. The fluctuating population of the young city of Lomé would certainly have lent itself to a similar trend. The precise identity of licensee no. 8, Robert A. Cole, remains a mystery, but it is highly unlikely that he was a longtime Lomé resident. The letterhead used in his appeal indicates that he was a merchant broker for a Manchester export firm, McClaren Brothers and Company, with bases in Sekondi, Cape Coast, and Accra, whereas the political officer's notes on Cole assert that he had recently come to Lomé to represent the same firm. It is most likely that he came from Sierra Leone, where a large Cole clan had been active in commerce since the mid-nineteenth century. Licensee no. 13 was a member of the Gaba family of Aného. The testimony of Emmanuel Koukou Dogbe supports the claim that many letter writers then were surely assuming a second or possibly even a third profession when they applied for licenses.[43]

Letter writing operated primarily as a for-profit business, although instances have come to light where licensees worked pro bono. Although Roberts was unable to establish the fee structure for Dakar's *écrivains publics*, Adewoye reports the regulation of fees in Nigeria. Two of his informants, A. A. Babalola and J. A. Oke-Owo, licensees in Ibadan, affirmed that from a financial point of view, the writing of petitions was "the soul of the business."[44] In Lomé there is no evidence of a set fee for a letter or a petition, but fortunately for the historical record licensees were expected to provide their name, license number, and fee charged at the end of each petition. Letters of one or two pages, handwritten or typed, cost on average two or three shillings. Depending on the nature and content of the letters, strong evidence suggests that letter writers considered the value of the service and its potential outcome when establishing their fees. Longer letters cost more, and the highest fee I have found was ten shillings, which was for a damages claim that, if successful, could have won the plaintiff forty pounds plus costs.

Letters seeking access to the courts are, of course, like petitions of appeal, formulaic documents.[45] In Lomé court records, an obeisant tone predominates. A petition generally began, "We the undersigned . . . have the honor most respectfully to submit to you the following petition." A letter of appeal against a native tribunal ruling usually began in a more abrupt manner, diving directly into the subject matter. Letters from chiefs defending their court rulings were not written by licensed letter writers, however, but usually by the chiefly linguist, clerk, or court recorder. At the end of each document, below the signature or mark of the plaintiff but above that of the licensee, was a passage indicating "the contents of the above letter have been explained to the plaintiff" and often translated into "the local Ewe language." The presence of an additional formulaic passage such as this suggests that at least 50 percent of those contracting the services of a writer were illiterate and/or nonconversant in English.

But while the language of petition texts conformed to established norms, the subjects of letters seeking access to courts were expansive. The substance of petition writing was conceptually at odds with letters gaining court access. In my initial survey of some two hundred or more letters deposited with the city tribunal, most were civil disputes. Chieftaincy and stoolship disputes often surfaced in the form of land and usufruct conflicts and less frequently as complaints about excessive labor requirements asked of villagers, such as in the building of roads. Marital disputes are regular subjects, ranging from battered wives seeking compensation for assault to cases of abducted daughters or elopements to incarcerated husbands demanding the return of their estranged spouses or at the very least return of bridewealth. Chiefs and court clerks wrote seeking special powers to punish recalcitrant subjects and hold others in contempt of court and once even for two sets of handcuffs to enforce a summons. Complaints of petty theft of livestock and money are numerous. There are also isolated demands for a form of restraining order. Finally, a number of disputants seized on the opportunity created by the new, entirely British jurisdiction over border regions. Whereas farms or chiefly authority had spanned the former British-German border, making litigation difficult, plaintiffs now desired that British courts right previous wrongs.

The numerous commencements of civil proceedings suggest the investment of high hopes in the interim British occupational force. To what extent these individuals were successful in their appeals, however, is largely unknown. As with the records of the Dakar *Tribunal de Première Instance*, there are no adjoining pages containing rulings. Occasionally petitions and letters have marginalia from various political officers indicating that this or that complaint was inadmissible for such and such a reason. At other times a senior political officer directed his junior to "deal with this matter," which suggests that plaintiffs often attempted to bypass the hierarchy of the court system by appealing directly to the superior authority. At other times the court receiver was ordered to reply to the plaintiff, shedding light on another important role of an African intermediary in the colonial court system. One member of the Tamakloe family, an important Anglophile Lomé merchant family with kin throughout Eweland, served in this role from mid-1914. As court receiver Theophile Tamakloe arranged petitions in the order he saw fit and even assisted his allies in their appeals. Although very little is known of this particular man, the role of court receivers in Lomé is a potential site of fruitful research.

Although the Secretary of Native Affairs in the Gold Coast, Captain Furley, had spent much of 1918 and 1919 traversing Eweland caucusing for evidence of significant pro-British sentiment and thus a reason to remain in the region, British control of Lomé and much of its hinterland ended on September 30, 1920.[46] Subsequently the capital and its environs came under French League of Nations mandate administration. The incorporation of Anglophile elements into the urban court bureaucracy was thus temporary, and soon after the establishment of French control, measures were enacted to encourage the spread of *la langue française* in the new quasi colony.[47] Perhaps because of the vague and inconclusive terms of the mandate and fears that the region might be merged with the British Gold Coast or worse, returned to Germany, French officers were anxious to replace Anglophilia and vestiges of pro-German sentiment with affection for France and all things French. To this end local clerks complained that imported *fonctionnaires* from Dahomey displaced them in the courts and other government agencies.[48]

The French administration was equally chary of a flood of civil legislation from its mandated subjects, but only further research will uncover to what extent officers drew upon the small Lomé cohort of public letter writers to act as Cerberus. The licensed letter writers of British Lomé were most likely dislodged by this current of change, and the presence of clerks, letter writers, and court reporters on the list of names of an Anglophile "Committee on Behalf of Togoland Natives" formed circa 1918–19 suggests their disenchantment was one factor leading to its establishment. This relatively mysterious organization met in the home of Alfred Acolatsé and championed the retention of British control over the region. Petitions from 1918 to 1922, directed at London, New York, and Geneva, called for the British to remain in Lomé. The pro-British lobbying of this group, a significant factor in the later relocation of many of its members across the border to British-controlled Aflao, underscores the important political role played by letter writers in early nationalist and anticolonial activity.

After the failure of its lobbying, however, this organization transformed itself into the more narrowly focused Lomé Union, and among its ranks remained several former clerks and letter writers.[49] The union championed the rights of clerks who had loyally served the British administration and was paralleled by organizational movements of clerks in other former German colonies, most famously the Tanganyikan Territory African Civil Servants Association (1918). The Lomé Union included Robert A. Cole, Henry Rue Gaba, and Theophile Tamakloe.[50] When this failed, petitions to the League of Nations mandates generally attacked the perceived injustices of the French and occasionally of the British. Many of these petitions, especially those arising from the Lawson-Adjigo dispute and the Bund der deutschen Togoländer, were authored by lawyers, such as J. E. Casely-Hayford, or previously licensed letter writers, such as Gaba. Furthermore, because paid letter writers were familiar with the names of government officials, the tendency to leapfrog the hierarchy of the court bureaucracy continued under the League of Nations mandate. In the case of land disputes in Nybongo and Woame spanning the new international frontier between British and French mandated Togoland, as well as land restitution claims by the people of the Agu-Kpalimé region, letter writers acting for local plaintiffs sent their petitions directly to Geneva. In terms of chiefly and "traditional" authority, the British treatment of petitions involving complaints arising from chiefly native tribunals and stoolship disputes prefigured their plan to amalgamate *dukowo* in the Eweland region with the goal of minimizing the number and cost of civil disputes.[51]

As to licensee no. 8, Robert A. Cole, he seems to be the archetype profiteer of which so many petitioners and colonial officers complained. If we conservatively estimate an average of only two shillings for each of the 1,072 letters and petitions he alleges to have written during a four-year period, he would have had a personal revenue of over 250 pounds sterling. Moreover, the number represents possibly five letters per week, which would be completely compatible with another occupation. With no direct taxation in operation in Lomé and the fact that he continued to serve as a broker for McClaren Brothers and Company, Mr. Cole was assembling a small fortune. Whether or not he succeeded in his appeal is immaterial as his premium service as an English language writer was redundant after 1922, when Lomé fell under French control.

But what did Cole do with this enormous sum of money? In a clever article that attempts to retrace the life of Wangrin's nemesis, Laurent Fourchard asserts that many administrative cadres in Ouagadougou,

Upper Volta, invested their wealth in urban property.[52] They were able to do so precisely because they were among the few people capable of negotiating the complicated terrain of urban property law. Emmanuel Koukou Dogbe's testimony also supports this view. Letter writers were "reasonable people" who invested in property and education.[53] While Fourchard's example does not pertain directly to the experience of the Lomé letter writers, it does provide a possible framework for understanding what came next.[54]

In 1922 a new series of petitions arrived on the desk of the District Political Officer in Denu, Gold Coast. The letters from British subjects resident in Aflao, the small village immediately on the other side of the international border that runs along the edge of Lomé, complained of a certain Cole who had been buying up large tracts of land and displacing the local people. They stated that for several years, Cole (whose first name is unmentioned) had sought to acquire territory against the wishes of the local community, and they asked the district officer to intervene in their plight. When we consult the records of companies active in Lomé in 1922, there is no longer any mention of McClaren Brothers and Company operating in the city. Could this be the same Robert A. Cole continuing the exploitative practices for which the British occupation of Lomé had so eminently prepared him?

Letter Writing in Eweland and Beyond

It remains to be seen what other social, political, and economic impact the British regulation of letter writers had on long-term developments in the Ewe-speaking region of the former German colony of Togoland. What can we make of the unusual step of regulating letter writing in British-occupied Lomé? Public letter writers, licensed or otherwise, provide an important service in communities with low literacy and little familiarity with legal procedure. But even in contemporary Europe and North America, few individuals would attempt any civil, let alone criminal, litigation, without the advice of an informed and educated legal authority, one whose documents have legal standing in the courts. In the litigious colonial Togoland environment, although adherence to civil legal procedure and precedent may have been less important, few plaintiffs could frame their own complaints or petitions. Some of the more sophisticated letter writers identified by Adewoye were able to challenge judgments on procedural grounds and cite numerous common law precedents.[55] In Lomé, however, there was no tradition of

British common law, and plaintiffs were less troubled with the legal niceties and more concerned with the urgency of their hearing.

Lomé was under British military occupation, and like all administrative decisions made between 1914 and 1920, the licensing of letter writers was a temporary measure. Although access to the courts was a fundamental part of all colonial regimes' attempts to legitimate colonial rule by providing for authoritative and accessible judicial review, wartime urgencies were paramount in the creation of the license system in Lomé. Determined to mitigate the inevitable flourish of civil claims that seem to have accompanied the creation of any new court system, the local officers determined that written appeals would have to come via preapproved learned individuals, and thus they created licenses for letter writers that provided for a fee-charging disincentive to appeal. Interestingly, a further Gold Coast (and by implication Lomé) ordinance was enacted on August 26, 1918, to regulate the preparation of legal documents. It specifically banned the preparation of "legal instruments" (i.e., deeds, wills, etc.) by persons other than "legal practitioners" (i.e., lawyers). A fine of up to fifty pounds for the first offense demonstrates that the activities of the entrepreneurial "bush lawyers" were not restricted to Southern Nigeria. It is only a matter of speculation what might have happened in Lomé had the British remained and attempted to put court access on a permanent statutory footing.

By 1915, then, partly in deference to the feelings of qualified legal practitioners, of which there were a not insubstantial number in Lagos, Accra, and Cape Coast, the Nigerian administration abandoned the system of licenses. Adewoye writes that although considered a necessary move at the time, "this measure was a step in the wrong direction. The issuing of licenses to letter writers did provide a means of exercising some control. . . . [T]he licenses were issued annually, and the renewal of a license could be made to depend on good behavior on the part of the licensee. Moreover, it would not have been too difficult to use the system to set some educational requirements for prospective letter writers."[56]

The history of letter writers and the regulation of the profession provide insight into the lives of colonial intermediaries and the Africans who turned to them for assistance in negotiating the colonial legal world. Although not employed by the state, the letter writer was in the position of acting as a go-between amid litigating parties and charged with the task of conveying a legal matter to the colonial authorities. Because letter writers functioned as intermediaries, albeit in a different capacity than that of interpreters and clerks and with a different constituency, they sparked concerns among colonial officials, necessitating regulation. The enactment of controls and the snapshots of the otherwise unremarkable life of Robert A. Cole speak more broadly to colonial concern about interpreters and clerks, for letter writers occupied similarly ambiguous nexuses of power and authority.

The role of colonial public letter writers in British, German, and French colonies is a central component of the social history of access to the colonial court system, and the life of Cole far transcends the confines of urban Lomé. Letter writing for hire operated as a mechanism whereby all colonial subjects—educated or illiterate—could have their grievances brought to the attention of the appropriate authority or administrator. The letter writers functioned as intermediaries in a complex environment, negotiating, shaping, framing, and reframing the illiterate plaintiff's language. To the African they represented an avenue to legal review for a reasonable expense. To the colonial official letter writers both facilitated and obfuscated colonial law. For the vast illiterate African majority, they were crucial to the court system, because written documents were far more likely to result in civil or criminal proceedings.

Notes

1. Evidence comes from Archives Nationales Togolaises (hereafter ANT) Lomé, box E-1 1916, Public Letter writers in box 8APA 264, 1917–18.
2. For *la loi bureaucratique,* see Roberts, "Case against Faama Mademba Sy."
3. See Marguerat, "Histoire et société urbaine."
4. I use the term "right" advisedly but with caution. Although British subjects were indeed "entitled" to petition the highest authority in the realm, no such privilege existed in Germany.
5. Groff, "Dynamics of Collaboration."
6. Chanock, "Making Customary Law"; Chanock, *Law, Custom, and Social Order,* 59; and Moore, *Social Facts and Fabrications.*
7. Groff, "Dynamics of Collaboration," 148.
8. Hampâté Bâ, *Fortunes of Wangrin.*
9. Groff, "Dynamics of Collaboration," 158.
10. Conklin, *Mission to Civilize.*
11. Roberts, "Text and Testimony."
12. The best discussion of the civil law tradition is that of Merryman, *Civil Law Tradition.*
13. Roberts, "Text and Testimony," 456. Roberts adds: "Although access to French law is supposed to be without cost, to those unable to initiate their own

written requests, potential plaintiffs had to weigh the costs of letter-writing against the possibility of the court's favoring their claim" (457).

14. Roberts, "Text and Testimony," 463.

15. For Britain, see E. P. Thompson, *Making of the English Working Class;* D. Thompson, *Chartists;* E. P. Thompson, *Customs in Common.* For the colonies, see, for example, Gocking, "Creole Society"; Rathbone, "The Gold Coast"; and Boahen, *Ghana.*

16. See *Laws of the Gold Coast Colony,* 1920, vol. 1, chap. 8, Ghana National Archives (hereafter GNA), ADM 4/1.

17. Akurang-Parry, "'Smattering of Education.'"

18. Osei-Tutu, "Petitions and Other forms of 'Peaceful' Protest."

19. Recently explored by Hawkins, *Writing and Colonialism.*

20. Akurang-Parry, "'Smattering of Education,'" 56; Sebald, *Togo,* 535–85.

21. Adewoye, *Judicial System,* 188–97.

22. See *Laws of the Gold Coast,* 1920, vol. 2, 1408–10.

23. For narratives on the Ewe migration, see Gayibor, *Les Aja-Ewe;* and Gayibor, "Agokoli et la dispersion de Notsé." See also Amenumey, *Ewe in Pre-Colonial Times.* For an explanation of the traditional Ewe structure, see Verdon, *Abutia Ewe of West Africa,* 46–73.

24. For a comparative study of tax regimes, see Knoll, "Taxation in the Gold Coast Colony and in Togo."

25. Education policy is discussed in Lawrance, "Most Obedient Servants"; Adick, *Bildung und Kolonialismus in Togo;* and Lange, *L'école au Togo.*

26. For German colonial rule, see Nussbaum, *Togo;* Knoll, *Togo under Imperial Germany;* Sebald, *Togo;* Maier, "Slave Labor and Wage Labor"; Avornyo, *Deutschland und Togo;* Erbar, *Ein Platz an der Sonne?;* Trotha, *Koloniale Herrschaft;* Napo, "Le Togo à l'époque allemande"; Schuerkens, *Du Togo allemand aux Togo et Ghana indépendants.*

27. Marguerat, "La naissance d'une capitale africaine."

28. Marguerat, "Histoire et société," 16, my translation.

29. Stoecker, "Position of Africans."

30. Knoll, *Togo,* 65.

31. Knoll, *Togo,* 47–49, 65–68.

32. Hans Georg von Doering, "Über die richterliche Tätigkeit der Häuptlinge," April 2, 1906, Conseil du Gouvernment, 1903–7, ANT, D.2.9. Cited by Knoll, in *Togo,* 180.

33. This is in sharp contrast to British policy from the mid-1920s. See Lawrance, "Bankoe v. Dome"; and Brown, "Politics in the Kpandu Area of Ghana."

34. For the role of the *Bezirksamtsmann* or *Bezirkschef,* see Sebald, *Togo,* 272–75.

35. Described by Knoll, *Togo,* 67–68.

36. Petitioning and complaining in German Togo is well documented. Sebald, *Togo,* 535–85, contains numerous examples of petitions and newspaper

articles and letters detailing abuses. Knoll, *Togo*, 62–64, restricts the discussion to the exchange between African elites and the German colonial office.

37. See Marguerat, "Histoire et société."

38. Ordinances governing the French courts in Dakar and the Four Communes (but not the native courts) required written letters to gain access. Because of the temporary nature of the wartime ordinances governing British Lomé, it is impossible to know with certainly that the services of a letter writer were required for access to civil courts. The quantity of letters written by licensed writers (over a hundred in number), however, strongly suggests that written documentation was privileged by the British and thus desired and sought after by plaintiffs.

39. A petition from a certain Avorgbedor, written by Mr. Gaba for the sum of four shillings, dated June 30, 1920, began with the statement, "[T]he order of the District Political Officer, was that, all cases which have been decided by the German Government, before the war must not be recalled and rejudged by any tribunal."

40. This approach was consistent with international treaties that were to come into force after World War I governing territories occupied in case of war. Under no circumstances could occupying powers modify legislation governing the country until a peace treaty officially awarded sovereignty to the victorious power. But while the British were anxious that all administrative questions should await a future peace treaty, the French acted quite differently. In the words of Yves Marguerat (personal communication), they considered "Togo as definitively theirs." To support this, between 1917 and 1918 the French administration produced paper with the letterhead "Colonie du Togo," conveying a legal status that never existed.

41. Cole, 1918, ANT, 8APA 264, 1917–18, box E-1 1916.

42. Adewoye, *Judicial System*, 189.

43. Interview with Emmanuel Koukou Dogbe, Hohoe, Ghana, July 6, 2002. He stated that many letter writers in the 1920s and 1930s in the Kadjebi area, on the border of the French and British mandated Togolands, came from Keta, Peki, and Accra.

44. Adewoye, *Judicial System*, 190. Interviews conducted in 1966.

45. See Davis, *Fiction in the Archives;* Roberts, "Text and Testimony," 455–56.

46. The testimonies from Lomé's leading men, Augustino de Souza and Octavianus Olympio, and many other statements, letters, and interviews conducted by Furley are to be found in the GNA, ADM 11/1/1620: Togoland Secret and Confidential Papers.

47. Lawrance, "Language between Powers."

48. The *Gold Coast Independent*, January 13, 1923, printed an article titled "The Gauls in Togoland," written anonymously by "A Togolander," in which the regime of Governor Woelffel was characterized as "whole importations of

French clerks . . . let loose like wolves upon an unprotected people and some became roving gents in the night." Archives de la Société des Nations (hereafter ASN), Geneva, R37 FMT(12226) No. 22291.

49. Sometimes also referred to as "The Committee on Behalf of the Chiefs and Inhabitants of Togoland." The two titles are from different sources. The former from a letter of J. T. Mensah, ASN, R20(3099) no. 4900. The latter is from a letter signed by the committee's president, Octavianus Olympio, Archives Diplomatiques Quay d'Orsay, Série: SDN, Sous-série: Sec. Gén.; Mandats Togo-Cameroun, Pétitions 1923–1938, no.: 622, dossier 3: Bund der deutschen Togoländer, 642.

50. ANT, 8APA, Cercle de Lomé, Rapport Mensuel du Février 1921. According to this report the other members included Abibu, Blavo Tsri, Alfred Nyonator, Christian Dorkenoo, Charles Okpatta, Nelson Domaki, Edouard Mensah, John Atayi, E. G. de Lima, John Mensah, Sam Ghartey, Bennett Cridjah, William Fumey, John K. Byll, O. Tosu, F. K. Anthony, E. S. Anthony, R. E. Nyatepi, L. S. Lawson, William K. Dadzie, J. M.Lawson, O. Sokpolie, B. M. Opoloo, Mathieu Adoky, Andreas Lawson, F. K. Agedjie, Johann Kenyi, Ayovi, Atodevi, and Innocentus d'Almeida.

51. See Lawrance, "Bankoe v. Dome."

52. Fourchard, "Propriétaires et commerçants Africains."

53. Interview with Emmanuel Koukou Dogbe, Hohoe, Ghana, July 6, 2002. He stated that some letter writers were lame or injured and could not farm, so they bought land and built houses. Many others spent their earnings on education for their children.

54. Marguerat, "À chacun son 'Chez.'"

55. Adewoye, *Judicial System*, 191–92.

56. Adewoye, *Judicial System*, 190.

Negotiating Legal Authority in French West Africa

The Colonial Administration and African Assessors, 1903–1918

RUTH GINIO

In the introduction to the volume *Law in Colonial Africa,* Richard Roberts and Kristin Mann emphasize the centrality of law to the understanding of colonialism in Africa. The enforcement of law by a system of courts, police, and prisons was crucial to the maintenance of colonial rule.[1] Law and the rule of law were the ultimate justification of the colonial project.[2] The colonizer, however, could not be the only actor in the legal drama. The colonized populations had an active part in it too, not only as those who approached the legal system or were prosecuted by it but also as assistants of the colonial regimes. Without the collaboration of colonial personnel, colonial legal systems could have not functioned effectively. In French West Africa, African employees such as assessors, interpreters, and secretaries were supposed to assist the French administration to mete out justice according to the local customs. However, the African court often turned into a battleground between colonial and African perceptions of the essence of the legal process.

This essay examines the role of the African assessor *(assesseur)*, or judge *(juge)*, as he was often referred to by the colonial administration. I will show that through careful reading of colonial documents, it is possible to reconstruct the ways in which these assessors perceived their role and their image, the extent of independence they possessed, and their negotiation of legal authority with the French colonial administration. The chapter focuses on the formative years of the native legal system in French West Africa from its establishment in 1903 until the end of World War I. During these years the French endeavored to shape a native legal system that would, on the one hand, reflect the values of French civilization and its contribution to the "uplifting" of the Africans and, on the other hand, serve as an effective instrument of control. The attempt to bridge these sometimes contradictory aims lay behind much of the administrative correspondence regarding the legal native system during this period. This is also the time when African intermediaries in the native courts enjoyed more autonomy and attempted to adjust to the new order while maintaining their precolonial social status. I first briefly outline the structure of this system and the place designed in it for the assessors. The French discourse on the African assessors will be discussed next. I then present the French colonial dilemma of enhancing the assessors' prestige and independence while wishing to control them. Finally, I analyze the extent of power that was in the hands of the assessors and the ways in which they were able to manipulate the legal process for their own ends and thus to become active players in the legal arena.

The System of the Native Courts in French West Africa and the African Assessors

Up until 1903 French courts in French West Africa existed only along the coast and adjudicated the cases of Europeans and Africans holding French citizenship who were concentrated in that area. No formal French legal system had been set up inland, and Africans continued to litigate their own disputes with little interference from the French administration. Then, along with further French expansion into the hinterland, the governor general's office in Dakar, the capital of French West Africa, had to decide whether to extend French law to the interior or to establish a different judicial system for Africans. The governor general decided to establish two parallel systems of justice: one for Frenchmen and Africans holding French citizenship, the other for the vast majority of African "subjects" who would bring their cases before African "magistrates" applying "customary" law *(loi coutumier).*[3]

During the period discussed here, two decrees shaped the structure of the native legal system. The first, which actually established this system, was that of November 10, 1903, and the second, which introduced certain modifications to the first, was that of August 16, 1912. According to article 75 of the 1903 decree, the judgments rendered by the native courts were to be based on the local customs as long as these did not contradict the principles of French civilization. The problem, however, was that the colonial administrators were totally ignorant of the local customs and languages in the regions under their control. This ignorance raised the question of codification of African customary law. During the decade following the decree of 1903, the colonial authorities attempted to create a body of customary law for the various territories. Governor General Ernest Roume (1902–8) recognized the diversity of African customs, which he noted varied even from village to village. Nevertheless, he expected his administrators to look for common traits and gradually to codify a rational and applicable legal system based on the fundamental principles of "natural law." William Ponty (1908–15), who succeeded Roume, continued to encourage the codification of customary law. During that time the lieutenant governor of French Soudan, François Clozel, commissioned Maurice Delafosse, a recognized linguist, ethnographer, and historian, to provide a synthesis of the customs of his territory. Delafosse's influential book, *Haut-Sénégal-Niger,* indeed advanced the task of codification by proposing that all Sudanese agrarian communities shared certain common legal principles. As Hervé Jézéquel shows in this volume, Africans had a part in this process of codification as interpreters, informants, and literate writers of short ethnographic monographs and digests of legal customs. Although usually their role was limited to collecting field data while its analysis was reserved for Western intellectuals such as Delafosse, they still had influence over the legal basis of the native courts system. In spite of all these efforts, though, the initial purpose was never fulfilled, and the local customary law remained mostly unknown to colonial administrators.[4] Thus, a paradox was created when administrators who served as judges in the native legal system had to rule according to the customary law about which they were totally ignorant. They thus had to rely on African assessors who were supposed to be acquainted with the local customs of their regions. Moreover, the courts system could not function without other African officeholders such as interpreters

and secretaries because of the lack of European personnel and the ignorance of colonial officials in local languages.

Another dilemma stemming from the principle of accepting local
customs as long as they did not contradict the principles of French civilization involved the definition of these principles in the colonial context. To what extent should the colonial regime intervene in the legal
disputes of its subjects? In other words, were Africans advanced
enough to be judged according to these "principles of French civilization," or should "local customs" be accepted even if they were not seen
as "civilized" in French eyes?

Although the new legal system for Africans that began operating in
1905 was supposed to be adapted to African traditions and cultures, the
hierarchical structure of the metropolitan legal system was imported
virtually intact into the African reality.[5] The lowest judicial authority
was the village chief, who had only the power to reconcile.[6] The next
level was the province court, later called the subdivision court. The
African chief of the province or canton presided over it and was assisted by two African assessors. These courts dealt with civil and commercial cases, and their verdicts could be appealed before the circle
court.[7] The circle court, serving as a criminal tribunal, tried all felonies
committed by African subjects and reviewed appeals from the province
courts. It was presided over by the circle commander, his deputy, or
possibly some other European official designated by the governor. Two
African notables, nominated at the beginning of every year by the head
of the colony on the advice of the attorney general, had a consultative
voice in the proceedings. Monthly accounts of these proceedings were
to be sent both to the lieutenant governor of the colony and to the attorney general in Dakar, who had the right to reopen any case. The administrator who presided over the circle court was a judge with virtually
unrestricted powers, as he served simultaneously as policeman, examining magistrate, public prosecutor, and the authority responsible for
executing the sentence. In theory he did not have to listen to the assessors, but his ignorance of the local customs according to which he was
to rule empowered these assessors to influence his decisions. All circle
court sentences exceeding five years' imprisonment were automatically
reviewed by the *chambre d'homologation,* a special department of the
French appeals court, based in Dakar and presided over by the vice
president of the appeals court.[8]

In this chapter I discuss the assessors of the province/subdivision
courts and those of the circle courts. As indicated in the introduction to

this volume, paradoxically, those Africans who were in the lower colonial bureaucracy and held positions bestowing little authority were often the most indispensable for colonial rule and in this case for the functioning of the native legal system. Because of the relative power these assessors possessed, they appear more often in the colonial documents than in those of the *chambre d'homologation*.

No matter the extent of their power, assessors at all levels of the native legal system were indispensable. To be valid every verdict handed down by a native court had to include the sentence: "After being deliberated and the native assessors consulted."[9] The colonial administration thus attributed considerable importance to the mission of recruiting assessors. The decree of 1903 shaped the process by which the assessors were to be recruited. The head of the colony, in the case of each province court, had to nominate two assessors from a list of at least five. He was advised by the attorney general. In the case of the circle court, the head of the colony chose the assessors from a list of at least four candidates. In regions where litigants claimed Muslim status, one of the assessors nominated to the province court had to be Muslim. In the circle court a supplementary Muslim assessor had to be available in case a Muslim appeared before the court. In the absence of the supplementary assessor, the local qadi was called instead.[10] The assessors had to be respected members of their communities; they usually held some social, religious, or political leadership position. They had to be acquainted with the local customs of their regions, or in the case of Muslims, with Islamic law *(sharia)*. Knowledge of French was required only of the two assessors who sat at the *chambre d'homologation* in Dakar; for others it was preferable but not necessary. The fact that most assessors did not in fact speak French meant that the administration had to invest efforts in the recruitment of interpreters and secretaries to write the verdicts in either Arabic or French.

The status of the assessors was perceived as extremely important, although status did not necessarily ensure that these individuals would be familiar with either local custom or Islamic law. In colonial Algeria, for example, candidates had to pass special exams to become judges, but no such selection procedure existed in French West Africa.[11] The only criteria by which assessors, even Muslim ones, were chosen in French West Africa were administrative reports on them and their authority among the local population, to the extent that such authority could indeed be evaluated. Therefore, there was no way the administration could verify that the assessors actually knew the customs by which they had to judge. This was especially true with regard to the non-Muslim assessors because the customs by which they had to give judgments were not written anywhere. According to Brett Shadle's study of the African court elders in Nyanza Province, Kenya, prior to the late 1930s the British chose African legal personnel by similar criteria as the French. They preferred "traditional" men thought to be well versed in customary law to younger, "modern" Africans, who they believed were more inclined to be corrupted "in modern ways." Shadle clarifies that the British in Kenya, just as in French West Africa, had little influence over the knowledge and moral attributes of the court elders they chose.

The assessors were thus a vital element of the native legal system. Without them this system simply could not function. The ignorance of colonial administrators at all levels regarding local customs denied them the tools to examine the assessors' professional capacities. Even after they succeeded in choosing seemingly appropriate assessors, their problems had just begun. They now had to deal with African notables to whom they had given considerable power within the arena of the native court.

African Assessors in the Discourse of the French Colonial Administration

French administrators often voiced their opinions regarding the African assessors and the way they functioned. Occasionally they exalted their ability to learn the principles of French civilization and gradually to endorse them.[12] They also praised their devotion and efforts to perform their duties well. Most colonial discourse on these assessors, however, was negative. It must be emphasized that the colonial administration did not see all African judges as one category. A clear distinction was made between Muslims and non-Muslims, sedentary and nomadic assessors, and between assessors residing in different colonies. Muslim judges were sometimes considered superior to the rest. E. Beurdeley, *chef de bureau* of the ministry of the colonies who was sent on a mission to French West Africa in 1913 to examine the functioning of the "Native Courts" system, stated that unlike their non-Muslim colleagues, Muslim judges were perfectly familiar with the law according to which they had to pass judgment.[13]

Nevertheless, the colonial view of the Muslim judges was rather ambivalent. The French feared that because Islamic law was written, it would be preferred over non-Muslim local customs and thus force the

Islamic religion on non-Muslim Africans.[14] This fear was also reflected in the debate over the issue of the language that should be used for writing verdicts in the province courts, which will be discussed later.

The colonial administration also made a clear distinction between African assessors who resided in different colonies. In general, Africans who lived in the colonies that were the last to be occupied, such as the military territory of Niger and the region of Timbuktu, were considered more distanced from the "principles of French civilization" and therefore were not appointed as presidents of province courts.[15]

One of the most common complaints regarding African assessors in general was their lack of enthusiasm for their role. French administrators were puzzled that African notables were not eager to become assessors and that when they did accept the appointment, they did not consider this honor to be sufficient. One of them stated that unlike French judges, who considered as sacred the privilege the law had given them to judge their peers, the mentality of African judges prevented them from understanding this and made them demand more concrete forms of compensation for their efforts.[16] The judges' "mentality" or "race" explained other faults as well: ruling in favor of rich and influential members of society, corruption, abuse of power, and an inability to understand the enlightened principles of French justice.[17]

The colonial administration thus found itself in a difficult situation with regard to African assessors. On the one hand, the French questioned the ability of these assessors to judge according to French standards, although they did believe that at least some of them were trying hard to perform their duties as well as they could, considering their "limited capacities." Because the French doubted African assessors' abilities, they wanted to control the judges closely. On the other hand, these same judges were the representatives of French civilization in the judicial sphere. To be influential and to attract Africans to the colonial courts, they had to be respected. Therefore, control over them had to be limited and the administration sometimes had to accept the fact that they could not be in total command of the "monster" they had created.

Who Controlled the Courtroom?

The dilemma of the French colonial administration was, then, how to maintain control over the judicial process without hampering the authority of African assessors. The picture that emerges from the colonial documents is one of constant negotiations over legal authority in the native courts, especially in the provincial courts, where often enough no European was present.

One member of the native tribunal staff who was highly relevant to these negotiations over legal authority was the court secretary. Under the terms of article 34 of the decree of 1912, the function of court's clerk (*greffier*) did not exist in the subdivision and circle courts. The presidents of these courts were to be assisted by a secretary in the editing of verdicts and court notes. Further instructions from September 22, 1913, added that the secretary had to be an African familiar enough with the French language or a French official. It was affirmed that the secretary would function only as a scribe and would not intervene in the debates. He would only be allowed to provide information about the formalities that should be observed and would have to inform his superior in case he noticed any abuses.[18] The administration discussed two main issues with regard to the secretaries, both closely related to the problem of control: the question of the language and the possibility of "planting" a European secretary in the subdivision court.

The instructions to recruit only Africans who could write in French did not exist in the decree of 1903. As Saliou Mbaye writes in an appendix to this volume, before 1911 African secretaries could also write verdicts and court notes in Arabic. This situation was often criticized in colonial correspondence. In 1909 the governor of French Guinea complained to Governor General Ponty about the requirement that in his colonies he recruit only secretaries who could write in Arabic. He agreed that this might be logical for regions that were predominantly Muslim, such as Futa Jallon. However, recruiting an Arabic-speaking secretary for regions where the judges were illiterate and Islam was not dominant was, according to him, a serious mistake. A secretary who wrote in Arabic in such regions would convey the message to the Africans that the French were paying homage to Muslim instruction and according it official prestige. The governor recommended recruiting secretaries among the young Africans who were attending French schools. He explained that the role of the secretary was more than just writing what was being said. The secretary had great influence over the Africans who attended the trials. His duty was thus to propagate the ideas that he represented. Therefore, it was vital that this be propaganda for French rather than Islamic values.[19] Ponty agreed and affirmed that although it was important not to express any hostility toward Islam and Muslims, it was equally vital to give the non-Muslim Africans the feeling that they were as respectable as the Muslims.[20]

In 1914 Ponty finally resolved the question of which language the re-cruited secretary had to know when he instructed the governors of the colonies to select only French-speaking secretaries. The use of Arabic in the native courts, even in Muslim areas, was to be suspended. Ponty gave several reasons for this decision, but it is quite obvious that he was concerned with control and supervision. He noted that as most French administrators did not read Arabic, they were incapable of exercising any control over documents written in this language.[21]

The second question the issue of secretaries raised was related to the possibility of recruiting European secretaries. In some cases this was seen as a golden opportunity to control the judiciary process, certainly in the subdivision courts, where Europeans had no formal role. How-ever, the presence of a European secretary in a court presided over by an African posed serious challenges to French authority. The French worried that Africans would interpret this as a situation in which an African judge was superior to a European secretary. Beurdeley, for ex-ample, was basically in favor of recruiting European secretaries, but he insisted that the instructions forbidding them to take active part in the debates be abolished. The presence of a European secretary in a court presided over by a native, he explained, put the white person in a state of inferiority that would be evident to all. Beurdeley asserted that by re-sponding to the judges, taking part in the debate, and playing a role, the European would at least save his dignity. If the European secretary was allowed to take an active part in the debates, he believed, his presence in the subdivision court might even be helpful. He explained that al-though the colonial policy was to allow Africans to implement their customs and to respect the independence of the judges, those judges still lacked the necessary education to be completely independent.[22]

The main fear of the colonial administration, then, was that the space in which Africans conducted the legal process mainly by themselves — the subdivision court—might sometimes escape colonial supervision. The subdivision courts were numerous and European personnel scarce. It was especially difficult to send Europeans to distant areas, and these were exactly the areas considered most problematic. Therefore, the co-lonial administration had to resort to other means of control, such as regular reports that the subdivisions' administrators had to send to Dakar. Although this measure was criticized as not efficient enough, a greater intervention was difficult if not impossible.[23]

Much of the independence of African assessors also derived from the way in which the assessors enforced customary law. As noted earlier, the French did not doubt the moral superiority of their legal system over African customary law, but they also believed that most Africans were not civilized enough to be judged according to this legal system. Customary law, as vague a notion as it was, had to be the legal basis for the native courts' judgments. I will now examine how the use of customary law and the hesitance of the colonial administration to reverse verdicts that were ostensibly based on it allowed the assessors a certain space to maneuver within the rigid colonial rules.

African Assessors and the Colonial Debate about Customary Law

The most important tool allowing African assessors a certain degree of independence was the vaguely defined "customary law." Despite several attempts to codify local customs and to render them clearly accessible to French colonial administrators, the French never succeeded in this task. Their ignorance regarding customary law gave the assessors certain power. We can best assess the extent of this power by examining a number of appeals to and protests against the judgments of the provincial courts. One of the motives for requesting assessors' verdicts to be reversed was the claim that the judicial process was faulty. A series of four complaints that Hacinthe Devès, a member of the General Council (conseil général), submitted to the lieutenant governor of Senegal on behalf of Africans reveals the administration's approach to this kind of intervention in the native legal system.[24]

The first case regarded the issue of slavery. Although French colonial rule officially abolished slavery in French West Africa in 1848, in the period discussed here slavery still existed in the territories of the federation because the French hesitated to disrupt the social structure of African society.[25] In this case a man named Yoro Ligore was accused of offending Déjé Gueye by calling him a slave. He was fined twenty-five francs. Ligore appealed the verdict to the circle court, and the fine was increased to one hundred francs. According to Gueye, Ligore told him: "Your old masters did not take charge of threatening me, dirty captive, vile slave." The defendant claimed that he did not use the words "captive" and "slave," but he admitted to having said the first phrase. There were no witnesses to the incident. The circle court decided not to ask Gueye to swear on the Quran that he had actually said these words, because the first sentence to which the accused had admitted was already insulting enough. Devès claimed that because the procedures of the trial were faulty, the verdict must be nullified. The attorney general, however, fully supported the court's decision. On the contrary, he believed that such verdicts could contribute to civilizing the Africans in the colonies and to the disappearance of slavery, which had been legally and judicially abolished sixty years before. He concluded that Mr. Devès should not have interfered in this case.

Another complaint Devès submitted regarded a case involving two contradicting systems of inheritance: that of Islamic law and that of the Sereer customary law. According to Sereer custom, the matrilineal nephew of the deceased was entitled to inherit; according to Islamic law, the son was the legal heir.[26] The case involved two Muslim nephews of the deceased, both of whom claimed to be his heirs. They presented their claims to the qadi of N'Diourbel, and he attributed the estate to one of them. The other one then appealed to another qadi who was considered superior to the first one. This qadi ruled that neither of the nephews was the heir as, according to the Islamic law, the estate went to Yoro Diouf, the son of the deceased. Mr. Devès claimed that the custom of the Sereer, the people of the quarreling parties, had been violated. The attorney general responded that he had no intention of examining Islamic law or the customs of the Sereer, as this was the duty of the province court to which either of the parties to this conflict could turn. The three parties should also have realized that verdicts of a qadi did not have the authority of a formal legal judgment and could be considered a valid solution only if the parties agreed to accept it.[27] Devès introduced two other cases as well, but they need not concern us here.

The refusal to reverse any of the four verdicts demonstrates that the colonial juridical authorities were not interested in questioning the assessors' knowledge of customs or the judgments of the lower courts. The attorney general was definitely not prepared to verify whether a specific decision was based on Islamic or customary law and had no intention of taking sides in the conflict between the two sets of law. As far as he was concerned, the principle behind the decree establishing the native court system was to alleviate the burden on colonial authorities to deal with such complicated legal questions.

On the other hand, colonial authorities were keenly interested if cases involved the sensitive issue of "public order." When native courts acquitted or lightly punished defendants who committed offenses that the colonial administration considered menacing to public order, officials rarely hesitated to intervene. However, as we shall see, even this critical motive of protecting colonial order did not always make intervention easy.

The colonial administration was very interested when a verdict given by the province court of Moyen Sassandra (Côte d'Ivoire) on February 1, 1907, acquitted three Africans who were accused of trade in firearms.[28] The motive for the acquittal was that according to the local customs of the region, arms trading was not considered an offense. On the contrary, local customs considered it a highly respectable activity. The court declared that it was aware of the fact that the colonial administration viewed such activity as an offense, but nevertheless it had to acquit the defendants. Otherwise their compatriots would rebuke them for not obeying the local customs. The administrator of the circle of Sassandra was unhappy with this verdict. He realized that this offense could not go unpunished, as it menaced colonial stability, but he also knew that the African judges had acted exactly as they had been instructed.[29] This paradox was the subject of a complicated and long correspondence between administrative and legal authorities in French West Africa. Governor General Roume suggested that in cases presenting a threat to public order, if the province court acquitted the defendants or the punishment given was not severe enough, the administrator of the circle would be allowed to transfer the case to his own court. There was one major problem with this suggestion: the administrator would also be the one to preside over the circle court. The attorney general did not like this solution at all as it contradicted the decree of 1903. His answer was to formulate a different decree. Eventually the decree of 1912 solved this paradox by transferring some infractions against the state to the circle courts. But this took five years, and the colonial administration could not allow stability to be challenged while the attorney general dealt with legal procedures. The interim solution, until a new decree was drafted, was the one the governor general had proposed. The only detail added was that the administrator would have to report to the governor general every time he decided to remove such a case from the jurisdiction of the subdivision court.[30] The obsession of the French administration with decrees and regulations and the long administrative correspondence that any legal dilemma entailed paralyzed the administration in the face of assessors who acquitted defendants who presented a real or imagined threat to the colonial regime.

A contradiction between customary law and colonial perceptions in cases of this kind continued to exist even after the introduction of the new decree of 1912. Two years later a case brought before the circle court concerning accusations of smuggling raised a strong reaction from the head of Senegal's customs service. In a letter to the governor of Senegal, he complained about the verdict of the Zinguinchor circle court and requested it be annulled because of the incompetence of the court to deal with this sort of offense. The following are the details of the affair: On the night of October 17, 1914, a group of five men and three women with children crossed the border from Gambia carrying merchandise and failing to report to the customs post in a place called Sélécty. A customs guard noticed them and gave chase. He managed to grab one package from one of the women and was consequently, according to his testimony, attacked by the group and beaten several times with a saber. The members of this group were arrested the following day. The main reproach the head of customs had toward the assessors in this case was that they had used the pretext of local customs to lighten the nature of the offense and thus managed to inflict the accused with the lesser punishment of short-term imprisonment. The offense committed in this case, according to him, was smuggling in a group while carrying arms (*importation frauduleuse avec attroupement et port d'armes*) and, therefore, was not under the jurisdiction of the native courts.[31] Using customary law, the assessors actually redefined the offense. They claimed that according to the testimonies of the defendants, they were not smuggling goods but had purchased them for their own personal use. Second, they did not really form a group as they had simply met by chance and decided to cross the border together. The third point, regarding the carrying of arms, is the most interesting, as it concerned the local customs of the Diola, the ethnic classification of all the defendants. The assessors ruled that in Diola culture sabers were considered agricultural instruments rather than weapons and were carried at all times by all male members of society. Their conclusion was that there was neither group smuggling nor carrying of arms. The only offense attributable to the group was refusing to obey the instructions of the guard, and for some of them, using violence against him. The assessors explained that according to Diola customs the punishment for disrespect for authority was fifteen to ninety days in prison, and the punishment for using violence was one to two years, and they ruled accordingly.[32] This decision enraged the head of customs, and he demanded that the case be brought to the *chambre d'homologation*. The governor of Senegal, however, refused to intervene. He said that the verdict conformed to the customs of the region and seemed to him totally impartial.[33]

These two cases demonstrate the ability of the assessors to maneuver within the colonial rules. In the first case the assessors ruled that arms dealing was not an offense, although they were certainly aware that this sort of activity threatened the colonial authorities. The reaction of the colonial administration to such cases was to change the rules of the game and transfer certain kinds of offenses—those they thought menaced colonial order—to the circle court, over which a European presided. The second case that occurred after these changes demonstrated that the assessors could use local customs to change the nature of the offense and to lighten the punishment in order to bypass the obstacle the authorities had tried to put before them in the amended 1912 decree. Here again the colonial administration found it difficult to intervene in a judgment based on local customs, even when these customs lightened the sentence of Africans who violently attacked a representative of the colonial order.

Maintaining public order was undoubtedly the foremost objective of colonial rule. But French colonialism was also committed to the civilizing mission. Article 75 of the 1903 decree, which stated that custom was to prevail as long as it did not contravene the principles of French civilization, nonetheless continued to confront French officials with ethical challenges. This dilemma was evident in the case of Niaka Sakiliba, who refused to accept the Khassonke custom of levirate and marry her brother-in-law after her husband was killed in an industrial accident. Despite the tremendous sympathy the colonial authorities, up to the level of Governor General Joost Van-Vollenhoven, expressed for the woman's plight, they found themselves unable to act against the native court's decision. The correspondence regarding this case reveals a real desire on the part of the colonial authorities to reverse the native courts' verdicts. It also shows that even when the colonial administrators at the highest levels vehemently objected to a certain verdict, they did not allow themselves to intervene as long as the verdict was in line with local customs.

This case is also intriguing in the way it reflects the plaintiff's ability to present her arguments in the "language" of the colonizer. Sakiliba brought her case before the province court claiming that she was a Muslim and marrying the deceased man's brother was not a Muslim custom. The province court ruled that she must marry her brother-in-law according to her ethnic group's customs. Sakiliba appealed the verdict to the circle court and was again denied. The court justified the rejection of the appeal by stating that it was very well known that

Khassonkes who became Muslims did not abandon their customary status, which continued to dominate their family affairs.[34] Sakiliba, however, did not despair. It is hard to know if someone else assisted her, or whether she had enough skill, initiative, and knowledge to act alone. In any case, she sent a letter of protest to the governor of Haut-Sénégal-Niger in which she pleaded with him to act on her behalf. She first raised her basic judicial argument, saying she should be judged according to Islamic law. Then she clarified to the governor that her brother-in-law did not care for her and her four children at all, an argument that would have been totally irrelevant in the native courts. She explained that customs were especially onerous on the weak and the deprived of society. Endorsing the discourse of the "civilizing mission," she wrote: "It is inadmissible that in a civilized country it would be possible to shed the skin of a poor woman with four children for the simple reason that she does not wish to cohabit with a person who is unkind to her."[35] The governor found himself unable to assist Sakiliba, although he was apparently deeply touched by her arguments. He forwarded the letter to his superior, Governor General Van-Vollenhoven, in the hope that his hands would be less tied. The governor general's main concern in this matter was that the verdict given in the native courts was harmful to the goals of the civilizing mission. The woman, he wrote to the attorney general, had exhausted all the legal means available to her. However, this was a woman who had been married for eleven years to a team leader of the Kayes-Niger railway. Her standard of living was higher than that of her native milieu, and she lived in constant contact with French civilization. She even received a railway pension that provided for all of her needs. She had obviously evolved toward a mentality and lifestyle that were more in harmony with her actual status. The governor general insisted in his letter that the verdict given in Sakiliba's case actually forced a woman who had distanced herself from the native masses to be returned to them and therefore impaired the objectives of the French civilizing mission.

Despite the sympathy the governor general had shown toward this "semicivilized" African woman who wanted to became "totally civilized," he eventually decided not to recommend the reversal of the original verdict. Ignoring local customs and reversing assessors' verdicts that were based on them, he explained, might create "serious inconveniences." Already, he reminded the attorney general, the case had raised some protest in the region from Africans who were worried that the colonial courts might ignore their customs.[36]

Sakiliba's ability to speak in a clear voice, use the colonial language, and reach the ears and even the hearts of high-ranking colonial officials was probably unique. That was one of the reasons her plea drew so much attention, even from the governor general. But as far as the governor general was concerned, her situation was not so exceptional, representing instead a much wider problem: the issue of Africans who did not completely assimilate into French culture but had gone a long way from the native masses. Another example of Africans who belonged to this category was the Senegalese *tirailleurs* who were lucky enough to return safely from the battlegrounds of World War I. The French colonial administration considered these soldiers, who had been exposed to French civilization during their stay in Europe, as an intermediate category between the native status that was dependent on custom and French status.[37] Following the case of Sakiliba, the governor general suggested recognizing a special status for those Africans who were not French citizens but had the benefit of a certain social evolution, thanks to their contact with the French. The attorney general rejected this proposal because of the problems it might cause whenever a case involved a "civilized" African on one side and a "primitive" one on the other. These special courts might have created, in his view, an inevitable and dangerous conflict between two opposite moral concepts—the "civilized" and the "primitive"—and thus pose a threat to public order. The only solution to the problem of "civilized" natives, according to the attorney general, was to award them French citizenship.[38]

In spite of her eventual failure, Sakiliba showed an impressive ability to manipulate French colonial justice and perceptions to her own advantage. Before turning to the colonial authorities, she tried to appeal to the logic of the native legal system in asking to be judged according to her Muslim status. When this failed, she appealed to higher levels. The two arguments she used were especially suited to French colonial ears: the rational one about the French civilizing mission and the emotional one about the absence of any feeling on the part of her intended husband toward her and her children. However, in spite of these skills and the sympathy she managed to evoke toward her case in the highest colonial authority of the federation, the assessors were still more powerful. It was the colonial administration that decided the rules of the game—rules giving the assessors the power to judge according to local customs, known or sometimes unknown to them only. These rules were meant primarily to maintain order and therefore to preclude social upheaval, even such that might promote the causes of the French "civilizing mission." After they had fixed the rules, it was hard for the colonial administration to act against them or to change them even when assessors' decisions seemed to them barbaric, incorrect, or even dangerous for colonial order. The decision to establish courts in which African assessors were allowed to judge according to local customs left the assessors with a certain space of control into which the colonial administration and even the governor general himself found it difficult to penetrate.

Conclusions: The Power of African Assessors and Its Limits

The creation of the native legal system in French West Africa forced the colonial authorities to rely on the collaboration of Africans. This system was arbitrary and coercive, but it also opened opportunities for certain ambitious Africans who were willing to participate in this colonial project.[39] In his article on the non-European foundations of European imperialism, Ronald Robinson refers to the dangers of colonial reliance on indigenous collaborators: "Collaborators, on their side, were concerned to exploit the wealth, prestige and influence to be derived from association with colonial government, to increase their traditional followings or improve their modern opportunities. For these reasons collaboration, as colonial rulers well understood, could be a dangerous game. It involved dealing some of their best cards to potentially overmighty subjects."[40] From the French point of view, the best cards were indeed dealt to the African assessors, especially to those who were able to control the judicial process without colonial supervision. Not every African notable who qualified for this position, however, was especially eager to accept the role of assessor. Many of them could do without these overly complicated duties that did not even offer a substantial financial return.

Those notables who became assessors found themselves in a position of certain power. This is especially true with regard to the province or subdivision court judges. But even assessors in the circle court had the ability to influence the verdict. The commandant of the circle could not give a verdict without consulting them. His ignorance of local customs gave the assessors power to decide what these customs were. The issue of language was also decisive here. Because most if not all administrators did not know the local language, they were totally dependent on the court interpreter.[41] When no European was present in court, they had only the secretary's word that his notes reflected what had actually happened inside the courtroom.

Colonial documents also reveal that African assessors were aware of their power to rule according to local custom. They knew of the reluctance of the colonial authorities to reverse verdicts that were based, ostensibly or not, on these customs. They therefore used this power even in cases when they knew that the administration would not like the verdict. After serving for a while under French administrators, they probably realized that changing the rules of the game took a long time, as these rules could only be changed by the formulation of new decrees and a great deal of legal work. This French obsession with legal procedures allowed the African assessors a certain amount of leverage.

In 1924 the French drastically changed the rules of the judicial game when a new decree entrusted the chairmanship of the subdivision court to the French head of the subdivision or to some other European official.[42] However, during the period up until the publication of this decree, the assessors sitting in the subdivision court had a high degree of control in civil cases.

During the formative years of the native legal system in French West Africa, African assessors could take advantage of the weakness of the French colonial state. These weaknesses derived from shortages in personnel but also from the French insistence on combining colonial domination with republican values—a mission that was soon proven impossible. Although African assessors were indeed indispensable to the functioning of the native legal system and to French colonial rule in general, they were not simply collaborators or pawns on the colonial chessboard. In fact, they were much more than that. They followed their own legal agenda, did not always play by the rules, and sometimes even tried to change them. Their power might have been limited, as the power of the colonized always is, but it was substantial enough to arouse the worst fear of the colonizer—the fear of losing control.

Notes

I would like to thank the Harry S. Truman Research Institute for the Advancement of Peace in Jerusalem for its financial support for the research on which this paper is based and to the editors of this volume and the anonymous readers for the University of Wisconsin Press for their helpful comments and suggestions.

    1. Mann and Roberts, "Law in Colonial Africa," 3.
    2. On the centrality of law to the maintenance of colonial empires, see also Kirkby and Coleborne, *Law, History, Colonialism*.

3. The Africans covered under the first system were mainly *originaires* of the four communes, Dakar, Saint-Louis, Gorée, and Rufisque, who were accorded some rights of French citizenship in 1848, and the few assimilated Africans who managed to gain French citizenship. On the implementation of the new legal system, see Conklin, *Mission to Civilize*, 86–87.

4. D. Robinson, "Ethnography and Customary Law in Senegal," 231–35. On this subject see also: Ed Van Hoven, "Representing Social Hierarchy," 180–81. On the influence of ethnographic research on French colonial policy see also: Ruth Ginio, "French Colonial Reading of Ethnographic Research." On the attempts of similar codification of local customs made by the British in Kenya see: Brett L. Shadle, "Changing Traditions to Meet Current Alerting Conditions."

5. Roberts, "Representation, Structure and Agency," 390, 398–401.

6. The decree of 1903 gave the chief the power to impose fines of one to fifteen francs or an arrest of one to five days. The decree of 1912 cancelled this authority, and the village chiefs were left with only reconciliation powers in civil and commercial cases. Beurdeley, *La justice indigène*, 4–8.

7. Beurdeley, *La justice indigène*, 4–6, 8–9.

8. Suret-Canale, *French Colonialism*, 334–35; Roberts, "Representation, Structure and Agency," 390, 398–401; Conklin, *Mission to Civilize*, 91. There was no right of appeal to the *chambre d'homologation*. This court decided alone whether it was necessary to intervene in verdicts handed down by native courts. For more on the performance and duties of the *chambre d'homologation* in the early twentieth century, see Sarr, "La chamber spéciale d'homologation."

9. Archives Nationales (hereafter AN), Paris, 200mi/1238 M/94/5.

10. Beurdeley, *La justice indigène*, 4–6, 8–11.

11. Christelow, *Muslim Law Courts*, 188–90.

12. For example, the attorney general reported to the governor general, Ponty, in 1914 that some of the assessors he had met during a tour complained about local customs that prescribed punishments that were either too light or too harsh. He indicated that this was a sign the assessors were evolving toward a higher stage of civilization. AN, 200mi/1240, M/89/43, Dakar, February 18, 1914.

13. Beurdeley, *La justice indigène*, 20–22.

14. This concern existed as well in predominantly Muslim regions such as North Africa. See, for example, Christelow, *Muslim Law Courts*, 6.

15. Beurdeley, *La justice indigène*, 8–9.

16. AN, 200mi/1237, M/98/211, June 23, 1908. According to Benjamin F. Martin, French judges in metropolitan France during this same period were highly frustrated by their low salaries. Benjamin F. Martin, "The Courts, the Magistrature, and Promotions in Third Republic France, 1871–1914," 982.

17. There are quite a few examples of complaints regarding these alleged faults. For instance, the administrator of the circle of Savalou (Dahomey) noted that if one of the relatives of the province court judges were involved in

a financial dispute, he would probably be acquitted. The judge would collaborate with the interpreter to change the verdict in favor of his relative or at least to lighten it. AN, M/98/90, Extrait de la letter du Procureur Général de l'AOF à Gouverneur Général de l'AOF, Dakar, June 27, 1907. In another case the lieutenant governor of Senegal was reluctant to bring a former interpreter who was accused of swindling before the province court in which he had previously worked so that the judges would not favor him. AN, 200mi/1237, M/98/89, November 28, 1906. The relation between the assessors' race and corruption is emphasized in a report of the commander of the circle of Djenné in Haut-Sénégal-Niger from 1914: AN, 200mi/1239, M/94/79, Rapport sur la Côte d'Ivoire, Dakar, November 21, 1906; 200mi/1237, M/97/49, Colonie du Haut-Sénégal-Niger, Cercle de Djenné, 1914, 2ème trimestre.

18. Beurdeley, *La Justice indigène*, 25.

19. AN, 200mi/1241, M/99/8, Le choix des secrétaires des tribunaux indigènes, Conakry, June 30, 1909.

20. AN, 200mi/1241, M/99/9, Le choix des secrétaires des tribunaux indigènes, Dakar, August 1909.

21. AN, 200mi/1239, M/96/1, May 8, 1914.

22. Beurdeley, *La Justice indigène*, 26–27.

23. The governor of Senegal complained about the inefficiency of such reports to the governor general: AN, 200mi/1239, M/94/51, Lieutenant-Gouverneur du Sénégal à Gouverneur Général de l'AOF, La transmission du justice indigène, April 10, 1909.

24. The General Council of Senegal included twenty members who were elected by the *originaires* of the four communes. In 1920 the colonial administration replaced it with the Colonial Council, which had forty-four members: eighteen elected and twenty-six appointed noncitizens who represented the canton and province chiefs. Morgenthau, *Political Parties*, 127.

25. Klein, "Slavery and Emancipation," 180–82.

26. On the inheritance rules in Islam, see Coulson, *Succession in the Muslim Family*. See also Klein, *Slavery and Colonial Rule*. In 1903 Martial Merlin, then secretary general of the government general, asked the administrators' opinions on how to deal with slavery but also requested that they avoid raising the collective consciousness of slaves. His stand demonstrates the ambiguity of the colonial view regarding the question of slavery.

27. Archives Nationales du Sénégal (hereafter ANS), 6M/298/28, Justice indigène, 1838–1954, August 25, 1906, Dakar.

28. On the French concern regarding trade in arms, especially in unstable areas such as Côte- d'Ivoire, see Suret-Canale, *French Colonialism*, 100–103.

29. AN, 200mi/1239, M/95/40, Côte d'Ivoire, cercle de Sassandra, Rapport trimestriel de M. le Capitaine Schiffer, de l'Infanterie coloniale, hors cadres, Administrateur du cercle de Sassandra, sur le fonctionnement de la justice indigène, March 31, 1907.

30. AN, 200mi/1239, M/95/41, Gouverneur Général à lieutenant gouverneur de la Guinée, A.S. de la transformation effectuée par les indigènes de fusils à silex en fusil à piston; M/95/42, Note sur la répression des infractions du Décret du 4 Mai 1903 sur les armes à feu., M/95/43, Dakar, August 7, 1908, Note sur la question des infractions prévues par nos règlements et non punissables aux termes de la coutume indigène. A similar debate emerged around incidents of revolts of African soldiers who had returned from the battlefields of World War I. The question was whether there was a danger that some of the Africans who participated in these revolts would be acquitted because the local customs did not recognize such rebellion as an offense; AN, 200mi/1239, M/95/78, Bamako, August 5, 1916, Lieutenant-Gouverneur du Haut-Sénégal-Niger à M. le Gouverneur-Général de l'AOF; AN, 200mi/1239, M/95/65, Bamako, November 8, 1916, Le Lieutenant Gouverneur du Haut-Sénégal-Niger M. le Gouverneur-Général de l'AOF; AN, 200mi/1239, M/95/66, Dakar, December 6, 1916; AN, 200mi/1239, M/95/82.

31. AN, 200mi/1238, M93/73, Affaire Arcine Sy. January 4, 1915. The basis for this claim is unclear as the 1912 decree transferred such offenses from the subdivision court to the circle court.

32. AN, 200mi/1238, M93/74, Copie du jugement rendu par le Tribunal du cercle de Ziguinchor, November 24, 1914,

33. AN, 200mi/1238, M93/72, January 21, 1915.

34. AN, 200mi/1238, M93/14, March 15, 1918.

35. AN, 200mi/1238, M93/12, 1917.

36. AN, 200mi/1238, M93/16, September 7, 1918.

37. On African soldiers in World War I, see Echenberg, *Colonial Conscripts*, 25–46; Lunn, *Memoirs of the Maelstrom*; and Michel, *Les Africans*.

38. AN, 200mi/1237, M93/18, 26 October 1918.

39. Groff, "The Dynamics of Collaboration," 147–48. In this same essay Groff presents an example of such an ambitious African who gained authority in the precolonial era and assisted the French upon their arrival. He was appointed an interpreter and then a court assessor and managed to acquire a great deal of wealth and power.

40. R. Robinson, "Non-European Foundations," 134.

41. According to William Cohen, until 1939 few of the administrators in French West Africa knew any African language, and therefore they had to rely on the services of interpreters: W. Cohen, *Rulers of Empire*, 126–27.

42. Suret-Canale, *French Colonialism*, 334.

The Maturing Phase
of Colonial Rule,
ca. 1920–1960

"Collecting Customary Law"

Educated Africans, Ethnographical Writings, and Colonial Justice in French West Africa

JEAN-HERVÉ JÉZÉQUEL

Shortly after the founding of the French West African Federation in 1895, the colonial administration was preoccupied with the codification of native customs. Such codification, the administration thought, would permit a better understanding of native societies and a better means of controlling them.[1] Codification of native customs was part of a larger project of generating knowledge about African societies. Professional scholars from France, colonial administrators, and amateur ethnographers eager for professional respectability were placed in charge. In terms of the production of colonial knowledge, these Europeans acted at center stage. In the background, however, several Africans cast shadows from their obscure secondary roles; they were interpreters, informants, and authors of short ethnographic monographs and digests of legal customs. The roles and works of these native figures are still poorly understood.[2] At first glance their secondary roles in the production of knowledge seem to have placed them in generally subordinate positions in this project. By the 1930s, however, this group of African intermediaries began to publish their first ethnographic studies in French West Africa.[3]

In examining these digests of customary law (*coutumiers*) published by literate natives, this chapter demonstrates that the production of knowledge by Africans can no longer be neglected.[4] These writings remain to some extent marginalized by European scholars' production of colonial knowledge, but their significance is far greater when the context of their production is analyzed in relationship to the authors' political and cultural strategies. Ethnographic writing, of which the production of the digests of legal customs is one of the most interesting forms, constitutes a form of privileged expression of these African intermediaries' different strategies for self-promotion. The study of these digests reveals how these African intermediaries dominated the field of colonial ethnographic science and deployed complex strategies transcending the production of knowledge per se. This chapter contributes to the growing literature that explores the role of African ethnography not only within the field of colonial knowledge but in relation to local political arenas.[5]

The first section of this chapter briefly describes the process that allowed the emergence of a native ethnographic literature and specifically the writing of *coutumiers* by African auxiliaries. The two following sections examine two *coutumiers* published in the thirties. The last section explores the writings produced by an African teacher that does not explicitly take the form of a *coutumier* but was intended to address problems in local customs. Comparing the itinerary of their respective authors and the contexts of production of these studies reveals the different strategies prompting these writings and the different ways in which local auxiliaries penetrated and made use of the colonial sphere of customary law.

African Informants and the Collection of Customs

As David Robinson argues, "[T]he concern for establishing custom emerged from administrators preoccupied with centralization, control and a strong paternalistic and interventionist approach to their African subjects."[6] Although Governor Faidherbe in the middle of the nineteenth century and Governor General Roume at the beginning of the twentieth century displayed strong interest in collecting customary law, the codification of West African customary law experienced its most important development in the thirties. In 1931 the new governor general, Jules Brevié, wrote a directive emphasizing the practical interest of studying customary laws. He wanted to improve the quality of the

tribunaux indigènes, the native courts organized by the colonial administration. Brevié created a customs and traditions committee (Comité des
coutumes), which was in charge of publishing the monographs written
by European administrators *(les broussards)* and also by literate natives,
such as West African schoolteachers.

Whereas literate natives in the British West African colonies had a
tradition of writing historical or ethnographic studies dating back to
the nineteenth century, with exceptions in nineteenth century Senegal,
the French West African colonies did not develop this tradition until
the early twentieth century. The first publications were actually promoted by the colonial administration, which wanted to understand
better the organization of the different societies it sought to rule. Beginning in the second decade of the twentieth century, a new generation of
ethnographer-administrators *(administrateurs-ethnographes)* took office
in French West Africa.[7] Looking for both social and academic recognition, they intended to build up a local infrastructure of knowledge production with its own associations, publications, hierarchy, and even
its own museum in Dakar. In 1915 Governor General Clozel, Maurice
Delafosse, and some of these ethnographer-administrators created the
Comité d'études historiques et scientifiques de l'Afrique Occidentale
française (CHESAOF).[8] In its first issues the bulletin of the CHESAOF
encouraged literate natives to conduct fieldwork and publish some of
their ethnographic writings. At the same time, a second local bulletin,
the administrative *Bulletin de l'enseignement de l'AOF,* published in Dakar and directed by Georges Hardy, a key member of the CHESAOF,
started to publish ethnographic works and brief historical accounts
written by African schoolteachers such as Dominique Traoré, Mamby
Sidibé, and Fily Dabo Sissoko.

Facing the necessity of collecting data on still little-known societies,
they considered the literate natives a useful and skilled workforce. A
division of scientific labor was thereby introduced: collecting field data
was a task allotted to local auxiliaries (lower-ranking administrators
and literate natives), whereas the far more prestigious and "complex"
art of analyzing data was reserved for Western intellectuals, such as
Maurice Delafosse, Georges Hardy, and Paul Marty.[9]

To some extent the role these African pioneers were expected to play
did not go beyond the tasks performed by the illiterate informants.
Both provided Western scholars with field data. Moreover, the scope
of their initiatives as ethnographers was often very limited. Western
scholars turned to them insofar as they were supposed to become

acquainted with their fellow men and their traditions. As a consequence the Africans were not really free to choose their field of research. Their writings were legitimate insofar as they dealt with the country and the people they came from. Hence there was a gap between African ethnographers and administrator-ethnographers such as Delafosse, who published studies on countries he never visited.

This division of unequal tasks remained unchanged during the colonial period. In the thirties some West African amateur ethnographers (e.g., Amadou Mapaté Diagne, Mamby Sidibé, Moussa Travélé) were appointed corresponding members of the Comité d'études historiques et scientifiques de l'Afrique Occidentale française. Governor General Brevié also created a prize for African authors in 1931. These rewards, however, remained purely honorific. Some literate natives, such as the Dahomean Maximilien Quénum or the Senegalese Mamadou Dia, began to complain about the lack of recognition.[10] But many others were still sending ethnographic studies to the colonial administration. Looking back at this ethnography, it often appears that the literate Africans who produced these works only played a marginal role in the production of colonial knowledge. In terms of number of publications as well as academic recognition, they did not compete with the ethnographer-administrators who dominated the ethnographic scene in interwar West Africa. Why then did they even bother collecting oral traditions and sending their texts to colonial reviews that did not recognize them as full members of the ethnographic scene? The next sections demonstrate that the writing of these texts also makes sense outside the field of colonial knowledge in which they were initially produced.

Codifying the Law to Confiscate the Land: Abdou Salam Kane's *Coutumier* on Fouta Tooro (Senegal)

Abdou Salam Kane was a well-known Foutanke chief who successfully managed to integrate his local leadership and political dominance into the new colonial order. His long domination over Damga lasted for half a century (from the French conquest to his death in 1955).[11] Such longevity in an area where political rivalries and land disputes were rife is quite surprising. Abdou Salam Kane's prolonged "reign" can be attributed not to his unquestioned legitimacy but rather to his ability to maintain the unfaltering support of the colonial administration. The strategies he developed to benefit from colonial favors were probably numerous and complex. This section focuses specifically on how he codified and reinvented customary laws to consolidate his control over land. I first describe the intricate land systems that characterized Fouta Tooro and then situate Abdou Salam Kane and his ascendancy within the local political scene and conflicts. Finally, an analysis of the *coutumier* he wrote illustrates how the manipulation of customary law consolidated Abdou Salam Kane's seizure of resources in Damga.

In Fouta Tooro the French colonial administration very early faced unending land conflicts and disputes over local political offices. Several factors contributed to this explosive situation. During the nineteenth century the ruling lineages of Fouta Tooro were constantly pitted against one another. The main political leaders, the *almamys,* were dismissed frequently. Many of them did not stay in office for more than a few months.[12] This political instability affected access to land as changing coalitions of aristocrats made contradictory claims over land. To the French who "pacified" the country toward the end of the century, the legitimate rules of access to land and political office appeared very confusing. Land disputes generated by lineage rivalries worsened with the conquest of French Soudan between 1890 and 1893 and with the pacification of Mauritania. Immediately after he conquered French Soudan, Colonel Archinard ordered the Foutanke followers of al hajj Umar Tall to return to their homeland in Fouta Tooro.[13] While these Foutanke had been trying to build their conquest state along the banks of the Niger, other Foutanke, who had refused Umar's rule and had rallied to the French, had seized their lands along the Senegal River. The return of the defeated Umarians generated serious conflicts over land and authority, particularly in the area of Kanel, Abdou Salam Kane's stronghold. To compound matters, toward the beginning of the twentieth century, the French pacification of Mauritania exacerbated land disputes along the Senegal River. In response to continuous raids by the Maures, the Foutanke had left these productive lands on the north bank of the river. After 1902 the French were determined to stop these raids. Their success led to the relocation of Foutanke peasants to the areas they had fled. This "return" created tensions over the ownership of land: many peasants hoped to escape their landlords by crossing northward over the river, and the aristocrats complained about this. At the same time, the various ruling lineages competed to assert their claims on these lands.

Disputes around the most productive flood plain land *(waalo)* were closely linked with the ebb and flow of the Foutanke population.[14] Faced with unceasing and seemingly inextricable troubles, the colonial administration quickly ordered local inquiries and tried to resolve the numerous misunderstandings.[15] These studies were designed to help resolve the land disputes in Fouta Tooro. However, the "traditional" Foutanke societies did not remain unchanged during the colonial era. On the contrary, Leservoisier demonstrates that the colonial era played a crucial role in the redefinition of land law. Africans played an active part in this (re)definition of customary laws on land tenure.[16] For instance, Abdoulaye Kane, a French-appointed chief and former interpreter, helped Henry Gaden, an administrator-ethnographer, collect data and write his articles on property in Fouta Tooro. Apart from these oral informants, some literate Foutanke wrote ethnographic and historical accounts.[17] In 1916 Abdoulaye Kane published a study on aristocratic patronyms in Fouta Tooro. However, the most interesting African writings came from Abdou Salam Kane, who published a major study on customary laws in Fouta Tooro in 1939 (discussed later).

Sheik Mamadou Mamoudou, Abdou Salam Kane's father, was a famous marabout and a great grandson of the first *almamy*. After his pilgrimage to Mecca, he returned to Fouta Tooro and settled in Maghama, a village situated on the northern bank of the Senegal River. His military talent against the Moors and his religious reputation helped him impose his rule over this very fertile area (the Littama). By this time the French were fighting against Abdul Bokar Kane, a Foutanke chief seeking to impose his rule over Fouta Tooro. Sheik Mamadou's connections with the French allowed him to be named chief in the Damga, Fouta Tooro's eastern province. In 1890 Abdul Bokar besieged Maghama and killed Sheik Mamadou. In 1891 Abdul Bokar was killed in turn, and the French imposed their rule over the Fouta. The same year Colonel Dodds gave Abdou Salam Kane land in Maghama as a reward for his father's services.

Abdou Salam Kane was born in Saint-Louis, the French capital of Senegal in 1879. His mother was the daughter of a Foutanke chief, Tamsir Hamat N'Diaye Ane, who joined the French in Saint-Louis. After brief Koranic studies, he attended French schools in Saint-Louis and in Tunis. He returned to Senegal in 1895 and was appointed district chief in Kanel (Damga) in 1897. This eighteen-year-old chief had never before lived in Fouta Tooro, and thus his authority initially appeared very weak. He belongs to a small group of young educated Africans that the colonial administration attempted to put in position of power as district chiefs just after the conquest. Most of them were quickly removed as local rivals contested their legitimacy. Kane, who also had to face rivals but managed to remain in power until his death in 1955, definitely stands as an exception. During the colonial era he became of the most important *chef de province* in Senegal. This successful tenure was the result of Abdou Salam Kane's ability to manipulate customary law to serve his interests. An example was his production of a *coutumier* in 1939.

Abdou Salam Kane's study was published in 1939 in the *Coutumiers juridiques de l'Afrique Occidentale Française,* a three-volume compilation of customary laws from territories under French domination in West Africa.[18] The texts were chosen by the Comité des coutumes, a committee charged with collecting studies on customary laws from every colony of the West Africa Federation.[19] Apart from being written by the only African author selected by the committee, Abdou Salam Kane's study was actually written in 1907. All the other *coutumiers* date from the beginning of the thirties. Thus, Abdou Salam Kane' writing is contemporary with the land conflicts generated by the French pacification of Mauritania.

Abdou Salam Kane's work explores topics such as family structure, matrimonial practices, and inheritance rules among the Foutanke. For our purposes, Kane's section on land law in Fouta Tooro is most important. According to Abdou Salam Kane, the Foutanke system of land tenure was based on "ancient" land distribution practices among the first Fouta Tooro's kings (the Satigui). After the Satigui were overthrown by the Islamic revolution (at the end of the seventeenth century), the first *almamy*, Abdoul Kaader Kane, implemented important land redistribution *(feccere Fuuta)* among leading families (or turban holders).[20] Since this time, according to Kane, there were no significant changes in the Foutanke system of land tenure.

Two points are particularly interesting in Abdou Salam Kane's description of land tenure. First, recent changes in Fouta Tooro's history are ignored. For instance, Abdou Salam Kane is oddly silent about land disputes that occurred at the end of the nineteenth century and the beginning of the twentieth century. He completely omits the reoccupation of the northern bank by the Foutanke in Mauritania. Although he briefly mentions the problem caused by the Foutanke's return following the Umarians' defeat in the French Soudan, he argues that it did not have any major effect on land tenure.[21] Second, and more important, Abdou Salam Kane's writing promotes a feudal conception of land tenure in Fouta Tooro. He was a key actor in what Jean Schmitz has described this invention of the Foutanke feudal system.[22]

French officers between 1905 and the beginning of the First World War produced the first sets of studies on land in Fouta Tooro. These works were ordered by the colonial administration, which was concerned about the constant land disputes in Matam and Kaedi's courts. These works sought to throw light on the system of land tenure. They consisted of a meticulous census of the Foutanke who owned land rights. In this first set of studies, Foutanke landlords were described as local community representatives. A second set of studies emerged in the thirties. In 1935 the *Bulletin du Comité d'études historiques et scientifiques de l'AOF* published three articles on the Foutanke system of land tenure.[23] In 1939 the Comité des coutumes published Abdou Salam Kane's study on Foutanke customary laws. These articles reflect the colonial administration's constant concerns about this area. Unlike the previous surveys done by the French military, these studies presented a more theoretical approach to land law. The main change lay in the way landlords were portrayed. They were no longer presented as the representatives of communities, but as feudal landlords who own hereditary rights from the *almamy*.

As Schmitz notes, these studies influenced later studies on Fouta Tooro. It was only in the 1970s that historians began to criticize the feudal myth.[24] They stressed the fact that the *almamys* were quite weak throughout the nineteenth century. The *almamys* depended on local turban holders rather than the other way around. Moreover, Schmitz shows that holding the turban was less a hereditary privilege than an elective function: of the 159 customary political offices he studied in Fouta Tooro, 127 proved to be elective functions. According to him, Fouta Tooro was less a feudal society than a system of village republics. If so, how can we explain the invention of a feudal Fouta Tooro during the colonial period?

From the French point of view, two main considerations led to the conceptualization of Fouta Tooro as a feudal entity. First, many administrators, including Henry Gaden, were fascinated by the Foutanke upper classes and were inclined to assimilate them into the Western aristocracy. Second, and more important, the invention of the feudal myth coincided with a crucial change in the French policy toward native chiefs. Alice Conklin has demonstrated that in the interwar era, the colonial administration developed a "more conservative vision of the *mission civilisatrice* . . . in which the prewar preoccupation with transforming African society yielded to a greater respect for the pre-colonial aristocracy—who were now to become associate in the civilizing process—and an emphasis upon power sharing generally."[25] To control the indigenous world and prevent social or political protest, the French developed a policy that supported, and sometimes invented, native chiefs and aristocracy. The colonial administration was, therefore, inclined to favor the conceptualization of a hierarchical and conservative feudal society in Fouta Tooro.

Abdou Salam Kane's goals were different, but they converged with the French point of view. Nor was his role in developing the feudal myth innocent. As I have argued, the French granted him land tenure over both the Damga (southern bank) and the Littama (northern bank). But his rule was not immune to conflict and protest. For instance, in Maghama, Littama's main village ruled by his father for ten years, he faced strong opposition. Part of the local population contested his right to tax land and decided to flee the village in 1903 and again in 1906. The production of his *coutumiers* in 1907, even if it was not to be published for thirty years, was closely linked with this situation. By defending the idea of a feudal system, Abdou Salam Kane defended his own interests. Paradoxically, he legitimated his recent domination of the area by referring to an ancient and fixed system of land tenure. The land belonged to the *almamy*, who gave it to the leading families to whom he belonged.

Hence, writing was part of the strategy Kane employed to strengthen his weak political and legal position on land tenure. His father's legitimacy derived from his status as a religious leader and his military talent against the Moors. Abdou Salam Kane did not inherit his father's religious mantle (he had been educated at the French school), and he never fought in any war. In addition, Kane wrote in French, thereby substituting the Latin letter's power for the Arabic script's aura. Whatever legitimacy he had lay in his effort to reinvent customary law.

As Max Gluckman states, "[C]odification was a powerful weapon in the hands of government to shape the course of economic, political, and social development."[26] In Fouta Tooro and particularly in the Kanel area, Abdou Salam Kane manipulated codification to support his own position. Even more important from our standpoint was that his manipulation, rather than occurring at the level of oral testimony, instead took the form of a written digest of legal customs. His success was long in coming, however. In 1908, following tensions about tax collecting in Maghama, Kane was apparently compelled to sign a deal with the French.[27] He was granted dominion over an extended Damga district, but at the same time had to resign from his position in Littama District. Kane's contribution to the production of customary laws is not unique. It illustrates a process that Terence Ranger documented a long time ago.[28] Yet the following sections suggest that this classical instance of "invention of tradition" should not overshadow alternative uses of ethnographic writings by educated Africans.

Social Promotion through Knowledge: Mamby Sidibé's *Coutumier du cercle de Kita* (1932)

In 1932 the *Bulletin d'études historiques et scientifiques du comité d'études africaines* published a long article (130 pages) written by Mamby Sidibé, an African schoolteacher. This was the first time that this review, founded in 1915 by Governor General Clozel, had published such a long work by a literate native.[29] The article, titled *"Coutumier du cercle de Kita,"* explicitly dealt with the codification of customary law in the region of the colonial town of Kita (French Soudan). This publication reflected the new policy encouraged by Governor General Brevié since his arrival in Dakar in 1931. Brevié wanted to promote the ethnographic and historical studies undertaken by literate natives and especially the graduates from École Normale William Ponty, the most prestigious colonial school in French West Africa. By promoting native ethnographic studies, Brevié and his main collaborators were pursuing two main objectives.

On the one hand, this policy, liberal and respectful toward African history and culture in appearance, was driven by very conservative motives. Since the beginning of the policy to promote an educated indigenous elite in French West Africa, the colonial administration was faced with a tricky alternative.[30] The French lacked financial means to administer the empire directly and needed to train a local elite that could perform duties at a very low cost (compared to the costs of supporting civil servants coming from the *métropole*). On the other hand, the administration feared that education would eventually produce a detribalized, educated elite that would contest its domination. To prevent social breakdown, they encouraged a Franco-African culture that would reconcile the educated elite with their native cultures. Thus, the colonial state's support of native ethnographic or historical studies was part of a larger policy promoted by Brevié and many colonial officials of the education service (e.g., Charles Béart, the William Ponty School director, Albert Charton, chief inspector of education).[31] Second, Governor General Brevié wanted to tap into local knowledge to produce digests of local customs that would help administer the empire more efficiently. Facing a shortage of scholars, however, the colonial administration relied on both administrators and literate natives to develop the knowledge of its territories.

This was the context in which Mamby Sidibé published his *coutumier*, just one year after Brevié signed his 1931 ordinance on the need to codify indigenous law.[32] Although the colonial expectations were now clear, the motives that led African civil servants to participate in these tasks remain to be explored. Mamby Sidibé was one of several literate natives to collect customary laws. Many other schoolteachers, such as the Senegalese Amadou Mapate Diagne in Casamance and the Dahomean Maximilien Quenum, wrote articles on customary laws in the thirties. Many of these works were never published but kept in regional colonial archives *(archives du cercle)*. For instance, Jean-Loup Amselle quotes a study commissioned by a *commandant de cercle* in Bougouni (French Soudan) and written by an African teacher.[33] The French administrator was trying to understand the rivalry between families competing for the cantonal chieftaincy *(chefferie de canton)*. This study helped him and his successors choose among rivals for local chieftaincies, but it remained unpublished.[34] The next section explores the way in which the sphere of justice constituted a place where two different interests converged: a powerful colonial administration handicapped by its myopia and its lack of resources in the bush, on one hand, and a growing group of lower-ranking African civil servants seeking social promotion through active cooperation with the colonial authority, on the other.

Promotion through Education

Unlike Abdou Salam Kane, Mamby Sidibé was born of very humble origins in 1891 in Niamefero, a small village of the Birgo, an area situated in the far south of Kita (French Soudan). His parents were free peasants and hunters belonging to the Sidibé Karamangue clan and were not linked with either formal political or religious power in the area.[35] At the end of the nineteenth century, his destiny changed when his family was forced to send him to the whites' school *(l'école des blancs)* in Kita. At that time schooling was not very popular among the Birgo inhabitants. The French administrator wanted the most important families of the *cercle* to send at least one boy to the school in Kita. To avoid this obligation the ruling Ba Sidibé family of Sirakoro (the principal village in Birgo) decided that a dependent village, Niaméfero, would support schooling. In turn, the elders of Niaméfero decided that the young Mamby Sidibé had to go to school.[36] Ba Sidibé secretly sent Mamby Sidibé instead of his son. This switch totally changed Mamby Sidibé's destiny: this young boy, working in the fields with his relatives, ultimately became one of the first Malian schoolteachers and an important political official during independence.[37]

The young Mamby Sidibé was sent successively to Kita (*école de village*), Bafoulabé (*école régionale*), Kayes (*école des fils de chefs*, sons of chiefs' school), and finally Saint-Louis (*école normale*).[38] He became a schoolteacher in 1913. Then the colonial administration sent him to Upper Volta, far from his homeland: Ouagadougou (the capital), Fada Ngourma, Goundam, Banfora, Bobo-Dioulasso (the second largest city in Upper Volta), Diébougou, and back to Ouagadougou, where he taught mathematics at the École primaire supérieure, the highest position available to an African teacher in Upper Volta.

While he was a teacher, Mamby Sidibé decided to collect folktales and to undertake ethnographic studies in the areas to which he was appointed. By doing so Sidibé was responding to the demands made by the service of education and the colonial administration. In 1918 the *Bulletin du Comité d'études historiques et scientifiques de l'AOF* published his first ethnographical article, "Monographie régionale de Fada N'Gourma." In the following years he published several articles in both the *Bulletin de l'éducation de l'AOF* and the *Bulletin du Comité d'études historiques et scientifiques de l'AOF*. His ethnographic activities enabled him to create a useful network within the colonial administration. His connections with Frédéric Assomption, a former teacher interested in ethnographic studies and chief inspector in French Soudan, surely facilitated his career.

After fourteen years in Upper Volta, Mamby Sidibé requested to return to his natal French Soudan. In 1927, thanks to Frédéric Assomption, he was appointed to the École primaire supérieure by Governor Terrasson de Fougères in Bamako. This was a position sought by both European and African teachers. Whereas most African teachers were sent to schools in the bush (*école de brousse*), Mamby Sidibé taught in the capital, a privilege usually held by Europeans: after fifteen years as a teacher, he now occupied a very prominent position and was one of the highest ranking African teachers in the colony. A few years after his return to French Soudan, he married the sister of an important district chief in Bamako. Like other African auxiliaries, he was well regarded by the population in Bamako, where his humble origins were less important (perhaps even unknown) compared to his professional situation.[39] This was the context in which he decided to publish his "Coutumier du cercle de Kita."[40]

"Distinguer les bons serviteurs des mauvais"

Sidibé's *coutumier* clearly followed the agenda contained in the questionnaire sent by the administration to codify West African customary laws.[41] In this study Mamby Sidibé describes family structures, matrimonial practices, inheritance laws, property, and so on. Knowledge of these elements would likely help the colonial administration guard against manipulation of custom within the native courts. As Mamby Sidibé points out, corrupt African magistrates often manipulated colonial justice. European administrators were unable to detect or defend themselves from this manipulation because they did not understand what was going on in the court. Mamby Sidibé intended to denounce the corrupt intermediaries but also to codify the Malinké customary laws to stop such corruption: "No more abuse should be accepted in the name of the 'Whites,' a name that the most dishonest men abominably soiled. 'To serve France loyally' should be the motto of the natives in charge of representing the colonial Authority."[42]

Unlike Abdou Salam Kane, Mamby Sidibé's *coutumier* was not written to defend property or to invent traditional claims to a particular local political office. He was now a respected and urbanized civil servant who would probably have been reluctant to return permanently to his native village. Unlike two other schoolteachers who were appointed "chefs de canton" in the forties (Simbo Keïta was appointed *chef du canton de Kita* in 1942 and Djigui Diallo *chef du canton de Birgo* in 1944), Mamby Sidibé never tried to become chief in the Birgo.[43] His humble origins probably prevented him from developing any ambition related to the chieftaincy, and Mamby Sidibé was looking for a different means of social promotion.

Unlike the former interpreter Abdou Salam Kane, Mamby Sidibé was not involved in a *stratégie de notabilisation*, a strategy that would eventually allow him to claim the rank of a local notable. His *coutumier* reveals the ambitions and interests characterizing the group to which he belonged, namely, a growing educated and urbanized elite. As a teacher and graduate of the William Ponty School, Mamby Sidibé belonged to an elite subgroup that received the best education available to an African in French West Africa. Nonetheless, despite the prestige given by their qualifications, African teachers were subject to relative deprivation and humiliation. A more or less explicit color bar forced them to remain among the colonized.[44] Moreover, within the social strata composed of different kinds of African intermediaries, they were often considered secondary auxiliaries. Interpreters, *chefs de canton,* guards, and even houseboys were sometimes more highly respected than teachers. The former were seen as close collaborators of the *commandant de cercle,* whereas teachers were isolated in their school far from the *résidence* (the *commandant de cercle*'s office). Many teachers complained of being considered *bilakorokuntigi* or *bambin barbu* (a bearded baby) by African populations that still massively rejected French schools in most of French West Africa.[45] In the colonial cities the educated civil servants had higher status than African teachers appointed to bush schools. Disappointed by the colonial realities, they developed strategies to improve their social and professional situation.

Writing constituted one of the means they used to advance socially. This is particularly clear in Mamby Sidibé's *coutumier.* First, by addressing the colonial need for useful knowledge, he gave himself a role that went beyond the responsibility of a teacher. His proficiency in both Western and local knowledge allowed him to claim the status of a privileged counselor. Thus he clearly considered his *coutumier* to be an expert work deserving a prominent place in the *commandant de cercle*'s library: "The administrator cannot know everything in his district. The study of native customary laws and their perfect interpretation would necessitate a thesis or a doctorate. Yet an administrator arriving in a new district can use the *coutumiers* as his bedside book."[46]

Second, Sidibé also used writing to denounce corrupt intermediaries who manipulated both the local society and the colonial administration: "We should not accuse the 'White man.' The truly responsible are the natives who stand around them. . . . The European administrator should be aware of these perfidious men who approach him in order to manipulate him. This is particularly true when an administrator is new to his position."[47] These quotes attest the anger that better educated but marginalized teachers had toward the illiterate or semi-illiterate auxiliaries who occupied better positions in the colonial administration than they did.

Ibrahima Diaman Bathily: Reforming Customary Law, "Modernizing" the Society

In the discussion of the two preceding *coutumiers,* I argue that writing supported two very different strategies of valorization. Whereas Abdou Salam Kane reinvented tradition to better serve his material interests,

Mamby Sidibé used writing to enhance his role as a privileged "counselor" of the colonial project and in so doing overcame his modest status as a schoolteacher. These two cases, on the one hand, a self-serving *chef de canton*, on the other, a socially aspiring professional and collaborator, do not exhaust the range of ways literate Africans used ethnographic writing in the colonial context. The last example, Ibrahima Diaman Bathily, a schoolteacher, underscores a different use of ethnography by literate Africans.

Ibrahima Diaman Bathily was born around 1896 in Tiagou, a village associated with Gadiaga in the Bakel region of Senegal. His father, who worked as an interpreter for the French, spent most of his career in the Soudan, where his son attended school. Ibrahima Bathily pursued his education at the School for the Sons of Chiefs in Saint-Louis and finally at the École Normale William Ponty, from which he graduated with a teaching diploma in 1917. Most of his working life was spent in the Soudan. He had a number of assignments, the last of which brought him to Macina. Bathily not only taught but also responded to the many calls for research and papers from the journal *Éducation Africaine*. According to his son, Diaman Bathily, he continually edited the notes for the volume and for a study of the Peul societies of Macina, which was published in 1936. His studies, however, did not meet with the same success as those of other teachers such as Mamby Sidibé or Bouillagui Fadiga.

In 1942, wishing to return to his natal region, he requested and obtained a post in Senegal. In 1944 he was approached by the administration in Dakar and by the Bathily family village elders to consider the post of *chef du canton*. From this post he began a series of social and economic reforms in an economically deprived region. At the same time he embarked on historical and ethnographic research into the Gadiaga people and the region of Bakel. The majority of his writings were not published during his lifetime. Some were sent on to the French administration. Indeed, Bathily used these documents to justify his arguments before the French authorities, particularly concerning land conflicts in the canton. In a manner similar to Abdou Salam Kane, Bathily cemented customary law in writing as a means of legitimating his claims before the French. Unlike Kane, however, Bathily, never sought to defend or invent personal or familial claims to land. His research seems to have served exclusively a personal project of social and economic reform in the Gadiaga region.

His writings about the history of the Bakel region helped frame his argument about the region's economic decline. He also wrote many letters to the administration in Senegal in which he tried to capture the economic and cultural dynamism of the precolonial period. In his ethnographic writing, Bathily strove to produce a corpus strongly denouncing "outmoded customary law," which he believed was blocking local development. As might be expected, Bathily quickly collided with the relatives of the prominent families of Gadiaga, who violently opposed his reformist orientation. He was only half-heartedly defended by an administration also disturbed by his activist agenda. Bathily, however, was never fooled by the apparent zeal of the colonial administration for the promotion of change and development in the Sarakolle society: "What good is it to expend vain effort in the accomplishment of a struggle endorsed by France but for which France is unwilling to provide the necessary support?"[48] His rivals accused him of homicide and misappropriation of official funds. Bathily committed suicide on June 26, 1947, with a shot to the head, two years after he was relieved of his duties as cantonal chief.

Despite his tragic end, the life and writings of Ibrahima Bathily shed light on the singular destiny of a man situated on the frontier of two worlds and at the junction of two value systems: the Sarakolle society and culture of which his family was a part; and the culture of France, which shaped him through his education and his profession as a teacher. His ethnographic endeavors were not born of a voluntary desire to enjoin the expectations of colonials; instead, during his final three years Bathily embarked on his own projects of social and economic reform. In this sense Ibrahima Bathily illustrates the broader phenomenon of the appropriation of writing and ethnography by African intermediaries for their own end. Along with Abdou Salam Kane and Mamby Sidibé, he further underscores the diversity of uses of writing and codification of custom by educated Africans during the colonial epoch.

The drafting of customary codes by indigenous authors may appear relatively marginal to the wider sphere of the production of colonial knowledge. The majority of the authors were indeed European themselves, although Diaman Bathily demonstrates that educated Africans contributed to the written codification of customary law despite the fact that they did not actively pursue publication of their work. This chapter has attempted in part to measure the impact of these works, not only in terms of the production of colonial knowledge but also with regard the socio-professional trajectory of their respective authors. It thus reconstructs the singular contexts that testify, each in its own way, to the importance of the diverse uses of writing in a literate milieu. This narrative is particularly important with regard to understanding the production of legal codes that played a vital role in the establishment of regional law and order in French West Africa.

African intermediaries employed by the administration manipulated not only the colonial judicial decision-making process, in the manner of Wangrin.[49] They also participated, albeit in a fashion contrary to the original intent, in the drafting of customary codes and other documents that established local authority in French West Africa (land tenure, chieftaincy, family law, etc.) and served as the written basis for tribunals presided over by Europeans. Upon examination of the context in which these diverse sources of customs were produced, it seems that the very act of establishing a custom or tradition in writing was simultaneously an act employed to support diverse strategies characteristic of the educated milieu: Abdou Salam Kane manipulated land tenure law to better defend his land claims; Mamby Sidibé attested to his mastery and knowledge of local traditions to entrench himself in the privileged role of counselor to the colonial administration. Finally, the tragic fate of Ibrahima Diaman Bathily illustrates that the appropriation of writing by educated Africans seeking to describe and subsequently "modernize" local customs and traditions could easily enflame other vested interests, especially those supporting the status quo.

Africans' use of writing and literacy cannot be limited to ruse and the manipulation of colonial justice. The diversity of uses to which they put written ethnographies and legal digests illustrate above all else the very complexity of this literate African community raised in the shadow of colonial domination. These narratives suggest some of the ways one can assess the complex connections between the literate elite and the production of customary law in French West Africa. This theme merits more serious attention. It requires the recovery of forgotten documents from local archives attesting to the riches of this literary production. These local archives contain a treasure of forgotten ethnographic, historical, and juridical literature condemned to slow and steady decay.

Notes

1. D. Robinson, "Ethnography and Customary Law."
2. For instance, Sibeud's recent study, *Une science impériale,* completely ignores their roles.

3. Jezequel, "Maurice Delafosse," 90.

4. In colonial terminology *coutumiers* are digests that identify, collect, and fix the so-called indigenous customary laws. These digests were designed to help colonial administrators rule local societies. For instance, French administrators were supposed to use them when acting as president of *tribunaux indigènes* (native courts). Unfortunately, the lack of studies on colonial justice prevents us from knowing to what degree these *coutumiers* were actually used.

5. See D. R. Peterson, *Creative Writing*.

6. D. Robinson, "Ethnography and Customary Law," 237.

7. Sibeud, "La naissance de l'ethnographie."

8. This committee, created in 1915 by Governor General Clozel, organized and promoted research in West Africa. It eventually became the French Institute for Black Africa (Institut Français d'Afrique Noire) in 1938.

9. Jézéquel, "Maurice Delafosse," 99–100.

10. Jézéquel, "Maurice Delafosse," 101

11. Damga is the eastern province of Fouta Tooro.

12. Before the colonial period the *almamy* was Fouta Tooro's most important religious and political leader.

13. Klein, *Slavery and Colonial Rule*, 106.

14. *Waalo* refers to the land liable to flooding; this is the most fertile land in Fouta Tooro.

15. Leservoisier, "L'évolution," 72. For instance, in 1904 colonial army officers were asked to gather information on land property in the Fouta Tooro.

16. This is hardly new, as Terence Ranger made this point a long time ago. See Ranger, "Invention of Tradition." However, our objective is not so much to assert once again that Africans took a part in the reinvention of their traditions under colonial rule as to suggest how this co-creation of tradition only unveils part of the reasons why literate Africans invested the ethnographic scene.

17. Literate here means literate in French. Many Foutanke marabouts and aristocrats were literate in Arabic.

18. Kane, "Coutume civile."

19. The committee received 123 studies between 1931 and 1935. It published only twenty-eight texts.

20. Abdul Kaader Kane was Abdul Salam's great-great-grandfather (Kane, "Coutume civile"). Regarding *feccere Fouta*, see Leservoisier, "L'évolution," 72. In Fouta Tooro, the turban is a symbol given to those who are named to a political office.

21. In a later article (1935), he emphasizes that the colonial administration decided to expropriate the Foutanke returnees from their land. It was a way of punishing their resistance to the French conquest. Kane no longer denies the problem caused by these returnees, but he rallies to the French position that favors him. Kane, "Du régime."

22. Schmitz, "Cités noires."

23. Two articles were produced by French administrators, Henri Gaden ("Du régime") and M.Vidal ("Rapport sur l'étude"). The last one was written by Abdou Salam Kane ("Du régime").

24. D. Robinson, *Chiefs and Clerics*.

25. Conklin, *Mission to Civilize*, 249.

26. Gluckman, *Ideas and Procedures*, 33.

27. We still do not have definitive evidence of it.

28. Ranger, "Invention of Tradition."

29. Usually the articles written by literate natives are seldom more than ten pages. Jézéquel, "Maurice Delafosse.

30. Bouche, *L'enseignement*.

31. Charles Béart also encouraged the Ponty students to write plays based on African history. See Jézéquel, "Le théâtre des instituteurs."

32. D. Robinson, "Ethnography and Customary Law."

33. Amselle, *Logiques métisses*.

34. It would be an interesting, albeit very difficult, project to inventory all these studies. Many of these unpublished ethnographies and local histories still reside in district archives.

35. The Karamangue are known to be good healers in the Birgo. The main religious offices are occupied by the Sangare family, whereas the—contested—Ba Sidibé family holds the political responsibilities in the Birgo. Interview with Colonel Bakary Sidibé, Bamako, Mali, February 1997.

36. At that time Mamby's father was dead, and it was probably easier for the elders of the village to choose him. Interview with Colonel Bakary Sidibé, Bamako, Mali, February 1997.

37. Interestingly, Mamby Sidibé's personal story shares a great deal with Yambo Ouologuem's novel *Le Devoir de violence, roman* (Paris: Editions du Seuils 1968).

38. In 1915 this school became the École Normale William Ponty, the most prestigious school in French West Africa. Jézéquel, "Les 'mangeurs de craies.'"

39. To draw a comparison we can refer to Awa Keïta's autobiographical book, *Femme d'Afrique*.

40. Despite living in Bamako, Mamby Sidibé returned to Niamefero a few times during his holidays. Interview with Bocar Cissé, Mamby Sidibé's former secretary, Bamako, Mali, February 1997.

41. The section title in English: "Distinguish good servants from bad ones." Sidibé, "Coutumier," 86.

42. Sidibé, "Coutumier," 90.

43. Nevertheless, in 1929 the colonial archives of Kita described him as an opponent of the Ba Sidibé chief of Sirakoro (Birgo main village). According to Colonel Bakary Sidibé, this chief (who was his father) was the boy who had been replaced by Mamby Sidibé at the French school. The same informant, who lived at Mamby Sidibé's house in Bamako, claims that Mamby Sidibé and Ba

Sidibé eventually reconciled. Interview with Colonel Bakary Sidibé, Bamako, Mali, February 1997.

44. For instance, there was a clear distinction between European and African teachers. Their respective careers were ruled according to different sets of rules : the Europeans belonged to the *cadre supérieur* (previously *cadre européen*) and the Africans to the *cadre secondaire* (previously *cadre indigène*). Until 1947 it was almost impossible for an African teacher to integrate the *cadre supérieur*. Jézéquel, "Les 'mangeurs de craies.'"

45. In French Soudan *bilakorotigui* means "chief of the uncircumcised," an insult to an adult.

46. Sidibé, "Coutumier," 93.

47. Sidibé, "Coutumier," 86, 93.

48. Bathily, "Notices," 34.

49. Hampâté Bâ, *Fortunes of Wangrin*.

Interpreters Self-Interpreted
The Autobiographies of Two Colonial Clerks

RALPH A. AUSTEN

Autobiographical writings by Africans who served as junior colonial functionaries are very rare, and the reasons for such near silence are not difficult to understand.[1] In political terms the position of intermediary between alien rulers and a subject population was problematic and thus awkward to recall either during or after the colonial era. Moreover, Africans proficient enough in European languages to produce such self-reflective writings usually found better employment than that of clerks, to say nothing of the less literate position of interpreter, and the majority of them came of age at the very end of the colonial era.[2]

The two authors under consideration here, Amadou Hampâté Bâ and Jacques Kuoh Moukouri, entered colonial service only in the 1920s, somewhat after the epoch when, according to Henri Brunschwig, interpreters were "indispensable for the French."[3] Their administrative tasks were thus more that of clerks than interpreters, and their exceptional talents eventually took both men well beyond this entire level of employment. However unrepresentative they may be, the books written by these individuals at least give some voice to the otherwise silent presence of clerks in most colonial documentation.[4] They offer unique insights into the experience of inhabiting such colonial roles (not only in their authors' own times) and raise questions that can only be answered by research into larger sets of records.

The Authors and Their Narratives

Before making use of these two works for historical purposes, one must understand something about the contexts—both sociogeographic and personal—from which they derive as well as how they are composed. What Hampâté Bâ and Kuoh Moukouri have in common is a roughly similar age (born, respectively, in 1900 and 1909) as well as periods of service (1922 to 1942 and 1926 to 1947) as subordinate officials within the French colonial system. In their places of origin, however, they represent the extreme poles of the western African spatial and cultural map. Hampâté Bâ was a Fulbe from the inland savanna of present-day Mali and spent the first decade-plus of his administrative career (the eleven years described in *OMC*) in Upper Volta (present-day Burkina Faso). Kuoh Moukouri was born to an indigenous family of the coastal port of Douala in Central African Cameroon and served the colonial government mainly in his own city and the inland capital of Yaoundé. Both books were written well after their authors had moved from being interpreters and clerks to more prestigious careers in the late- and post-colonial eras.

Although the two authors entered the colonial administration at about the same rank with the same middle-school level of formal French education (the prevailing standard for clerks) their paths into European culture and beyond such employment also differed significantly.[5] Hampâté Bâ was forcibly recruited from a Koranic school into a French one at the age of twelve, dropped out for some years after elementary school, and only finished the next level when he was twenty-one. He had been designated to go on to more advanced education and a "professional" career at the pinnacle of the French colonial school system, the Ponty School at Gorée, but refused at his mother's insistence. As punishment he was dispatched in the capacity of *écrivain expeditionnaire auxiliaire* (probationary clerk) to the remote and newly established colony of Upper Volta.[6] From 1934 to 1942 he served in relatively senior administrative positions in Bamako, Mali but got into political trouble because of his connection with the suspect Hammalist Islamic movement.[7]

Hampâté Bâ subsequently shifted to service with IFAN (l'Institut Français [now Fondamental] de l'Afrique Noire), the main research organization in French Africa, thus beginning his longer career of scholarship and writing. At independence he became Mali's ambassador to Côte d'Ivoire and also a member of the Executive Council of UNESCO. In 1970 he officially retired to a permanent residence in Côte d'Ivoire, where he wrote both *L'étrange destin de Wangrin* and his memoirs.

Kuoh Moukouri, whose family was at least nominally Christian, entered colonial schooling voluntarily and finished the two available stages of education in the new French mandated territory of Cameroon at the age of seventeen.[8] He immediately received an appointment in the financial services as an *écrivain-interprète* (clerk-interpreter), although in most of the book he refers to himself exclusively as *écrivain*. By 1933 he had risen to the rank of *commis d'ordre et de comptabilité* (senior clerk and bookkeeper/accountant) and immediately after World War II rose to *rédacteur principale des services civils et financiers* (senior office administrator).[9]

As a result of postwar reforms in the colonial system, Kuoh was promoted, from 1947 on, to a series of territorial administrative posts previously reserved for Europeans. In 1950–51 he also undertook postsecondary studies at the Paris École Nationale de la France d'Outre-Mer and in 1957 formally moved into the senior ranks of the French Overseas (formerly Colonial) Ministry.[10] During these years he also spent tours of duty on the central office staffs of government ministries both in Yaoundé (for the nascent Cameroonian national regime) and in Paris (for a European Cameroonian delegate to the National Assembly who held several metropolitan cabinet positions). At Cameroon's accession to independence in 1960, Kuoh became ambassador first to France and the European Community and then to the United States and Canada, a post from which he wrote *Doigts noirs*.

The differences in location and broader careers of the two authors are also reflected in the social tone and literary character of their respective autobiographies. Hampâté Bâ inhabited a Mande-Fulbe space in which colonialism accommodated itself at least partially to elaborate indigenous hierarchies of rulership, caste, and religion. His own position within this world was rather privileged, and he insists on its recognition (by others regarding him as well as by himself for those to whom he owes deference) throughout the narrative. In part because of this sensitivity to a complex African social order, Hampâté Bâ is clearly a more major intellectual figure then Kuoh Moukouri, and his memoirs are arguably the finest autobiographical texts in the African literary canon. This commercially successful work was preceded by the even more widely read "novel" *Wangrin,* which tells the story of a true (although atypically well-educated) *interprète* from the generation of Africans who entered the colonial administration before World War I.[11] The memoirs themselves are as rich in humor and drama as *Wangrin,* although, for present purposes, their concerns sometimes range quite far from the issues of what it meant to be a colonial clerk. In retrospect Hampâté Bâ shows himself less concerned with the authority and income deriving from his administrative position than with the issues that became his later professional as well as personal objects: the collection of oral traditions and the cultivation of Islam.

The southern Cameroonian world of Kuoh Moukouri had no centralized states, little precolonial contact with Islam, and a status hierarchy based mainly upon rather conflicting issues of slavery versus freedom, priority of contact with Europeans, and regional/ethnic rivalries.[12] Not many of these issues enter explicitly into *Doigts noirs,* perhaps because the time of writing as well as the author's ambassadorial position demanded a more homogeneous representation of the new nation state. This small volume (201 pages as opposed to Hampâté Bâ's 508) is the first and only book published by Kuoh Moukouri, although he later produced another valuable manuscript, "Le Cameroun et ses références," on the history of his own Duala people.[13] Kuoh Moukouri's intellectual and artistic stature is clearly not equal to that of Hampâté Bâ, and his literary devices of writing in the third person and not introducing the details of his own identity until very late are both enriching and frustrating.[14] During the early chapters, which provide all the intimate details of life as a clerk, it is not entirely clear whether the author is recounting his own experiences or that of an unnamed predecessor, "Le pionnier méconnu" (the unrecognized pioneer), who began his colonial administrative career at the starting point of the French Cameroon regime in 1916.[15] As in the case of Hampâté Bâ's *Wangrin* (and we may assume that Kuoh Moukouri also got his information directly from the man—or men—he represents), this move allows us to learn about a wider historical experience than that of the author himself. In a later section Kuoh Moukouri also introduces a *Kanzlist,* that is, an even older man who served as a clerk in pre–World War I German Cameroon. Unlike Hampâté Bâ, Kuoh Moukouri does not indicate any vocation other than the ones linked to his formal employment, although he devotes much of the second half of the book to political matters, most of them occurring after the end of his time as a mere clerk.

The Role Remembered: Description

The history of African colonial functionaries is undoubtedly best constructed from archival records and, where possible, interviews with a wide range of incumbents and those who witnessed their activities. The written memoirs of two rather exceptional figures can only suggest, confirm, or amplify such information and are perhaps most valuable, as will be seen later, for telling us what it felt like to be a colonial intermediary. But even with such limited empirical goals in mind, it is worth examining how Hampâté Bâ and Kuoh Moukouri describe the work, politics, and related social situations that they experienced, observed, or recorded from the memories of older colleagues. It will be obvious in what follows that the two autobiographies do not always deal with matching issues and that Hampâté Bâ provides much more detail on most subjects. But in many respects the narratives complement each other and, when supplemented by citations from the few other writings of this kind and some contemporary documents, do give us some sense of what colonial clerks actually did or were expected to do.

The Division and Hierarchy of Office Labor

One reason for the lack of autobiographies by African colonial *fonctionnaires* is that their work consisted mainly of banal and generally petty bureaucratic chores. However, in the colonial context such tasks provided those who performed them with considerable power; they, more than the segregated and monolingual European commandants, were the "gatekeepers" of this regime. It is thus of interest to see how specific responsibilities were allocated. Hampâté Bâ offers the best account of colonial administrative office structures, due not only to his literary skills and commitment, but also because he served much of his time in rural posts, where such issues are more dramatically presented. Thus when the commandant of Tougan was faced with a major tax collection problem

He immediately called together his personal general staff, consisting of the interpreter, who was at once his mouth, his eyes and his ears; the chief clerk, who was the keeper of his seals and the writing instrument of his sultanic decrees; and the police sergeant [*brigadier-chef*], who was his archangel, head of the guardian angels of Hell, which is to say the prisons. (*OMC*, 352)

The *grands interprètes* whom Hampâté Bâ finds stationed outside every district office are still important figures to whom he needs to show respect; but of the five he describes (*OMC*, 60, 71–72, 102–3, 189, 338–42), only one has attended any school, most speak only a pidgin French, and all seem of rather humble origin.[16] Soon after Hampâté Bâ's arrival in Upper Volta, these men literally become relics of an earlier era. In an *arreté* of December 31, 1923, the lieutenant governor formally abolished further appointments of "illiterate natives" to the local administrative cadres and announced that the functions of interpreters would be merged with those of clerks under the new title of *écrivain-interprète*.[17]

It was thus neither desirable nor possible for Hampâté Bâ to emulate Wangrin (who also had a middle-school education and was originally assigned as a schoolteacher) and take over the job of interpreter. While the frequently held notion that *Wangrin* is itself an autobiographical invention must now be rejected, it is clear that the well-born and educated hero of this earlier work is closer to Hampâté Bâ in many of his social characteristics than he is to the earlier generation of interpreters. He may be closest of all to Kuoh Moukouri, with at least his title of *écrivain-interprète*.[18]

We do not learn directly from Kuoh Moukouri's account how much interpreting he actually undertook, but Hampâté Bâ does indicate the situations when he had to play this role: while traveling with Europeans; while working for very high officials such as the lieutenant governor of Upper Volta; and during one very delicate negotiation over a tax revolt against a local chief. In this last case Hampâté Bâ did not actually speak the language of the local (Tougan) peasants, although they understood the Bamana into which their statements were translated by the very chief against whom they were complaining. Along with translating the chief's Bamana into French for the commandant, Hampâté Bâ was able to offer his own suggestions about how to resolve the problem (*OMC*, 358–75).

Beside making a great story, this incident nicely illustrates the corresponding limitations of interpreters and clerks. The former cannot be moved beyond the areas of their language competency and are unlikely to have the cultural skills to discuss administrative matters directly with their European superiors, while African clerks may themselves become dependent on interpreters for communicating with local populations when posted away from home.

Kuoh Moukouri, despite the subtitle of his book, does not have much to say about the status or function of interpreting. His own work (as opposed to that of the *pionnier méconnu*) was exercised entirely in the urban offices of the financial services rather than in district administration, which he only undertook under the very different conditions that followed World War II. But the consequent stress on French language and administrative skills again accounts for his early ascent through the clerical ranks.

The levels to which clerks could be promoted within the colonial hierarchy were obviously quite limited, and I will discuss the issues engendered by such racial restrictions later. However, in comparison with interpreters, clerks could move over a considerable range of positions and on occasion (if only temporarily and without the corresponding privileges) actually replace Europeans.[19] Hampâté Bâ describes a period of about one year (1930–31) when he functioned as the commandant of a subdivision (Tougan) in Upper Volta, although he notes that during this entire time he still worked out of his original chief clerk's office (*OMC*, 393–410). Kuoh Moukouri, who would become a fully recognized senior administrator in the post–World War II era, cites an earlier case of an African who is temporarily made a bureau head in a technical branch of the governor's office (*Doigts noirs*, 39–41).[20]

Both Hampâté Bâ and Kuoh Moukouri describe their normal work as essentially the keeping of records and transmitting of correspondence. This command over the written word not only confers status and occupational mobility but also provides opportunity for the manipulation of information in interests other than those of their employers. *Wangrin* is full of stories about self-serving chicanery, but Kuoh Moukouri never addresses this issue, and in the account of his own administrative career, Hampâté Bâ admits to no dishonesty.[21] He even insists that a case of embezzlement by a postal employee in 1932 is the first such accusation against any public employee in Upper Volta since the founding of the colony in 1919 (*OMC*, 414).

There are, however, several examples in *Oui mon commandant* of information being delayed or transmitted from government sources into private channels. Hampâté Bâ even admits that

The native functionaries had woven a sort of personal network [*reseau amicale*] that allowed them to operate under the very nose of the administration so as sometimes to put matters on a slightly different course or even prevent certain ill-intentioned administrators or heads of political bureaus from achieving their goals. (*OMC*, 345–46)

However, the cases he presents of such behavior involve the concerns of Europeans as well as Africans (in one instance giving advance notice of his punishment to an administrator whom he has helped convict; *OMC*, 291–93), Moreover, the only public interest ever damaged is the principle of secrecy.

If clerks were, according to both these accounts, essentially honest, they nevertheless appear to have felt great pressures to spend money on the support of dependents, the maintenance of a prestigious standard of living, and the entertainment of various guests. Could this be managed on their official salaries and emoluments, or did it require extra sources of income, which, in works like *Wangrin* or *Mister Johnson*, take mainly illegal forms?

Kuoh Moukouri devotes an entire chapter of his book to the "economic role" of the clerk (*Doigts noirs*, 52–62) and is quite explicit about the need for more money than was paid by the government (he also describes frequent dockings of this pay for various perceived infractions). Furthermore he (or the third-person character at this point in the text) is forbidden to carry out any private business. The solution is to take up agriculture, which meets with the approval of his European superior, and he even founds a local cooperative, which is in accord with central government policy but not that of the local commandant and the indigenous chief.

Hampâté Bâ also founded a cooperative while in Upper Volta, but this is presented as more a political and moral than an economic initiative.[22] The account of his years in this colony given in *OMC* implies that he was able to maintain his family and what appear to be many other expenses by combining his government income with the patronage of more senior Africans at his various posts;[23] none of the latter, however, make illegitimate demands on him. However, in unpublished correspondence from the 1940s concerning his employment with IFAN, Hampâté Bâ indicates both a strong desire to hold on to the financial benefits attached to his *"cadre d'origine"* and severe difficulties in meeting his now extensive familial obligations with the income (and especially the expected pension) of *"un agent indigène."*[24]

The contradictions between what is published by Hampâté Bâ (and to a lesser extent Kuoh Moukouri) and what archival evidence reveals may tell us something about the nature of performed memory. More immediately it suggests a lived contradiction in the historical position of colonial clerks. They were at once privileged by their assimilation into the formal prerequisites of European office and tormented by the limitations of these rewards in relationship to what their own society expected from them.

Politics in a *Beamtenstaat*

Although neither of these books is really a political work (there was little scope for public politics in the periods when the two men served as clerks), they both discuss struggles over power in a number of contexts: status within the African bureaucratic cadres, relations with European superiors, popular resistance to government impositions, religious questions, unionization, and some elements of early nationalism. The first four of these issues are treated mainly by Hampâté Bâ and the last two by Kuoh Moukouri.

Nothing in Hampâté Bâ's memoirs approaches the bitter battles waged between Wangrin and his various adversaries in both the African and European government ranks. He represents himself (and the impression is confirmed by those who knew him) as a very congenial person whose ambitions may occasionally involve some bending of rules but do not require the displacement or extreme manipulation of others alongside or above him on the administrative ladder. However, he does ascribe Wangrin-like trickery to some of his peers. A temporary clerk at his first rural post, Dori, tries to embarrass Hampâté Bâ but is halted when the latter threatens to reveal his bribe taking (*OMC*, 188–219). Just before the point at which his memoir ends (*OMC*, 496–97), another "intrigue on the part of certain colleagues" forces Hampâté Bâ to abandon his dream of being posted in his home city of Bandiagara. In this case he simply relents on the advice of the religious mentor, Cerno Bokar, who tells him not to create enemies in Bandiagara and instead take advantage of what will, in fact, turn out to be great opportunities offered by employment in the territorial capital, Bamako.[25]

Both Hampâté Bâ and Kuoh Moukouri make frequent references to the near absolute power held by French administrative officers. Kuoh Moukouri particularly notes the refusal of Europeans to recognize their African subordinates as *fonctionnaires* and points out how a French noncommissioned officer was allowed to publicly assault the closest Cameroonian equivalent to Hampâté Bâ, the writer and clerk Isaac Moumé Etia (*Doigts noirs*, 27).[26] Hampâté Bâ himself calls the administrators *dieux de la brousse* (gods of the bush) and shows the *petits commandants* as often more annoying than their seniors; but he also reveals the methods by which clerks could at times manipulate these Europeans and even defend other Africans against them. The main weapon was always information, but Hampâté Bâ never resorts to the favorite tool of Wangrin: intimacy with, or even provision of, *moussos* (literally "women" but in this context African concubines). Instead he makes use of friendly interpreters or even *plantons* (guards/office boys) to learn how he must handle particular officials.

Hampâté Bâ also presents two cases in which he helps nonofficial African notables win contests with European administrators. The first, involving a chief who faces the prospect of being unjustly displaced, is managed by the delayed delivery of the local commandant's telegram to the governor; the latter can thus hear the African side of the story before he takes any action (*OMC*, 253–54). The second is a more complex and engaging story about a marabout who physically attacks a commandant because the latter is forcing his wife into sexual relations (*OMC*, 258–96). Here, in a scene recalling a similar (but less morally motivated) episode from *Wangrin*, the marabout's defenders withhold a critical piece of evidence until the climax of their court case.[27]

Neither of the books in question deals with any major uprisings against colonial rule. We do get an account of one such case from the otherwise very thin memoir of the Ghanian "senior interpreter" Robert Cudjoe, who assisted the Nigerian government in putting down the 1929 Igbo women's riots in Nigeria. His account is not very sympathetic or insightful: "The Riots from my personal experience were an unfortunate game played by the men of the affected villages and clans who thought they could incite the women with all sorts of false stories so as to get the tax stopped altogether in the country."[28]

Hampâté Bâ was involved in a similar but less severe event in Upper Volta, when the peasants of a Tougan canton (village group) claimed they were being unjustly taxed by a chief who, like those in Eastern Nigeria of the same period, was an outsider chosen unilaterally by the colonial authorities (357–388). Hampâté Bâ also sees a conspiracy behind the protest, which he calls a *fronde des tirailleurs* (meaning local veterans of colonial military service) and he is instrumental in convincing the commandant that the "dynamic and intelligent chief" in question deserves to retain his "turban."[29] However, he also recognizes the unjust burden placed on peasants by annual taxation as well as by obligations to provision passing officials (including *blancs-noirs* like himself). Hampâté Bâ even proposes a less onerous system for meeting such needs and gains the approval of his immediate superiors, although the plan is rejected by the central administration.

Islam became a major political issue for Hampâté Bâ in the last phase of his administrative career, which is dealt with in the third, yet unpublished volume of the memoirs. In *Oui mon commandant* we only see foreshadowings of this conflict, which do not involve the author's administrative role. First, he gives a general account of the persecution of Hammalists throughout French West Africa, including the Upper Volta *cercle* of Ouahigouya while he is stationed there.[30] However, thanks to the restrained actions of a wise and humane local French administrator, Hampâté Bâ is spared any anguish in this matter (*OMC*, 421–27). During his leave in Bandiagara, which ends this book, Hampâté Bâ manages to alienate an unnamed but powerful "grand marabout" of the mainline Tijani order. His error is a display of greater respect for his own teacher, Cerno Bokar (eventually himself a Hammalist), than toward the marabout. The latter had earlier disappointed Hampâté Bâ by advising him that his spiritual duty was "to be loyal and obedient toward the representatives of France" (*OMC*, 462–69).[31]

The more immediate religious conflicts experienced by Hampâté Bâ during the 1920s all involved the Catholic Church. During his initial posting in Ouagadougou, he attempts, along with several other African administrators, to form a produce-purchasing cooperative. This venture is denounced by the archbishop of Upper Volta as a subterfuge for converting peasants to Islam and soon has to close (*OMC*, 343). Later in Tougan he is personally blamed by the local Catholic mission for the reconversion of the commandant's interpreter to Islam, and an official inquiry is launched into the possible broader consequences of such an event (*OMC*, 338–46). When Hampâté Bâ subsequently takes sole charge of this subdivision, he again clashes with the missionaries: first over a request that he recruit young girls for their nursery school; and again when he registers a protest over sermons that imply the souls of all Muslims are destined for hell (*OMC*, 394–97, 407–10). In all these Tougan conflicts, Hampâté Bâ's position is supported by the government, which may be due to the correct administrative behavior that he describes but also to the general tensions between church and state under France's Third Republic. However, in deference to the church authorities, Hampâté Bâ is transferred to another administrative post.

Had these accounts dealt with British, rather than French Africa they might have said a good deal about the formation of unions among colonial clerks, since this took place in a number of British colonies well before World War II.[32] Martin Kayamba, the only British colonial clerk to have left an extended autobiography, unfortunately omits from it all reference to his leading (and well-documented) role as a founder of the Tanganyika Territory African Civil Servants Association in 1922.[33] Instead Kayamba speaks of establishing a sporting club; ironically this is the only kind of organization that, Kuoh Moukouri tells us, his commandant would allow. An effort was made to establish a Cameroonian *syndicat* of indigenous *fonctionnaires* in 1931, but the government never gave its authorization (*Doigts noirs*, 43–44).[34]

Not even Kuoh Moukouri, who speaks of himself as a "patriot," ever claims that he or other clerks seriously thought about overthrowing colonial rule until well after World War II. However, assertions of that kind had been made by other Duala elites well before this time.[35] This apparently precocious nationalism can be ascribed to the peculiar situation of Cameroon as a territory that had changed hands after World War I and was threatened with German reoccupation during the latter 1930s. Thus, Kuoh Moukouri quotes a lengthy political discussion with one of the numerous Duala Germanophiles and describes both himself and the unspecified older Francophone clerk who is his narrative alter ego as choosing to show their loyalty to the current colonial rulers by joining the government-sponsored Jeunesse Camerounaise Française. In effect this organization proved to be a bridge to more fully anticolonial nationalism. However, Kuoh Moukouri makes no claim that he or his administrative colleagues took a leading role in such initiatives.[36] In describing his own extensive involvement with post–World War II politics, he attests to having always maintained a moderate position and sought to advance the interests of his compatriots mainly by representing them in ever higher echelons of the colonial structure.

Hampâté Bâ's published memoirs take us only up to 1933, so there is even less indication here of whether or to what degree he and his administrative colleagues ever became involved in nationalism.[37] However, for both authors, the autobiographies are less valuable as sources of political information than they are indices of the affect of living so intimately within the colonial experience.

Self-Definition as Colonial Intermediaries

Both Hampâté Bâ and Kuoh Moukouri address themselves frequently and explicitly to the issue of colonialism. What they have to say here is worth noting, but it is also very much shaped by the events that have taken place between the lived experience and the time of writing. The more authentic "archive" of this experience lies in their accounts of attitudes toward work, language, and cultural practices.

Hampâté Bâ's several pages of reflection on French rule (*OMC*, 439–44) are ambiguous at several levels. In his explicit evaluation he shifts between a philosophical detachment ("colonization has certainly existed at all times and in all climes, and there are few peoples, great or small, who are totally innocent in this area") to an obligatory denunciation ("nevertheless this does not justify it, and its principles remain hateful"). This is perhaps the attitude one would expect from someone who is the heir of Sudanic empires that competed for conquest with the French and also comes from a country that underwent (especially up to the 1980s, when this book was composed) a very unhappy experience of postcolonial regimes. Hampâté Bâ credits the philosophical side of his posture to the best-known of his translated Fulbe initiatory tales, *Kaèdara,* and its lesson that "every existing thing bears two faces: a nocturnal, pernicious face and a diurnal, favorable face."

Neither in this summing nor in the memoir as a whole is there any "colonial nostalgia." Hampâté Bâ rather tries to recapture the ambiguity of the epoch itself and notes the capacity of Africans subjects less learned than himself to overcome their sufferings through "humor, that great weapon of the *'Africains 'noirs-noirs.'"* This spirit is expressed first through a rich catalog of nicknames that capture the varying character of colonial officials, including some "quite malevolent *blancs-noirs.*"

Hampâté Bâ concludes this mini-essay with a long anecdote about forced road labor not unlike many of the story chapters of office life preceding it. His account centers on the sarcastic songs composed about a European taskmaster by his "happy workers" and ends with the eponymous punch line (from the mouth of an interpreter validating the administrator's total misunderstanding of what he has just heard): "Oui mon commandant!"

Kuoh Moukouri presents his own "portrait gallery" of commandants, seen more from the perspective of their clerks than that of the general population. The experience amounts to a "Calvary" of abuse and humiliation (including a brief arrest for violating "pass laws"), only occasionally interrupted by benevolence (*Doigts noirs,* 27–37). Rather than humor, the weapon of the oppressed and enslaved populations with which the narrator identifies (citing the Haitian writer Jean Price-Mars) is "dissimulation, lying and the mask" (*Doigts noirs,* 27). Kuoh Moukouri's colonialism shows far more of its evil face, and he comes to see his "career as a clerk" as "no more than a means and not . . . an end in itself" (*Doigts noirs,* 41). But the goals to which he dedicates himself remain closely identified with the European *mission civilisatrice.*

Although neither author presents administrative work as "an end in itself," both indicate great pride in the skills which allow them to function as the "pen" of the commandant.[38] Hampâté Bâ, however, more clearly defines the noncolonial purposes to which he wants to apply these capacities or develop other ones. Thus, while he undoubtedly made some efforts to improve his French, the only subjects he tells us he studied while a clerk are Islamic religion and the Arabic language. He does, however, credit earlier French education and his administrative career for aiding him in his second great calling, the recording of oral traditions. Colonial schooling provided him with functional literacy. The administrative requirement of keeping a journal during his initial voyage from Bamako to Ouagadougou taught him to use this skill for inscribing what he was told by learned but illiterate fellow Africans. Finally, French became his vehicle for "communication in a universal language" (OMC, 35).

Hampâté Bâ's lifestyle during these years in the colonial administration is presented as far more African then European. At each of his stations he establishes ties with local notables, thus reinforcing his position within Sudanic society and also acquiring places to live and eat while still a young bachelor. Once married and thus required to build his own home, he does so with the allotted support from government funds, but in a style (a compound) and in a place (near his senior "relatives"), which accords with local African norms. He does report one major moral lapse during his initial period in Ouagadougou, when he frequents courtesans and develops a taste for alcohol. However, he is saved from this situation by an awakened religious conscience and the timely consummation of a marriage already arranged for him by his family.

The one moment where Hampâté Bâ falls into the classic "Mister Johnson" caricature of the colonial clerk as a dandified ape of European manners and clothing occurs at his second posting, in a "bush" district. He describes in great detail the "European dress outfit" that he wears for his first day as senior clerk but also notes the "pride and stupidity" that blinds him to the reaction of the people he meets on his way through the market place and the subsequent warnings at the office door by the commandant's planton (OMC, 187–94). Although Hampâté Bâ hereafter dressed almost exclusively in Sudanic robes, this is likely not the only time in his career that he overplayed the role of indigène évolué.[39] But in representing the practice through such an extended story, he doubly transcends this cultural trap of the colonial intermediary: first, by stating an awareness of its nature, and second, by displaying a true command of the European language abilities that are claimed by such self-displays.

Kuoh Moukouri gives us a less engaging but in some respects more revealing account of how "he" went about acquiring European culture beyond the formal schooling needed to enter the clerical ranks. It is important, however, to consider whether the life described is Kuoh Moukouri's own or that of his "class of 1916" predecessor, *le pionnier méconnu*. If the latter is the intended subject (as formally denoted by the position of these passages in the narrative), Kuoh Moukouri has also established some distance between himself and the figure who naively but enthusiastically dedicates himself to the goal of personal and collective "modernization" rather than studying religion or African culture.[40] He practices proper French phrasing by memorizing the reports of his commandants and learns the rules of behavior and dress from observing Europeans as well as reading an instructional book, *Savoir vivre* (*Doigts noirs*, 38, 44–47). His role models are Africans and African Americans, but they are also derived from books rather than figures in his own world: "Great Men . . . who did not start out as great intellectuals. . . . 'Booker Washington,' 'Dr. AGREE,' 'Blaise DIAGNE,' etc." (*Doigts noirs*, 41).

Within his home community, *l'écrivain* presents himself as a general champion of European values against "superstitions" such as traditional healing and witchcraft beliefs and feels he is "on the good road toward 'enlightenment' *(lumière)* for his country" (*Doigts noirs*, 50–52). He unapologetically tells of his pride in owning and wearing European clothing, eating from a table in the European manner, and acquiring such items as a kerosene lamp, a phonograph, a rifle, and "a masonry house *(maison en dur)*, a white person's house" (*Doigts noirs*, 43–49).

In imitating Europeans so closely, the clerk represented by Kuoh Moukouri is in some respects remaining true to his own version of African tradition since "'he" (and this applies to both personae of *l'écrivain*) is a Duala. The coastal Duala people have a long history of mediating between Europeans and the Cameroon hinterland, a history that includes the very early adaptation of much European culture. However, it is in the one area of personal life most linked to European religious proselytization, marriage, that Kuoh's hero falls into more traditional practices. He does insist on the "social revolution" of choosing his own wife (although from his home "village") but then pays a dowry, offers several years of entertainment to his in-laws, and takes on the costs of an expensive wedding, all in the interest of "social prestige" (*Doigts noirs*, 48). He attempts to further this status by remaining monogamous "not so much on the grounds of Christian faith but as a mark of civilization." However, he eventually finds himself with a second wife, something that does not hurt his reputation within the local African community but is deeply regretted as a form of backsliding, which he still hopes somehow to transcend (*Doigts noirs*, 50).

Hampâté Bâ, although a committed Muslim, is "assimilated" enough to express a preference for monogamy. He is therefore doubly embarrassed when his family arranges a second marriage for him without even his knowledge. After much soul-searching and consultation with his Islamic mentor, the new wife is accepted on the grounds that refusal would show disrespect to both his elders and his teacher (*OMC*, 449–56).[41]

These two autobiographies recall very different experiences of being a colonial clerk. Hampâté Bâ presents an almost ideal (and perhaps idealized) balance between the European culture needed to carry on this task and an African identity that, despite its colonial redefinition as "tradition," can still be lived out in a very rich and satisfactory manner. Kuoh Moukouri describes a more classical struggle to live up to the colonial ideal of "civilization" while recognizing the ill will or at best condescension of the Europeans who are its exemplars. The triumphs in this effort are revealed as petty, and its goals conflict with other social demands that are increased by the very status derived from office in an alien regime.

It is impossible to decide, from the evidence in and around these texts and the present state of scholarship on the social history of colonial African *fonctionnaires*, which of these two accounts comes closest to capturing the average experience of such a life. We obviously need to supplement them with further research in more broadly representative sources. Yet ultimately there is no way to establish a statistical norm for such varied and subjective phenomena. Because of their richness, candor, and contrast, the autobiographies of both Hampâté Bâ and Kuoh Moukouri thus stand as authoritative, if not conclusive, statements about the possibilities of inhabiting the interface between African society and European colonial authority.

Notes

1. Very few sources of this kind are cited in Derrick, "'Native Clerk,'" and Brunschwig, "Rois." The two collections of African autobiographies compiled during the 1930s, Perham, *Ten Africans*, and Westermann, *Autobiographies*,

include only one account of such a figure, Martin Kayamba, which will be cited in this discussion along with Cudjoe, "Some Reminiscences."

2. The self-written accounts in Perham, *Ten Africans,* and Westermann, *Autobiographies,* are mostly by teachers, as are other memoirs produced after independence by men of this era. See also Austen, "From a Colonial to a Postcolonial African Voice," 1–2.

3. Brunschwig, "Rois," 122. "Native court" interpreters-assessors continued to be important, especially in British Africa, but appear to have been an even less-schooled category of functionaries; Afigbo, *Warrant Chiefs.*

4. Hampâté Bâ, *Oui mon commandant!* (hereafter *OMC*); Kuoh Moukouri, *Doigts noirs.*

5. There were attempts in the early 1920s and from 1935 to 1947 to train indigenous administrators at the advanced Ponty School in Gorée; but graduates of this program accounted for less than 10 percent of African clerical cadres and were not guaranteed significantly higher employment than products of the local *écoles supérieures primaires;* Sabatier, "Educating a Colonial Elite," 373–74.

6. All of this is described at great length in Amadou Hampâté Bâ, *Amkoullel,* and summarized in Austen, "From a Colonial to a Postcolonial African Voice." The *Journal officiel de la Haute Volta* for this period provides documentation of his advancement up the bureaucratic ranks of *écrivains* and then *commis* (literally "agent" but more accurately "senior clerk").

7. This period is not covered in *OMC* but is treated in the yet unpublished third volume of Hampâté Bâ's memoirs. The main outlines are presented in Devey, *Hampâté Bâ;* and Sanankoua, "Hampâté Bâ"; both of these authors have looked at Hampâté Bâ's personal archive, which was not accessible for purposes of the present essay.

8. No Cameroonians appear to have been admitted to Ponty before 1933 and only three between then and 1949 (Sabatier, "Colonial Elite," 217–18).

9. This trajectory, along with evaluations by European supervisors (almost always highly positive) are contained in his main personnel file Centre des archives d'outre-mer (CAOM), Aix, France , EE/11/7574. I am also very grateful to Aimé-Gaston Kuoh for providing me with biographical information on his late father and making other useful comments on this paper.

10. This last promotion accounts for the presence of his file in the archives of the ministry. Kuoh retained his formal status as a French bureaucrat until he reached the age of retirement.

11. There can be no doubt that Wangrin was a real person, known variously as Samba Traoré (in private life) and Samako Gnembélé (in government records), whose career is fairly accurately depicted by Hampâté Bâ; see *Journal officical de la Haute Volta* 4–5 (December 12, 1919) through 105 (March 1, 1924); *OMC,* 389–95; and Fourchard, "Propriétaires et commerçants," 456–57.

12. The issue of priority of contact with Europeans is also cited by Hampâté Bâ, who is theoretically at a disadvantage vis-à-vis Senegalese Africans (who

may even be citizens of France); however, this distinction ultimately plays less of a role in his self-regard than do internal savanna hierarchies.

13. Jonathan Derrick and I both knew Kuoh Moukouri and received much help from him on both the history and culture of the Duala and their region. Unfortunately for present purposes, we never questioned him about the details of *Doigts noirs*.

14. The literary legacy of Kuoh Moukouri lives at least through his children. One daughter was one of the first African women to publish a novel; Thérèse Kuoh-Moukoury, *Rencontres essentielles* (1969; New York: Modern Language Association, 2002); another, Grace Etonde-Ekoto, was a professor of literature at the University of Yaoundé.

15. According to Aimé-Gaston Kuoh (e-mail, April 18, 2002), "All the 'écrivains-interprètes' recruited from 1916 to 1934 are 'pionniers méconnus.' They all shared common experiences. J. KUOH MOUKOURI [my father] recruited in 1926 is among them. . . . the author, then tells the experiences that were recorded and collected from the lives of various 'écrivains-interprètes' of the period as if they were lived by the symbolic character representing them all whom he has called 'le pionnier méconnu.' Some of those experiences might have been his own, but most of them are not. . . . He didn't state the real names of the people having lived those various experiences."

16. Even the one educated interpreter was recruited into a Catholic mission school and forcibly converted there, which implies low family status.

17. *Journal officiel de la Haute Volta* 6, no. 102 (January 15, 1924): 6.

18. According to Jézéquel, "Les 'mangeurs de craies,'" African schoolteachers constituted "une aristocratie de la fonction coloniale" in principle but in practice often suffered from very limited opportunities for professional advancement or monetary gain, thus making a position of clerk or even interpreter more attractive. Mamadou Gologo describes his own rejection while at Ponty of either the difficult life of a "bush" schoolteacher or, despite the greater power enjoyed by clerks, the tedium of "Madame Remington" (the typewriter); he thus chooses to study medicine (*Le rescapé*, 45–49). It was only the advent of decolonization that opened up new horizons for Africans with the relatively advanced literary education of teachers.

19. This is the initial attraction of the position for Mamadou Gologo (*Le rescapé*, 47).

20. There is no indication in his personnel file of Kuoh himself holding such a post, although he did occupy middle-management posts previously filled by Europeans. Another African clerk, Martin Kayamba, served for over three years as assistant secretary in the Tanganyika Secretariat, a job normally reserved for "a young but unusually promising European political officer"; Iliffe, "Spokesman," 82–84. Kayamba himself, however, never mentions this post in "The Story of Martin Kayamba," in Perham, *Ten Africans*, 173–99. As a result of union action, several Nigerian clerks were also appointed to such posts from the early 1920s; Okonkwo, "Nigeria Civil Service Union."

21. For earlier Duala interpreters and their subterfuges under the German regime in Cameroon, see Austen and Derrick, *Middlemen of the Cameroons Rivers,* 104, 113.

22. On multiple private enterprises by Wangrin and other interpreters in Bobo-Dioulasso during this period, see Fourchard, "Propriétaires et commerçants," 455–57.

23. The annual salaries paid to the upper ranks of interpreters, *écrivains,* and *commis* in Upper Volta during the 1920s ranged from F 7,600 to 3,500, which exceeded payments to the lower ranks of European personnel; *Journal officiel de la Haute Volta* 2, nos. 22–23 (September 1–15, 1920): 138–39. There are similar indications for the positions occupied by Kuoh Moukouri; *Journal officiel du Cameroun* 18, no. 309 (April 1, 1933): 175.

24. Regarding his desire to retain *cadre d'origine* benefits, see Hampâté Bâ to Théodore Monod, March 20, 1941, Fonds Monod (Louis Brenner very kindly provided these documents). He discusses his financial difficulties in a letter to Monod on September 30, 1946 (most of this letter is printed in Brenner, "Amadou Hampâté Bâ," 309–10). As an apparent result of a request attached to these complaints, Hampâté Bâ was promoted in 1947 into a more senior echelon of IFAN employees; Devey, *Hampâté Bâ,* 100. Kuoh Moukouri also made a lengthy and somewhat acrimonious argument against the racial barriers within the French bureaucratic hierarchy prior to his advancement into the senior ranks of the colonial administration; this statement is not mentioned in his autobiography, but see Kuoh Moukouri, "Réponse au Bureau d'Études de la Direction de Personnel," n.d. (ca. November 1952), CAOM, EE/II/7951/1266. In the cases of both men, the legal barrier to promotion was their lack of the requisite educational credentials.

25. Cerno Bokar plays a similar role in Hampâté Bâ, *Amkoullel,* 335–36, when he advises the author's mother not to resist the French demand that her son go to their school rather than his own. Although there is no reason to doubt the truth of these events, they are clearly laid out by Hampâté Bâ so as to lend a harmonious destiny to the complex directions of his life.

26. The official French decrees establishing the *cadres indigènes* of the colonial administration do refer to their incumbents as *fonctionnaires* and provide them with privileges of promotion, travel allowances (including family members), leave, and pensions associated with such a position. "Arrêté portant organisation d'un cadre indigène de commis d'ordre et de comptabilité," Yaoundé, December 10, 1924, in *Rapport annuel,* 1925, 163–64.

27. Although Kuoh Moukouri provides no examples of manipulating government records, in a pre–World War I situation, when the German government sought to expropriate large tracts of valuable urban land, the relevant files appear to have been stolen by Duala clerks and now reside in the private archive of the principal family involved; Austen and Derrick, *Middlemen,* 125, 221.

28. Cudjoe, "Some Reminiscences," 161. The standard historiography makes the clerks and interpreters in African warrant chiefs' courts the major

villains of the uprising and gives the women greater agency; Afigbo, *Warrant Chiefs*, 215–39, 274–82. Cudjoe worked directly for the European administration and thus neglects these "indirect rule" aspects of the conflict along with its social base.

29. It is typical of the rich complexity of Hampâté Bâ's narrative that the canton in question had been part of the chieftaincy of his stepfather, who was deposed by the French before World War I as the result of another conspiracy. Some of the peasant protesters actually name Hampâté Bâ as a replacement for their present chief. He refuses to consider the offer mainly, he tells us, on the grounds that his stepfather is still alive and would be insulted.

30. The Hammalists were a new branch of the Tijani Sufi order that French administrators saw as a source of disorder and a threat to Tijani sheiks allied with the colonial regime; Launay and Soares, "Formation of an 'Islamic Sphere.'"

31. The marabout in question is definitely Seydou Nourou Tall, later instrumental in Hampâté Bâ's persecution for "Hammalism"; Sylvianne Garcia, "Al-Hajj Seydou Nourou Tall, 'grand marabout' tijani: l'histoire d'une carrière," in Robinson and Triaud, *Temps des marabouts*, 262–63; and Sanankoua, "Hampâté Bâ," 399–400.

32. Derrick, "Native Clerk"; Mason, "History of Mr. Johnson," 196–217; Okonkwo, "Nigeria Civil Service Union."

33. Iliffe, "Spokesman,"73–74"; cf. Kayamba, "Story."

34. Kaptué, *Travail et main-d'oeuvre*, 192–93. Kayamba's organization did not represent itself as a labor union, and Kayamba himself felt that "'Politics' and 'strikes' were bad words"; Iliffe, "Spokesman," 83.

35. Austen and Derrick, *Middlemen*, 144–50.

36. For the political limits of clerical organizations even in the more volatile situation of interwar British Nigeria, see Mason, "History of Mr. Johnson"; Okonkwo, "Nigerian Civil Service Union."

37. Sanankoua, "Hampâté Bâ," 405–6, describes a brief and not very happy foray into party politics while on leave from his (still formally administrative) IFAN position in 1946.

38. Kayamba, "Story," 197–98, also offers at least these kinds of reflections on clerical duties. In the French case, it should be noted, that advancement to the higher *commis* ranks required the passing of rather extensive and competitive examinations in general knowledge, French language skills, mathematics, bookkeeping and office management. The essays and exercises which the twenty-four-year old Kuoh Moukouri produced on this occasion are preserved in his main personnel file (CAOM, EE/11/7574) along with the quite strict grading of his examiners.

39. In a July 2, 1945, letter to Théodore Monod from Conakry he makes special mention of wearing European clothes because in Guinea "functionaries dressed in native style [*à l'indigène*] are not accepted." Fonds Monod.

40. Even if this picture depicts Kuoh Moukouri himself in his clerical years, it is evident that in later life he took great interest in Duala culture.

41. During his retirement in Abidjan he reached the Islamic marriage limit by taking two more wives, including the French woman, Hélène Heckmann, who edited his memoirs. He is reported to have maintained a tranquil household and defended polygamy on the grounds that it allowed a man to act out his sexual desires without falling into sin (Lilyan Kesteloot, private communication).

African Court Elders in Nyanza Province, Kenya, ca. 1930–1960

From "Traditional" to "Modern"

BRETT L. SHADLE

Scholars well appreciate how essential colonial legal realms were to the everyday lives of Africans. Investigations into the creation, recreation, and uses of "customary law" have suggested that courts were central arenas for battles between men and women, young and old, wealthy and poor. As such it is imperative that we understand the structure of African courts and who staffed them. Yet we know little about these men (all of them were men)—their backgrounds, how they were appointed, or how they carried out their duties. At best, scholars have described them as neoconservatives, dedicated to strict patriarchal control over women and junior men and relatively unconnected to the wider world of education, wage labor, and the "modern" milieu more generally. For colonial officials looking to shore up "tribes" via senior male power, scholars suggest, the appointment of "traditional" elders was worth concerted effort.

In this chapter I examine the history of court elders in colonial western Kenya. Much of what we have heretofore believed of court elders, I argue, is incorrect. Beginning in the late 1930s, new court members were likely to be educated, younger, Christian, and experienced in government and/or business. Far from being "traditional," these men were among the most "modern" and "progressive" of the region. This was so for two reasons. First, rather than promoting older, "traditional" men as elders, colonial officials favored "modern" men. Second, because colonial officials knew so little of local conditions, they relied largely on the advice of Africans—especially elite Africans—for selecting elders.[1] Thus "modern" Africans significantly influenced the composition of the benches, generally advancing allies and men from their own class. Among the administrators' primary goals in attracting these new men was to eradicate corruption, but rarely were they successful. If elite Africans and colonial officials together created new benches, in some regards African elders continued to operate their courts much as they wished.

This chapter examines two districts in Nyanza Province, western Kenya: South Kavirondo (on which I have done the most research) and North Kavirondo (Nyanza replacing Kavirondo in 1950). Most of the evidence comes from documents in the Kenya National Archives, including administrative reports and letters of application and of complaint from Africans. The courts were known as native tribunals until about 1950, briefly as native courts, and thereafter as African courts.

Origins of the African Courts and Elders' Biographies

African courts in Kenya were hybrid institutions: they were created and backed by the British government, fully African in staff, and employed a mixture of "customary law" and colonial law. From their establishment in the 1890s all courts in the land—African and otherwise—were officially subordinate to the Supreme Court; nonetheless, on a day-to-day basis administrators oversaw the operations of the African courts. This *de facto* control became *de jure* in 1951, when the tribunals were fully separated from the judiciary.[2]

Authority to hear local, intra-African disputes was first granted to government-appointed headmen in 1902, although this was transferred to councils of elders by 1913.[3] Early on, tribunals in Nyanza served locations, which were administrative units under the rule of one chief. Restructuring the courts in 1937, the administration consolidated the many locational courts into a few divisional ones. In South Kavirondo the reform reduced the number from thirty-nine to nine, in North Kavirondo from twenty-five to six.[4] The size of the benches was reduced as well, from dozens of elders in the 1920s to three in the 1950s. A president and sometimes a vice president served each court; they were to be (but did not always restrict themselves to being) *primus inter pares,* guiding cases and sometimes transcribing them, for which they earned higher salaries than other court officials. Elders served on courts within their home area; occasionally presidents or vice presidents were rotated to other courts, but only within their "tribal" areas. African appeals courts were gazetted in the 1930s. Litigants still unsatisfied could appeal further to a district officer and ultimately to the provincial commissioner.

Into the 1930s the administration filled the courts with elder, "traditional" men thought to be the most well versed in "customary law" (those whom scholars have envisioned as typical court members). Younger men knew little, officers believed, and were more likely than their elders to have been corrupted by the modern ways. Britons thought even less of educated youth. In previous years, explained administrator Arthur Phillips in his 1943 study of Kenya's African courts,

It had been felt that these educated young men would be out of touch and out of sympathy with the masses, that their ideas of progress would be ill-balanced, that they would be individualists, likely to exercise an influence prejudicial to the healthy development of the body politic and inimical to what was best in the traditions of the tribe, that they would be hostile to the existing native authorities; in short, that they would be a disturbing element, calculated to introduce disharmony and unrest into the tribal society and to precipitate its disintegration.[5]

Times were changing, however, and administrators began to lose faith in the efficacy of "traditional" elders. As South Kavirondo district officer C. Farquhar Atkins explained in 1944, "On the whole the tribunals fulfill their present functions very adequately, but it is increasingly evident that the standard of education of Presidents and Vice-Presidents requires to be raised more and more to enable the tribunals to carry out properly their functions as criminal courts."[6] Even more desirable were literate men. For district officers to review cases and to avoid the inconvenience and cost of appeals being heard *de novo,* relatively detailed transcripts were required of the tribunals. Some courts employed recording clerks, but—for reasons of economy and to prevent clerks from dominating the courts (a telling acknowledgment of the power of "middle men")—administrators preferred elders able to compose transcripts themselves.[7] A North Nyanza district officer in 1955 expressed his wish that recording clerks be done away with but admitted that this was impossible until educated, literate elders filled the bench. This was surely not the case at the time; indeed, the benches were cluttered with "dead wood."[8]

Increasingly, administrators sought Western-educated and literate elders. Former colonial officials who had in the 1950s overseen the African courts recall that, while some elders steeped in customary law were always wanted on the bench, "progressive" men would compose the majority.[9] Administrators sought out schoolmasters, church elders, public servants, and artisans to serve as elders. Admittedly, such men had little knowledge of customary law, but it was thought that with their broader experiences they had the ability to learn it on the job.[10] Thus, already by the time of Arthur Phillips's 1943 *Report*, the tribunals in Meru (Central Province) had both "ancients" and "moderns," while in South Kavirondo tribunal membership was "representative of the present transitional stage of development, for it include[d] some elders of the old-fashioned illiterate class and others of the modern educated types."[11]

Examining elders' biographies reveals that in the 1940s and 1950s tribunal benches did indeed include increasing numbers of "young progressives."[12] Many elders had taken biblical or Western names, indicative of association with missions and Western schooling and thus also of elite status.[13] The shift toward greater numbers of Christian elders began as early as 1936 in South Kavirondo, and by the next decade elders with Western names composed a majority of new appointments.[14] For example, during a major reorganization of tribunal membership in 1947 at least 19 new men joined the tribunals, 17 of whom had Western names. All told, of the over 200 South Kavirondo elders who served in the 1940s and 1950s for whom we have information, at least 57 percent carried Western names. Another 10 percent are listed only by last names or have first names of indeterminate origin. Combining North and South Kavirondo districts, out of 185 elders who served in the 1940s, 58 percent had western names; of 121 who served in the 1950s, it was 62 percent.

Some elders had not only converted but had also become leaders within their churches. Four elders from South Kavirondo had been Seventh-day Adventist (SDA) teachers. One of these men along with three Christians from North Kavirondo had risen to become elders in their respective churches. The president of the Kisii Appeal Tribunal in 1944 had formerly been an SDA evangelist, while in the same year Pastor Okeyo resigned his tribunal position to return to his true calling.[15]

Only three elders appear to have been selected primarily for their knowledge of "customary law." Primarily, but not solely: they also had knowledge of the local courts system, having served as assessors for the district officer's appeal court. Similarly, another set of elders included an assessor and a former member of an *etureti* council (a Gusii informal dispute-resolution body), evidence of their knowledge of customary law. Yet both men also had other notable achievements on their resumes, making their knowledge of customary law only one of their strengths.

Most court elders had proven themselves through service to the state.[16] Three elders in South Kavirondo had worked in the courts in positions that required bureaucratic knowledge and literacy: one had been a process server, two had been court clerks. Seven men (all of South Kavirondo) had been "indirect rulers": one a headman, three each subchiefs and chiefs. Daniel Murunge, for example, had served successively as translator, chief, and member of the Suba-Kuria Native Tribunal.[17]

Other elders had served on local legislative or advisory bodies. Seven had been members of location advisory councils (LACs) ("democratic and progressive bodies," the South Kavirondo district commissioner said of them in 1947). LACs were chaired by chiefs, and with the taxes they imposed, promoted primary schools, infrastructural improvements, "community development," and so on.[18] At least three elders of North Kavirondo and four of South Kavirondo sat on the more powerful districtwide local native councils (LNCs) (later, African district councils), which the administration held up as training grounds for African leaders. LNCs issued trading licenses, extended loans, imposed taxes, and controlled large sums of money. Councilors were the emerging and quite powerful elite.

Several elders combined church leadership, government employment, and private business, making them among the most "modern" men in colonial western Kenya. Consider the lives of six men, four of South Nyanza and two of North Nyanza:[19]

Thomas Matwetwe, appointed April 1953; formerly SDA teacher, subheadman, trader.

Janai Marita, appointed April 1953; formerly SDA teacher, evangelist, clerk in Medical Department, clerk at Manga African Court, ADC beer canteen manager, LAC member, trader.

Jafeth Guonda, appointed April 1953; formerly SDA teacher, evangelist, *etureti* elder, LAC member, trader.

Ezekiel Mbori, appointed April 1953; formerly tax hut counter, SDA teacher, clerk at cotton store, LAC member.

Joseph Obare, appointed March 1953; formerly in railway administration, 15–20 years Church Missionary Society elder, church instructor, Jeduong Gwen, LAC member.[20]

Samwell Cheptum, appointed May 1954; four years as appeal court assessor, member of the agricultural committee of LAC, ADC roads supervisor in his location.[21]

Isolated from the new colonial world they were not.

Selecting Elders

Despite the importance administrators attached to engaging the right kind of elder, they never developed a single, colony-wide policy for doing so. In fact, methods of selection differed from district to district, from year to year. Provincial commissioners held the final authority to appoint and remove elders but in practice rubber-stamped their district commissioners' recommendations. District commissioners themselves were not always aware of tribunal membership: in 1940 officials in North Kavirondo discovered that their lists of elders were hopelessly out of date, as for some time tribunal members had simply coopted local men when necessary.[22] Even the appointment of a judicial advisor in 1945, charged with shaping tribunal policies, could not harmonize the haphazard local policies.[23]

District commissioners employed myriad methods of identifying potential elders, none ever proving satisfactory. Most sought African input. A few held "elections" in open *barazas* (public meetings) but quickly determined these to be failures. In the late 1930s in Nyeri district (Central Province), open elections were scrapped when it appeared that people had voted for fellow clansmen, giving no weight to (what officers considered to be) candidates' qualifications. The district commissioner of nearby Embu district reported, "[The elders] are really chosen by the chiefs and missionaries, however much we like to think that they are elected in open *baraza* by the people."[24] Administrators also turned to LACs, LNCs, and chiefs for advice. In North Kavirondo, district commissioners consulted chiefs in appointing tribunal presidents and vice presidents; in turn, the presidents, chiefs, and headmen selected the other members.

A more detailed history of South Kavirondo tribunals illustrates the regularity with which administrators adopted and discarded methods of selecting elders. In 1937 at Manga Native Tribunal, a district officer wrote, elders were elected by "popular vote," but who voted and how he did not say.[25] The district commissioner in 1940 took advice from a LNC subcommittee, although within two years the full LNC was involved in the selection of elders. This plan too was discarded. Early in 1943 District Officer Atkins undertook a procedure suggested by the provincial commissioner and approved by the LNC, and one that quickly attracted popular complaints. In February Atkins and his translator traveled to the tribunals to meet with the chiefs and headmen of each jurisdiction. At these conferences chiefs put forward names, most of which were, despite some initial dissension, agreed to unanimously. Several former elders were not returned to the bench at Manga, including former chief Muriru and the former interpreters Nyakundi and Kiriago. Ibrehemu Onyangi of Kuja Native Tribunal was the only tribunal president not retained; his name was in fact not even advanced to be a member of the court.[26]

Complaints were lodged quickly enough. Onyangi wrote to the provincial commissioner, K. L. Hunter, distressed over his initial meeting with Atkins. He had inquired of Atkins what his mistake had been that he had not been retained. Atkins told him that it was not the district commissioner but the chiefs and headmen who had made the decision. If that were so, Onyangi explained to Hunter, he understood full well why the chiefs had voted him down: Onyangi had always refused their incessant demands for preferential treatment. For his part, Atkins informed Hunter that Onyangi had been "suspected of corrupt practices." In his reply to Onyangi, Hunter reiterated that it was not the administration but his own African leaders who selected elders; perhaps, he told Onyangi, "you did not please them."[27]

A longer letter of complaint to the provincial commissioner came from anonymous persons under the jurisdiction of the Manga Native Tribunal. On the day announced for selecting elders, the letter went, large crowds assembled awaiting Atkins's arrival. Rather than address the throngs, however, Atkins retired with the chiefs and subheadmen. When they emerged later, the people asked when the selection of elders would begin. Atkins told them that the matter had been completed, climbed into his vehicle, and drove off. As the car disappeared, mutterings of discontent came from the crowd. The chiefs simply laughed. What had caused the masses to grumble and the chiefs to gloat? The new elders received their appointments, the anonymous petitioners charged, because they had proffered bribes to the chiefs. The bribes paid off handsomely, since the chiefs had "the strength and cunning to have the leaders of government listen to everything they say!"[28]

Little satisfaction would come to the disgruntled subjects. They first wrote to Atkins, but as with Onyangi, he dismissed their complaints. The petitioners had concluded, they told Hunter, that Atkins could do nothing to help them "because he agree[d] with every false word which the chiefs [told] him." Hunter was unmoved. In his reply (to whom it was sent is unclear, given the writers' anonymity), he pointed out that the system had been agreed to by their representatives on the LNC. The provincial commissioner challenged them to bring forward specific examples of corruption but warned that if they made false charges they would be called to justice. He turned away their complaints of Atkins's inaction: "Know that it is the custom of the government, if you write me a letter it must go through the hands of Bwana D.C."[29]

The administration continued to cast about for a satisfactory procedure by which to identify potential elders. In 1947, the district commissioner and the district officer detailed to courts work suggested that names be put forward by LACs and in open *barazas*. From among these the district officer, in consultation with the newly formed Native Tribunal Advisory Committee, would select tribunal members.[30] This method appears not to have been employed, however. A few months later elders were selected via the "queue method," by which people lined up behind their favored candidate—although the district commissioner insisted that these "elections" were simply a means of gauging public opinion.[31] Nonetheless, the situation remained confused. In 1949 the provincial native courts officer queried the district commissioner about an entirely new bench recently "appointed" to Kuja; the district commissioner explained that of those "nominated for reelection" only the best were "re-elected."[32] The next year, in a report titled "Election: South Nyanza Appeal Tribunal," a district officer "recommend[ed]" a list of those who should be retained or retired.[33] Later in the decade it appears a more regularized system was in place, with district commissioners selecting elders for three-year terms after discussions with LACs or the LNC.[34]

What remained constant was the administration's reliance on the input of elite Africans, who also favored "progressive" elders. In North Nyanza the Kimili LAC nominated as elders three fellow LAC members (one of whom was also a teacher and another an employee of the chief's office), two traders, one former tribunal member, and two "volunteers" (the meaning of which is unclear). For vice president and president of the tribunal, the LAC recommended a former tribunal vice-president, an "ex-olukongo" (headman), a "volunteer," a warrant officer of the East African Command, and Benjamin Kaptain, who was school supervisor, secretary to the LAC, and a member of the Northern Nzoia Joint Local Council. All thirteen—save, perhaps, one—had Western names.[35] Similarly, to choose from among the names advanced by the North Nyanza LNC, the district commissioner called a "selection committee," perhaps, as elsewhere, composed of chiefs and headmen. The committee thought Samwell Cheptum and James Chepkoi "easily the best candidates." The latter, although "a man of integrity and fairly knowledgeable about indigenous law," was "hardly literate and rather too old and slow." Cheptum, in contrast, "appeared to be both knowledgeable on indigenous law and quicker witted." His four years as appeal court assessor, service on his LAC's agricultural committee, and current employment as ADC roads supervisor put his candidacy over the top.[36] Thus it was that "progressive" Africans joined with administrators to remake the courts in their own image.

Letter Writers

Some members of the "modernizing" class also applied directly to the administration requesting appointment. These letter writers were all of the type with which the administration hoped to fill the courts: literate (many in English), often government or church employees. Nonetheless, the administration had no use for these men.

As did administrators, letter writers pointed out the tribunals' need for younger, literate, educated men with experience in the new world and economy. As one wrote, "I am fully aware of all the radical changes which are at present operating [in] the country and the causes of them."[37] Benjamin Kaptain (who would be nominated by the Kimili LAC) wrote, "[a]s we all know . . . Government wants educated people who are good, keen and skilled in the work."[38] Hudson Sanja asked the provincial commissioner for a seat on a tribunal, pointing out, "All educated citizens have greatly supported my application of becoming a member to their court. They are of opinion that this court at this time ought to have an educated member with modern views, who has a wide scope about the decision of any case." He suggested that, if he were appointed, he "might try to give [older members] fair advices about some cases where errors usually occur."[39] George Otieno, writing in support of Esau Khamati, pointed to illiteracy as one factor that "impede[d] African progress," complicating "law in a changing African society": "Illiterate or semi-literate elders versed only in existing customary law, are not well fitted to create or cope with principles of law in civil cases of a new type, such as those which arise out of commercial intercourse." As did administrators, however, Otieno admitted that younger men could not entirely supplant "traditional" elders, else "the tribunal [might] lose the confidence of illiterate and backward people."[40]

The letter writers' backgrounds were much the same as those who served on the courts. Given that they were literate—they had written their own letters—all had had some level of schooling, and many had worked or were currently working for the government. The applicants included:

Joel Owanda, letter of April 2, 1948, requesting position on Mbale Native Tribunal: educated at Government African School, Kakamega; after five years passed Standard VI; poll tax clerk for five years; past three years senior clerk at a sisal estate; thirty years old.[41]

Pascal Nabwana, letter of February 6, 1948, requesting presidency of North Kavirondo appeal tribunal: taught at mission 1915–35; teacher at Jeannes School, 1936–41; member, LNC since 1931; member, District Education Board; member, Finance Committee, Joint Nyanza LNC; forty-six years old.[42]

James Agola, letter of April 15, 1950, requesting position on Nambare Native Tribunal: Kenya police 1918–30, retired as sergeant; member, Municipal Council, Eldoret, 1931–37; currently Nairobi municipal African housing officer; chairman of Baluhya Association; member, African Starehe Village Committee; fifty years old.[43]

Despite their pleas—or, rather, because of them—not a single letter writer appears ever to have served on the tribunals.[44] Administrative officers were often brusque in their replies, if they replied at all. In response to Hudson Sanja's 1948 letter, the provincial commissioner affirmed that appointments were never made without consultation with the local people. In February 1952, Sanja again requested a tribunal seat; he was "forced to write" another missive in April, however, noting, "as a matter of fact I have heard no reply." Gently, he acknowledged, "[I] had been doubting whether my letter safely reached your hand."[45] His February letter and a copy of a response are in the archive, but the administration appears entirely to have ignored his April letter.[46] Another man, requesting that Daudi (i.e., David) Were be returned to the bench, was told by the provincial commissioner that "unless there were very good reasons, [he] would certainly not interfere" with the recommendation of the LNC. Were could expect no sympathy: "If Daudi has not been selected, he must accept the position and seek employment elsewhere."[47]

At first blush the administration's response to the letter writers is surprising. These men clearly had the qualifications the administration sought: they were educated, had wide experience in the "modern" world, and had served in leadership positions, often with the government. Their letters were uniformly polite, even supplicating. In his February 1948 letter, Sanja promised, "I shall do all I can to see that I work as a faithfull [sic] servant to my government, with the view of being a helpful servant to the government as well as my people." He ended with the standard administrative closing, "I am your most obedient servant."[48]

Put in the larger context of colonial Kenya, administrative dismissal of letter writers is less surprising. In part, this was due to the policy of soliciting African advice in selecting elders; at best applicants were advised to set their names before their LACs for consideration.[49] The rejection of letter writers was also a manifestation of a long-standing distrust of Africans who approached British administrators directly rather than through their African "indirect rulers." Officers appreciated leaders but not politicians; they appointed men for whom the populace voted but distrusted those who canvassed for votes. If LACs or LNCs had been delegated the authority to provisionally select elders, then select they would. Men who applied instead to the administration challenged state policy and the methods of indirect rule itself. Such men were "politicians," the most threatening of the administration's perceived enemies.[50] "Politicians" were those who refused to accept their position as subjects not just of the Crown but also of their chiefs and established councils. Letter writers and politicians presumed to approach the administration, if not as equals, then as men of a class: literate, Christian, "modern," and perhaps not constrained by the limits placed on the "backward" masses.

Men already loyally serving the state had better luck applying for court positions. Paul Nyangoto Ogeturenga had been a subchief in Gusiiland since the 1930s. In 1957 he called on the district commissioner and queried how he, a literate subchief, could earn only two shillings per month, the same as a lowly state-employed cook. The district commissioner took Ogeturenga's request for a seat before the local elders, who approved of him. As a final test, the administrator asked Ogeturenga a particularly difficult question pertaining to inheritance, one that might come before the courts. Ogeturenga answered correctly, and he took up his post at Manga African Court.[51] Similarly discontent with his salary as subchief, Nyasani Omanua came to the district commissioner to tender his resignation. The district commissioner, intent on retaining a good employee, placed a stack of bills on the table for Nyasani and asked him to remain on as subchief. Unimpressed, Nyasani turned and walked out of the office without touching the money. Nyasani's courage in refusing the money and defying Bwana was celebrated in song. Nyasani's integrity struck the district commissioner as well, who later called him for an interview. As Nyasani's character had already been proved, the interview consisted only of demonstrating his literacy by way of writing the district commissioner's name. He proceeded to join Manga African Court in 1953.[52]

Corruption in the Courts

If Nyasani's integrity was beyond reproach, this could not be said of all his fellow elders. Among British observers reports of bribery in the courts were quite common. One district officer in 1938 noted that one of his duties when visiting native tribunals was hearing *shauris* (disputes) involving the tribunals themselves.[53] According to the Nyanza provincial commissioner in 1946, "bribery . . . amongst the [Gusii] tribe, [was] one of the causes of [public] dissatisfaction" with the native tribunals.[54] One former colonial official (who served in the 1950s) recalled that some elders accepted bribes, but that it was not a major problem; a colleague of the 1940s and 1950s thought bribery rather common, and the administration had constantly to be on guard against it.[55] Phillip and Iona Mayer, anthropologists in Gusiiland in the late 1940s, observed that bribery was common in all Gusii litigation, especially land cases.[56] Even those who defended the courts did so only half-heartedly. In 1955 the South Nyanza district commissioner considered the tribunals to be honest, perhaps the most honest in Kenya, but he readily admitted that some of them made unfair judgments.[57]

Only a handful of court elders, however, were ever convicted of corruption. In 1941 District Commissioner D. Storrs-Fox checked a boundary dispute previously heard by Eliazaro Okwoyo of the Kisii Appeal Tribunal. Storrs-Fox "found that the judgment was so contrary to justice and to common sense" that he asked Okwoyo if he had been bribed. Okwoyo "admitted this fairly readily and seemed ashamed of himself." Okwoyo's contriteness served him well as the district commissioner recommended only a temporary suspension.[58] Storrs-Fox also requested the dismissal of Kurate, president of Suba-Kuria Tribunal, for two offenses: falsifying records by wrongfully adding nine head of cattle to the record; falsifying the record of a case in which he was cited as defendant by causing his name to be deleted and the name of another person substituted. Following procedure, the provincial commissioner recommended that they both be tried before a European magistrate and, if convicted, fined.[59]

The attempt to punish Kurate and Okwoyo and, it was hoped, discourage other elders from exploiting their powers failed in the face of the legal "technicalities" that so distressed administrators. Okwoyo withdrew his admission of guilt, and on technical grounds (involving who was and was not present at the time) his confession was declared inadmissible. Left with only circumstantial evidence (which could suggest either corruption or "mental deficiency"), the district commissioner instead bypassed the judiciary and used his administrative prerogative to keep Okwoyo on suspension.[60] Kurate was convicted and fined three hundred shillings, but on revision the Supreme Court struck down the judgment. Nonetheless, the administration decided that Kurate had been involved in other "irregularities" and dismissed him from his post as tribunal president. The absence of suitable men, however, prevented the administration from taking harsher methods. Kurate was given the opportunity of returning as a tribunal member after one year. Okwoyo also survived. The provincial commissioner firmly believed him to be "an undesirable character to have as a member of a Native Tribunal." Nonetheless, he told the district commissioner, "[u]nless you know of a better man, he may be reinstated when his year of suspension has run out."[61]

Not just Britons but Africans as well believed the courts thoroughly corrupt. Older Gusii today are virtually unanimous that court elders were open to bribes. Thus the poor and the weak were less likely to prevail than the wealthy and powerful, and those on principle unwilling to bribe went down in defeat. Africans clearly distinguished between bribes and the customary gifts litigants presented to precolonial councils of elders. Gifts were presented in public and signaled respect. Bribery, in contrast, was done in private and was intended only to influence the elders' decisions. One informant recalls having given a sixty-shilling bribe in relation to a land case, not to honor the elder but to assure himself of victory. The distinction between gifts and bribes was clear to litigants, the public at large, and certainly the elders as well.

Some commoners filed complaints with the state. Nyabiya of South Kavirondo charged that Chief Musa Nyandusi, his headmen, and the wealthy were "involved in confusing many cases." "[P]oor people," in contrast, could not afford bribes and thus "frequently [lost] their lands." The elite were "sometimes misleading the Administration," Nyabiya continued, "by falsehood methods."[62] Lawrence Aroga alleged that only by bribery could one get a positive result from the South Nyanza Native Appeals Court.[63] Two men of North Kavirondo complained that in transcribing cases tribunal president Samwel twisted litigants' words and invented evidence, thereby "robbing" them of their "shambas [farms]." Moreover, the other elders deferred to Samwel as president. "Alas!" the petitioners wrote, "Did the Government put him there to help other people or to rob them of their shambas? Is that justice?"[64] But without firm evidence administrators rarely followed up on such complaints.[65]

If a few letter writers could not move the administration, more widespread public outcry could. In late 1946 the South Kavirondo administration established the Native Tribunal Advisory Committee (NTAC). It was staffed by Paulo Mboya (the most trusted "progressive" in the province), chiefs Musa Nyandusi and Gideon Magak, John Kebaso (a local politician whom the administration was trying to coopt), Paulo Ondiek (member of the South Kavirondo Appeal Tribunal), Charles Wedo (president of a Luo court, Bura Rongo), and Asha Onyiego (by 1956 chief of Majoge). The large number of appeals made from Gusii tribunals to the South Kavirondo Appeals Tribunal was the first issue put before the NTAC, and a subcommittee (of Magak, Onyiego, and Kebaso) was formed to investigate the matter.[66] The subcommittee held several public meetings and quickly concluded that appeals were so common because bribery in the courts of first instance was so rife. "People informed us," the committee wrote, "that the source why there are so many appeals [from the Kuja Native Tribunal] is because bribe matters and not justice." Moreover, at a meeting held in regard to the Manga Native Tribunal, the first item put forward by the attendees "was that no one could be heard by Tribunal Member unless he paid bribe."[67]

The subcommittee's conclusions were not challenged. The full NTAC strongly endorsed their findings, and District Officer Low, charged with overseeing the local courts, came round to the same opinion.[68] Previously he had tended to consider rumors of corruption "exaggerated since there [were] so few complaints" made to the administration. On the other hand, he mused, the actual exchanges were normally conducted in secrecy, and since all the parties could be prosecuted, to lay a complaint would be to incriminate oneself. Moreover, Low himself had recently held public meetings to discuss corruption in the courts, and "[i]nevitably [attendees] brought the discussion round to bribery." Several had offered specific examples, one man in fact admitting to having twice bribed tribunal elders. Low concluded that bribery in the Manga Native Tribunal "was common," at least "between the elders and uneducated litigants."[69] Low's district commissioner did not disagree, and later that year the provincial commissioner concurred that the courts were rotten with corruption by way of bribery.[70]

Administrators devised many (ultimately ineffectual) methods of eradicating bribery. In 1936 a district officer forced the elders at the Kuja Native Tribunal to take an oath involving the sacrifice of a sheep rather than the less powerful "solemn oath" they preferred.[71] The provincial commissioner in 1947 suggested that greater pageantry would emphasize the gravity of elders' duties. Oaths of office, administrators hoped, might also prevent bribery. The 1949 induction ceremony in South Kavirondo was to be attended by the district commissioner and the provincial commissioner. Court elders were to take their oaths from an SDA pastor, a priest, or (if "pagan") from a district officer:

I . . . do swear by Almighty God that I will well and truly serve His Majesty King George in the Office of Tribunal Elder. I bind myself to be impartial in all cases; and not to favour either party to any suit; but honestly and fearlessly to every case according to its merits.

I solemnly swear that I will never accept any bribe directly or indirectly from any party to any dispute whether such suit has or has not been filed.

So help me God.[72]

In 1955 the provincial commissioner called the swearing-in ceremony "an occasion of some importance," one for which he would "wear full dress."[73] Although Europeans found the ceremonies impressive, court elders were not impeded from accepting bribes directly or indirectly.

Administrators thought that reforming elders' terms of service might help eradicate bribery. The NTAC explained that the rotating panel system contributed to bribery since "those elders who ha[d] been waiting at home for a long time" without regular pay took bribes upon being recalled to the bench "because they need[ed] the money."[74] Low, the DC, and the PC all concurred that the panel system must be replaced by permanent benches appointed for three year terms.[75] Raising pay rates, administrators hoped, would also eliminate elders' financial dependence on bribes and might also help attract and retain the more educated Africans who might otherwise seek employment elsewhere.[76] Some advocated identifying promising youth and educating them for future courts work, perhaps even sponsoring some to Makerere College in Uganda.[77] Administrators encouraged Africans to think of courts work as a career rather than as a steppingstone toward other government positions.[78] That accusations of bribery continued unabated reveals the ineffectiveness of these reforms.

The only anticorruption measures that achieved any real success were undertaken by Africans rather than by Britons. Upon his appointment to Manga African Court, a celebration was held at Nyasani Omanua's home. Beer was brewed and animals slaughtered. The local elders pulled Nyasani aside to advise him on how to settle cases and to offer him their blessing. The elders also vowed that curses would befall him if he indulged in corruption. That his family had prospered, Nyasani's wife pointed out in 2002, demonstrates his honest dealings as a court elder. In contrast, an appeal court elder known for taking bribes and unjustly imprisoning people ended his days mentally unhinged and eating produce otherwise left to rot in the market, considered by many to be his just reward.

The African court system in western Kenya (and undoubtedly elsewhere) involved two sets of intermediaries. The first were the court elders themselves, who mediated commoners' access to the authority of the state. Marking land boundaries, reclaiming bridewealth cattle, asserting custody over women and children—all of these were done through the African courts. Moreover, the African courts could call on *askaris* (state-employed police/armed retainers) to attach property, detain suspects, and imprison convicts. Complaints of corruption illustrate just how important the courts were: one does not bribe the powerless.

The second set of intermediaries were the elite Africans who advised Britons on whom to select as elders. These men—chiefs and headmen, translators, members of LACs and LNCs—generated the knowledge on which officials drew to make "informed" decisions. In contrast Africans unable to enter into a regularized, bureaucratic relationship with the state had little hope of becoming court elders. Those forced to write letters of application wrote in vain.

Court elders in Kenya were not culled from the group of men we might have assumed. Neither were they chosen by the methods we might have suspected. They were of a new generation who were not selected to and did not intend to act as bulwarks against the collapse of the "traditional" world. While they tended to favor the claims of senior men over women and junior men, they did not do so unquestioningly.[79] This is not to say that court elders were impartial. Bribery deeply compromised the dispensation of justice. Similarly, examining cases involving immovable property might expose class bias, as is shown by Maurice Amutabi. Court elders were powerful intermediaries; this essay is a step toward a better understanding of them and their place in African history.

Notes

My thanks to Richard Roberts, Emily Lynn Osborn, Benjamin Lawrance, the other members of the Stanford conference, and the anonymous readers for the University of Wisconsin Press for their comments and suggestions. Thanks also to Calvin White Jr. for his editing assistance. At various points support for the research that produced this essay came from a Graduate Fellowship, Academy for Educational Development, and the College of Liberal Arts, University of Mississippi.

1. See the chapters by Ginio and Amutabi in this volume.
2. I provide a more detailed history of the courts in "Administrative Policy and African Courts in Colonial Kenya," unpublished paper, September 2002.
3. Hailey, *African Survey*, 389; Morris and Read, *Indirect Rule*, 141.
4. Phillips, *Report on Native Tribunals*, 17.
5. Phillips, *Report on Native Tribunals*, 187. Officers in South Kavirondo also passed out tribunal seats as "consolation prizes to former Government employees who ha[d] outlived their usefulness." Kenya National Archive (hereafter KNA), Nairobi, Kenya, South Kavirondo District Annual Report, 1939. Wilson reported that court elders in Central Kavirondo also included former loyal government servants. Wilson, *Luo Customary Law*, 3.
6. Quoted in Phillips, *Report on Native Tribunals*, 33, and see also 27, 34.
7. Provincial African Courts Officer Nyanza to District Commissioner South Nyanza, January 28, 1953; District Officer North Nyanza to Provincial Commissioner Nyanza, January 21, 1955; Provincial Commissioner Nyanza to District Officer North Nyanza, January 26, 1955, all in KNA, L&O 2/1. On the power of court clerks, see Amutabi, this volume.
8. District Officer North Nyanza to Provincial Commissioner Nyanza, January 22, 1955, KNA, L&O 2/1. Similarly in 1953 the South Nyanza DC complained of "too much dead-wood" in the ranks of the chiefs. KNA, South Nyanza District Annual Report, 1953. The shift toward more "progressive" elders proceeded along with appointing more "progressive" chiefs. At least four

elders, however, left the courts for more lucrative positions as chiefs: two men resigned from the South Nyanza Appeal Tribunal (in 1946 and 1955), while Mateyo Ratemo left his position as vice president of Kuja African Court to begin a fourteen-year rule as chief of Bassi.

9. Personal communication, Oliver Knowles, December 11, 1997; personal communication, "E" (anonymity requested), January 23, 1998; personal communication, T. A. Watts, January 27, 1998.

10. District Officer North Nyanza to Provincial Commissioner Nyanza, January 22, 1955, L&O 2/1; Personal communication, T. A. Watts, January 27, 1998.

11. Phillips, *Report on Native Tribunals*, 97, 32.

12. Most of what follows comes from KNA, L&O files 1/1/4/1, 2/1, 2/1/1, 2/13.

13. As late as the 1950s very few South Kavirondo Africans had converted to Christianity, especially among the Gusii. As churches almost exclusively controlled schooling (the key to the best-paying jobs), Christian elders were among the most elite men in the region.

14. Regarding the shift in South Kavirondo, see K. L. Hunter, Record of a baraza, Kitutu, October 26, 1936, KNA, Adm 12/4/1; Lists of Baraza Elders, June 1936, KNA, L&O 1/1/2/2.

15. Phillips, *Report on Native Tribunals*, 32.

16. We know of only one man who had served in the military, Stephen Akuma of South Kavirondo. In uniform from 1942 to 1947, Akuma excelled, rising to the rank of sergeant by the time of his discharge at the relatively young age of twenty-nine. Untitled document, c. April 1953, KNA, L&O 2/1/3.

17. Kjerland, "Cattle Breed, Shillings Don't," 99.

18. KNA, South Kavirondo District Annual Report, 1947; South Nyanza District Annual Report, 1959.

19. The first four come from an untitled document, ca. April 1953, KNA, L&O 2/1/3.

20. District Commissioner North Nyanza to Provincial Commissioner Nyanza, March 2, 1953, KNA, L&O 2/1/1.

21. District Commissioner North Nyanza to Provincial Commissioner Nyanza, May 19, 1954, KNA, L&O 2/1/1.

22. Phillips, *Report on Native Tribunals*, 19.

23. Shadle, "Administrative Policy."

24. Quoted in Phillips, *Report on Native Tribunals*, 79.

25. Hunter, Safari Diary, August 1937, KNA, Adm 12/4/1.

26. Atkins, Memorandum on the Election of the New Native Tribunals in February 1943, in District Commissioner South Kavirondo to Provincial Commissioner Nyanza, March 29, 1943, KNA, L&O 1/1/4/1.

27. Onyangi to Provincial Commissioner Nyanza, March 20, 1943; handwritten note by District Commissioner on copy of letter; Provincial Commissioner to Onyangi, March 30, 1943, all in KNA, L&O 1/1/4/1.

28. "Nyaribari, Kitutu, and N. Mugirango," to Provincial Commissioner Nyanza, April 22, 1943, KNA, L&O 1/1/4/1. The names are those of the locations under Manga's jurisdiction.

29. Acting Provincial Commissioner Nyanza to "Mr. Nyaribari, Kitutu, and N. Mugirango," May 4, 1943, KNA, L&O 1/1/4/1. For at least one location, however, some good may have come of their complaints. In April the district commissioner wrote a letter to the provincial commissioner, titled "Election of Native Tribunal Elders." An alteration of boundaries between two subheadmen required a reapportionment of court elders. When one new elder refused to take the oath of office, "a substitute was called for" and "the people chose another man." Public input had been achieved after all, at least for that moment. District Commissioner South Kavirondo to Provincial Commissioner Nyanza, April 20, 1943, KNA, L&O 1/1/4/1.

30. District Commissioner South Kavirondo to Acting Provincial Commissioner Nyanza, March 18, 1947, KNA, L&O 2/1/3.

31. *Sauti ya Bomani,* July 6, 1947, 1; District Commissioner South Kavirondo to Acting Provincial Commissioner, July 31, 1947, KNA, L&O 2/1/3. During the 1930s and 1940s LNC members were elected in the same manner. Mboya, *Utawala na Maendeleo,* 8–9.

32. Provincial Native Courts Officer Nyanza to District Commissioner South Nyanza, January 14, 1949, and reply, February 7, 1949, both in KNA, L&O 2/1/3.

33. District Commissioner South Kavirondo to Provincial Commissioner Nyanza, November 9, 1950, KNA, L&O 2/1/3.

34. Provincial Commissioner Nyanza to District Commissioners Nyanza, January 20, 1953, KNA, L&O 2/1. Oliver Knowles, a former district officer in charge of courts in South Nyanza, recalled that elders in the 1950s were appointed by the district commissioner in consultation with the African district council. Personal communication, December 11, 1997.

35. Chief Henry Nakisa to District Commissioner North Nyanza, February 17, 1951, KNA, L&O 2/1/1.

36. District Commissioner North Nyanza to Provincial Commissioner Nyanza, May 19, 1954, KNA, L&O 2/1/1.

37. Letter to Provincial Commissioner Nyanza, February 16, 1948, KNA, L&O 2/1/1. The author is unknown, as the second page of the letter is missing.

38. Benjamin Kaptain to District Commissioner North Nyanza, February 17, 1951, KNA, L&O 2/1/1.

39. Hudson Sanja to Provincial Commissioner Nyanza, April 3, 1952, KNA, L&O 2/1/1.

40. George Otieno to District Commissioner North Nyanza, May 1950, KNA, L&O 2/1/1.

41. Owanda to Provincial Commissioner Nyanza, April 2, 1948, KNA, L&O 2/1/3.

42. Nabwana to Provincial Commissioner Nyanza, KNA, February 6, 1948, L&O 2/1/3.

43. Agola to District Commissioner North Nyanza, April 15, 1950, KNA, L&O 2/1/3.

44. Terence Gavaghan, who served as a district officer in North Kavirondo from November 1947 to October 1948, recalls having "met a politically active Local Native Councillor and Native Court Chairman [President?] called Pascal Nabwana. His name and influence cropped up constantly in all kinds of dubious connections." I have found no archival evidence, however, of Nabwana having served on a court. Gavaghan, *Of Lions and Dung Beetles*, 113.

45. Hudson Sanja to Provincial Commissioner Nyanza, April 3, 1952, KNA, L&O 2/1/1.

46. Hudson Sanja to Provincial Commissioner Nyanza, n.d. [but February 16,1948]; Provincial Commissioner Nyanza to Hudson Sanja, March 1, 1948, KNA, L&O 2/1/1.

47. Provincial Commissioner Nyanza to Daniel Zakaria, May 3, 1948, KNA, L&O 2/1/1.

48. Sanja to Provincial Commissioner Nyanza, n.d. [but February 16, 1948], KNA, L&O 2/1/1.

49. Only one letter writer, Benjamin Kaptain, had also gained LAC approval, but its recommendation appears to have been vetoed by the administration. Kaptain to District Commissioner North Nyanza, February 17, 1951; Chief Henry Nakisa to District Commissioner North Nyanza, February 17, 1951, both in KNA, L&O 2/1/1.

50. Hudson Sanja understood administrative prejudices and hoped to placate them. In his April 1952 letter, he assured the provincial commissioner, "I am entirely out of the political arena. As I told you, I am no longer interested in the today's politics, now operating in N[orth] N[yanza] District."

51. Interview with Ogeturenga by Ben Omwega, October 24, 1997.

52. Interview with Nyasani by Omwega, October 22, 1997; interview with Nyasani by Ben Omwega and Brett Shadle, June 2002.

53. KNA, South Kavirondo District Annual Report, 1938.

54. Provincial Commissioner Nyanza to District Commissioner South Kavirondo, February 4, 1946, KNA, L&O 2/1/3. At the end of the year, however, the district commissioner reported that nearly all the complaints of corruption were too general to follow up on. KNA, South Kavirondo District Annual Report, 1940.

55. Personal communication, Oliver Knowles, December 11, 1997; personal communication, "E" (anonymity requested), January 23, 1998.

56. Mayer and Mayer, "Land Law in the Making," 68.

57. KNA, South Nyanza District Annual Report, 1955. Such opinions were not limited to Nyanza Province. The district commissioner of Kiambu (Central) reported in 1949 that he had turned out all tribunal elders, despite his desire to

keep the better ones. Accusations of bribery were so widespread, he wrote, it had become impossible to know which men were guilty and which were innocent. District Commissioner Kiambu to Provincial Commissioner Central, ca. Jan. 1949, KNA, MAA 6/33.

58. District Commissioner South Kavirondo to Provincial Commissioner Nyanza, May 2, 1941, KNA, L&O 1/1/4/1.

59. Provincial Commissioner Nyanza to District Commissioner South Kavirondo, May 7, 1941, KNA, L&O 1/1/4/1.

60. District Commissioner South Kavirondo to Provincial Commissioner Nyanza, May 20, 1941, KNA, L&O 1/1/4/1.

61. Provincial Commissioner Nyanza to District Commissioner South Kavirondo, September 4, 1941, KNA, L&O 1/1/4/1. One year earlier a district officer had discovered several men who had been imprisoned for some weeks. The district officer wrote that he "strongly suspected victimization" of them by the tribunal president and the chief. The only action taken was to demote the president. District Officer South Kavirondo, "Complaint," December 13, 1940, in District Commissioner South Kavirondo to Provincial Commissioner Nyanza, December 14, 1940; Provincial Commissioner Nyanza to District Commissioner South Kavirondo, December 18, 1940; District Commissioner South Kavirondo to Provincial Commissioner Nyanza, December 27, 1940, all in KNA, L&O 1/1/4/1.

62. Nyabiya s/o Anyona to Registrar, Supreme Court, October 1, 1952, KNA, ARC (MAA) 2/9/16 I. See also N. R. Arina, African Assistant Administrative Officer, Kericho, to Chief Native Commissioner, July 23, 1951, KNA, RR 1/4.

63. Lawrence Aroga to Sub-Committee of the Native Courts Bill, July 20, 1951, KNA, RR 1/4.

64. Manueli Odera and Nyogeza Lejoi to Chief Native Commissioner, January 16, 1953, KNA, ARC (MAA) 2/9/16 I.

65. KNA, South Kavirondo District Annual Report, 1946.

66. Minutes of NTAC meeting, 12 Feb. 1947, KNA, L&O 2/1/3.

67. "Report of the sub-committee," January 24, 1947, KNA, L&O 2/1/3.

68. Full NTAC endorsement is recorded in Minutes of NTAC meeting, February 12, 1947, KNA, L&O 2/1/3.

69. Low to District Commissioner South Kavirondo, March 4, 1947, KNA, L&O 2/1/3.

70. District Commissioner South Kavirondo to Provincial Commissioner Nyanza, March 18, 1947, KNA, L&O 2/1/3; Provincial Commissioner Nyanza to District Commissioners Nyanza, October 6, 1947, KNA, L&O 2/1.

71. Safari Diary, 1936, KNA, DP 30/24.

72. Winser, District Officer, "Swearing in Ceremony," February 22, 1949, KNA, L&O 2/1/3.

73. Acting Provincial Commissioner Nyanza to District Commissioner North Nyanza, May 14, 1955, KNA, L&O 2/1/1.

74. Minutes of NTAC meeting, February 12, 1947, KNA, L&O 2/1/3. See also Phillips, *Report on Native Tribunals*, 100.

75. Low to District Commissioner South Kavirondo, 4 Mar. 1947; District Commissioner South Kavirondo to Provincial Commissioner Nyanza, 18 Mar. 1947; Acting Provincial Commissioner Nyanza to District Commissioner South Kavirondo, 2 Apr. 1947, all in KNA, L&O 2/1/3. See also remarks of Nyeri District Commissioner, quoted in Phillips, *Report*, 41.

76. Regarding increased pay as an incentive, see Provincial Commissioner Nyanza to District Commissioners, October 6, 1947, KNA, L&O 2/1. The point regarding better pay as a means of retaining educated Africans was also made in regard to clerks assigned to chiefs. KNA, South Nyanza District Annual Reports 1951, 1952.

77. Phillips, *Report on Native Tribunals*, 187, 194; Nyanza District Commissioners' Meeting, April 5-6, 1945, KNA, Adm 3/2/2. See also Phillips, "Future of Customary Law in Africa," 99.

78. Native Courts Officer to District Commissioner Kiambu, July 2, 1951, KNA, MAA 6/22; Provincial Commissioner Nyanza to District Commissioners Nyanza, November 15, 1952, KNA, RR 1/6; R. E. Robinson, " Administration of African Customary Law," 162.

79. Shadle, "Bridewealth and Female Consent."

Power and Influence of African Court Clerks and Translators in Colonial Kenya

The Case of Khwisero Native (African) Court, 1946–1956

MAURICE NYAMANGA AMUTABI

In this chapter I historicize the power and influence of African court officials in colonial Kenya. I problematize judicial bias as it was unleashed upon uneducated Africans by their privileged kindred within the colonial courts. Colonial courts and other judicial issues constitute an insufficiently studied area of Kenyan history. The records of African officials at the African Court at Khwisero in colonial Kenya and the broader dynamics of the colonial system reveal how courts were susceptible to manipulation by African elites. This flies in the face of the prevailing notions in Kenyan colonial history, where the colonial court system has often been portrayed as an instrument of whites, where only whites were manipulative. Such discourses have presented colonial courts as well meaning and properly organized institutions that competently discharged their duties of maintaining law and order efficiently and effectively within a settler society that favored white interests. In these narratives all African actors are often portrayed as victims, effectively masking the violence of African perpetrators and leaving hierarchies and layers of difference intact. They do not interrogate sites of privilege and domination among and between the Africans in the courts.

The colonial courts operated under the national chief executive (governor) and did not function as separate entities under the judiciary until independence in 1963.[1] Rather, the colonial courts were centers of power and privilege, feared sites, replete with structures of patronage and favoritism, many of which privileged the emerging African elite at the expense of the underprivileged Africans in effectively exploited social networks. In this chapter I adduce a dramatic court case involving two African protagonists. One is Washington Atamba Lusuli, who was educated, spoke Swahili and English, and had worked as a medical assistant in the colonial army. The other is Ariton Amuchuku Estambale, whose occupation—other than as church leader—was that of a thatcher. At the center of this drama was a court official, Caleb Asituywa, who epitomizes the power of African intermediaries. These two, Lusuli and Estambale, did battle at the Khwisero Native Court, where Asituywa worked. I use Asituywa to problematize the role of intermediaries in the colonial system in Kenya. While not claiming that this manipulation of the justice system by intermediaries was typical of all courts in colonial Kenya, I argue that Lusuli's education and knowledge of English and Kiswahili and his connection to the court officials gave him an advantage over uneducated Estambale. I contend that this relationship—of educated over uneducated, of connected over unconnected, as well as mediation and influence by those in the service of the colonial system— is a historicization of binaries that existed in colonial Kenya and can be transposed to other colonial situations in Africa.

What one finds is that intrigue, chicanery, and partisanship took place and were witnessed at the Khwisero African Court during this case involving the two factions of the African Interior Church (AIC). The case aroused much interest in the whole of Western Kenya, as the AIC had acquired many followers.[2] The African court clerks took sides in this case. My interest lies with the problems of translation, transcription, interpretation, and clerical inaccuracies emanating from African officials in the colonial courts at Khwisero between 1946 and 1956. This evidence is cross-checked against oral testimonies of litigants, both victims and beneficiaries of the "justice" system.

Underlying my exploration of this court case, filed at Khwisero by the erstwhile Lusuli against the unsuspecting Estambale, are two sets of theoretical assumptions that I would like to make explicit. The first concerns the assumption of binaries of class and race that have been pursued in the historiography of Kenya. I seek to discredit the idea that the colonial court system in Kenya pitted whites against Africans and contend instead that serious divisions existed among Africans themselves. I do not deny that whites enjoyed privileges, but rather that this factor has been overemphasized in previous studies, sometimes at the expense of other levels of privilege, including those in the court system that I examine in this chapter. This court case confirms that some African court officials subverted justice and manipulated the court system in their own interests.[3] The second set of assumptions deals with the power of translation in colonial settings. Emily Apter has also asked the question I wish to address: "How does interpretation affect a work of history?"[4] Apter considers several factors concerning questions of language and the broader concept of translatability. I not only explore the politics of translation as such but also examine the difference between the court records and oral sources, the evidence of bias, and the presence of (class) self-interest.

Intimidation by African court officials remains underexamined in legal scholarship. Whereas the functions of the colonial chiefs and catechists were visible and their roles pronounced and therefore easily scrutinized, those of the African court officials are not easy to unveil. Because few colonial administrators had the linguistic skills to control what actually took place in the courts, they relied on African translators.[5] This chapter is based on a close reading of the court records and oral testimony about those records.

Law in Colonial Africa

Richard Roberts and Kristin Mann examine the colonial court system as an important area where power, dominance, and hegemony played out and interacted with other sectors, observing that "because of its centrality to colonialism, law provides an excellent window through which to view the colonial period." Law not only affected nor was it only affected by engagements between Africans and Europeans. Rather, struggles between Africans were central as well. Indeed, "in the colonial period Africans met one another on the legal battlefield far more often than they did Europeans." Roberts and Mann continue, "[T]he legal discourses and debates, disputes and conflicts among Africans were as important as those between Africans and Europeans in shaping the colonial social order."[6] Mahmood Mamdani has also argued that the "civilizing" project of colonial powers in Africa revolved around the rule of law and that "the torchbearers of that civilization were supposed to be the colonial courts. The courts were intended neither just as sites where disputes would be settled nor simply as testimony to effective imperial control; rather, they were to shine as beacons of western civilization."[7] This notion is echoed in a memo written by a colonial governor in Kenya in 1910, detailing the role of provincial commissioners (PCs) and district commissioners (DCs), who were the initial custodians of courts in colonial Kenya:

"Generally speaking it will [be] his [PCs] endeavor to rule through Chiefs and Elders and to educate them in the duties of rulers according to a civilized standard; to convince them that oppression of the people is not sound policy, or to eventual benefit of the rulers; to bring home to their intelligence, as far as may be, any evils which destroy individual responsibility, ambition, and development amongst their people; and to inculcate the unspeakable benefit of justice, free from bribery and open to all."[8] Mamdani contends that such claims lay in shreds, however, as more forceful structures of power and coercion were created to find ways of controlling the multitudes on the ground, necessitating a shift in perspective from civilizing mission to the administration of law and order.[9]

Recovery, interpretation, and construction of history via court transcripts and reports are new neither in Kenya nor elsewhere. Gayatri Spivak problematized the colonial archive as a product of certain interests.[10] This shift in the understanding of the archive also reflects a growing awareness of its power, as scholars become increasingly sensitive not only to its central role in the day-to-day function of empire but also to the symbolic weight it carried in the broader cultural and political projects of imperialism. Historians of Africa know that the archives reflect the interests of the colonial project and must therefore be attentive to the distortions and omissions in them.

Tony Ballantyne has argued that the colonial archive was itself the site where the "transformative power of colonialism was enacted and contested."[11] It was here that the processes of self-preservation took place, as the archive was meant to ensure the legacy and posterity not only of the colonial official but also of the colonial project. This speaks to the contemporary court system in Kenya, to Kenya's cultural and social dilemmas, and to the antithesis of center-periphery relations more generally, where the British legacy still persists in Kenya. But perhaps one of the best examinations of court processes, officials, and witnesses and the way they inform cultural history is the discussion by David W. Cohen and E. S Atieno-Odhiambo of the burial of SM Otieno.[12] Facts were selectively included and consumed in the courtroom to suit the intentions and positions of the various parties and actors involved. Moreover, the protagonists were paraded against each other by the media and the judicial officials, generating hostilities that did not previously exist. Cohen and Atieno-Odhiambo also address questions pertaining to the influence of power, gender, class, and the state in the courtroom and how these determined the outcome of the SM Otieno case.

Cultural aspects of the colonial courtroom and its proceedings have not been as thoroughly investigated. Only the cases involving politically significant figures such as Jomo Kenyatta or Tom Joseph Mboya have attracted scholarly attention. In fact Kenyatta's Kapenguria trial has been most romanticized and popularized in works of fiction and nonfiction alike, equaled only by the witchcraft trials of Ukambani. Case studies that have examined ordinary African court cases, focusing on ordinary individuals such as Lusuli and Estambale, are rare.[13] These two individuals belonged to the same clan and therefore ethnic group. Their differences were not even generational, as they belonged to the same age group. They were, however, differentiated by class, education, power, and privilege.

Eugene Cotran's *Casebook on Kenya Customary Law* and Cohen and Atieno-Odhiambo's *Burying SM* address issues in the independent Kenyan courtrooms, where litigants may have knowledge of either Kiswahili or English. The problems of translation and transcription that are so rampant in colonial courts do not affect the post-independence Kenyan court system in the same way they did the colonial court, where English and Kiswahili were still the preserve of a few. Whereas the colonial court privileged individuals based on race, ethnicity, class, power, and gender, the courts in independent Kenya have evolved different structures of privilege that are not always easily discernible. It is against this background that I emphasize language and education, class, and gender difference as areas of interest in the colonial courtroom in Kenya, as sites of stratification, and finally as factors that defined power as it emerged in Khwisero African Court.

The Court System in Colonial Kenya

Her Majesty's Government took over judicial matters in the East Africa Protectorate (consisting of Kenya and Uganda) in 1895. In 1896 it appointed the first judicial officer for the protectorate under the Africa Order in Council. The jurisdiction of this official over natives was provisionally unlimited, save for the right of appeal to the commissioner in charge of the East African Region. The East Africa Order in Council of 1897 created a new court for the entire protectorate known as Her Majesty's Court of East Africa, or alternatively as the Protectorate Court. This court had jurisdiction over all British subjects, foreign nationals, and Africans ("natives"). The order also provided for the establishment of provincial courts.

The court system in colonial Kenya was part of the central government, where the executive, judicial, and legislative roles were combined until August 16, 1907, when the first legislative council meeting was held at Nairobi. In 1910 the governor, Sir E. P. C Girouard, issued memoranda to provincial and district commissioners detailing their administrative and judicial roles. The role of Africans, especially in the administration of justice, features very prominently in these directives. Khwisero was one of the eight African courts that were established in Kakamega District in colonial Kenya to adjudicate over African affairs. The others were at Butere, Butali, Hamisi, Ikolomani, Lurambi, Mumias, and Vihiga. These courts were presided over by district officers (DOs) who doubled as magistrates. At the district level the DCs ran the courts, and the court of Kakamega District was based in Kakamega town.

In the functioning and operations of the colonial government, the judiciary was one of the executive departments placed under the direct command of the governor in Nairobi. When they filled these judicial roles, the DOs and DCs were discharging both executive and judicial duties. These officials were jacks-of-all-trades, supervising education, agriculture, and health and attending to security matters and to the interests of other sectors. Later when more officers became available, magistrates came under the direct control of the PCs, who were regarded as their superiors. The DCs and DOs were left to concentrate on administrative functions.

Thus, the entire judicial department had an executive approach to its duties. It was guided more by the concern for the maintenance of order than for the administration of justice. It is against this mired background that those Africans who were recruited by the colonial government within the court system found ample opportunities to exercise power and authority. Africans were hired as translators/interpreters because court business was often conducted in English and Kiswahili, knowledge of which many Kenyans still lacked, especially judicial English and Kiswahili. African court clerks transcribed court business from the vernacular to English and kept the court records. The white DOs and DCs relied on these translations, interpretations, and transcriptions in adjudicating. Only those with knowledge of English and Kiswahili could follow and comprehend court proceedings.

Caleb Asituywa

Caleb Asituywa was an African court official at the Khwisero Native (later African) Court. After attending primary school at Ekambuli, he had proceeded to the Kima Mission School. He was later employed as a court clerk by the colonial government in Kenya. Asituywa recalls, "I was more known than Kulali and Okinda [long-serving chiefs of the East Bunyore and the Kisa West location, respectively, in the 1950s]." He says further, "There were always long lines of people seeking to consult me on legal issues at my home, which made Okinda and Litunya [Asituywa's location chiefs] very envious at times. My wife and children were constantly bothered by these crowds, until I built a shop at Ebukambuli, where these consultations shifted."[14] The shop became Asituywa's operation base outside his official office at Khwisero. People interested in Asituywa's assistance on various legal issues often visited him at Ebukambuli.

For many years Caleb Asituywa served as a court translator, clerk, messenger, and processor and sometimes acted as a cultural specialist at the Khwisero African Court. He combined roles that are filled by three or more people in the court system in Kenya today. He was revered, feared, and respected by his peers outside judicial circles. At this time the courts presided over many cases because colonial order exacted many demands on the relatively conservative Abaluyia people, who, unlike the Kikuyu, were among the last to come under complete colonial subjugation. The new rules and laws brought with them confusion and conflicts. Litigants swamped the courts with cases involving taxes and their regulations, cases regarding distinctions between modern land adjudication and the communal and ancestral land system and between modern marriage and traditional marriage, cases concerning the creation of a new elite based on education rather than age and patronage, and finally cases concerning new religions and denominationalism coupled with syncretism.

Asituywa and his fellow clerks were at the center of this activity and became very influential. Without doubt he was aware of his powerful position. Like other African colonial employees, Asituywa was exempted from paying hut and poll tax. He admits that he was very wealthy, that people sought favors from him, and that he indirectly influenced the outcome of court cases.[15] Perhaps that is why his popularity and fame grew far and wide. In his dealings with so many people and in the way he manipulated cases, he epitomizes the power of African intermediaries.

The Court Battle between Estambale and Lusuli

Events leading to this conflict started the afternoon of December 25, 1945, at the Kima Mission of the Church of God (COG), which was run by the white missionary J. S. Ludwig. The mission station witnessed a unique phenomenon that no doubt shocked a significant portion of the Christian community in colonial Kenya.[16] On that day a group of young Africans led by Pastor Livingston Omukwangu Imbira from the Emmang'ali Parish of the COG seceded from the Kima Mission in one of the boldest moves ever made by a local group.[17] The Reverend J. S. Ludwig promptly declared the secession illegal and got court orders barring the group from using all COG churches and facilities including buildings and schools. The African "rebels" mobilized their own resources, built their own schools and churches, and were soon self-sufficient.[18] Soon after breaking away, however, the "rebels" became embroiled in their own differences over leadership of their new church, which led to another schism that resulted in two separate groups, one led by Pastor Ariton Amuchuku Estambale and the other by Pastor Washington Atamba Lusuli, successor to Pastor Livingston Imbira.[19] Imbira had been upstaged in the internal rivalries within weeks after leaving Kima Mission.[20] Various attempts to reconcile Estambale and Lusuli having failed, the African Court at Khwisero became the last resort. Thus the protagonists (Lusuli and Estambale) took their differences to the African Tribunal at Khwisero in January 1946, in a case that would drag on for close to a decade. At the end of the proceedings in 1956, the group led by Pastor Washington Lusuli emerged "victorious" with judgment pronounced in its favor.

The court battle was long and intense. Throughout the court transcriptions, one notices that the sections for Lusuli and his group were clearly worded and presented very articulately, whereas those of Estambale and his group were vague, disjointed, unclear, and in several places, self-incriminating. True, Lusuli was better educated than Estambale, but the work of the court officials was supposed to narrow the

gap in such advantages and bring litigants to the same level before justice. The court officials' job, in part, was to make it possible for all litigants' views to be heard by the courts as clearly as possible. It is clear
that such was not the case here. Lusuli was even referred to as Bwana
("Mr.") in the recorded court proceedings, a title usually reserved for
whites and very respected Africans in colonial Kenya. This appellation
indicates that Lusuli and his group were obviously more privileged
than Estambale and his constituents. Based on the information that Asituywa revealed later, these translations, transcriptions, and misinterpretations were intentional and meant to confuse the white DO/district
magistrate.

The misinterpretations reveal that the semiliterate litigants not favored by the court clerks suffered violence in the colonial courts in
Kenya. Perusal of other court cases, especially the renderings of the
translations, reveals that court clerks wielded considerable power as
intermediaries between Africans and the colonial power. They clearly
indicate why serious miscarriages of justice were occasioned by either
incompetent or conniving African court officials. Examination of the
Khwisero Court records covering the AIC case reveals evidence of calculated misrepresentation and mistranslation.[21]

Charge: Refusing to release church property and embezzling church funds;
claiming to be the leader of the African Interior Church.
> Q. Court to Estambale (Defendant) and group: Do you admit that you refused
> to relinquish church leadership according to your church's constitution
> and that you also embezzled £2,000 being property of the AIC, Bunyore?
> A. No.
> Q. What do you know about these accusations, Estambale?
> A. The constitution of the church was not endorsed by the AIC General
> Assembly in my presence.
> Q. (To Estambale): Why are you rebelling against your leader?
> A. Estambale: It is only the members of the Church as a whole who can
> answer. [The clerk recorded that Estambale did not seem to know the
> answer to any question put to him. "He is just an agitator."][22]
> Q. How many members are with you?
> A. Twenty.[23]
> Q. Where is this money that was collected by the church and which you are
> keeping?
> A. I did not keep a lot of money as Lusuli took all the collections.[24]
> Q. Mr. Lusuli, what happened?
> A. Plaintiff Lusuli states: The Estambale together with others have refused
> to hand over church property and still claim [kujidai, which actually

means "boast"] to be officials of the church despite their having been
rejected by the congregation in our last church elections.

Q. (To Lusuli): Since when did you start having problems with Estambale's
group, Mr. Lusuli?[25]

A. Ever since we left the Church of God (in 1946) when he became treasurer
and has never accounted for church funds.[26]

There followed months, then years of testimonies, counter-testimonies, and evidence from both sides similar to that above. Throughout this period the government took over the operation of the AIC-sponsored schools under the District Education Board in Kakamega. In the AIC church buildings, the status quo remained, and in this the Lusuli faction controlled twenty-four out of the church's twenty-nine congregations, thus clearly controlling the majority.

One chilly morning in May 1956, a curious and anxious crowd gathered outside the Khwisero Native (African) Court, awaiting the ruling in a case that had dragged on for a decade. Among the onlookers in the crowd were two partisan groups, one supporting Washington Atamba Lusuli and the other Ariton Amuchuku Estambale. Lusuli and Estambale were the two chief antagonists in the case. Lusuli proudly recalled that day in 1956, when he said that many in his party had arrived on bicycles from Bunyore, their native location, whereas those of Estambale had covered the twenty-kilometer distance on foot. Bicycles marked status. Lusuli, like many in his party, wore jackets, also a status symbol.

Lusuli had his Medal of Honor strapped near the upper pocket of his jacket.[27] He also proudly displayed his war veteran's badge, having served as a sergeant major during the World War II in the King's African Rifles (KAR). Indeed, Lusuli was one of the three highest ranking Kenyans in the KAR during World War II. During the same war, Estambale had served under the successor to the World War I Carrier Corps, spoken of and known locally in Kenya by its corrupted form of Kariako. The KAR was more respected than the Carrier Corps. Lusuli was famous in the region, but Estambale was unknown beyond his village of Esibuye. Estambale lacked modern skills; he worked as a village hut repairer, specializing in thatching leaking roofs. He had attended formal schooling at Esibuye Sector School for only two years, just enough to be able to read the Bible, which enabled him to become the lay leader in the COG, beginning at Esibuye.

From the outset Lusuli was confident that his side would win the case and had many reasons for believing so. He had summoned credible witnesses, including Ludwig Krammer, a white man. He also had many educated Banyore men such as James Nasiali, Zadock Imbeba, Julius Opanga, and Erastus Olwamba testifying for him. Since he was better educated than Estambale, he had corresponded on behalf of the church and as such had kept all the church records and significant documents before the differences with Estambale surfaced. Lusuli had also personally testified in court. There was tension in the air on that occasion. Estambale arrived to find Lusuli and his supporters already waiting. He recalled, "[They were] conversing in *olufotifoti* (English) with people we did not know. We immediately knew that we would lose the case. We could not understand what they were saying but occasionally they pointed towards our direction. We then knew that they were talking about us, even if we did not understand *olufotifoti*."[28]

In May 1956 the Khwisero court, under District Officer/Magistrate III John O'Brien, entered judgment, allowing Washington Atamba Lusuli and his team to take over AIC church leadership and making Ariton Amuchuku Estambale subordinate to Lusuli. Estambale was ordered to hand over all church property to Lusuli and refund all dues. Estambale and his group were devastated. They immediately mounted an appeal against the ruling to the DC, but from the beginning, the appeal was doomed to fail. Appeals rarely succeeded because success inferred a lack of confidence in the presiding officer, the white district officer/magistrate. For Estambale, even if he had a chance, the appeal process was problematic because the African court officials also manipulated the transcripts of the case. If an appeal went through, their tampering was also likely to be exposed; hence they ensured that this did not happen, and, indeed, it did not. Three months later the appeal process was concluded, and Lusuli's group was still declared victorious.

From this case at Khwisero, it is evident that education was a gateway to many opportunities in colonial Kenya and offered many advantages, including the possibility of "hijacking" the justice system. Moreover, men were privileged over women in the native courts in colonial Kenya. The case records are not always very useful in understanding the nature and events surrounding the cases they covered. They are at times vague and confusing, a result not of legal jargon but of the inadequate translation and the way situations were portrayed, for example, when rape is described as "loving by force" or "sharing blankets by force."[29]

These instances indicate how vernacular expressions influenced the process of translation. Someone without knowledge of the Oluluyia language may not easily understand the meaning of words. In the Oluluyia language rape of a woman is *"okhutila omukhana,"* which literally translates as "to catch a woman," without any reference to forced sexual intercourse. Although I can thus empathize with these early court officials, I fault them for not moving toward a conceptually more appropriate understanding of the real meaning behind the vernacular. Caleb Asituywa, a former court official at Khwisero, conceded that limited education was to blame for some of the linguistic problems that I unearthed in the 1990s, and I could not agree with him more.

While conducting field work in 1990, I was lucky to meet extremely helpful and friendly people in the field: people in the AIC churches, former and present church ministers who were involved in the court battles as witnesses or as sympathizers of the factions, the former court official, and others who knew about the case. They clearly indicated that they did not in fact consider that anything was amiss or wrong with what I was showing them from the case books. Many said that the Estambale faction had lost the case, and they had resignedly accepted defeat and thus forgotten about it. When I read Estambale some of the court renderings of his utterances in court from about forty years earlier, he looked very disturbed. Gasping for air and lifting his frail, old frame, he looked firmly in my face and retorted, "If that is what he [the African translator] told the magistrate that I said, then he lied. I believe that is how we lost that case."[30]

In lengthy interviews I went step by step with Estambale through much of the court archives. Certain details emerged that Estambale had been contemplating for some time. He was aware of Lusuli's privileged position in the court at Khwisero. It was not lost on him that two court officials who directly participated in the court case at Khwisero had attended Kima School with Lusuli. Estambale was also aware of the possible influence that Lusuli's position on the Native Council of Emuhaya could have had on the case.[31] But Estambale and his group had believed the white DO or his representative to be an impartial arbiter and expected justice. They underestimated the role of the African "middle men," who served as conveyers of justice.

The way the court transcripts presented Estambale's case rendered his testimony very weak compared to Lusuli's. Estambale had explained as clearly as he could remember that the problem with Lusuli was that he had falsified the church constitution. Lusuli had singlehandedly changed the constitution, making himself the head of the church for life. Indeed, Lusuli died in office as head of the church in

1989. Estambale said that Lusuli had not married in church as was expected of a church official and therefore he should have been legally barred from officiating at marriages. My interview with Lusuli's widow, Eunita Lusuli, confirmed that indeed Lusuli had not married her in church and that they had never had a formal wedding, contrary to what Lusuli had told the congregation.[32]

Education, Social Networks, and Court Officials

One can unearth a great deal about the colonial encounter by studying what transpired in the colonial courts. From the court files and oral testimonies of the trial at Khwisero, one can conclude that knowledge of English was a symbol of status in colonial Kenya. It provided a privileging platform to those who spoke it. Those who spoke English were able to navigate, negotiate, and weave their way through complex colonial institutions. Next in line was knowledge of Kiswahili, which was the official language in the colonial public space. Lack of knowledge of either language presented serious obstacles to individuals who ventured out of their cultural area. The further one went out of his or her cultural space or into the colonial institutions such as schools and courts without knowledge of these two languages, the more difficult it became to negotiate and function within them.

Africans who spoke Kiswahili and English were employed in many sectors within the colonial enterprise, as mediators and bridges between colonial statutory law and traditional African practices and laws. The colonial court became a place feared by those without the requisite linguistic knowledge. Of the two litigants, Lusuli was more privileged as he had knowledge of both English and Kiswahili. He was a member of the Emuhaya African Tribunal, a sister tribunal to the Khwisero Tribunal within Kakamega District, under the auspices and jurisdiction of the same DC. His case was heard at Khwisero. In modern judicial jargon, he would be *amicus curiae* at Khwisero. He had attended the same school with some tribunal members at Khwisero, including Caleb Asituywa, Liboyi Omwoha, and Enock Sikalia.

In contrast Estambale was unknown beyond his village of Esibuye, which might well have worked against him. His profession as a village roof repairer was one of the lowest in the pecking order of village occupations. Thus, while Lusuli understood and closely followed all that transpired at Khwisero, Estambale had to rely on translators to pass on to him what had transpired and to convey his views and elicit a response from the court. In the transcribed translated text of the proceedings of this case, Lusuli spoke 1,654 words to Estambale's mere 713 words. The questions the court officials asked Lusuli were friendly and clear, whereas those posed to Estambale seem hostile and complicated. Even when he answered appropriately, the transcription and translation renders his answers vague and in some instances incriminating.

Semiliterate as he was, Estambale pointed out to me the anomalies and problems of misrepresentation evident in the court records from Khwisero. Three other litigants on both sides of this case and whose excerpts I do not include here, disagreed with the court versions of their story, as represented by Asituywa and his team of African court officials. As I moved between the archival records and tracked down the living litigants for corroboration of their accounts, miscarriage of justice due to "mistakes" introduced by the court officials became very apparent.

There were disparities between the spoken and the written testimonies. The court clerks, interpreters, and translators wielded much power and influence, perhaps unknown to their white superiors. It was the African court officials who manipulated these testimonies and put forward the versions that suited their courses and served their partisan interests. These men predetermined the outcomes of court cases, yet the white officials who often relied on them might not have been aware that they were being manipulated. Only litigants who knew English and possibly Kiswahili and were therefore able to address the tribunal or court officials directly had a chance of receiving favorable verdicts without bribing the African court officials or seeking their patronage. But those who used Kiswahili and the vernacular were always at the mercy of the clerks and translators, who had the power to decide what to tell the white officials.

The Khwisero Tribunal records reveal that it suffered from extensive and deliberate mistranslation, misinterpretation, and misrepresentations by African court officials. The court records were inaccurate and biased depending on the officials handling them and their interest in the cases. I located only three of the many African court officials at Khwisero, and only one, Caleb Asituywa, agreed to an interview. His testimony confirmed my suspicion that the colonial court system in Kenya was partial, not only because of cultural and linguistic divisions between the white administrators, the magistrates/judges, and African customs, but also mainly because of the partisanship of the African officials. Caleb Asituywa said that there was no way Lusuli, their "friend," was going to lose that case, and I believe him.[33] A perusal of the record book reveals ignorance on the part of the court officials. They were simply not fair mediators in law.

My analysis highlights the convoluted court processes of colonial Kenya. Through court records I have addressed multiple issues that emerged from an examination of the operations and functions of African court officials. Such issues include class differences, the role of education, the social network, cultural identity, cultural differences, and cultural community in colonial Kenya. The establishment of the judiciary as an independent arm of government at independence did not change the bias inherent in the courts. The judicial officers continued to regard themselves as part of the executive arm and never appreciated the need to operate independently of the state's directions. The government's closest ally in oppressing the Kenyan people was the judiciary and the police. Through incompetence and willful subservience to the executive branch, judges and magistrates twisted the law to support the government, thereby betraying the judiciary's constitutional goal as a guardian of the people's fundamental liberties. Although the court records are not accurate and therefore cannot be used as exact records of what happened in the courts, I have demonstrated that cultural history of the colonial courts has much to contribute to our understanding of the current decay in the judicial system in Kenya, especially with regard to issues involving corruption. I believe that addressing the interests of court officials and their role in Kenya's colonial past has been pivotal in understanding present-day corruption and inefficiency in the judiciary in Kenya and much of Africa, where deepening patterns of corruption and abuse of justice have become entrenched as a "cultural practice."

Because they were biased against the illiterate, the semiliterate, and the poor, the court records in colonial Kenya, I have argued, are unreliable sources of cultural, social, and political history unless corroborated by oral testimonies and other sources. The court records were produced under distinctive power structures and were very susceptible to different forms of corruption.

In light of the postcolonial trends assessed earlier, it is increasingly difficult to view the archive as a store of transparent sources from which the total image of Kenya's past can be recovered or assembled; instead the archive must be reimagined as a site saturated by power, influence, and corruption, a dense but uneven body of knowledge scarred by the cultural struggles and violence of patron-client relations, as played by

Asituywa, a typology that perhaps has been replicated everywhere in the colonial spaces.[34] This chapter has shown that the stumbling block and obstacle to Estambale's access to justice was not John O'Brien, the white colonial magistrate, but Asituywa, his fellow African.

Notes

This essay, first presented at the Eighth Stanford-Berkeley Law and Colonialism Symposium, has benefited from comments from Richard Roberts, Ralph Austen, Martin Klein, Tabitha Kanogo, Benjamin Lawrance, Emily Osborn, and Bernard Sihanya.

1. Ghai and McAuslan, *Public Law and Political Change.*
2. Amutabi, "History."
3. Anderson, "Policing, Prosecution and the Law."
4. Apter, "On Translation."
5. See Ginio, Shadle, Osborn, and Jézéquel in this volume.
6. Mann and Roberts, *Law in Colonial Africa,* 3–4.
7. Mamdani, *Citizen and Subject,* 109.
8. Mungeam, *Kenya,* 99.
9. Mamdani, *Citizen and Subject,* 107.
10. Spivak, "The Rani of Simur," 263.
11. Ballantyne, "Re-reading the Archive and Opening up the Nation-State."
12. Cohen and Atieno-Odhiambo, *Burying SM.*
13. Throup, "Crime, Politics and the Police." See also Mutungi, *Legal Aspects of Witchcraft.*
14. Interview with Caleb Asituywa, Ekambuli, November 5, 1990.
15. Interview with Caleb Asituywa, Ekambuli, November 5, 1990.
16. American Missionaries from Anderson, Indiana, set up the Church of God Mission at Kima in 1901. The first missionary, James Wilson, came with three other missionaries and their wives. The mission was progressive compared to other foreign missionaries in Bunyore, such as the Anglican Church at Maseno, which started in 1895.
17. Pastor Livingston Imbira, the first African minister of the Church of God's Emmang'ali parish, was semiliterate, only able to read and write in vernacular (Oluluyia).
18. Amutabi, "History," 173.
19. Like Imbira, Ariton Estambale was semiliterate, and this proved very costly during the court case; in court Lusuli had the advantage of English, and many of the court officials not only knew him personally, as he served in the African Tribunal at Emuhaya, but also had attended the same mission school with him.

20. Washington Atamba Lusuli was educated to class eight at Kima Mission School and spoke English quite well. He used English in many of the court sessions. He had served in World War II, rising to the rank of sergeant major. He was well known to the court officials, many of whom were his former schoolmates. He was also privileged in understanding court processes and procedure, as he served as an elder in the Native Tribunal at Emuhaya (later African Court at Emuhaya).

21. Kenya National Archives (hereafter KNA), ADM 61/4/1, Kakamega District Record Book, Lusuli v. Estambale, March 27, 1947, Khwisero, 172.12.1692.

22. "Agitator" is a term the colonial government used to refer to nationalist politicians such as Harry Thuku in 1922. Being an agitator in colonial Kenya was tantamount to criminal behavior.

23. This information incensed Estambale, garnering the retort, "If that is what he told the Magistrate that I said, then he lied." He said that the number he gave for his followers was "amakhumi tisa" (translation "nine tens" or ninety). Thus, the court officials chose to reduce the number of those on the side of Estambale perhaps to make his case weak and portray him as a leader of a small faction.

24. Estambale's recollection was that he said he did not keep any money, as Lusuli kept all the money, contrary to the clerk's record, which stated that, "I did not keep a lot of money."

25. "Mr." or "Bwana" (its Kiswahili rendering) was a title used for whites and on very rare occasions for respected Africans holding positions of authority. By referring to Washington as Bwana, the court was privileging him over Estambale. Lusuli was thus given more dignity and honor and hence advantaged.

26. There is neither documentary evidence nor acceptance of liability by either party to the suit in court to back the court's "findings" and claims against Estambale. The court arbitrarily chose to believe Lusuli and not Estambale.

27. Interview with Julius Opanga, Ebunangwe, Bunyore, October 12, 1990.

28. Interview with Ariton Amuchuku Estambale, Esibuye, October 11, 1990.

29. See Resident Magistrates Court, Kakamega. KNA, NNM/104/146 / 1948—Case no. 104. Shivachi v. Ambundo, August 5, 1948; Resident Magistrates Court, Kakamega, KNA, NNM/KSO/75/1949—Case no.75. In the Native Tribunal, Khwisero, July 12, 1949, Crown (CrC) v. Amuhinda Amukhobo; KNA, ADM 71/5/1, Kakamega District Record Books. Silas Amuka v. Ngamia Omusula, March 27, 1950. 172.12/1796, on the charge of assault and causing actual bodily harm.

30. Interview with Ariton Amuchuku Estambale, Esibuye, October 11, 1990.

31. Kima School was the first formal school for boys established in Bunyore in 1904 by the COG. In 1926 the school became coeducational. In 1946 the boys' school was transferred to Ingotse in Lurambi, and Kima (later Bunyore) was designated for girls.

32. Interview with Omusiele Eunita Lusuli, Mukhombe, Bunyore, November 14, 1990.

33. Interview with Caleb Asituywa, Ekambuli, November 5, 1990.

34. See Richards, *Imperial Archive.*

The District Clerk and the "Man-Leopard Murders"

Mediating Law and Authority in Colonial Nigeria

DAVID PRATTEN

The equivocal social and political position of colonial clerks offers a window on the changing modalities of colonial rule and on the influence of Africans in the mediation and application of colonial law and authority. In the sphere of "working misunderstandings" between the colonial state and society, the scope for African auxiliaries to exercise their own initiative, creativity, and power was broad. An expanding bureaucracy meant that where district officers were distant and aloof, clerks, letter writers, and interpreters became part of the local social landscape and part of new personal networks.[1] Clerks controlled the gateways to colonial courts and bureaucracies and hence exercised great influence over these important sites of struggle for access to resources and the meanings of social relationships and authority. Exactly how important their role was and the precise nature of the balance they struck between self-interest and official service have been the subject of the albeit limited literature on colonial clerks in West Africa.[2]

Two dominant perspectives on African clerks and intermediaries are of central relevance to the events in southeastern Nigeria just after the Second World War that are discussed here. The first concerns the way that colonial clerks are perceived within a dichotomy of collaboration and resistance. Some commentators stress the oppressive role of collaborating colonial functionaries. E. A. Ayandele, for instance, writes that intermediaries in colonial Nigeria were veritable oppressors.[3] He argues that the pinches of colonial rule were felt from the hands of the letter writer, the sanitary inspector, the policeman, the warrant chief, the court clerk, the interpreter, and the tax gatherer. Other perspectives stress what we might call a model of ruse and an image of clerks engaged in self-serving chicanery. In representing local rather than colonial concerns and individual rather than public interests, clerks and other functionaries provided a counterpoint to a stereotypical image of an all-seeing colonial administration confronting passive African societies. Those involved in carrying out the day-to-day requirements of colonial rule could challenge colonial attempts to reshape African societies. Collaborators or resistors? Tricksters or loyal civil servants? Although the intermediary role of clerks offered opportunities for accumulation and personal promotion, this story illustrates that they might also be held to account by the multiple constituencies for whom they were brokers. This essay is a counterpoint to interpretations of functionaries as tricksters. They could overreach, and the room for maneuver at the interface between customary, civic, and state spheres was finite.

The second point is that clerks formed part of the literate elite and hence part of a wider political trajectory involving the educated elite's changing relationship to colonial rule. Forms of organization and mobilization coalesced around clerks, and many early unions were founded by them. They formed the secretariat and members of the "ethnic unions" who, along with the local press, championed their cause. After the 1940s one of the most widespread nationalist demands was for Africans to be able to advance from the clerical to the upper ranks of government service. In this sense clerks, although intimately part of the colonial order, constituted an important element of the nationalist elite who ultimately undermined that order and assumed power from it. Yet this simple narrative trajectory—from collaborator to resistor—overlooks the difficulties that clerks faced in negotiating the contradiction. It ignores the personal tribulations of those engaged in coming to terms with moments when the room to maneuver an already tricky terrain was constrained. This was particularly apparent during the Second World War years, when political nationalism extended beyond a narrow group of radicals to be taken up by the "reading public" at large.

To understand these points we need to situate our observations within cultural frameworks, within the fine grain of individual motivations, and of course historically. The situation for clerks and other intermediaries in southeastern Nigeria, where this story is set, is much cited, largely because of A. E. Afigbo's seminal work on the modalities of indirect rule.[4] Throughout the second and third decades of the twentieth century, clerks in the southeastern Nigerian provinces gained a dubious reputation. Indirect rule provided what Jean-François Bayart has called an "academy for improvisation" in which these "auxiliary tricksters," the interpreters, messengers, and clerks, could profit from their function as political and cultural intermediaries.[5] After Frederick Lugard's reforms of 1914, the ascendancy of the court clerk was determined by the infrequent presence of political officers and the use of English on the forms and records of the court. The warrant chiefs depended on the court clerks' favor. They paid bribes for their seats on the bench and addressed the clerks as "master."

The fallout of the Women's War of 1929 and the administrative reforms introduced by Governor Cameron in 1933 led to a rapid multiplication of courts and councils and with them a new set of problems. New clerks had to be found and trained. Candidates attracted by the relatively low salaries did not have the highest educational qualifications. Hence, the district officer at Abak reported that although the court clerks of this period learned to keep cash books and to issue processes, they learned little about court procedure and less about the law. With the outbreak of the Second World War, clerks were laid off, others left the service in favor of the profits of trade, and those who remained struggled to make ends meet against a plummeting exchange rate with the local manila currency. Civil service positions of the period were synonymous with corruption, especially when the literate elites, the "reading public" took up anticorruption campaigns during and after the war.

This story is set within the fast changing postwar political landscape and focuses on events described in the British press during 1947 as "the strangest, biggest murder hunt in the world."[6] Between 1943 and 1948 almost two hundred mysterious deaths were recorded in a remote corner of southeastern Nigeria. By the end of the investigation, seventy-seven men had been executed by the British colonial authorities for murder. The deaths took place in southern Annang territory in the districts of Abak and Opobo under Calabar Province and were among the last murders in Africa to be publicly attributed to the human-leopard society or any of the continent's other theriomorphic cults.[7] The subterfuge of a leopard-style attack, with copycat mutilations, created doubts about the identity of the killer, whether man or beast, from the outset. The shape-shifting powers that the killers were said to invoke (in Annang they were known as *Ekpe-Owo,* "the leopard men") only heightened an air of mystery that was compounded by contradictory and fragile evidence. Toward the end of the investigation, those closest to it feared that the origin of the outbreak of "leopard" murders would probably never be discovered with any degree of certainty.[8]

During the three years of investigations, hundreds of police officers were drafted into the districts; special sessions of the Supreme Court were held to hear "man-leopard" cases; pathologists were flown-in from Lagos; and forensic tests were carried out in London. Yet, like every good detective story, the case hinged on just a few personalities, their pet theories, and their petty intrigues. This handful of characters included the district officer at Abak, Frederick Kay, who first pursued rumors of human leopards and is credited with setting the investigation on its course; the senior police officer, D.S. Fountain, whose weekly reports filtered and analyzed the evidence; prominent local chiefs such as Obong Udo Ekong, who earned great credit for his unswerving support for the administration during the crisis; leading Annang and Ibibio elites, such as Dr. Egbert Udo Udoma, the president of the Ibibio Union, who became embroiled in the investigation and dragged its controversial fallout into the nationalist politics of the 1950s; and the district officer of the "leopard area," John McCall, whose secret reports in late 1947 threw the entire investigation into turmoil.

This chapter focuses on another of the pivotal figures in the investigations of the man-leopard murders, Usen Udo Usen. An Ibibio from Ikot Offiong in Itu Division, Usen had been an interpreter since 1926 for M. D. W. Jeffreys, a district officer who later became an academic anthropologist. By 1947 Usen was the district clerk in Uyo, the headquarters of the predominantly Ibibio Uyo Division. Outside office hours Usen was a prominent member of the leading "progressive union" in the province, the Ibibio Union. Formed in 1928 by traders, schoolteachers, and clerks from the six Ibibio and Annang districts of Calabar Province, the Ibibio Union had become a powerful political force by the early 1940s, gaining credibility from its self-funded education projects and its direct engagement in the local and national political sphere.[9] Usen Udo Usen joined the Ibibio Union at its inaugural meeting and was appointed its general secretary in 1933, a post he would hold until the events of 1947. It was in both these capacities, as district clerk and as secretary to the Ibibio Union, that Usen Udo Usen would become involved in the leopard murder investigation. And it was precisely as a result of this peculiar position that his predicament arose. By the end of the investigation, Usen Udo Usen had fled Calabar Province after being publicly ostracized by the Ibibio Union. But just a year later he received the Certificate of Honour from the government for his part in bringing the murders to an end. The certificate itself was awarded posthumously, however, as Usen died under suspicious circumstances in Enugu in 1949.

Was Usen Udo Usen a stool pigeon who betrayed his own people for promotion, or a scapegoat who fell victim to political intrigue? The background to the incidents in which Usen Udo Usen's career was both made and lost was extraordinary, though the problems he, like other clerks, confronted in mediating law and authority during this period were not. Usen positioned himself at the center of a complex of forces aligned rhetorically as civic power with its characteristic defense of rights in the public sphere, customary rule that fused "every moment of power" in the office of chieftaincy and between both these spheres and the local colonial state.[10] Yet during the events of 1947 authority and the claims on which it was based shifted quickly and unpredictably. Political authority was contested by chiefs, diviners, district officers, the police, and the new elites, and by unlikely alliances of these groups. Judicially colonial legal codes based on forensic evidence would abut customary practice based on the performance of oath and ordeal. And culturally colonial rationality would both collide and collude with secrecy and the supernatural. This chapter focuses on two aspects of Usen Udo Usen's role in the leopard murder investigations: on his part in peace-keeping ceremonies conducted in Annang villages at the height of the murders, and on the political fallout of a report he presented on the killings. Usen's story illustrates how clerks employed a range of discourses and devices from customary, civic, and colonial spheres simultaneously to secure consent within the relationships they mediated.

The Crime Scene

The "man-leopard" murders occurred in a landscape of flat, dense oil palm on the west bank of the Qua Iboe River. Some 130 Annang villages within an area just ten miles in diameter were affected. Located between two of the "oil" rivers flowing south to the coast, this Annang territory lay adjacent to Ogoni and Igbo communities across the Imo River to the south and the west, and to the Ibibio across the Qua Iboe River to the northeast. Dialectically distinct from their Ibibio neighbors, Annang nevertheless shared with them a common political, economic, and cultural fabric. In the lineage-based Annang society, the powers of village heads and councils were counterbalanced by those of secret societies, especially the leopard society *(ekpe)*, the ancestral masquerade *(ekpo)*, and the warrior cult *(ekong)*.[11] Despite the economic significance of this oil-palm hinterland, the villages in which the murders occurred constituted a remote administrative backwater far from the political and commercial hub of Calabar. The borderland between Opobo and Abak Division gained a reputation for lawlessness and resistance, which came to a head, so far as colonial opinion was concerned, in the spread of the Women's War into these districts in late 1929.

In the years preceding the outbreak of the Second World War, Calabar Province was subject to radical political, economic, and religious upheaval. Reforms to the local courts and councils in the aftermath of the Women's War designed to resolve an emerging intergenerational rift instead turned the courts and councils into spheres of intense political contest. Native court benches intended for lineage heads were usurped by former warrant chiefs and "other thrustful energetic and unscrupulous young men who ha[d] arrogated to themselves the power and right of trying cases."[12] The control of local taxation revenue made representation on the council, like seats on the bench, a prize for new elites and elders alike, and the "committee class" of young men who made up the "vociferous, letter-writing minority" formed progressive welfare societies publicly to expose corruption within the Native Administration and privately to usurp its perquisites. Economically the rising cost of living, the slump in the palm-oil price in the late 1930s, and the declining exchange rate with the local manila currency in the early 1940s affected commodity producers and civil servants alike.[13] Complaints of acute economic hardship had indeed surfaced during a women's tax riot in the neighboring district of Ikot Ekpene in November 1944. And in the religious context, three factors marked the war years: the perception of a resurgence of secret societies resorting to vigilante justice; concerted mission pressure to criminalize these societies; and an apparent crisis among the Annang divination order of *idioŋ*, whose monopoly on prognostication was challenged by the emergence of "spiritual churches" such as the Christ Army and Sabbath churches.[14]

These developments, along with the direct consequences of the war, of commodity shortages, cut-backs in administrative personnel, and demobilization, made up the social landscape against which the "leopard" murders took place. But it was the physical landscape that determined their features. The dense oil-palm belt of southern Annang territory was natural leopard habitat, and it was hard to distinguish between real leopard attacks and those that simulated them. The victims appeared to have been killed in the same way a wild leopard attacks its prey, from behind and biting at the throat. The murders were linked in the style of the assault and corpse mutilation, with arms and heads severed and flesh scraped off, and in the location of the attacks, always on an isolated bush path at dusk. Forensic investigations were further complicated by the suspicion that the killers used a set of clawlike blades to commit the murders and placed leopard hair, droppings, and pad marks made by carved wooden sticks ("leopard shoes") to disguise the scene of the crime.[15]

Persistent rumors and press articles that strange deaths had been caused by a "leopard society" were largely ignored, and the leopard style of murder had apparently duped the resources of forensic pathology since 1943. It was not until 1945 that the authorities began to investigate local speculation that these deaths were part of a series.[16] In March 1945 the district officer at Abak, Frederick Kay, was alerted to local suspicions, published in the *Nigerian Eastern Mail*, that Dan Udofia, who died at Ikot Okoro after being attacked while tapping palm wine, had fallen victim not to a leopard, as the principal witnesses claimed, but rather to members of a man-leopard society. The victim was the houseboy of the head court messenger at Ikot Okoro, Okon Bassey, on whom the finger of suspicion fell. Seriously wounded, Udofia had found his way back to the court compound after being attacked, but Bassey prevented the local dispenser from seeing him, failed to report his death, and buried Udofia himself. This strange behavior, coupled with details of a previous dispute between the men, secured Bassey's conviction.[17] He was hanged in Abak in March 1946, the first of seventy-seven "man-leopards" to be executed.

Despite initial skepticism about the existence of a human-leopard society, officers began to investigate postmortem and police reports in "leopard" killings prior to the Udofia case, and by December 1945 they claimed there was conclusive evidence that a leopard society had committed the murders in the Ekparakwa, Ikot Ibritam, and Ibesit Native Court areas. In early January 1946, a ninety-five-strong police detachment was drafted into the area and given extensive additional powers to conduct its investigations the following month when Abak and Opobo were declared "proclaimed districts" under the Peace Preservation Ordinance.[18] Over 100 deaths were under investigation at the beginning of 1946, yet by June only thirteen convictions had been secured, and the killings continued. Calls for more forthright action were met with public executions that began in September 1946, a dusk to dawn curfew, and the dispatch of a two-hundred-strong "leopard force," which was billeted in villages where murders had taken place to act as a deterrent to further killings and as a form of collective punishment.[19] By the end of 1946 some 157 murders had been investigated. Of these 64 were classified as probable, and 93 were possible "man-leopard" murders.[20]

The Motives

With the subterfuge of the killings apparently exposed, the mutilations inflicted on the victims became subject to intense scrutiny. A number of questions arose: Why were the mutilations so precisely copied in so many cases? And why were the mutilations so elaborate? Was the removal of flesh from the bodies part of the disguise or part of the reason for the murders? For three years these questions sparked a debate as to whether these were ritual or revenge murders.[21] In the early stages of the investigation, it was believed that the mutilations at the murder scene were linked either to a "master-juju" reminiscent of the Long Juju of Arochukwu or to a series of small village shrines before which the killers performed appeasement ceremonies.[22] Rumors surfaced that the killers were selling flesh and body parts to buyers for prominent shrines in neighboring Ogoniland and to the Annang *idioŋ* society of diviners.[23] The leopard men, it was suggested, were contracted as the agents of *idioŋ* priests who sought organs of the body to satisfy the demands and enhance the power of their shrines. Hence *idioŋ* would divine the cause of their client's ill luck or illness or of a relative's death and would "encourage and counsel the commission of murder as the only means of settling a grievance, real or imaginary and afford the murderers every assistance in the preparation of the crime."[24]

By 1947 no firm evidence had been uncovered to corroborate this view, however, although suspicion still hung over the diviners as likely accessories to murder. As the investigation explored alternative lines of inquiry, analysis of the *ekpe-owo* cases during 1946 revealed that the accused had a personal motive for killing the victim.[25] As a result official opinion shifted away from the belief that an organized society was directing the murders for ritual purposes and toward the idea that those accused of committing murder were part of, or had hired, a band of professional assassins, a "native form of "Murder Incorporated," compelled by the "Corsican vendetta."[26] Of the ninety-seven cases confirmed as "leopard murders" by November 17, 1947, the investigation revealed revenge and jealousy, especially linked to unresolved court cases concerning brideprice, land, and debts, as the prime motives for the leopard murders.[27] Innovations in customary law and frustrations in the courts led people to take matters into their own hands, and it was argued that "one of the main underlying causes of the outbreak of murders in this area was an existing need by these people for a speedier and more ruthless form of justice than that provided by the British System."[28]

As evidence of vendetta-style assassinations was mounting, a murder on January 25, 1947, shifted the thrust of the investigation once more.[29] The murder was that of one of the investigating police officers, P. C. Evans Chima, and the circumstances surrounding his death appeared for the first time to confirm suspicions that the *idioŋ's* part in the murders was malicious. This particular case was notable as it concerned the only death of a serving officer in the colonial administration and inevitably raised the question of whether the colonial regime was itself a target of the "leopard men."[30] Its real significance, however, was that it was the most high profile death in which explicitly ritual motives were reported. Confession evidence extracted from one of the four accused killers stated that they had killed P. C. Chima in order to remove his lips for empowering an *idioŋ* shrine.[31]

Senior police officers thought this evidence was the breakthrough their investigation desperately needed and that *idioŋ's* involvement might be the "missing link in the chain connecting all the murders."[32] Though the confession was problematic and no remains were found at the suspected *idioŋ* shrine, this case was fundamental to the colonial argument that these were "medicine murders."[33] As a direct result the *idioŋ* society was prohibited in February 1947.[34] On February 27 the police mounted a dawn raid in which over three hundred *idioŋ* shrines were destroyed, and the diviners themselves were taken to police camps for questioning. Cases in which *idioŋ* members were implicated in providing information leading to revenge killings had caused the provincial administration to consider a ban on *idioŋ* once before.[35] In 1940, however, the resident of Calabar Province was hopeful that the practice of consulting *idioŋ* to determine the cause of death would be held in check by "public opinion coupled with energetic action by District Officers."[36] The government was reticent to act more firmly against *idioŋ* because it was reluctant to weaken the authority of the many chiefs in the region who were *idioŋ* initiates themselves.

In 1940 the government sought the advice of the Ibibio Union about this question but ignored the union when the question resurfaced in 1947. The Ibibio Union had consistently opposed the ban, and the prohibition of *idioŋ* in 1947 was to be the source of a long-running and very public dispute. The union maintained that the laws of *idioŋ* prevented initiates from shedding blood, that *idioŋ* would lose the power of divination if they committed murder, that the ban had been applied to an order of *idioŋ* known as *ifa*, which was not involved in divination, and drew attention to the contradiction that local "spiritual" churches, including the Christ Army Church, was also offering prophesy and divining motives for revenge but had not been prohibited. A further line of argument was based on the right of religious freedom. Nyong Essien, the Calabar Province representative in the Regional House of Assembly, asserted in a speech during the legislative council meeting in March 1947 that *"Idioŋ* should enjoy the protection which other religions in Nigeria enjoy under the law."

The Ibibio Union and "Civic Duty"

Just days before the police raid on the *idioŋ* shrines, the Ibibio Union had held its annual conference and resolved to demand from the provincial authorities that it be allowed "to take the matter into their own hands . . . with the view of stamping out the obnoxious society from Ibibiolands. It [was] also requested that the Government be good enough to provide transport for native Chiefs and important citizens of the six districts of Ibibioland who [were] to come with their traditional emblems to restore order and peace in the affected areas."[37] The governor, suspicious of the impression conveyed by the authorities' admission of failure, framed the union's proposal for a delegation to tour the villages of the "leopard area" in a subversive light: "The Union's motives are largely political, with the object of diverting from Government to themselves the credit for putting a stop to these crimes."[38] Yet the

government feared that the murder rate during the early months of
1947 was increasing, and was persuaded by local police officers who
thought that the Ibibio Union's peacekeeping ceremonies would prove
to be "the culminating factor in reducing the existing murder rate."[39]

Though these circumstances were extraordinary, the Ibibio Union's
actions were not unprecedented. They echoed attempts to prevent the
spread of the Women's War in 1929 and 1944 and extended the idea of
the touring delegation that conducted "enlightenment" and antibribery
campaigns during the early 1940s. The idea of touring the district drew
directly on colonial administrative practice and had been similarly appropriated by other figures of the urban middle-class such as the newspaper editor J. V. Clinton. Indeed, the proposed tour was consistent
with a longstanding discourse the Ibibio Union espoused in its relationship with the colonial state. In 1940 the Ibibio Union had outlined to the
governor its desire to be considered part of the administrative structure
and represented its role as that of a mediator:

> To go hand in hand and interpret the policies of the Government to natives,
> To see that the laws and orders of the Government were kept, and,
> A medium through which the government can speak to the Ibibio tribe as a
> whole.[40]

The union's tour of the man-leopard villages was an exercise of these
civic responsibilities. Here was an opportunity for the Ibibio Union to
"demonstrate its national feeling—to do its civic duty; to help the innocent victims of the murderers; to redeem the good name of Ibibioland,
nay the Calabar Province."[41] The difference on this occasion, however,
was that the union's civic agenda was articulated not in literate and
"civilizing" form but in an alliance with the most prominent provincial
chiefs ostensibly in defense of another bastion of the conservative rural
hierarchy, the *idioŋ* "priests."

The union's touring deputation was mandated under the Native Authority Ordinance of 1943 to compel villagers to attend public meetings,
which they did in over eighty meetings organized during May, June,
and July 1947. Usen Udo Usen was appointed as the permanent secretary to the tour and along with his assistant, W. K. Ekanem, coordinated
the logistics with the police and district officials. D. S. Fountain, the senior police officer in charge of the investigations, would later write that
in Usen Udo Usen the union had appointed a remarkably good leader:
"Usen devoted the whole of his energies to his task and showed a most
unusual determination to put a stop to the murders at all costs. As an

Ibibio himself, he felt that the situation in the area was a stigma on the good name of his tribe and that it was incumbent on him to wipe it away."[42]

During the tour Usen received deputations, settled minor disputes, and heard public grievances. He recorded this in a tour diary of over two hundred typed pages of entries compiled from each of the village meetings, copies of which were submitted at intervals to the authorities. Every murder case was itemized, and local opinions, usually those of the elders, were given as to the cause of the killings. Diary entries reveal that several villagers gave Usen clues as to possible links between the murders and various secret societies. The diary also demonstrates that Usen publicly defended the government's position. When confronted by the village head and former *idioŋ* member in Inen Ikot Esien, who asked if the government was justified in destroying his *idioŋ* shrine when he claimed to have no knowledge of the man-leopard killing practice, Usen replied, "When the cases of many killings under the guise of Leopard by your people was brought into book, it was proved beyond doubt that Idiong diviners were the cause of the many killings. . . . I consider that the Government was right in the measures taken to prohibit Idiong Cult at the time, but in the case of destroying I reserve my opinion. . . . The answer I give you in connection with Idiong is my personal opinion which has nothing to do with the general opinion of the Ibibio people."[43] "It must have taken considerable courage," one officer wrote, "for Mr Usen to speak out so forthrightly."[44] This speech, along with other passages from the union's tour diary, was cited extensively by the government as evidence justifying the continued ban on the *idioŋ* order. The authorities also believed that such a forthright view must have indicated unanimity among the touring delegates, though this would prove to be a presumptuous conclusion.

The tour delegation comprised thirty-six chiefs, representing the six Ibibio and Annang districts, each possessing "the ancient judicial rights in capital offences, homicide and manslaughter."[45] Some of the delegates, such as Chief Udo Ekong, had been involved in the investigations previously as members of District Officer Kay's Native Authorities Investigating Committee. On this occasion, however, the chiefs were there to see that every tax-paying villager pledged an oath that he would not aid or join the leopard men.[46] Initially, Usen had assured the Resident of Calabar Province that the customary *mbiam* oath "in the true sense" would not be sworn, but in fact in each of the villages Christians swore on verses of the Bible and non-Christian villagers were made to swear *mbiam*.[47] Reports of the oath-swearing process are contradictory, but notes submitted to the authorities recorded the ceremony as starting with the burying of a palm frond *(eyei)* across the road leading to the village, after which an elephant tusk *(nnuk enin)* was blown three times. Salt, sand, and water from the village were mixed and poured over the buried palm leaf. Villagers then walked across the buried palm leaf in order to undertake the "solemn agreement" that they would not join or hide *ekpe-owo*.[48]

Colonial and Annang epistemological paradigms and divergent conceptions of agency and causation began to collapse into one another during the murder investigations. In this context, where secrecy and oaths shrouded certainties and truths, the performative constitution of local knowledge was key. Annang concepts of truth are acquired through the process of testing *(ndomo nse,* "to test and see"). Oaths *(mbiam)* and ordeals *(ujang)* are the performative devices through which hidden truths are determined. *Mbiam* has a mutable character, and its meaning varies according to context, variously oath, ordeal, and poison.[49] Usen Udo Usen therefore grasped the significance of combating ambiguity and secrecy with the most familiar device of the Annang and Ibibio cultural repertoire, the oath. In paternalistic fashion Fountain reported that while Usen had a fairly high standard of education, he nevertheless "firmly believed in the actual supernatural powers of the jujus of his people." *Mbiam* was both lie detector and deterrent. Failure to swear and illness attributed to false swearing were signs of guilt, and mass oath-swearing created a baseline placing the population on notice.

The conjunction of customary and colonial codes of justice employed during the tour was not lost on observers. Assistant Superintendent Williams later wrote that "with hindsight these counter-measures appear to have been more effective than the normal process of a civilized law and criminal jurisprudence."[50] The killings continued even as the tour proceeded, and eleven more deaths would be reported, but news of the efficacy of the oath and the effects of false swearing began to spread. On July 25, 1947, villagers in Ibiana heard of a man from Ikot Akpabong who had begun to suffer from a strange sensation after taking the oath and had offered a cow and six hundred manilas to have the oath revoked.[51] Optimistic about the deterrent effect of such news, the union was able to proclaim the tour a success, and the authorities could justify its approval. Police officers like Williams reported that the "bizarre turn" in the eradication of the killings was therefore brought about by the use of more powerful spiritual means in the oaths overseen by Usen, which had effectively neutralized "the Idiong juju of Ekpe Owo."[52]

Aftermath and Accusations

"It is difficult to assess the effect of the tour in preventing or reducing the murders," the resident reported, "but it resulted in the collection of much useful information and calming of public opinion."[53] Despite the official success of the Ibibio Union's tour, for those involved it ended in controversy. Dr. Egbert Udo Udoma, the union president, claimed that Usen Udo Usen had submitted a report on the tour to the authorities without prior approval from the union and without it being discussed or signed by other members of the delegation. Whether this was a deliberate ruse or an accidental oversight, the consequences were significant. Usen's report corroborated the police's inquiries in key respects, notably that *idioŋ* divination and charm preparation had contributed to the murders, and he therefore lent backing to the authorities' decision to ban *idioŋ* and undermined the union's opposition to its prohibition.

Usen's report was only loosely based on the evidence compiled in the tour diary, and it seems likely that he had access to police files before he completed his report. The suspects named in Usen's report were already well known to the police, but he told them a convincing story about how the murders began that drew together previous loose ends. Usen claimed that an *idioŋ*, Akpan Ekpedeme, and his sister's son, Akpan Nyoho, had both kept company with a gang of highway robbers for whom Akpan Ekpedeme prepared protective charms. One gang member was being harassed by a creditor, and another suspected his wife of adultery, so the robbers, Usen suggested, decided to use their charms to eliminate their enemies. Their success and apparent immunity from detection led them to become hired assassins, with agents who would approach people known to have grudges or disputes asking for fifty manilas for a consultation fee and one hundred manilas for the "leopard men" to eliminate their opponent. Usen further suggested that an *idioŋ* member, Ukpong Eto of Ediene Atai, had consulted Akpan Ekpedeme to procure a new human head for his oracle and as a result not only became familiar with the various charms used by the leopard men but also found a market for the sale of body parts (heads, arms, and genitalia) from the victims by selling them to new *idioŋ* members as a condition of their initiation.[54]

Usen's theory was that *idioŋ* used their knowledge of existing personal rivalries and of court disputes over land, brideprice, and debts to identify victims for the leopard men. He thus argued that the ritual and revenge theories that the police had been oscillating between were not mutually exclusive but overlapped. Most of this had long been suspected by the police, but coming from Usen, the man who had visited every village affected by the murders, who had off-the-record evidence, and who was an Ibibio speaker himself and apparently understood the nature and meanings of charms and rituals, it was adopted as clear proof of the police's stance. As a result Usen was immediately seconded to the police detachment on special duties and became their leopard murder specialist. Indeed, his conclusions became the linchpin of the police's case. The prohibition of *idioŋ* had failed to stop the killings, and after six months the government's stance was not only unproved but was also subject to widespread criticism. From their side the police cited events from fifty years earlier involving human leopard killings in Sierra Leone in support of the assertion that these were ritual murders. Senior officers in the Nigerian investigation had only a limited knowledge of these events, however, as they tried in vain to consult an out-of-print account of the trials in Sierra Leone at Foyles bookshop in London. This left Usen's evidence, which was cited directly by the police in their effort to assure themselves (the Criminal Investigation Division commissioner in Lagos and the House of Commons in London) that they had not blundered in their decision to prohibit the *idioŋ* diviners.

The Ibibio Union, meanwhile, summoned Usen to appear before a public assembly in Ikot Okoro in March 1948 to justify the claims made in his report. Passages of the report in which he had accused prominent persons of being members of the man-leopard society were read aloud in English, and the union members in turn questioned Usen directly about the accusations he had made against these men. The atmosphere was tense, and Usen had to be protected by a police cordon when the crowed tried to break through and attack him. The most dramatic moments of the meeting arose in a cross-examination of Usen by Ukpong Eto, the man Usen accused of carrying on Akpan Ekpedeme's role of procuring skulls for new *idioŋ* initiates. A record of this conversation appears in Udoma's memoir, written with distinct prejudice against Usen and which cannot be corroborated. It is revealing nevertheless and suggests that relationships during the tour were not all they had appeared. It claims that Usen and the chief were friends and that on the three occasions on which Ukpong Eto had been arrested Usen had stood bail for him:

UKPONG ETO: If you knew that I was a member of the man-leopard society, being one of the original founders with Akpan Ekpedeme then dead, why did you volunteer to take on my bail?

USEN UDO USEN: Having associated with you for a long time I had always
    entertained doubt as to your being concerned with the man-leopard
    society. . . .
UE: I appeal to you in the name of God to reveal the name of your informer.
UUU: I cannot now remember his name.
UE: I suggest you are lying because no one ever gave you such information.
UUU: No answer.
UE: Are you prepared to take a solemn oath that I am a member of the
    man-leopard society?
UUU: I cannot swear.[55]

With this palpable irony, namely, that the man who had sworn the inhabitants of eighty villages would not himself be sworn, the plot thickened. At the Ibibio Union meeting on May 29, 1948, a resolution was
passed suspending Usen from the union and calling for everything
possible to be done to bring him to justice for his conduct: "Feelings ran
high when it was discovered that certain portions of the report contain
serious but fantastic and groundless allegations against Ibibio chiefs
and the Idioŋ Society. It is believed that Mr Usen, for his own personal
advancement and in order to earn honour and promotion from Government, had secretly forwarded the report to Government well knowing
that the serious allegations contained in the report are entirely baseless."[56] According to police reports, the Ibibio Union sought to discredit
Usen Udo Usen further by accusing him of acting as a police agent, of
taking bribes from chiefs so as not to expose them as *idioŋ*, and of embezzling union funds. A committee of Ibibio Union members formed to
investigate Usen's report claimed that it was "a carefully planned imaginative fabrication clothed in the garb of realism and half-truths. . . . Unless Mr Usen Udo Usen was himself a member of the so-called man-
leopard society . . . he could not have been in a position to disclose all
that the report contained."[57]

The Ibibio Union passed resolutions and signed petitions over the
next five years for a commission of inquiry into the man-leopard murders and for the authorities to provide proof to justify the ban on *idioŋ*.[58]
There was considerable speculation as to the reason for this apparently
unlikely alliance of the self-styled "intelligentsia" with the forces of
rural conservatism and why the mission-educated elites of the union
supported the *idioŋ* diviners so vehemently and for so long. A number
of reasons presented themselves. The union's defense of *idioŋ* was assumed to be influenced by senior figures within the Ibibio Union who
were themselves *idioŋ* members, including Obong Ntuen Ibok of Essene in Opobo District. During the police raid of February 1947, his

idioŋ paraphernalia was destroyed, he was detained in Calabar for three months, and he claimed that he had been robbed of £1,200 in the process. Ironically, prior to his arrest he had accommodated police during their investigations in Essene, and it was Ntuen Ibok who had proposed the tour of the "leopard area" to restore the peace. Because of these connections the authorities believed that senior members of the union who were *idioŋ* diviners, like Ntuen Ibok, were using the union and the devices of colonial law at the disposal of its "intelligentsia" to fight the ban. In July 1947, for instance, a former clerk, Udom, was alleged to have collected £122 from *idioŋ* members to finance a petition against the ban and had asked Dr. Udoma to write it.[59]

Events at the Ibibio Union's annual conference held in August 1948 were keenly observed. Undercover Special Branch police reported that Dr. Udoma had come to an agreement with the *idioŋ* members of the union that "in the event of getting the Idiong Cult restored the Union would waive the repayment of a loan advanced to him for his legal training—a sum believed to be in the region of £2,000."[60] It was reported that Usen "was the first victim sacrificed in Udoma's campaign" and that he had ordered a former journalist, S. E. Hezekiah, to smear Usen in the press. The police claimed that no device to discredit Usen was left untried and that the Union threatened to bring criminal charges against Usen for embezzling union funds while he was general secretary unless he agreed to make a public withdrawal of his statement incriminating the *idioŋ* cult.[61] At the conference Usen was dismissed from membership in the Ibibio Union for life, and it was resolved that he be ostracized by Ibibio people everywhere for having "plotted the destruction of leading personalities by deliberately picking them out, well-knowing that they were innocent, and accusing them falsely of being members of the man-leopard society."[62] No evidence suggests whether it was seen as a credible threat, but the police report from the union conference further claimed that "Native doctors were employed to prepare charms against him [Usen] in order to bring about his death."[63]

The union's condemnation of its own former secretary coincided with a dramatic twist in the murder investigations. During the Ibibio Union's tour, a new district officer was appointed to administer Opobo Division, John McCall. Initially concerned about the number of acquittals in supreme court cases, he found serious discrepancies in eyewitness statements when he reviewed the evidence and was shocked at the paucity of hard evidence for the existence of the man-leopards. His point was quite simple, that the man-leopard episode had been conjured up not by the *idiog* society but by mass hysteria and that the killings were not elaborate simulations but genuine bush leopard attacks. The district officer and his assistant, Dennis Gibbs, tested this theory when they organized a leopard hunt.[64] It was not the first hunt of the investigations, but it was more extensive than previous efforts and successfully trapped a number of leopards, including a seven-foot "man-eater" that had suffered an injury to its paw and was therefore unable to kill its normal prey. McCall's theory appeared all the more probable as only one "leopard" killing was reported after the hunt, and this was outside the "leopard area."

McCall's allegations turned the whole investigation on its head. He was adamant that even if his theory about the leopards was wrong and that the deaths were the result of murder, then the colonial criminal justice system had hanged the wrong men. His reports were evidence of a rift that had emerged between the police and the district administration. McCall criticized Fountain's police investigation and questioned the faith he placed in the speculative findings of Usen's report. McCall's knowledge of the murder cases was not comprehensive, nor was his acumen for forensics more than amateurish, but the questions he raised concerning the use of material evidence were devastating. Why had the police relied on the confession evidence in the P. C. Chima case when it had not held up in court and the accused had been acquitted? And why, he asked, had police attention focused squarely on the use of body parts when in the vast majority of cases they had never been removed from the scene of the crime? Usen's report had suggested that murders were performed to obtain male and female genitalia and skulls for ritual purposes, but there was never any evidence that genitalia had been touched nor that skulls had ever been removed. McCall questioned Usen on this very point, who replied that he was "referring to killing custom which pertained in very olden time, and not during the present series of killings."[65]

Sixteen convicted men were due to be executed when McCall urgently submitted a series of secret reports detailing these reservations in the days before Christmas 1947. McCall insisted that his correspondence be passed to the secretary of state, and his allegations therefore threatened to undermine the reputations of all those involved in the investigations. Indeed, in November 1947, when McCall's views surfaced, the colonial secretary had already been asked in the House of Commons to justify the "vast number of death sentences passed."[66] The government's response was predictable. McCall was given twenty-four

hours to leave his post and was ordered to refrain from drawing attention to his transfer to Lagos.[67]

McCall's reports of December 1947, however, had become general
knowledge, and chiefs from Opobo sent telegrams to London petitioning against his hasty transfer. Crucially for the chiefs and the Ibibio
Union, McCall's allegations enabled them not only to deny *idioŋ* involvement in the killings but more generally to redeem the good name
of Ibibioland by dismissing any suggestions that the killings were conducted by the man-leopard society for ritual purposes at all: "It sur-
prises the bulk of the Ibibio people to hear that the Idiong society, a
society as old as the hills in Ibibioland, has connection with the recent
man-leopard menace, there being no society in Ibibioland known as the
'Man-Leopard Society.' . . . [W]e humbly pray to government to repeal
the legislation against this purely religious society of the Ibibio people,
as freedom of worship constitutes good government."[68] While these
events unfolded in the early months of 1948, Usen Udo Usen had been
working with the Nigeria police contingent based in Ikot Okoro. Usen,
it was claimed, continued to voice his anti-*idioŋ* sentiments, and the Ibibio Union's campaign against him "did not deter Usen from his self-
imposed task . . . he gave up his weekends and most of his other spare
time to visiting different parts of the area, using his very considerable
influence with the local people and continuing to supply most useful
information to the police."[69] Backed by local court and council members, Usen embarked on a second tour of the man-leopard villages in
1948. He was convinced that murderers had evaded the effects of the
mbiam oath sworn the previous year by use of an antidote, and despite
the inconclusive results of the previous tour, he was sure that oath
swearing was the only means by which the killings would finally be
stopped. Hence, Usen set about obtaining from "medicine men" various medicines and charms, and thus armed he held meetings and repeated the oath-swearing ceremonies in nearly every one of the affected Annang villages. Fountain reported that from the start Usen was
well received and that his second tour was an acclaimed success.

The final twist came on February 21, 1948, when Akpan Ukpon
Eto, the son of Chief Ukpon Eto of Ediene Atai, with whom Usen had
clashed over the contents of his report, died suddenly. An exhumation
order was obtained by the medical officer, who was unable to certify
the cause of death. The chief's son was rumored to have been a leading
"man-leopard" himself and had been accused of but never charged
with the murder of P. C. Chima the year before. He had taken Usen's

oath when he visited the village a fortnight previously during which the *mbiam* was held against his chest, back, and head, parts of the body where Akpan Ukpon Eto complained of pains before he died. Rumors spread that he died of swearing a false oath and that he had confessed this before his death. Usen's reputation, Fountain claimed, was redeemed, and apart from the single death in March 1948, the murders stopped. Among the various factors that had broken the murder cult, Fountain wrote that "the work of Mr Usen may certainly be given a high place on the list."[70]

The provincial authorities deemed that a formal inquiry into the man-leopard murders would prove politically unsettling. At a meeting with the chief commissioner of the eastern provinces in March 1950, the Ibibio Union was told that a commission of inquiry into the killings would have led to "a great deal of unpleasant publicity and . . . endless complications."[71] Partly this would have appeared to concede to the Ibibio Union's demands, and partly such an enquiry would have had to address McCall's potentially embarrassing concerns. Hence, in conspicuous contrast to other major incidents in the eastern provinces, such as the Women's War of 1929 and the Enugu Colliery shootings of 1949, the man-leopard murder investigation simply petered out.

After his secondment with the police, Usen reverted to the provincial administration and was transferred first to Ikot Ekpene, then to his home district of Itu, and finally at his request to the headquarters of the regional administration in Enugu. In the margin of a report that referred to Usen's death after a short illness in Enugu, Frank Williams, a junior police officer with the investigation, wrote "Was Poisoned!!" In an article he wrote later for a police journal he expanded: "[T]his District Clerk died mysteriously shortly afterwards. It is quite probable that he was poisoned for his disclosures, he had obviously incurred the disfavour of some of his fellow tribesmen. The cassava root, grown extensively in the area and the staple diet, is edible only after lengthy processing. In its early stages of preparation for food, it is poisonous and a well-known insidious means in the disposal of unwanted persons."[72] Usen, along with the handful of Annang court members who supported the investigations in 1948, was awarded the Certificate of Honour on the king's birthday in 1949. The Ibibio Union claimed that the posthumous award was a "face-saving device."[73]

Honored by the colonial authorities but publicly outcast from his own community, had Usen Udo Usen betrayed his people, or was he a political fall guy? Several points can be made concerning the events narrated here that also have a central bearing on how clerks mediated law and authority in colonial Africa. The first touches on modes of justice and knowledge, the second relates to Usen's attempt to mediate between the various parties engaged in the murder investigations, and the third concerns something of the man and his motivations.

The Ibibio Union would condemn Usen's report on the grounds that he had intended to exploit the gullibility of expatriate administrative officials by a display of his knowledge of the social structure, norms, and beliefs of the Ibibio people.[74] Usen Udo Usen, then, was portrayed as the "man who knew too much." Indeed, the murder investigations demonstrate that knowledge and ways of knowing were critical. Usen's part in the murder inquiries was crucial not only because of the structural and personal way in which he brokered between institutions but also because of the way he mediated between different ways of knowing. For the authorities the man-leopard society was a knowable object of colonial rationality that had, so officers mused, evaded detection during the extensive 1930s inquiries for the clan intelligence reports. Indeed, throughout the campaign the police called for a specialist, an anthropologist, to be hired to investigate the "leopard society." The names of S. F. Nadel, Audrey Richards, Phyllis Kaberry, and J. S. Harris were all mentioned in connection with the proposed anthropological investigation, which, like the formal inquiry, was called off as political sensitivities increased.[75]

Usen, in fact, had gained a unique insight into colonial modalities of the ethnographic method as Jeffreys's interpreter, and his report was a product of it. Yet if a "man-leopard" society had existed, neither the police's thumbscrews nor the anthropologist's observations stood much chance of penetrating its secrets, and Usen knew it. Usen grasped the significance that in this context truth was established by testing and that guilt was determined not in a courtroom trial but in trial by ordeal. Because of this over fifty years later those who remember the events of 1947 and 1948 in the former Abak Division say that it was the oaths Usen and the chiefs administered that brought the killings to an end. Usen's response demonstrates Karen Field's point that those who move effectively into insurgencies understand the significance of the knowledge and practice of routine cultural patterns in reestablishing order.[76] One of the most potent and contradictory images from these events must be that of the district clerk who championed the campaign against the *idioŋ* diviners, but who undertook this campaign with the use of charms and substances acquired from specialists in precisely the same arts.

Usen's actions demonstrate the improvisation with which colonial clerks subverted colonial modes of authority and how they were translated into locally effective terms. On the political level, however, his career also shows how their room for maneuvering could evaporate. In terms of the second point regarding Usen's institutional loyalties, it is evident that events overtook him quickly both in the micropolitics of the investigation and within the broader sweep of national political change. During the war years clerks had to negotiate the increasingly difficult political contradiction of being from the educated class, which criticized colonial rule, while at the same time being among those who helped to enforce it. In southeastern Nigeria 1947 was in fact a key moment for these political trajectories. Specifically, these few months represented the cusp of a fundamental change in relations between "improvement unions" like the Ibibio Union and the colonial state.[77] In the twenty years Usen had been a member of the Ibibio Union, no single issue before the ban on *idioŋ* had ruptured relations between its leaders and the resident of Calabar Province. The provincial authorities, indeed, had consistently sought to nurture the union as the body around which one day an amalgamated Ibibio Division could be organized. Yet coinciding with the Local Government Dispatch of 1947, a secret review was underway in the eastern provinces of the political threat of the improvement unions of whom the authorities had lost sight during the war, and who were buoyed by their recent affiliation with the National Council, which was led by the country's leading nationalists. By this time, then, the Ibibio Union had become a significant political force and was recognized as such both by local communities and by the authorities.

The more explicitly political and anticolonial trajectory of the unions and their more confident and strident tone of criticism toward the government from this moment in 1947 put those among their members who were part of the colonial machinery, such as clerks, in a potentially awkward position. Underlying the tension was an increasingly dismissive view among the intelligentsia toward government service, which was especially vehement when those in receipt of scholarships funded by the improvement unions entered the colonial administration. Once the lawyers and newspaper men of the union seized on the apparent injustices of the man-leopard murder inquiries, especially the ban on the *idioŋ* society, which they described as a gross infringement of religious liberties, they would publicly and persistently attempt to put the colonial administration on trial. Usen had therefore found himself on the wrong side over an issue that may have seemed innocuous enough to him at the time he submitted his report but that was progressively being recast not in the colonial context of law and order but in a nationalist framework of rights and freedoms.

Despite the shifting ground of political alliances, the idea that Usen was a victim of circumstance nevertheless fails to tell us the whole story, and a key puzzle remains. Since Usen knew better than most that the Ibibio Union's line on the *idioŋ* prohibition was resolute, why did he persevere in support of the government and why did he therefore allow himself to be set up to be despised by and ostracized from his own people? This question brings us to the final issue, which relates to his personal motivations. As a colonial clerk was Usen the collaborator or the trickster? Annang and Ibibio conceptions of the intermediary also draw on this distinction. Of those who insert themselves within a privileged site of brokerage to "make trouble so that they can eat" and to "take from each side," Annang say *siguongo inyongo* ("what comes out will not pass"). Such a term is used in opposition to the conception of *adaufot*. Precolonial economic and political links between villages were maintained by intermediaries called *adaufot* (literally "in-between"). This term *adaufot* has continued to refer to an upstanding person who mediates and hears from both sides in order to make peace. In local terms Usen represented himself as such an intermediary figure in opposition to the "tricksters." He was among those senior, long-serving clerks who not only stood apart from the criticism leveled at ill-educated bribe takers within the service, but also were themselves part of an emergent middle-class and members of associations who opposed bribery and corruption.[78]

Usen had been in colonial service for at least twenty-three years. He knew his Bible well probably from his schooling in the United Presbyterian Church of Scotland in Itu, and in his controversial report he left a record of his views on local people. These fragments combine to suggest the profile of a man whose ethical and political outlook was distinctly shaped by both mission teaching and colonial duty. His view of the local Annang population in the man-leopard villages was of "savage men who were clever only in practising wickedness." He noted passages of sermons from interdenominational church services that were held on each Sunday during the tour and attacked what he called the barbarous work of the new "spiritual churches" who engaged in faith healing. And he drew attention to those whom he called "men of character" and to distinguished church reverends, village heads, and court clerks who displayed that "high sense of duty and honesty" of which he himself was so proud.[79] In short he had become not only an agent of but a champion for the colonial order.

His was not as glamorous or as high profile a profession as the lawyers and journalists who were increasingly making the news, but for the duration of the first tour Usen was untouchable. The most prominent chiefs in the province, the resident, the district officers, the police, the court clerks from two divisions, not to mention the hundreds of local people he confronted each day—all were hanging on his word. As a clerk Usen was clearly flattered by and thrived on the attention. And while Usen and the tour party were met with grim findings and grave responsibilities at many of their stops, at others they were met with school children performing dances, and in one instance Mrs. Usen, who had joined him for a few days, was asked by a Catholic Church school to hand out the cups on prize day. This was the stuff of a district officer's or a resident's tour. In his report and his later correspondence, he would point out the deplorable state of the roads in certain villages, the illegality of particular local customs, the commendable achievement of mission schools, and how a village group might be better organized to be closer to court. These were precisely the observations and recommendations of senior colonial staff. The Ibibio Union Tour Delegation was part peacekeeping mission and part imperial pageant, and it is difficult to see how this could not have boosted Usen's sense of his own self-importance and ultimately his misplaced sense of where his own prospects were best served.

Notes

I am grateful to the Economic and Social Research Council and the British Academy (Postdoctoral Research Fellowship and grant SG-32993) for their support of the research on which this essay is based. My sincere thanks to John Peel, Richard Rathbone, the participants at the symposium, and the editors for their comments on earlier drafts.

1. Although I am distinguishing here between official roles—letter writers, clerks, interpreters—we should also be mindful that these categories often overlapped and people's roles were often improvised. Robert Cudjoe, a Ghanaian, worked in southeastern Nigeria during the second decade of the twentieth

century as an interpreter, though his official role was district carpenter (Cudjoe, "Some Reminiscences").

2. Derrick, "'Native Clerk.'"

3. Ayandele, *Educated Elite.*

4. Afigbo, *Warrant Chiefs.*

5. Bayart, "'Social Capital,'" 46.

6. *Daily Mail* (London), June 30, 1947.

7. Several coastal West African states, including Liberia, Sierra Leone, Gabon, and Senegal had, from the 1880s to the 1920s, witnessed fatal assaults that were disguised by simulating the injuries inflicted by wild animals on their prey and that were linked to societies of human-leopards, human-alligators, and human-baboons. Court confessions suggested that these were secret clubs whose members consumed human flesh and used it in the preparation of charms to make themselves rich and powerful. Other "big-cat killings" revealed motives of political assassination. In the Congo in the early 1930s, the Belgian authorities waged an intense campaign against man-leopard killers, known as *wahokohoko*, who were specialist assassins hired by prominent chiefs during an interclan conflict. Concurrent with events in Nigeria during 1947, 103 deaths in the Turu region of Singida Province in central Tanganyika were attributed to human-lions *(mbojo).* For an overview, see Lindskog, *African Leopard Men;* and Joset, *Les sociétés secrètes;* on the murders in Calabar Province, see Nwaka, "'Leopard' Killings.'"

8. Nigerian National Archive, Enugu NAE, ABAKDIST 1/2/88.

9. Noah, "Ibibio Union"; Nwaka, "Ibibio Union."

10. Mamdani, *Citizen and Subject.*

11. During the initial colonial enclosures in the second decade of the twentieth century, very few patrilineal clan heads, *okuku*, were recognized or "warranted," though the title has since become widely employed by village heads.

12. NAE, CSE 1/85/4905A.

13. See Naanen, "Economy within an Economy."

14. Cases emerged in the 1940s of *idioŋ* suing their Christian heirs for lost initiation fees (NAE, CALPROF 3/1/1955). The Christ Army Church and the Sabbath Church spread into the Annang hinterland from the commercial ports of Bonny and Opobo by capitalizing on the formalism of the Qua Iboe Mission and the syncretic charismatic impulse of the Spirit Movement, which had swept across the province in 1927 and annually throughout the 1930s. See Abasiattai, "Oberi Okaime Christian Mission."

15. In the Ibibio dialect the killers were referred to as *Ekpe Ikpa Ukot,* the "leopards who walk in shoes."

16. Inspector Ntima, in charge of the Opobo Police Detachment, was transferred in disgrace on suspicion that the chiefs of the "leopard area" were behind the killings and had bribed him to classify previous murders as wild leopard killings (NAE, OPODIST 1/10/8).

17. Okon Bassey's wives reported how he had shown them leopard pad marks on Dan Udofia's grave and that he had said, "A leopard always dances on the grave of its victim" (NAE, ABAKDIST 1/3/2).

18. The administration of Abak and Opobo Divisions was reformed with the creation of the "leopard area" in February 1946, which comprised eight native court areas from Abak and Opobo Divisions.

19. Widespread rumors that death sentences in previous cases had not been carried out and that the convicts had been conscripted or sentenced to hard labor convinced officials to conduct executions in public.

20. Rhodes House (hereafter RH), Oxford, U.K., MSS Afr.s.1784 (18).

21. The ritual and revenge motives were the predominant though by no means the only theories attributed to the murders both at the time and subsequently. The killers have been linked to Igbo blacksmiths (by the Ibibio Union), to demobilized soldiers (Okon, "Man-Leopard Society"), and to a revival of the *ekpe* secret society (Nwaka, "'Leopard' Killings").

22. This theory may also be linked to the fact that during a previous posting in Ogoja Province in 1938, the district officer F. R. Kay had investigated head-hunting murders in Obubra and was struck by the similarity of the mutilation with the leopard killings, particularly that facial tissue was removed from the victims in both cases (NAE, ABAKDIST 1/3/1).

23. Comments made in the earliest ethnographic accounts by Jeffreys had suggested a precolonial link between *idioŋ* and the Long Juju at Arochukwu, which served to heighten this speculation (cf. Afigbo, "External Contacts and Relations").

24. Public Records Office (hereafter PRO), London, CO 583/294/3.

25. CALPROF 13/1/8. The fact that no strangers were killed during *ekpe-owo* seemed to confirm that the killings were "personal matters."

26. Quotations respectively from RH, MSS Afr.s.1784 (18); NAE, CALPROF 17/1/1595.

27. In the case of 60 additional deaths that were investigated, making a total of 157, the motives were uncertain.

28. NAE, ABAKDIST 1/2/88.

29. This observation also reflects a common assumption that the killings occurred in two distinct phases, firstly by authentic "leopard-men" who employed all the various devices (costumes, medicines, and claws) to disguise their acts, and second, by those who effected crude imitations of the "leopard-style."

30. The parallel with previous acts of rebellion in south-eastern Nigeria was raised at the time of the killings. Nyong Essien, for instance, claimed that, "the Leopard Society was caused by a similar situation which gave rise to the Aba riot" (*Eastern Nigerian Guardian*, 2 April 1947).

31. NAE, ABAKDIST 1/2/90.

32. NAE, CALPROF 17/1/1598.

33. On the typology of such killings, see R. Law, "Human Sacrifice". Cf. on

"medicine murders," see Gocking, "Chieftaincy Dispute"; Murray and Sanders, "Medicine Murder"; Rathbone, *Murder and Politics.*

34. NAE, CSE 1/85/9284.
35. NAE, CSE 1/85/9284.
36. NAE, CALPROF 3/1/1955.
37. NAE, OPODIST 1/10/5.
38. PRO, CO 583/294/3.
39. NAE, CALPROF 7/1/1418.
40. NAE, ABAKDIST 1/2/80.
41. *Nigerian Eastern Mail,* October 11, 1947.
42. RH, MSS Afr.s.1784 (18).
43. NAE, CALPROF 7/1/1418.
44. NAE, OPODIST 1/1/47.
45. NAE, OPODIST 1/10/6.
46. The use of "counter-charms" against *ekpe-owo* was reported as a popular response to the killings. In August 1946 Chief Sampson Akpan Ekpo of Ikot Ibak in Opobo Division had paid eight pounds to a "native doctor" for the preparation of a charm that was guaranteed to protect his village against *ekpe-owo* and that would ensure the immediate arrest of the murderer if a killing was to occur (NAE, CALPROF 17/1/1598).
47. It was no coincidence that during the man-leopard murders the Qua Iboe Mission was reportedly "flooded" with new converts. And its cause was further promoted when its new rival the Christ Army Church was implicated (albeit indirectly) in the murders and "[t]he burning of the idols of the *Idioŋ* by the police gave the Church a wonderful opportunity for witness" (Public Records Office of Northern Ireland, Belfast, U.K., D/3301/GC/9/3).
48. The process of stepping over an object is common in Annang ritual practice. *Ekong* masquerade players, for instance, must jump over a net to signify that they are true initiates. No two reports of the substance used in the oath are the same, with references to villagers touching a pen, a doll, and a brass door knob, and to consuming or smearing on their bodies a clear liquid. It is possible that the delegation did not wish to elicit official consternation over the use of *mbiam* and therefore used innocuous objects. It is also possible that the substances were switched between villages to prevent the manufacture of an antidote from the same source. *Mbiam* can be of any substance, but crucially its origin should be secret (hence a preference for saltwater).
49. Similar features of the *hale* of the Mende are described in Jedrej, "Medicine, Fetish and Secret Society."
50. RH, MSS. Afr.s.1784 (18).
51. NAE, CALPROF 7/1/1418.
52. RH, MSS Afr.s.1784 (18).
53. RH, MSS Afr.S.1505.2.
54. NAE, OPODIST 1/10/6.

55. Udoma, *Story of the Ibibio State Union,* 166.

56. *Nigerian Eastern Mail,* July 10, 1948.

57. Udoma, *Story of the Ibibio State Union,* 142.

58. The prohibition on *idioŋ* was extended in 1951 to include the worship and invocation of *idioŋ,* and it was further recommended that the ban be extended to the whole of Calabar Province following a murder in Eket.

59. Udoma refused but another barrister, Ibeziaku, wrote the petition for a fee of 30 guineas (NAE, OPODIST 1/1/47).

60. NAE, OPODIST 1/10/3.

61. NAE, OPODIST 1/10/3.

62. Udoma, *Story of the Ibibio State Union,* 178.

63. NAE, OPODIST 1/10/3.

64. McCall reported that Gibbs kept a pet leopard in order to establish its feeding and killing behavior. McCall had been an administrative officer in the eastern provinces for eleven years. Gibbs, a former wing commander with the Royal Air Force, had a distinguished war record.

65. NAE, OPODIST 1/10/3.

66. *Evening Standard* (London), November 19, 1947.

67. McCall stood by these claims, particularly the wild-leopard theory in the British press and in response to academic writings (McCall, "Comment").

68. *Nigerian Eastern Mail,* July 3, 1948.

69. RH, MSS Afr.s.1784 (18).

70. RH, MSS Afr.s.1784 (18).

71. NAE, CALPROF 5/1/308.

72. RH, MSS Afr.s.1784 (18).

73. RH, MSS. Afr.s.1784 (18).

74. Udoma, *Story of the Ibibio State Union,* 163.

75. In addition Meyer Fortes and Raymond Firth were both asked to propose candidates for a Colonial Social Science Research Council–funded project in 1948 and 1949 that aimed to shed light on the murders while posing under the camouflage of a more general and innocuous study (PRO, CO 583/294/4).

76. Fields, "Political Contingencies," 593.

77. We need to be wary of here, however, of a teleology that would equate the "progressives" of the 1930s with the "political class" of the 1950s, since there was, as Peel notes, "a disjunction as well as a linkage between 'nationalism,' *qua* the national anti-colonial movement, and the local political tendencies related to it" (Peel, *Ijeshas and Nigerians,* 179).

78. Usen, for instance, had accompanied the Ibibio Union delegations in 1941 and 1942 around the district offices and court houses of Calabar Province, "enlightening" court and council members and his fellow civil servants against bribe taking. Groups specifically organized around this issue, such as the League of Bribe Scorners, would emerge some years later.

79. NAE, OPODIST 1/10/6.

Cultural Commuters

African Employees in Late Colonial Tanzania

ANDREAS ECKERT

The Mimic Men

New interpretations of the colonial state transcend the old dichoto-mous view of this state either as an "intelligent bulldozer," a powerful instrument of political rule and structural transformation, or as a weak state, characterized by its lack of resources and limited drive, con-stantly shifting between massive threatening of the local population and offers to cooperate.[1] To add further insights into the debates on the colonial state, a closer look at those Africans who staffed the adminis-trative apparatus of the state promises to be useful. One could even refer to Max Weber, who compared the modern state with a factory and insisted that "the real power, the power which has an impact on daily life, inevitably is in the hands of the bureaucracy."[2]

This chapter will thus focus on the activities, social structures, and mentalities of African colonial employees in Tanganyika after World War II in the context of state structures, projects, and practices. But why these particular people in the case of Tanganyika? Would it not be more relevant to look at the interactions that took place between colonials and peasant farmers? In Tanganyika peasants formed the great majority of the population; they bore the brunt of colonial domination and colonial exploitation and paid a terrible price. The Maji Maji War, for instance, was among the most brutal and the most costly in terms of lives.[3] The victims of huge and often disastrous development projects such as the notorious groundnut scheme especially after 1945 were mainly peasants.[4]

The importance of the colonial employees in Tanzania hails from the fact that they, although constituting a small group, became the champions of political modernization and later important protagonists of anticolonial nationalism before inheriting state power at the end of colonial rule. It is instructive to see that a considerable number of the Tanganyikan cabinet members in 1963 had worked at some point for the colonial administration.[5] Survey research done in the 1960s clearly demonstrated that the rulers of independent Tanzania were overwhelmingly salaried administrators. A private research firm found that more than half of the members of the elite in 1967 had "higher civil servant" as their primary occupation.[6] According to Steven Feierman, the salaried class with its roots in the colonial administrative service "was so powerful in the early years of independence that it was able to prevent the emergence of alternative nodes of power, whether among the traders . . . or among the trade unions."[7] The African employees were among the first individuals who—at colonial schools and in the workplace—were familiarized with the values of the colonizers. In their new positions they spread what they had learned. Moreover, this group was at the center of British attempts to impose discipline in school and administration, to regulate time, space, clothing and food—of "character training," as the British called it.

Of course, in colonial times the government of Tanganyika was by definition European, as were the higher ranks of the administration. But because of their weak presence, the so-called "thin white line," the British had to rely on a growing number of local staff members.[8] Most of these locals were employed in auxiliary services; some of them, however, were put in charge of local affairs in distant places. And some of them, such as the ubiquitous government interpreters working with European district officers, were even at the very center of things. Although they had no position of official authority, they had the power to influence things merely by their language skills. In Tanganyika until the late 1950s, the colonial administration needed interpreters espe-cially in those areas where little or no Swahili was spoken by the local population.[9]

However, the importance of interpreters in the context of colonial administration in post–World War II Tanganyika was probably fairly small, as Swahili as the lingua franca became increasingly dominant, and British officials usually had sufficient knowledge of Swahili to use it in administrative procedures and court cases. On the other hand, in this period the colonial need for African employees in general rose con-siderably. In the face of its rapidly melting Asian empire, Great Britain launched in Africa (as did France) a "developmental colonialism," which was supposed to be of immediate economic use to Britain and to grant Africans the "maturity" deemed necessary for independence.[10] Even in formerly imperial backwaters such as Tanganyika, the British made public investments on a larger scale, considerably extended the local administrative apparatus, and introduced new bodies of political participation. Thus administrative fields of activity opened up for a growing though still relatively modest number of Tanganyikans. At the end of the war, the British in Tanganyika faced a severe dilemma. They knew that things could not go on as before. The system of indirect rule, based on "tribal structures" and the alliance with supposedly tradi-tional rulers, had proved to be unsuitable for adequately coping with political and economic problems in the territory. Still, the government in Dar es Salaam did not share the enthusiasm of the Colonial Office, which propagated the cooperation with African urban "educated elites" in order to slowly prepare African territories for independence. It was hoped that by giving Africans a greater share in administration, the co-lonial governments would secure the cooperation and assistance of the educated and politically conscious Africans for a final and extended period of preparation for internal self-government and independence.[11]

Most colonial officials in Tanganyika, however, made considerable effort to circumvent related directives from London. These officials were prisoners of existing local power relations, prisoners of their own racist prejudices, too, but they were also very much aware of the difficulties of putting into practice the modernization project designed in London. They responded with resistance and activism, in the hope of saving the old power alliances with only slight modifications. They played for time. Although after 1945 more and more development experts arrived in Tanganyika, "determined to drag its people into the twentieth cen-tury," most administrators were keen to preserve tribal structures.[12] For financial as well as ideological reasons, the wonderful announcements in colonial memoranda were only partially and reluctantly translated into action. Thus both training and career patterns of African employees in late colonial Tanzania remained comparatively restricted.

African employees formed a rather heterogeneous group with different goals and conflicting interests. We could think of the conflict between bureaucratic ideals with its emphasis on achievement, division of labor, and impersonality, on the one hand, and the loyalty to local political culture, on the other hand, not to mention the influence of chiefly politics with their emphasis on accumulation, generosity, and personal loyalty. These employees manipulated and succumbed to manipulation. But for all their differences, they had one thing in common: their situation betwixt and between, or between tradition and modernity, as it was called in the 1950s and 1960s. British officials in Tanganyika, for instance, constructed their African employees usually as individuals torn between two worlds, as individuals whose unlimited access to the promises of modernity would for a long time to come be prevented by the "atavistic Africa" still in them. As one district officer in Dar es Salaam noted about his clerk: "He is one of the new Africans, the type created by European-style education and ideas. He and others like him face stresses and tensions Europeans find hard to imagine, for they are torn between two worlds. One foot is in the Western world, with all the dazzling advantages and opportunities to offer. The other is anchored in the old Africa of bush villages and primitivism and female circumcision."[13]

School (and sometimes university) education and their profession led the employees to a position between the local and the global, between old and new, to a position of intermediary ambivalence. They acted as cultural commuters or brokers, as mediators between different worlds. This positioning, however, did not necessarily mean they were torn between these two worlds, but, as Cooper rightly emphasized, "in between is as much a place to be home than any other."[14] Their function as brokers created for these Africans new possibilities of influence that sometimes went far beyond the realm assigned them by colonial organization charts. Moreover, this function enabled them to play with different cultural registers and repertoires and to establish numerous networks in an in-between space characterized by hierarchies, rejections, and contradictions. From that resulted a specific understanding of authority, power, and culture, neither traditional nor modern, but rather a specific *bricolage*.[15] The African employees rationally combined diverse attitudes and practices to develop and foster their own way of life. They mediated between apparently incompatible positions while never forgetting their own advantages. As will be shown, this *bricolage* characterized especially those employees who became late colonial chiefs.

The peculiar position of African employees is also reflected in the sources available. The British in London and Tanganyika produced splendid programs and bold reports. They left statistical skeletons and legislative texts en masse. Thus in many ways the colonial archive is a monument to both the fragility of bureaucratic utopia and its orientation toward a distant future. It is extremely difficult, however, to extract from these sources information about administrative routines and practices.[16] This is because the colonizers usually relied—whether out of necessity or by inclination—on oral information rather than on the written word. Moreover, the British colonial officials tended to ignore or overlook everything they did not want to see. Finally, even a cursory look at the source material shows that the British had the utmost difficulties in coming to terms with their African employees on an intellectual level. In general they depicted them in very derogatory terms that boiled down to the stereotype that all of them were half-educated at best and corrupt to the bone, arrogant cheats and indolent idlers at worst. V. S. Naipaul, the Trinidadian writer of Indian descent and a Nobel laureate, who received his university education at Oxford, called them the "mimic men."[17] Admiration and respect were reserved, if at all, for chiefs and peasants, not for employees, the further removed from colonial culture the better. No doubt these stereotypes were mainly a result of the hybrid position of the employees as pupils, collaborators, and competitors of the British.

Last but not least, it must be mentioned that African employees in late colonial Tanzania were overwhelmingly male. As was the case nearly everywhere in colonial Africa (and at that time in Europe as well), the world of the administrative offices in this East Africa territory was a male world. At least through the backdoor, however, the female part of the population began to enter the working environment. Already in the 1920s the British insisted in their education programs on the training of women by emphasizing their role as housewives and mothers. Reasonably well-trained women at least would ensure "that clever boys, for whom higher education is expedient, [could] look forward to educated mates."[18] The British ideal of an African bureaucrat thus implied a sufficiently educated wife "by his side." Until the end of the colonial period, however, aside from courses in sewing and housekeeping, there were few possibilities for women to enjoy higher education, let alone access to administrative jobs. And some colonial officials went so far as to regard supposedly uneducated wives as an obstacle to the fuller social integration of their African employees. J. C. Cairns, for instance, district officer in Dar es Salaam, concluded, "The African wife, of course, is the great barrier to natural social relations between the races. With the husband, conversation is often easy, and inter-racial relationships enjoyable. But what can be done about the wife, who sits miserable, speechless, ill at ease, unable to enjoy the food, unable to use a knife and fork, unable either to join in or understand the conversation."[19]

Employees In-Between

On the eve of independence a senior administrative job offered the greatest promise. In May 1960 the newspaper *Mwafrika* published a letter to the editor written by a clerk from Tabora, in which he proposed that clerks should be promoted to higher administrative posts while women should take over poorly paid clerk jobs: "These days we see that many Africans who do not come from among the clerks . . . are taken to study in Europe, and others are given high positions here in Tanganyika without going to Europe to study. The thing which distresses us, for our part as clerks, is that it is our brothers who are not clerks will get the benefit of important positions like Field Officers, Labour Inspectors, Co-operative Officers, Public Relations Officer and so on. . . . Clerks are people who have special knowledge of work in offices, and therefore ought to be thought of for higher positions and to leave the clerks' jobs for women."[20] As Feierman adds, "[t]he clerk's proposal became, to some degree, a reality."[21] In fact, after independence male employees soon made a career in the party and state bureaucracy and occupied important political positions.[22]

Who then were the African employees of the decolonization period occupying leading positions in independent Tanganyika? As will be shown, these African employees operated beyond the binary colonial patterns that neatly differentiated between "old" and "new," between "indigenous" and "Western," or between "tradition" and "modernity." The in-between space in which the employees acted offered many opportunities but at the same time repeatedly revealed the limits of the hierarchical colonial order.

African teachers and government employees experienced the years of World War II as a period full of privation. Although many started in a position of relative affluence and were anxious to preserve their superior status, they soon found that inflation drastically reduced the value of their salaries. Staff shortages forced them to work harder but did not bring faster promotion. British officials noted an increasing bitterness among the employees struggling to maintain their standard of living. This bitterness grew greater at the end of the war, because returning soldiers were often financially better off than the government clerks and were sometimes even promoted first.[23] The loyalty shown during the war (even if sometimes grudgingly) elevated employees' expectations of a more prosperous postwar period. They wanted to take the Europeans at their words; they wanted the state bureaucracy with its laws and decrees to become more transparent; and they themselves wanted to take the role as mediators and, above all, to take responsibility. In the columns of *Kwetu* as well as in diverse petitions and pamphlets of the African Association appeals to the duty of Africans to improve still could be found.[24] Calls for better opportunities, however, became more vocal. The employees suggested, for instance, more and better education, especially higher education, which was a prerequisite for positions in higher administration. They also hoped that the end of war would also mean the end of racial discrimination and racially based inequality. This hope had to be abandoned. G. G. Mhina, a government clerk, stated, "At one time I thought that Tanganyika was a little island in the ocean of colour bar, but recent events have dispelled such thoughts from my mind. Colour bar is now spreading like a forest fire. . . . All departments today reek of it and as long as our standard of life is at a low water mark the foreign element . . . will find grounds for its existence and perpetuation. We can combat it by having an elevation in salaries, standard of life and education, and so it is our chief duty to ask our 'Government' to raise those essential weapons against colour bar."[25]

After the war new complaints were added to the ones already raised in the 1930s, which had revolved mainly around low salaries and the lack of pension rights.[26] To reduce the chronic shortage in staff, the government increasingly filled administrative posts for which many Africans believed themselves to be qualified with Asians. Moreover it created the new position of "district foreman," a coordinator for development projects in the districts. Only "non-natives" had access to these jobs.[27] The rising number of British officials and the continuous refusal to recruit Africans for higher administrative posts reinforced the feeling of discrimination. The Tanganyika African Association (TAA) complained that the government always referred to the absence of qualifications of African candidates without providing a framework to raise these qualifications: "Plans for more education have so far fallen on practically deaf ears. . . . Government should find a new excuse instead of the lame old ones of 'lack of funds' alternating with 'lack of teachers' that has now [become] threadbare."[28]

In the 1940s the Tanganyika African Government Servants Association (TAGSA) became the mouthpiece of employees' demands. The organization claimed to represent the interests of all African government employees, "from road sweeper to the African holding the highest position in the government."[29] By its own account TAGSA had 1,820 members in October 1944, spread over Tanga, Mwanza, Arusha, and Dar es Salaam. In the following year twenty-three other branches in various districts were created.[30] In 1952 the membership had swollen to 3,000 individuals, although a third of them did not pay their membership fees, as the chairman complained.[31] During the first decade after World War II, TAGSA was the most stable and best organized association representing an occupational group, but formally it was not a trade union. It did not strike but instead delivered petitions complaining about the high costs for accommodations, newspapers, books, and cinema tickets.[32] The British preference for Asian employees remained a thorny issue, and resentments against Asians were widespread among African employees.[33]

In the meantime the government in Dar es Salaam retarded the recruitment of Africans for higher administrative posts until the last minute. The British attitude expressed itself, for instance, in the "Report of the Commission on the Civil Services of the East African Territories," published in 1954.[34] From the observation that only few Africans were sufficiently qualified for administrative service, the commission simply concluded that for a long period to come officials from Britain would have to serve in East Africa. Only with the Tanganyika African National Union's (TANU) government participation in 1959 did the Africanization of higher administrative ranks speed up. At that time, Julius Nyerere rightly emphasized in an interview with a British journalist that "[i]n West Africa the Colonial office made its policy clear from the beginning and a local service was trained in good time. Here events ha[d] moved suddenly so quickly that there simply [were] not enough local people with the necessary training available."[35]

It is true that since the late 1940s the number of African government employees continuously rose. In 1960 more that 26,000 Africans were employed by government.[36] Among the 299 administrative officers, however, only 7 were Africans. Dunstan Omari, a Makerere graduate, was appointed in 1959 as the first African district commissioner.[37] There were a further 47 assistant administrative officers. These individuals had no university degree and were not allowed to work autonomously. Even in mid-1961, a few months before independence, there was not a single African provincial commissioner, and there were only 2 district commissioners. Among 4,887 posts in the higher and middle ranks of the administration, only 616 were occupied by Africans.[38]

With the rise of anticolonial nationalism, African employees found themselves in a politically precarious situation.[39] On the one hand, they were cut off from their local roots; on the other hand, following British public service traditions, they were prohibited from taking part in politics and from becoming members of a political association.[40] Government employees with secondary educations who held the highest administrative posts open to Africans usually stayed for only a few years at one place before moving on. Thus it was extremely difficult for them to establish local political bases. Only a few important leaders stayed outside the civil service in the 1950s to work full time for TANU; Julius Nyerere and Oscar Kambona were the most notable of these. Numerous educated Africans working for the administration, however, had to remain—at least outwardly—apolitical.[41] In 1958 TANU began to bureaucratize itself. The party headquarters in Dar es Salaam appointed secretaries for the various local party branches and mainly considered well educated clerks who replaced the local "founding generation" consisting of traders or lower administrative ranks such as messengers. The new forces seemed better equipped to translate orders from the headquarters into action and to deal with the fast-growing correspondence. Soon TANU had nearly 1,000 employees on their payroll, and another 950 individuals received expense allowances or fees.[42]

Although sources are extremely limited and thus general statements are difficult to make, African employees seem to have treated modern bureaucratic administrative norms concerning discipline, clothing, punctuality, and rhetoric (in administrative correspondence) in a pragmatic way. In interviews former employees often raised the ideals of cleanliness, dress codes, and punctuality.[43] The acquisition of European clothes, furniture, a radio, or a gramophone offered the possibility to appropriate selected elements of European culture. These, in turn, made it possible for the employees to distance themselves from other Africans (and Asians).[44] Efforts aimed at separation can also be found in the spatial context. For instance, the TAGSA complained about the lack of separate rooms for African employees in the Sewa Haji Hospital in Dar es Salaam. In a letter to the chief secretary the organization requested a number of privileges: "[T]his Association takes the opportunity of representing the question of admission into hospitals of African Government employees. As a rule a separate compartment should be set aside for Government employees as well as for their families. . . . This Association strongly submits that . . . Government hospitals should spare a compartment—spacious and sufficient enough—for African Government employees and that those entitled to higher privileges on the railways should have them when admitted to hospitals."[45] Demands of this kind were heavily criticized by some Europeans, such as the British trade unionist Norman Pearsons, who sensed ungratefulness. Pearsons characterized educated African employees as irresponsible egoists who claimed advantages for themselves at the expense of the poorer classes (in both Tanganyika and England):

[W]hatever the circumstances of the case most educated Africans are convinced that they are not being fairly treated, and this is one of the things which brings the counter-charge of ingratitude. In any case the truth is that they are doing the exploiting—exploiting their more backward fellow-Africans and, indeed, exploiting many a poor British citizen worse off than they are and who has to keep on digging deeper into his pocket to pay for their welfare among other things. . . . Educated Africans like to claim economic equality with the British as an inherent right. They claim that they have the right to the same sort of food, the same kind of house, the same kind of clothes, the same kind of social conditions. They make their claim, however, not with the bottom classes, who are the types they commonly see in Tanganyika. Although they can see no reason why all British classes, poor included should not foot the bill for the benefit.[46]

Although the employees often made efforts to distance themselves from other Africans and Asians, they called for treatment equal to Europeans on several occasions. This request was seldom met. For instance, the Tanganyika European Civil Servants' Association strictly refused to accept Africans as members, although even the chief secretary had strongly advised the association to do so.[47] The British official in charge of a proposed canteen for government employees insisted on different mealtimes, because, as he explained: "Africans are rather aggressive eaters and drinkers, usually very crude in the way they use common utensils."[48] Residential areas everywhere usually remained segregated. Only very few African employees succeeded in settling in European quarters.[49] The segregation between European and African employees also seemed to have been the rule in the private realm, confirmed by some exceptions.[50] At the Arnautoglu Centre in Dar es Salaam a "multi-racial" discussion group was created in the early 1950s, which included British officials as well as Asian and African employees and teachers (such as Julius Nyerere, Rachidi Kawawa, and Zuberi Mtemvu).[51] Some years later smaller circles were set up in Dar es Salaam in which African employees made efforts to adapt European ways of life. Lorna Dorothy Hall, the wife of a British colonial officer, reported: "A rather exclusive Society has been formed for educated Africans, its twenty or so members are encouraged and helped by an Administrative Officer in his spare time. They meet to discuss a wide-ranging list of subjects and learn about European food and manners. They also like their wives to meet and talk with white women and learn about European food and manners."[52]

On the occasion of official events, African employees seem to have sought personal relationships with higher British officials. J. R. Allen, a mission teacher, noticed that during Governor Twining's visit at Kondoa Irangi, local employees attempted to position themselves besides Twining at the first opportunity.[53] The district officer in Tanga received massive criticism from African employees and teachers who complained that during the Remembrance Day festivities they had to sit too far away from Europeans.[54]

African employees in late colonial Tanzania can also be characterized by their ambivalent conventions of self-representation. A relatively positive attitude toward the many opportunities that came with the colonial order was accompanied by contradictory strategies to present "African tradition" as a limited and conservative sphere of influence. On the other hand, politically ambitious employees increasingly attached to "tradition" a value as a cultural resource and tried to use it for political purposes. In this context a number of employees showed off the production of so-called tribal histories. Already between the wars the colonial administration had made efforts to encourage chiefs to draft tribal histories to strengthen the system of indirect rule.[55] After 1945 the British government continued this initiative and increased their related efforts, for instance, sponsoring through the East African Literature Bureau a number of smaller publications in the series Customs and Traditions in East Africa. By promoting particular ethnographies, the British attempted to counter "detribalization" and nationalism.[56] One of the best examples of this ambivalent genre is *Historia, mila na desturi za Wagogi (The Gogo: History, Customs, and Traditions)*, by Mathias E. Mnyampala, published in 1954 by the East African Literature

Bureau in Nairobi, in which the author, a tax clerk, intended to demonstrate to "the Gogo" that their culture and history could be adapted to
the "modern world."[57] The mixture of tradition and change characteristic of his book is apparent in the following passage: "Perhaps today
some Wagogo are surprised to see that there are still people who listen
to the elders of old. Perhaps they regret the useless savagery of the past
and its things. Truly, each nation and every tribe in its past was in dark-
ness and was different from what it is today. Yet all people need a memory of the past. It is through comparison of such a memory with the
way things are today that we can see our progress. If we are backward
or things hold us back, we should support changes that lead people to
progress."[58]

Chiefs as Bureaucrats, Bureaucrats as Chiefs: Thomas Marealle

Mnyampala ran the Ugogo Union with other employees and teachers,
and it saw itself as a local counterpart of TANU. The union called for
speedy political independence and promoted development and modernization.[59] For its members, as for many other nationalists, chiefs were
political opponents slowing down modernization; chiefs embodied a
reactionary past and therefore had to go. Consequently in 1963, soon
after independence, chieftaincy was officially abolished and replaced
by "local authorities."[60] Far more explicitly than before World War II,
British officials regarded chiefs as part of a colonial bureaucracy in
which the latter were supposed to carry out specific administrative
(and political) tasks, such as the oversight of tax and local government
affairs. Especially those chiefs who presented themselves as being open
to the new were regarded as important partners on the supposedly long
way to self-government and independence. For instance, the British
preferred chiefs as African representatives in the Legislative Council.
On the other hand, they only reluctantly went along with the still small
urban elite. On the national level it was even thought necessary to push
back the "coat and collar boys in the towns" in favor of educated and
"enlightened" chiefs.[61]

It would be wrong, of course, to assume that the "enlightened"
chiefs so cherished by the British supported the British colonial project
without reservation. In late colonial Tanzania numerous chiefs at least
partially shared the visions and goals of the nationalists. This is not surprising considering that a number of those individuals who were

elected and inaugurated as chiefs during the 1950s had been well educated, had occupied higher posts within the colonial administration, and had played an important role during the early period of anticolonial nationalism. Thomas Marealle is a model case of an African employee turned into an "enlightened" chief.[62] Born in 1915 to an important chiefly family of the Chagga in Kilimanjaro area, Marealle entered the colonial administration in 1934. For ten years he served in seven different districts. He became a member of the African Association and emphatically supported *Kwetu* by collecting donations, soliciting subscriptions, and contributing articles. However, although editor Erica Fiah became more radical and critical toward the government during the war, Marealle gradually retired from his collaboration. He took care that the British regarded him as a promising government employee.[63]

Thanks to a government grant, Marealle spent two years (1944–46) in the United Kingdom, studying "social welfare" at the University of Wales in Aberystwyth and completing courses in "social government and administration" at the London School of Economics. Soon after his return to Tanganyika, he was appointed social welfare officer, responsible for several provinces. In 1949 Marealle was nominated program manager of the Dar es Salaam Broadcasting Station (Swahili Service). In this capacity be came a well-known radio "personality" throughout Tanganyika Territory. He was also active in politics, in both the TAA and TAGSA, of which he became president. During the late 1940s, Marealle also intensified his relations with the Fabian Colonial Bureau (FCB), an influential liberal, moderately anticolonial British pressure group with excellent contacts to important British politicians.[64] Around 1950 he was definitely among the best-educated Tanzanians of his generation. In a letter to FCB headquarters he proudly listed all his duties:

I have been appointed, nominated or elected to the following Committees and Boards since my transfer to Dar es Salaam in September, last: Patron of the Chagga Association; President of the Chagga Association, President of the Tanganyika Civil Servants' Association, Committee member (African and Asians) Promotional Board, Member of the Government Employees' Provident Fund, Member of the King George V Memorial Museum, co-opted member of the Rising Cost of Living Committee and Warden of the Lutheran Church of which I am a member. . . . I have been asked to start Tanganyika's B.B.C. right from scratch which means not only the founding of an acceptable system of programs but making up several stories of local texture for filming; editing original ones from other people, scouting for talent (musicians, cartoonists for rural development projects, singers, actors and actresses and Heaven only knows what else . . .).[65]

In the late forties a number of political parties emerged in the Kili-manjaro region, the territory's main coffee-growing area. The Kiliman-jaro Chagga Citizens Union in particular carried the struggle against the system of divisional chiefs, introduced after the war as part of the local government reform.[66] The union was able to push through the change that there should be a paramount chief, or *mangi mkuu*, of all Chagga, elected for life, and it persuaded Thomas Marealle to run for this position. He was indeed the perfect candidate. As grandson of Chief Marealle of Marangu, he had the essential chiefly blood. More-over, he was a university-educated modernizer with much administra-tive experience. Marealle won the election handily. A few days later he wrote in a somewhat pathetic mood to the Fabians: "I am therefore by the Grace of God, the wishes of the Chagga people and approval of the Government Marealle II, Paramount Chief-elect of the Wachagga."[67] Marealle himself never commented on his decision to give up his bril-liant bureaucratic career and to become chief, and the sources available provide hardly any hint. He probably hoped that his effective rule in one of Tanganyika's most important economic regions would facilitate access to political positions on the territorial level.

In January 1952 Marealle was solemnly inaugurated as *mangi mkuu* by Governor Twining. In his speech Twining emphasized the adminis-trative functions of the new chief and his role as "principal mouthpiece of the Chagga people and their liaison with Government."[68] Marealle's formal political power remained fairly limited. Thus he made consider-able efforts to symbolically strengthen his position and at the same time to establish himself as a driving force behind administrative and eco-nomic reforms. The administration of the district closely followed the British model. For instance, Marealle set up numerous subcommittees with their own budgets and meticulously copied the format and style of British administrative correspondence.[69] He promoted the continued educational and economic advancement of "his people" and the solid-ification of his own power by cloaking his authority in cultural nation-alism. The date of Marealle's inauguration was celebrated annually as Chagga Day, and a Chagga flag and anthem were created.[70] Thanks to this unique combination of neotraditionalism and the ethos of modern-ization, Marealle could promise that he would lead the Chagga to greatness as an independent sovereign. He would restore respect to the clans and clan leaders and abolish corruption in the administration. He would speak with authority to government, and it would be forced to listen.[71]

It is true that Marealle stood for two central aims of the government in Dar es Salaam: political reform through democratizing local government bodies, and the establishment of a "multiracial" order.[72] However, Marealle situated himself not far from TANU's aspirations, and he felt very close to Nyerere. In his speech to the United Nations in June 1957, Marealle supported Nyerere's political aims and defended him against his critics.[73] Shortly afterward he wrote to Hilda Selwyn-Clarke of the FCB: "Julius Nyerere and I have a lot in common."[74] Marealle repeatedly offended the nationalists though. For instance, he told *Time:* "The accomplishments of the Chagga will do more for the nationalists' cause than any amount of ranting and agitation. . . . We're making it possible for the nationalists to say: 'Look what we can do.'"[75] At this time Marealle's star was already on the wane. Declining coffee prices, accusations of corruption and autocracy, and suspicion of collusion with the government slowly but surely fueled a campaign against him, led by young Chagga intellectuals. In 1960 Marealle had to leave office. Some time later, after independence, he sued the Kilimanjaro District Council for breach of contract, claiming that local government was obligated to pay him the salary and benefits for a lifetime in office. In October 1963 the high court awarded Marealle the considerable sum of nearly 100 million shillings. Six months later the government introduced a bill in the National Assembly to overrule the court's decision. "Government," Prime Minister Rachidi Kawawa stated, "must have the power to stop a few people who want to suck the blood of many others."[76] From this event on and until very recently, Marealle's image was that of the prototype of a decadent and greedy chief who had firmly collaborated with the British rulers.

After independence other chiefs with important administrative and political careers fell out of favor as well. Among them was Patrick Kunambi, for a time a close ally of Nyerere and present at the legendary inaugural meeting of TANU in July 1954.[77] Kunambi had a degree from Makerere College (Uganda) and worked for a while as a schoolteacher before Governor Twining appointed him a member of the Legislative Council in 1955. Kunambi was a keen TANU activist and member of the party's organizational committee. At the same time, he accepted the newly created office of deputy sultan in Morogoro, where his uncle Sabu Sabu was sultan. According to government sociologist Henri Fosbrooke, Kunambi was the perfect cultural commuter: "There is a strong feeling for traditionalism in Kunambi, and he has easy and pleasant relations with the tribal elders and with Sultan Sabu, who is his uncle.

Nevertheless, Kunambi would like to see the Luguru make a greater advance in the modern world: they should abandon some of the customs, but not by force or decree and without losing their essential character. Kunambi is also a bridge with the European leader; he lives in Morogoro in a Western-type house in an area predominantly European, and his wife drives a car."[78] This position as cultural commuter also created conflicts. Kunambi's critics reproached him for striving for the best of too many worlds—high offices in local government, in territorial politics, and in the nationalist party. During violent manifestations against soil conservation and forced terracing, Kunambi fell between two camps. The anger of the local population was also directed against him, because as representative of colonial power he had to carry through forced terracing. Kunambi's relations to TANU cooled considerably, and after independence there was no place for him in the new political order.

On the other hand, Erasto Mang'enya never suffered because of his position as mediator between nationalist party and chiefly institutions backed by the British administration. After 1961 he became Tanganyika's representative at the United Nations, occupied several high positions in government, and served until his retirement in 1975 as speaker of the National Assembly. In his memoirs *Discipline and Tears*, published in 1984, he portrays himself as a Tanzania nationalist and staunch anticolonialist. However, he did not mention his involvement in the "tribal" Bondei Central Union (BCU) and thus avoided mentioning activities that might be seen as "tribalist," or as collaboration with the colonial state.[79] Mang'enya had already worked as a teacher for twenty years when he was elected *Jumbe Mkuu* of Muheza (Northeast Tanzania) in December 1958.[80] Although he spent most of his professional life outside Muheza, Mang'enya always maintained firm contacts to his home area. Immediately after World War II, he drafted some short essays on the "social development of the Bonde."[81] Comparable to the government memoranda of the period, Mang'enya's writing called for democratization of local government and the consolidation of "tribal structures," sketched five- and ten-year plans for the development of the region (with special emphasis on education and social welfare), and finally, held that chiefs should be educated to follow bureaucratic standards: "They must learn to keep the following records: A Diary, a Log Book, Birth and Death Registers and Cash Book." He garnished his writings with quotes from William Shakespeare, Thomas B. Macaulay, and Winston Churchill. During his office as *Jumbe Mkuu*, Mang'enya devoted—like Marealle—much time and energy to "reinventing" traditional regulations. He did not have much time left, for in Bondei too chieftainship ceased to exist just after independence. However, unlike in Kilimanjaro or in Morogoro, there were never serious conflicts between TANU, trade unions, and the "tribal" BCU in Bondei. The teachers and government employees who formed the BCU leadership easily reached an accord with TANU. And Mang'enya convinced himself as well as TANU that he always supported anticolonial nationalism.[82]

Employees as Rulers

The colonial state in Tanganyika, as elsewhere in Africa, was an authoritarian bureaucratic apparatus of control and—despite official rhetoric, especially after 1945—not intended to be a school of democracy. Although state power was generally weak, British officials struggled to maintain the facade of omnipotence and omniscience. They had a clear sense of being a legitimate and uniquely capable ruling class, a sense they passed on to their successors, to those Africans who had graduated from secondary schools and sometimes universities, who were employed as teachers or clerks by the colonial administration, and who were trained "not to run capitalist enterprises, but the apparatus of the bureaucratic state."[83] The state-administrative elite in independent Tanzania, many of them former colonial employees, formed a heterogeneous group. However, they shared the conviction taken over from their British predecessors that they alone knew the solutions for the many problems of the country.[84] They thus retained from the colonial period their familiar role as cultural brokers and mediated to the people strategies and projects that they thought would bring prosperity and justice. Their view of their own position was that skepticism, criticism, or even resistance against the state projects would threaten the still fragile national unity as well as the progress of society. Their "in-between" position now was far more comfortable than during the colonial period, as it was far easier to put ideas into practice. To substantiate their efforts to order rural life, the state elite adduced a mixture of constructions of a traditional African socialism and technocratic-economic visions of rural development deriving from the World Bank.

Finally, the close nexus between government, TANU, and administration resulted in a bureaucratic practice characterized by a certain autism. One of the most striking continuities between the British rulers and the rulers of independent Tanzania was the conviction of having a monopoly on useful knowledge and the view of peasants as obstacles on the way to progress. From the peasants' perspective, the despotism of the state simply continued.[85]

Notes

The research on which this essay is based was funded by the Deutsche Forschungsgemeinschaft through two large research projects on which I collaborated for certain periods. The interviews in 1996 quoted in the essay were conducted together with Katrin Bromber (now with the Center for Modern Oriental Studies, Berlin). I also want to thank Elias J. Tarimo for helping to arrange and conduct interviews in Dar es Salaam and Moshi in 1999. Special thanks must finally go to the late Albert Wirz (Humboldt University, Berlin), with whom I discussed many ideas relevant to this piece. He died, far too early, in May 2003, and I wish to dedicate this chapter to him. Throughout this essay I use Tanganyika and Tanzania interchangeably, though the latter formally only designates the country after the unification of Tanganyika and Zanzibar in 1964.

1. Bayart, *l'Etat en Afrique*; Berman, *Control and Crisis;* Berman, "Perils of Bula Matari"; Engels and Marks, *Contesting Colonial Hegemony;* Young, *African Colonial Stat.*
2. Weber, *Wirtschaft und Gesellschaft*, 825.
3. Iliffe, *Modern History of Tanganyika*, chap. 6.
4. Hogendorn and Scott, "Very Large-Scale Agricultural Projects."
5. *Who's Who in East Africa;* S. Nye, *Pan-Africanism*, 32.
6. McGowan and Bolland, *Political and Social Elite.*
7. Feierman, *Peasant Intellectuals*, 240.
8. Kirk-Greene, "Thin White Line."
9. Tanzania National Archives (hereafter TNA), Dar es Salaam, 43287: Confidential Note Chief Justice, August 31, 1953.
10. Cooper, "Modernizing Bureaucrats."
11. Hyam, introduction.
12. Westcott, "Impact of the Second World War," 239.
13. Cairns, *Bush and Boma*, 149.
14. Cooper, "Conflict and Connection," 1539.
15. Amselle, *Branchements.*
16. Albert Wirz, "Körper, Raum und Zeit," 30.
17. *The Mimic Men* is the title of one of Naipaul's novels, published in London in 1967.
18. Colonial Office, *Education Policy*, 8.
19. Cairns, *Bush and Boma*, 164.
20. Quoted in Feierman, *Peasant Intellectuals*, 238.
21. Feierman, *Peasant Intellectuals*, 238.

22. Bienen, *Tanzania;* Tordoff, *Government and Politics.*

23. Westcott, "Impact of the Second World War," 299.

24. The Swahili newspaper *Kwetu* (Home), the first African-owned newspaper in Tanganyika, was published for the first time in November 1937. Its founder, Erica Fiah, was one of the most radical political activists in Tanganyika during the 1930s and 1940s. He was strongly influenced by Pan-Africanist thought, especially that of Marcus Garvey, and established ties to anti-imperial organizations in the United Kingdom. *Kwetu* adopted a very critical attitude toward the colonial administration without being subversive. See, among others, Westcott, "East African Radical." The African Association was founded in the late 1920s (the exact date is disputed) and represented the effort to connect African government employees with leading representatives of other social groups. During the 1930s the organization more or less abstained from political activities. Iliffe, *Modern History of Tanganyika,* 406–35.

25. TNA 571/52: G. G. Mhina to Secretary African Association Dodoma Branch, March 16, 1945.

26. On the very restrained complaints of African employees about low salaries before World War II, see Eckert, *Herrschen und Verwalten,* chap. 2.

27. TNA 304/238: Chief Secretary to All Provincial Commissioners, December 20, 1948.

28. Public Record Office (hereafter PRO), London, CO 691/208: Tanganyika African Association to Dugdale, Colonial Office, August 30, 1950.

29. TNA 11051/II: Minutes Special Meeting of TAGSA, 2.2.1945; Chief Secretary to All Provincial Commissioners, November 8, 1944.

30. TNA 11051/II: TAGSA: Report and activities of the association for the year 1944; J. B. Matovu (Gen. Secr.) to Chief Secretary, May 13, 1946; Iliffe, *Modern History of Tanganyika,* 396.

31. PRO CO 822/660: Meeting with representatives of the Tanganyika African Government Servants Association, Dar es Salaam, August 18, 1952.

32. TNA 41527/1: Secretary TAGSA [Ally Kleist Sykes] to Chairman Cost of Living Committee, February 26, 1951.

33. Brennan, "Nation, Race and Urbanization," chap.4.

34. *Report of the Commission on the Civil Services.*

35. Quoted in Pratt, *Critical Phase in Tanzania,* 92.

36. *Report by His Majesty's Government,* pt. 1, 26.

37. *Who's Who in East Africa,* 29. See also Rhodes House Library (hereafter RH), Oxford, MSS Afr. s.1887: Peter Hope Johnston, Draft memoirs of colonial service in Tanganyika, 1938–1965, n.d. [ca.1980], who in the context of Omari's appointment could not avoid the following remark: "first posting Manyoni where nothing would go wrong" (17).

38. PRO CO 822/2689: Prime Minister's Office, Africanisation of the Civil Service—Progress Report No. 2, July 19, 1961. Slightly different numbers that

express the same trend can be found in Mueller, "Historical Origins," 479; Iliffe, *Modern History of Tanganyika,* 573; Pratt, *Critical Phase in Tanzania,* 92f.

39. Feierman, *Peasant Intellectuals,* 223–44.

40. TNA 47/A6: Government Circular No. 5 of 1953: Membership of Political Associations, August 1, 1953.The government in Dar es Salaam repeatedly made clear that it would use this decree. See, for instance, PRO CO 822/1364: Telegram Governor Twining to Secretary of State for the Colonies, June 1957.

41. After 1958 many of them joined TANU secretly. Several people I interviewed told me more or less the same story; that they were stopped by police while in possession of not only their own membership card but the cards of the entire local TANU branch. Of course, they succeeded in hiding the papers from the police. This story—whether true or not—obviously became an important part of the biographies of numerous African employees.

42. Iliffe, *Modern History of Tanganyika,* 558; Bienen, *Tanzania,* 113ff.

43. Personal interviews with, among others, Charles Hisis, Muheza, March 11, 1996; Mzee Karlo, Muheza, March 12, 1996; Job Lusinde, Dar es Salaam, July 12, 1999; Francis Xavier Mbenna, Dar es Salaam, August 10, 1999; Balozi Mhina, Dar es Salaam, February 28, 1996; Valentin Mtema, Mkuzi, March 12, 1996; E. C. Mzena, Dar es Salaam, August 6, 1999.

44. Personal interviews with Francis Damian, Dar es Salaam, August 11, 1999; Hashim I. Mbita, Dar es Salaam, August 10, 1999; Thomas Marealle, August 20, 1999; Valentin Mtema, Mkuzi, March 12, 1996; Chande Othman, Tanga, March 6, 1996.

45. TNA 33116: Tanganyika African Government Servants Association to Chief Secretary, April 11, 1945.

46. RH MSS Afr. s.394: Norman Pearsons, Trade Unionist on Safari, n.d. [1949], manuscript, 87, 123.

47. RH MSS Afr. s1546: Minutes Annual General Meeting Tanganyika European Civil Servants' Association, March 21, 1958.

48. RH MSS, Afr. s395: Memorandum on proposed restaurant for Government Employees, n.d. [ca.1950].

49. Personal interviews with Donald Barton, Oxford, September 10, 1995; David Brewin, London, September 8, 1995; Samuel Shadrack Kimei, Moshi, August 18, 1999; Patrick Kunambi, Dar es Salaam, August 7, 1999; Massam Omari Mongi, Moshi, August 16, 1999; Chande Othman, Tanga, March 6, 1996.

50. Some of the former African employees interviewed insisted on their excellent relationship with their British superiors, whom they also associated with after working hours. Personal interviews with Martin Kivumbi, Dar es Salaam, August 8, 1999; Francis Xavier Mbenna, Dar es Salaam, August 10, 1999; Daniel S. Mhando, Dar es Salaam, August 9, 1999; Julius A. Zacharia Mneney, Moshi, August 20, 1999; Israel Saul Tarimo, Moshi, August 16, 1999.

51. Hatch, *Two African Statesmen,* 91–93.

52. RH MSS Afr. s.1834: Lorna Dorothy Hall, "A Bushwife's Progress," manuscript, n.d.

53. RH MSS Afr. s.598: Report Mrs. Allen: The Governor of Tanganyika, Sir Edward Twining, visits Kondoa Iringa, n.d.

54. Tanzania Regional Archives Tanga T.A.4/7C1/4: District Commissioner Tanga to Provincial Commissioner Tanga, September 14, 1955.

55. Geider, "Swahilisprachige Ethnographien," 53–57.

56. TNA 32525/IV: Director of Education to Member for Social Services, January 11, 1952.

57. For an extremely useful introduction to this text, see Maddox, "Ironies of 'Historia.'"

58. Mnyampala, *Gogo*, 121.

59. Maddox, "Ironies of 'Historia,'" 25–29.

60. R. Martin, *Personal Freedom*, 57.

61. PRO CO 822/559: De Hall to Rogers (Colonial Office), January 30, 1953.

62. For a brief biographical sketch of Marealle, see Eckert, "Kulturelle Pendler." Personal interviews with Marealle were conducted in Moshi, February 4, 1996; August 20, 1999.

63. Rogers, "Search for Political Focus," 869.

64. For related correspondence, see RH MSS Brit. Emp. s.365/121. On the FCB and its role in decolonization, see Howe, *Anticolonialism in British Politics*.

65. RH MSS Brit. Emp. s.365/121: Marealle to Marjorie Nicholson, March 14, 1951.

66. Iliffe, *Modern History of Tanganyika*; Samoff, *Tanzania*.

67. RH MSS Brit. Emp. s.365/121: Marealle to Marjorie Nicholson, November 23, 1951.

68. Chagga Council and Whitlamsmith, *Recent Trends*, 6.

69. Stahl, *Tanganyika*, 33.

70. TNA 471/1019: Marealle to Provincial Commissioner Northern Province, November 24, 1952.

71. Iliffe, *Modern History of Tanganyika*, 493.

72. Pratt, *Critical Phase in Tanzania*.

73. Extracts of Marealle's speech can be found in PRO CO 822/1459.

74. RH MSS Brit. Emp. s365/121/4: Marealle to Selwyn-Clarke, July 27, 1957.

75. *Time*, August 21, 1958, 21.

76. Quoted in Martin, *Personal Freedom*, 57–58; also Feierman, *Peasant Intellectuals*, 229.

77. The following paragraph is based on two interviews with Kunambi in Dar es Salaam, February 27, 1996, and August 7, 1999.

78. Young and Fosbrooke, *Land and Politics*, 94.

79. Willis, "Administration of Bonde," 63.

80. See various documents in TNA 481/A2/8.

81. TNA 481/A2/8: "Social Development among My People, the Bondeis," n.d. [1946]; "Social Development of the Bonde," n.d. [1947].

82. Willis, "Administration of Bonde," 65–67.

83. Berman, "Ethnicity," 329.

84. Scott, *Seeing like a State,* chap.7.

85. For a forceful though not convincing analysis of the continuity of state despotism after independence, see Mamdani, *Citizen and Subject.*

Afterword

African Participation in Colonial Rule

The Role of Clerks, Interpreters, and Other Intermediaries

MARTIN KLEIN

Scholars have increasingly come to realize that even in absolutist states, rulers did not have absolute power and that supposedly totalitarian regimes never quite achieved total control of their subjects. If this is true of Nazi and Communist regimes, it was much more true of colonial regimes.[1] That does not mean that colonial regimes lacked power. Africa was conquered by relatively small forces, and after 1907 rebellions did not pose a serious threat to any colonial regime. Those whom Amadou Hampâté Bâ called the "gods of the bush" had virtually absolute power over their employees and their subjects. They could determine who held office and could arbitrarily deprive people of their liberty and usually of their lives. Hampâté Bâ knew that some of his attempts to manipulate decisions of colonial administrators could have ended his career.[2] And yet this was a very limited state, what Frederick Cooper calls a gatekeeper state: "They had weak instruments for entering into the social and economic realm, but they stood astride the intersection of the colonial territory and the outside world."[3] Colonial regimes were limited in the resources they could use and in their knowledge of the peoples and lands they ruled. Colonial administrators could exert nearly absolute power, but only in very limited spaces.

The chief reason for this limited state was fiscal constraint. The partition of Africa took place at a time when all major European powers had elected parliaments with control over purse strings. These parliaments were generally willing to allow the colonial interests their little wars, but they were reluctant to subsidize sustained conflicts and the administration or the development of the colonies. This was particularly true of Britain and France, the countries with the largest empires, which could have been a heavy burden on the domestic taxpayer. There was little public investment in African colonies before the 1940s.[4] Thus, the men who conquered Africa did so with African troops, who were much cheaper than their own nationals, and often compensated for low wages by rewarding their African soldiers with booty.[5] They also often depended on strategic alliances with African allies.

The refusal of European parliaments to underwrite the colonies meant that colonial governors were expected to run their colonies on local tax revenues. This was difficult in societies with very limited surpluses. The vast majority of Africans worked the land with a hoe, but the most that a hoe-wielding peasant could work was usually about a hectare of land. Most of any peasant's labor went to producing subsistence. Thus even in the more prosperous colonies, there was little productive activity to tax. If tax revenues were inevitably low, there was little local revenue to pay for expensive European administrators. In the early years of empire, freedom of action and sexual freedom drew a very eclectic bunch to Africa, but as colonial systems became more bureaucratic after World War I, salaries, pensions, medical care, and working conditions became important.[6] Few able men were willing to spend much of their lives in isolated and unhealthy outposts of empire. They had to be offered benefits attractive enough to lure them to Africa. The largest item in most colonial budgets was the personnel costs for a very small cadre of Europeans. Anthony G. Hopkins claims that in West Africa, almost half of the cost of government was the salaries and pensions of European staff. African employees were much more numerous but usually paid a fraction of the salaries of Europeans. This meant that staff was stretched thin and that there were usually few Europeans at any post. With few European administrators and few resources, European ardor to remake Africans into the wage laborers envisioned in Europe waned in the 1920s. "Colonial officials," Cooper argues, "were convincing themselves that their policy should be not to 'civilize' Africans, but to conserve African societies in a colonizer's image of sanitized tradition, slowly and selectively being led toward evolution, while the empire profited from peasant's crop production or the output of mines and settler farms."[7]

The colonial administrator was generally a jack-of-all-trades and often the master of none. In a letter home Joyce Cary wrote, "I am the Censor as well as the Builder, Surveyor, Road Constructor, Police Inspector, Assessor and Collector of Taxes, Magistrate, Meteorologist and Doctor."[8] While government work in Europe became more technical and more specialized, African administration remained in the hands of generalists.

Administrators were divided between those who sought development and those who feared it. In *Mr. Johnson* the administrator, Rudbeck, is a road builder, but his predecessor and the Waziri, who runs the native administration, fear that a road will bring in people from outside, who would not be easily controlled. These concerns extended into the administration of justice. Maurice Amutabi is correct in arguing that many administrators were "guided more by the concern for the maintenance of order than for the administration of justice." Similarly, Andreas Eckert argues that when authorities in Britain were convinced that change was necessary, many in Tanganyika were unhappy.

The conservative and cautious nature of colonial rule heightened the dependence on unspecialized intermediaries with limited education.[9] Chiefs usually chosen from traditional ruling families provided the base of the administrative structure. Colonial rulers exploited the chiefs' legitimacy but also pushed a contradictory modernizing agenda.[10] In 1946 Robert Delavignette explained: "We are caught up on certain necessary contradictions; on the one hand, we feel strongly that it is indispensable that we leave unchanged the traditional nature of the *chef de canton*'s authority and take advantage of the feudal spirit that persists; on the other hand, we are led by the force of the same colonization to bend him to our administrative mentality."[11] Colonial regimes often wanted chiefs literate in the metropolitan language, but not so well educated that they were cut off from their subjects. Chiefs' interests made them subservient to colonial rulers. The colonial state was not always happy with the results of education. For example, in Nioro du Rip (Senegal) after conquest in 1887, Insa Bâ, a brother of the ruler, was taken hostage and put in the School for the Sons of Chiefs.[12] When he did well, he was sent off to North Africa, much like Abdou Salam Kane (see chapter by Hervé Jézéquel), to get a lycée education. On his return he worked briefly as a teacher and then replaced his brother as chief. Timid by nature, he performed poorly, did not have his subjects' respect, and was dependent on an older brother, Ousmane, who was an Islamic scholar. The French briefly considered exiling Ousmane but instead made him the chief and were pleased with his performance.[13] Chiefs became salaried bureaucrats and whether educated or not, tended to be a conservative lot, dedicated to preserving their privileges and those of their families. As Jézéquel describes, Ibrahima Diaman Bathily may have been an exception because he had spent his adult life as a schoolteacher. Despite its efforts to preserve tradition, colonial rule nonetheless eroded traditional social controls. As a result colonial regimes struggled to maintain authority, becoming more conservative as African elites became more assertive. Brett Shadle describes how a younger, Christian, and progressive group of elders asserted themselves in egalitarian Kavirondo, but district officers were often scornful of the popular will and preferred to choose elders by consultation with chiefs and senior elders.

Administrators may have liked their chiefs tradition-bound, but they depended on modern intermediaries, the clerks, interpreters, and messengers.[14] Chiefs and clerks were not completely separate. In French Africa the sons of chiefs were often educated and given administrative positions until the time came for them to succeed. In British Africa, as Shadle demonstrates, indirect rule often led to struggles between educated, progressive candidates for office and more traditional ones.[15] Literacy, however, was essential to the work of the clerks. The interpreters and messengers were often illiterate. The French used the latter two positions to reward veterans. The relative importance of clerks and interpreters probably depended on their respective personalities and the administrative structure. In *Mr. Johnson* there is no interpreter, and the clerk is clearly the administrator's key aide.[16] In the French posts, as described by Hampâté Bâ, the interpreter guarded access to the administrator and was the conduit for information to and from the administrator. In Hampâté Bâ's satirical novel, the major rival of his picaresque hero, Wangrin, is Romeo Sibedi, who is clearly based on the real interpreter, Moro Sidibé. Both the fictional Sibedi and the real Sidibé spoke a soldier's pidgin French but excellent Bambara and Poular. They were able to use the intermediary role to achieve a position of wealth and influence in the community.[17] Ralph Austen argues that with the development of literacy in French, the interpreters gave way to people like Hampâté Bâ, who were both clerks and interpreters.

As with the chiefs, there was what Ronald Robinson called a "bargain of collaboration," but the situation of the intermediaries was carefully circumscribed. The dilemma of the colonial administration was compounded by the belief that social distance was necessary, that they had to maintain the prestige of white skin if they were to maintain their ascendancy with a small corps of European personnel. Emily Lynn Osborn tells us that Lucien Hubert, the commandant of the Futa Jallon, would not sit down at the table with Boubou Penda even though Boubou Penda was the trusted aide of his immediate superior and his collaborator in a corrupt enterprise. Hampâté Bâ tells us that Leenhardt, a progressive administrator on temporary contract, invited the commandant and the African staff to lunch. Soon after that, he was transferred to the capital and then left the colonial administration.[18]

The colonial state was also reluctant to give any African authority over Europeans. Ruth Ginio tells us that E. Beurdeley, who wrote on French law, had difficulty imagining a situation in which African judges ranked above French secretaries. Years ago I met Mabika Kalanda, the first Congolese to become a colonial administrator in the Belgian Congo. In 1959, when he entered the colonial service, he was assigned to a staff position, not a field position. He knew that even at the twilight of empire, the Belgians did not want a black man dealing with local people in the uniform of a colonial administrator.[19] Austen reminds us that when Hampâté Bâ served briefly as acting commandant, he did not actually move into the commandant's office. When the French wanted to reward a loyal and skillful clerk or interpreter, they sometimes made him a chief, though not always with success.[20] Archinard, the most important military leader in the Soudan, actually made Mademba Sy, a Senegalese who spent years constructing telegraph lines, a king and then created a kingdom for him.[21]

What Africans in the colonial service did successfully was to use colonial authority for their own ends. This involved ensuring their economic well-being and their social status. In *Things Fall Apart,* Chinua Achebe describes a group of clerks and messengers who increased the amount of a fine and kept the difference for themselves. Hampâté Bâ tells a story that took place when he was going by boat to his first posting. A large former soldier in the employ of a white merchant tried to keep his boat from docking in a space he was guarding for his employer. He and his companion, a guard, retreated into their boat and put on their uniforms, which marked them as *blanc-noirs.* Faced with a pith helmet, the symbol of white authority, the former soldier became a groveling, submissive figure, and the boat docked without difficulty.[22]

During the early colonial period, a common scam was for armed men, often former soldiers, to pass themselves off as representatives of the colonial state and use the nominal relationship to power to extract goods and services from villagers. This does not mean that the colonized stood in awe of their European rulers. African sculptures, the songs they sang, and the nicknames for colonial administrators indicate a frequently mocking attitude toward authority. The administrator's houseboy and his concubine were often a source of information about his character and his peccadilloes.[23]

Distance did, however, mean that few administrators ever had close relations with ordinary Africans. Interaction was usually highly structured. Lugard drew up rules about who was to sit, stand, or be offered a chair in the presence of an administrator, and officials were told that they could only interview Africans in the presence of a representative of the colonial authority.[24] When research was demanded by higher authority, the administrator usually relied on those around him or summoned those with the needed information to his administrative office. In the 1904 inquiry on slavery in French West Africa, only one administrator, Jules Brevié, seems to have talked to slaves.[25] To be sure, some administrators, like Noirot (see Osborn's chapter), formed personal friendships with Africans, but they were probably few and not approved of by their colleagues. For most administrators the closest tie they had to Africans was to a concubine or lover. Few administrators knew African languages. In the French system administrators were often moved around too often to maintain facility in languages. Pierre Alexandre had studied Wolof in France but was never assigned to a Wolof-speaking district.[26] In the British colonial service, a man was more likely to spend all or a large part of his career in the same colony or even in a region and had a better chance to learn its language and culture.

In almost all situations European colonial administrators' access to intelligence was circumscribed. They depended on intermediaries to get information for them, to tell them what others thought, and to carry out their decisions. It is striking that the colonial administration was never really certain that the leopard men existed (see chapter by David Pratten). Like Wangrin, Caleb Asituywa (see chapter by Amutabi) was able to convert his control over language into wealth and power. Shadle describes the reluctance of British administrators to punish the corrupt elders who staffed the courts. Osborn writes about a major scandal in which there was extortion, rape, murder, and bribery, and yet, it went on for years before any action was taken against the culprits. Information is power, but control over it offers even more power. Those who control it can accumulate benefits for themselves and also shape policy. Hampâté Bâ's *Oui mon comandant!* and *L'etrange destin du Wangrin* are almost text books on how subaltern officials can shape official action. The administrator was encouraged to spend a lot of time on tour, but even on tour the information he received was filtered through his interpreter and his clerk. With time an increasing number of people were able to speak to the colonial ruler in his own language, but getting access was always a problem. In an earlier book I described a case that took place while Nioro du Rip in Senegal was under military rule. The commandant was always a lieutenant and rarely spent more than six months in his post. His guards, who had been in this post for a number of years and married there, controlled access to him. The wall of silence—what Osborn has termed "circles of iron"—became known only when a peasant with a grievance could not get in and instead went to see Noirot, who was then in the adjacent *cercle* of Sine-Saloum.[27]

Austen suggests that the clerk's responsibility "consisted mainly of banal and generally petty bureaucratic chores," but these chores made him a central person in the local power structure. Caleb Asituywa told Amutabi that there were always large numbers of people wanting to see him on court matters. Wangrin was a figure of wealth and power. For many this was a direct result of collecting bribes. Hampâté Bâ and Kuoh Moukouri do not admit to selling their favors, but both seem to have lived beyond their salaries. Hampâté Bâ even owned a horse for a while and raced that horse in local competitions. He received gifts, and like Wangrin and Moro Sidibé, he entertained. The clerk or interpreter was not inhibited by the necessity of social distance. He invariably knew more about what was happening in any crisis situation than the administrator. Even while heading to his first post, Hampâté Bâ was given hospitality and gifts, which reflected not who he was but what he might become. During much of his first trip to a distant posting, he had to walk, but a horse was often provided by a village chief. When stopping at a post, he might be housed and fed by the interpreter.

Both European and African networks within the colonial state were marked by solidarity. Everywhere Hampâté Bâ went, he established bonds with people who knew his father or stepfather, with classmates, with relatives of people he had once lodged with, or simply with fellow Fulbe. He came from a distinguished Futanke family.[28] He several times used a joking relationship between the Bâs and the Diallos. When traveling he had to present his papers at every post he passed. In Mopti he was directed to the assistant commandant because the commandant was in a meeting. He was warned by the interpreter that the *petit commandant* did not like Foutanke and was told how to behave. After a brief but nasty interview, he got his papers signed and was able to move on.[29] After arriving in a new post, Hampâté Bâ made contact with local authorities and religious figures. Wherever he was, Hampâté Bâ studied with a local marabout. While this reflected his religious commitment, it also integrated him into his adopted community. When Hampâté Bâ's religious faith led to colonial surveillance, the postal clerk told him that his correspondence with his religious guide, Cerno Bokar of Bandiagara, was being read.

This does not mean that everything was sweetness and light. Every time Hampâté Bâ arrived in a new post, he investigated the quirks of the administrators and determined whether he threatened any existing staff. In his first post, Hampâté Bâ's superior status threatened the acting clerk he was supposed to replace. The acting clerk encouraged him to take an extra hour away from the office during Friday prayers, knowing that would anger the commandant. Then when Hampâté Bâ had to prepare the tax rolls, the acting clerk fed him incorrect information, which got him a reprimand. Hampâté Bâ in turn found out that the clerk was taking bribes and threatened to expose him.[30] As in any bureaucratic system, politics in a colonial state could be nasty, often involving planted accusations or work sabotaged so the responsible individual received a negative assessment.[31]

The essays collected here also point to several other conclusions. The first is the role of intermediaries in situations other than those of colonial administration. Roger Levine's chapter underlines the degree to which the establishment and development of missions was the result of work done by African catechists, evangelists, and aides. Without Jan Tzatzoe, John Read would have been able neither to negotiate with African chiefs nor to communicate with those he wanted to convert. Though no essay in this volume deals with commerce, Jeremy Rich has written elsewhere about the role of clerks in commerce, in the timber industry and in the colonial state in Gabon.[32] And Harry Bloom's novel *Episode in Transvaal* deals with a relationship between a wily but taciturn clerk and the administrator of a residential location in South Africa.

There were also important intermediaries outside the formal structure of the colonial state. The most important were the letter writers discussed for Togo by Benjamin Lawrance. They wrote letters for illiterates, but they could also frame grievances and generally knew where to address those grievances. The more important, like the Senegalese Mody Mbaye, had contacts with human rights organizations and newspapers in the colonial capital and in the *métropole*. Wesley Johnson speaks of the letter writer as "a kind of rural notary, an embryonic lawyer and a public tribune."[33] The letter writers were one of the few checks against the arbitrariness of colonial authority. They could, of course, only appeal to higher authority, but they were one way that higher authority could be informed about the petty acts of their officials. There was, for example, a case in which the resident of Siin in Senegal was on tour. A peasant complained that the resident's tents were planted on his fields, destroying his crops. It is probable that the peasant was an enemy of the village chief, who chose the site, but the resident was insensitive to what was happening. The peasant was able to get his complaint aired by Galandou Diouf, later a deputy to the French parliament, but then a member of Conseil Général.[34] Of course, as Lawrance makes clear, many administrators did not like the letter writers and did their best to restrain their activities. Still, the letter writers served an important function for the colonial state by providing an outlet for persons with grievances.

There were other intermediary groups. There were technical people. Mademba Sy had risen from a clerk's position to direct construction for the telegraph line. He was also occasionally pressed into military service. There were doctors. In British West Africa many were graduates of Edinburgh Medical School; in French Africa the *médecins africains* were licensed only to serve in the African colonies. And there were the schoolteachers. Jézéquel tells us that they had lower status than the intermediaries. Nevertheless, in colonial situations where few career options existed, most of the intellectuals became teachers or clerks. Though lacking advanced degrees, many of them were very able, and quite a few, as Jézéquel tells us, collected histories and ethnographies, and some wrote them up. They were also important in the nationalist movements. I remember meeting Mamby Sidibé (see Jézéquel) when I visited Mali in February 1964. Then an old man, he had been given a position by the Union Soudanaise regime and was respected for the rich historical knowledge he had collected in different posts.

There were also servants and concubines. None of them have written memoirs, though they appear in novels. Colonial administrators generally did not discuss their relations with African women, but they were common, particularly in French and Portuguese Africa. Empires were generally built by men. Before the early twentieth century, wives

were usually not brought to Africa. All Europeans had a version of
what the French called *mariage à la mode du pays,* temporary marriages.
Some colonial officials pursued predatory relationships during the
early colonial period, even sending out guards to round up girls for
their sexual gratification. Most, however, had regular unions. Some
even married African women, but most left their partners behind when
they moved on.[35] The interesting question, which may be hard to answer, is how important these women were as an intermediary group.
Were they merely a source of sexual gratification and domesticity, or
did they provide language training and information about local cultures and contacts? There were also servants. Most administrators had
at least one, sometimes several. During the period of conquest military
men appreciated their servants and often rewarded them with booty,
particularly slave women. The White Fathers in the Soudan were frustrated that the young men they trained found attractive positions as
servants in what the missionaries saw as the dissolute world of the administration.[36] On several occasions servants were given chiefly posts,
but we cannot infer much from that. Boubou Penda was originally
Noirot's servant (see Osborn chapter).[37]

Thomas McClendon presents us with an unusual case of white intermediaries. Shepstone and his disciples could become interpreters because they were white Africans and spoke African languages. Though
Shepstone sought African consent for his efforts to organize their affairs, in later years, the demands made by the South African state were
so harsh that they could only be enforced by the heavy use of police
power and modern technology. The other colonial regime that used Europeans to exercise direct control over Africans was the Congo, which
created the densest European presence of any colony. The presence of
both priests and agricultural monitors in the villages gave the state eyes
and ears, and it enabled the regime to maintain a more direct control
over population than elsewhere.[38] This was the domain of Crawford
Young's *Bula Mutari,* alternatively a destroyer and a stern but protective father. And yet both crumbled under pressure. In the Congo the
first meaningful protest took place in January 1959. Within a year colonial administrators in many parts of the Congo could not make their
writ accepted without the approval of politicians who had been incon-
sequential a year earlier. In South Africa, when the authority of the state
crumbled in the mid-1980s, African intermediaries were often killed or
had to flee to the protection of the state. The state won back control of
African locations only by a very heavy use of force.

Even the most coercive states could not do without, in fact, did not want to do without African intermediaries, but these states were so onerous that those intermediaries were at risk. Even in South Africa and certainly elsewhere, Africans could only be ruled by making some Africans a part of the colonial state. The colonial state could not have been effective without them. Racism and a belief in social distance limited African access to major posts but made them all the more important in the actual running of the colonial state. The individual clerk or interpreter could easily be punished, but as a group they were indispensable. If there was a bargain of collaboration, the African intermediary gave his service but in return received two things. First, he was allowed to guarantee his well-being. Often this involved turning a blind eye to illegal activities. Second, it involved the creation of an elite community, within which intermediaries had status and could create their own lifestyle.

Creating their own self-conscious status involved a potential to challenge the colonial state. The African clerk sitting in the outer office and the schoolteacher, who was not directly involved in power, were often convinced that they could run the show. In some cases, such as the Congo, where decolonization was abrupt and there was no time to train new officials, that is exactly what happened. The clerk moved from the outer office to the inner office and often performed quite credibly in the process. The sergeant became a captain and, in the case of the Congo, often a general. The clerk became a commandant. Where there was a slower buildup to independence, the intermediaries provided the cadres of the nationalist parties. Any glance at the first cabinets formed after independence shows a high percentage of clerks and schoolteachers. In relying on African intermediaries, colonial officials created candidates for their replacements.

Notes

1. Peterson, *Limits of Hitler's Power*; Getty and Naumov, *Road to Terror*.
2. Hampâté Bâ, 1994. *Oui mon commandant!*, 199–227.
3. Cooper, *Africa since 1940*, 5.
4. Cooper, *Africa since 1940*, 17–18; Berry, *No Condition Is Permanent*, chap. 2; Hopkins, *Economic History of West Africa*, chaps. 4 and 5.
5. Kanya-Forstner, *Conquest of the Western Sudan*; and Echenberg, *Colonial Conscripts*.
6. W. Cohen, *Rulers of Empire*, discusses the difficulties the French had in staffing the colonies, the mediocrity of many of the administrators, and the eclectic nature of the early administrators. The British had more of a colonial tradition

and though they had a massive empire to staff, seem to have had an easier time staffing it with qualified men. See especially Kirk-Greene, *Britain's Imperial Administrators;* and Kirk-Greene, *On Crown Service.* The Germans and the Belgians had the same problem of transition from an eclectic and often brutal band of free spirits to a more orderly administration. The Belgians had only one colony, but it was rich in resources. Both Leopold's regime and its Belgian successor were able to reap rich profits, which paid for the densest administration in Africa.

7. Cooper, *Africa since 1940,* 18.

8. Kirk-Greene, *Britain's Imperial Administrators,* 146; see also the chapter by Amutabi.

9. Crowder and Ikime, *West African Chiefs;* and Klein, "Chiefship in Sine-Saloum."

10. Crowder and Ikime, *West African Chiefs.*

11. Delavignette, *Service africain,* 134. My translation.

12. Klein, *Islam and Imperialism,* 211–13.

13. One of the central characters in Cary's *African Witch* is an Oxford-educated son of an emir, who mistakenly assumes that a British university degree entitles him to social equality. He is accepted, however, neither by the African community nor by the British rulers.

14. Derrick, "'Native Clerk.'"

15. See, for example, Soyinka, *Isarà.* This is a novel about Soyinka's father, who was involved in just such a struggle.

16. Cary, *Mister Johnson.*

17. Hampâté Bâ, *l'etrange destin de Wangrin;* and Hampâté Bâ, *Oui mon commandant!*

18. Hampâté Bâ, *Oui mon commandant!,* 264–67.

19. During the nineteenth century many Creoles held high office in the British colonies, but by the early twentieth century they were gradually but not completely eliminated. See Ajayi, "Nineteenth Century Roots." Only in the nineteenth century or toward the end of colonial rule were Africans able to compete for European positions. Even as administration became more complex and new roles were introduced, Africans could in most cases not hope to rise to European positions or European salaries. Personal communication, Mabika Kalanda, Kinshasa, 1968; see also Kalanda, *Remise en question.*

20. See Klein, *Islam and Imperialism,* 205–9, for a case of a successful clerk who is made into a chief with disastrous results. To support an entourage, he raided and committed extortion. When there were complaints, he was fired and given another appointment as a clerk, where he remained for the rest of his life.

21. Roberts, "Case against Fama Mademba Sy."

22. Hampâté Bâ, *Oui mon commandant!,* 40–45.

23. Oyono, *Houseboy.*

24. Kirk-Greene, *Principles of Native Administration,* 81–88.

25. Klein, *Slavery and Colonial Rule,* 134.

26. Alexandre, "Chiefs, *Commandants,* and Clerks."

27. Klein, *Islam and Imperialism,* 153; Emily Lynn Osborn, "Circle of Iron."

28. The Futanke were descendants of Fulbe who migrated to the Sudan to participate in the jihad of al haj Umar Tal. Hampâté Bâ was not a Tal, but his stepfather was an important chief.

29. Hampâté Bâ, *Oui mon commandant!,* 49–51.

30. Hampâté Bâ, *Oui mon commandant!,* 143–70.

31. In *Islam and Imperialism* I describe a number of cases of such rivalries. There was also a tendency for administrators to have their protégés and to catch peculation by the protégés of their predecessors.

32. Rich, "Troubles at the Office."

33. Johnson, *Emergence of Black Politics,* 133.

34. Klein, *Islam and Imperilismn,* 214–16.

35. White, *Children of the French Empire.*

36. The complaints were common. See for example, *Diaire,* Segou, April 1896, Archives of the White Fathers, Rome. This was a period when the Sudan was under military rule. Many of the soldiers kept a small harem.

37. When I studied Noirot's activities in Sine-Saloum (1890–96), Boubou Penda did not appear in either archival or oral sources, but once Noirot arrived in the Futa Jallon, Boubou Penda had a more public role. I have always suspected a homosexual relationship between Noirot and Boubou Penda. When I raised the question at the conference that produced this book, the idea was not well received. Many suggested that close but platonic friendships were common in the colonies. I, however, have not seen one in the archival record that was marked by such intensity. I do not have hard evidence, but the link between the two was very emotional, and Noirot behaved at times irrationally. There were many homosexual relationships in the colonial services, but usually they were quite discreet.

38. My first two experiences in Africa were in Senegal and the Congo. In Senegal, where I researched my thesis in 1963 and 1964, I became convinced that most Senegalese rarely had direct contact with white representatives of the colonial state and that colonial authority general expressed itself in an indirect way. In 1968 and 1969 I taught at Lovanium University in Kinshasa. When I asked students how colonial authority manifested itself in their villages, they talked about the agricultural monitors who controlled what they could grow, and the priests, who sometimes called on the colonial state to enforce Catholic morality and in particular monogamy. It also became clear that in the Congo, there was great control over who could study what, where people could go, and what they could do. That is what disintegrated in 1959.

Appendix

Bibliography

Contributors

Index

Appendix

Personnel Files and the Role of Qadis and
Interpreters in the Colonial Administration of Saint-Louis,
Senegal, 1857–1911

SALIOU MBAYE

All the chapters in this volume examine African intermediaries. Most of
these individuals worked for colonial states and were considered employees. Especially for those who worked for the French colonial administration in Senegal and the French West Africa Federation, which was
established in 1895, the National Archives of the Republic of Senegal has
a vast trove of personnel files classified as "series 1 C: Dossiers du personnel." The quality of evidence within these personnel files varies considerably, but these files can be used to trace the careers of African colonial employees. By law, however, personnel files for employees of the
state are closed for one hundred years following the birth of these employees. Requests for personnel files that fall within the one-hundred-
year period are permitted, but the approvals are exceptionally rare.

In addition to these personnel files, the Senegalese archives contain a
subseries on personnel issues that is not restricted. Classified as "series
3 C: Distinctions honorifiques," these records provide precious information on colonial employees who were nominated for special recognition of their services rendered to France. Organized originally by Na-
poléon Bonaparte in 1802, the Legion of Honor contained several levels:
knight *(chevalier)*, officer, commander, high officer, and High Cross of
the Legion of Honor. African employees had to be nominated by French

colonial officials, who were required to provide extensive reports on the services that their nominees had rendered and explain why they warranted honors. Records of individual African employees in this series begin only when the individuals are nominated, and in general these dossiers contain reports that present the individual in the best possible light.

Students of the lives of these colonial officials should also consult the notarial records, which are an excellent source for the reconstruction of social and economic history, the transfers of wealth across generations, and for *la vie quotidienne* generally. Indeed, the kinds of evidence available in these notarial records, including aspects of family life (number of wives and children), personal possessions, and real estate, are not available in the other, more formal personnel files. These notarial records are especially good for the study of qadis and interpreters in Saint-Louis, since many of these individuals were important members of the community. Evidence of these qadis and interpreters also appears in the very large collection of General Correspondence of the colony from 1779–1959, organized as series B in the Senegal archives. Records of these qadis and interpreters also appear in the deliberations of the Council of Administration and in the Private Council of the colony, conserved in the subseries 3 E. As I will demonstrate, students of the lives of African employees must pursue a research strategy of triangulation on each individual employee using sources from several different archival collections.

French Colonialism and the Role of Arabic

Following the Treaty of Paris in 1814, France regained legal rights of its tiny outposts of Gorée, Saint-Louis at the mouth of the Senegal River, and a handful of posts along the river but took possession only in 1817. In Saint-Louis the majority of the African population was Muslim, and few were literate in French. Those who were literate were so in Arabic. Much more so than the island of Gorée, Saint-Louis was part of a wider regional system on both sides of the Senegal River. After the abolition of the transatlantic slave trade in 1815, Saint-Louis emerged as the most important entrepôt for France's trade with the region, and gum Arabic was its primary export. To function within this multilingual regional system in which Muslims were the dominant actors, the French administration of Saint-Louis adopted Arabic as its official language of diplomacy. Since few French colonial officials were conversant in Arabic, they relied on Arabic-speaking interpreters to conduct the business of the administration.

In the 1850s the colony of Senegal was threatened by al hajj Umar's jihad. To build a stronger base of support in Saint-Louis, the administration of Saint-Louis sought to demonstrate that it was a protector of Islam. The administration honored local Muslim spiritual guides, especially the *tamsir,* who served the community as the imam. The *tamsir* served not only as head of the Muslim community of Saint-Louis but also as qadi.[1] David Robinson argues that "[t]he leaders of the translation service and the Muslim tribunal burnished the Islamic image of Saint-Louis. They gave substance to the French claim of tolerance. They were able to work for the Government without compromising their Islamic practice or their standing among most Muslims in the Senegal—Mauritanian zone."[2] Indeed, the French went so far as to pay for several Muslim notables of Saint-Louis to complete the pilgrimage.

In 1856 Governor Louis Faidherbe established the École des Otages, which evolved into the School for Sons of Chiefs and Interpreters. Arabic was one of the languages of instruction. The next year Faidherbe established a Muslim tribunal as part of the French colonial legal system in order to give Muslims the right to have their family disputes adjudicated by a qadi, who was officially appointed as a colonial employee. Muslim litigants could appeal their judgments before the colony's Cour d'Appel.[3] Governor Faidherbe also began an aggressive campaign to increase the size of the colony, which resulted in the incorporation of new territories as protectorates.

After 1843 the colonial administration began to develop more formal administrative offices when it established the Bureau of External Affairs, which became operational in 1846. This division was charged with maintaining political relations with chiefs of the region, and it did so in part through written correspondence. All such correspondence was conducted in Arabic, and the division was charged with translating French letters into Arabic and Arabic letters sent to the governor into French. By 1863 the Senegalese administration had created the Corps des interprètes to meet the increasing need for translation. Interpreters were nominated by the director of the Political Affairs Bureau, appointed by the governor, and divided into two ranks: qualified interpreters and auxiliary interpreters. Qualified interpreters were regular, salaried employees, and they could advance from second- to first-class ranks, depending on their experience and ability. Auxiliary interpreters were recruited as needed, divided into four classes, and paid considerably less than qualified interpreters. All interpreters were required to read and write in French and Arabic, and all were attached to the Bureau of Political Affairs.[4] Arabic remained the official language of the Bureau of External Affairs and the diplomatic language of the colony until 1911, when French became the official language of all communication within the colony and the French West Africa Federation.

Lives of Two Interpreters

Among the dozen interpreters and qadis of Saint-Louis whose lives I have reconstructed, I am selecting two individuals—one at the beginning of our period and one at the end—to demonstrate the sources that are available to students of colonial employees in Senegal.[5]

BOU EL MOGHDAD SECK (1826–1880)

Bou El Moghdad Seck was part of an extended Saint-Louisian family that had long supported the colonial administration. Bou El Moghdad was the brother-in-law of Hamet Ndiaye Ann, who was chosen by Faidherbe to be the first qadi of the Muslim Tribunal in 1857. Bou El Moghdad had served the French in different capacities since the governorship of Protet in the early 1850s but became a salaried interpreter ten years later. In 1857 Bou El Moghdad was appointed assessor to the qadi, and in 1880 he became qadi and *tamsir*. When Bou El Moghdad approached the director of the Political Affairs Bureau in 1860 with a request to subsidize his pilgrimage to Mecca, the colonial administration, faced with the growing threat of al hajj Umar, granted his request. The colonial administration hoped that once Bou El Moghdad returned with the prestigious title of *al hajji*, it would "have favorable results in terms of the maintenance and expansion of [French] influence with the people of Senegal."[6] The colonial administration was pleased with its investment in Bou El Moghdad. "Before becoming a salaried employee, M. al hajji Bou El Moghdad served different governors for ten years. He completed several missions, sometimes alone, sometimes in the company of French officers, but always to the complete satisfaction of the administration. He has assisted us in twenty-two combat missions or expeditions and since 1869, after twenty-three years of service, he is an Officer of the Legion of Honor."[7]

Bou El Moghdad retired from the colonial administration in 1879, and several months later he was named *tamsir* and qadi in Saint-Louis.

He died shortly thereafter in October 1880. Governor Brière de l'Isle wrote to the colonial minister in Paris that Bou El Moghdad was "a devoted servant [to our cause], eminently intelligent, and for [the colonial administration] became a powerful force in our relations with the Maures, with the Damel of Cayor, and with the sultan of Segou."[8]

Despite Bou El Moghdad's death in 1880, the influence of the Seck family within the colonial administration did not wane.[9] His three sons served the administration. Mohamadou Seck was chief interpreter in the Adrar region of Mauretania and an Officer in the Legion of Honor, Souleymane Seck served as qadi of Saint-Louis, and Doudou Seck served as principal interpreter of the colony and also became an Officer in the Legion of Honor.

FARA BIRAM LO (1869–1926)

Fara Biram Lo's administrative career spanned the era of the interpreters, and following the decline of Arabic as the diplomatic language of the colony in 1911, Fara Biram continued to serve the French as they regularized their territorial administration of the expanded colony. Fara Biram was born in Saint-Louis in 1869, son of a qualified interpreter first-class who was also the former qadi of Podor. His mother was the daughter of the chief of Saint-Louis. Fara Biram attended secondary school in Saint-Louis, and in 1887 he was recruited into the colonial administration as interpreter third-class. With the expansion of colonial conquest after 1879, the opportunities for advancement in the administration were great, and Fara Biram advanced rapidly. He was charged with a dozen important missions between 1888 and 1910, including a two-year appointment as Resident of Djoloff in the court of Bour Samba Laobé Penda. When the Minister of colonies, André LeBon, toured the new federation of French West Africa in 1897, Fara Biram was appointed as his interpreter. While he was Resident at Djoloff, he provided the government with crucial information that was used to arrest and deport Ahmadou Bamba, who was beginning a new Muslim brotherhood, which the French feared.[10]

Fara Biram served as chief of Meringhem province of Dagana district from 1904 to 1907, before he was appointed clerk to the Dakar Police Department. In 1911 he returned to territorial administration as chief of Keur Bassine province and returned as chief of Ross-Meringhem province in 1913, where he remained until 1922. In 1915 Governor Martial Merlin nominated Fara Biram as an Officer in the

Legion of Honor. "In renewing my appreciation for the interpreter Fara Biram Lo, whom I have known for twenty-seven years, [I state that] he is very intelligent, very discreet and always devoted. He has above all a very sound judgment and much experience. He is erudite, speaks and writes easily and with elegance French, Arabic, and all the dialects of the colony. I recommend in the strongest manner that he be promoted Officer of the Legion of Honor, a high distinction that he has earned in all regards."[11]

In 1922, however, Fara Biram Lo was accused by the inhabitants of Ross-Merinaghem of "numerous exactions, abuse of power and indelicate acts." Following an investigation of these complaints, the commission concluded that most of the accusations were well founded and proposed that Fara Biram Lo be forced into retirement as a means of foreclosing judicial actions against him. The administration proceeded leniently in part because of his long service and because in 1921 he had become stricken with hemophilia. He died in 1926.[12]

For more than fifty years, Arabic was used within the colonial administration of Senegal for the administration of justice among the Muslim population of Saint-Louis and as a means of diplomatic exchange with neighboring African chiefs. During this period France presented itself as a guardian of Muslims in the face of more militant Muslim messages. By 1911, however, education in French had made dramatic advances. In 1904 there were 4,909 students in French schools in Senegal; by 1911 the number had increased to 6,132.[13] The federation of French West Africa had established its control over the territories of West Africa conquered by the French and imposed a civilian administration. In 1911 Governor General William Ponty issued two crucial decrees that limited the roles of Arabic-speaking translators. The first mandated that French be employed in all administrative correspondence, and the second required that French be substituted for Arabic in rendering the judgments of the Muslim tribunals, which facilitated judicial review by French officials.[14] The strategic importance of interpreters in the colonial administration did not end with these two decrees. On the contrary interpreters remained important to the colonial administration until Senegal became independent in 1960. These decrees merely ended the special place given to Arabic within the colonial administration of Senegal during a strategic moment of Islamic religious fervor during the second half of the nineteenth century.

Notes

1. *Tamsir* is a corruption of the term *tafsir:* it referred to a leader of the community who not only had memorized the Quran, but also was capable of commenting on it. A council elected the holder of this position.

2. D. Robinson, *Paths of Accommodation*, 80.

3. Schnapper, "Les Tribunaux musulmans."

4. The Corps des interprètes was reorganized on November 27, 1893. *Bulletin Administratif du Sénégal*, 1893, 435–36. See also Niang, "La Politique coloniale."

5. See Mbaye, "Cadis et interprètes."

6. Letter, Ministre de la Marine et des Colonies Chasseloup, to Gov. Senegal, July 22, 1861, Archives Nationales du Sénégal (hereafter ARS) 1 B 79, letter no. 154.

7. Letter, Gov. Senegal to Ministre, September 23, 1878, ARS, 2 B 52. Unless otherwise noted, all translations are mine.

8. Letter, Gov. Senegal to Minister, October 25, 1880, ARS, 2 B 52.

9. For an inventory of Bou El Moghdad's possessions, see Inventaire après décès de Bou El Moghdad du 11 nov. au 31 dec. 1880, ARS, 4 Z2 (56).

10. Dossier personnel de Fara Biram Lo, ARS, 1 C 5905.

11. Gov. Merlin, recommendation for Fara Biram Lo, ARS, 3 C 7, 3 C 12, 3 C 64.

12. Dossier personnel de Fara Biram Lo, ARS, 1 C 5905.

13. Rapports de l'Inspecteur de l'enseignement, ARS, 2 G 1904, 1911. See also Bouche, *L'enseignement dans les territoires français*.

14. Circulaires May 8, 1911, and September 8, 1911, respectively.

Bibliography

Abasiattai, M. B. "The Oberi Okaime Christian Mission: Towards a History of an Ibibio Independent Church." *Africa* 59 (1989): 496–516.

Achebe, Chinua. *No Longer at Ease*. London: Heinemann, 1960.

———. *Things Fall Apart*. New York: Ballantine, 1959.

Adewoye, Omoniyi. *The Judicial System in Southern Nigeria, 1854–1954: Law and Justice in a Dependency*. Atlantic Highlands, N.J.: Humanities, 1977.

Adick, Christel. *Bildung und Kolonialismus in Togo: Eine Studie zu den Entstehungszusammenhängen eines europäisch geprägten Bildungswesens in Afrika am Beispiel Togos (1850–1914)*. Basel: Weinheim, 1981.

Afigbo, A. E. "External Contacts and Relations: An Overview." In *A History of the Cross River Region of Nigeria*, edited by M. B. Abasiattai. Calabar, Nigeria: Harris, 1990.

———. *The Warrant Chiefs: Indirect Rule in Southeastern Nigeria, 1891–1929*. London: Longman, 1972.

Ajayi, J. F. A. "Nineteenth Century Roots of Nigerian Nationalism." *Journal of the Historical Society of Nigeria* 2 (1961): 196–210.

Akurang-Parry, K. O. "'A Smattering of Education' and Petitions as Sources: A Study of African Slaveholders' Responses to Abolition in the Gold Coast Colony, 1874–1875." *History in Africa* 27 (2000): 39–60.

Alcaraz, E. "Translation and Pragmatics." In Alvarez-Rodríguez and Vidal, *Translation, Power, Subversion*, 99–115.

Alexandre, Pierre. "Chiefs, *Commandants*, and Clerks: Their Relationship from Conquest to Decolonisation in French West Africa." In Crowder and Ikime, *West African Chiefs*, 2–13.

Allman, Jean, Susan Geiger, and Nakanyike Musisi, eds. *Women in African Colonial Histories*, Bloomington: Indiana University Press, 2002.

Alvarez-Rodríguez, Román, and M. Carmen-Africa Vidal, eds. *Translation, Power, Subversion*. Philadelphia: Multilingual Matters, 1998.

Amenumey, D. E. K. *The Ewe in Pre-Colonial Times: A Political History with Special Emphasis on the Anlo, Ge and Krepi*. Ho, Ghana: E. P. Church, 1986.

Amselle, Jean-Loup. *Branchements: Anthropologie de l'universalité des cultures.*
    Paris: Flammarion, 2001.
————. *Logiques métisses.* Paris: Payot, 1990.
Amutabi, Maurice N. "A History of the African Interior Church, 1946–1990."
    Master's thesis, University of Nairobi, 1993.
Anderson, David M. "Policing, Prosecution and the Law in Colonial Kenya,
    1905–39." In Anderson and Killingray, eds. *Policing the Empire,* 183–200.
Anderson, David M., and David Killingray. *Policing the Empire: Government,
    Authority and Control, 1830–1940.* Manchester: Manchester University Press,
    1991.
Apter, Emily. "On Translation in a Global Market." *Public Culture* 13 (2001): 1–12.
Arcin, Andre. *Histoire de la Guinée française: Rivières du sud, Fouta-Dialo, région du
    sud du Soudan.* Paris: A. Challamel, 1911.
Atkins, Keletso. *The Moon Is Dead! Give Us Our Money!: The Cultural Origins of an
    African Work Ethic, Natal, South Africa, 1843–1900.* Portsmouth, N.H.: Heine-
    mann, 1993.
Austen, Ralph A. "From a Colonial to a Postcolonial African Voice: *Amkoullel:
    l'enfant peul.*" Roundtable on Amadou Hampâté Bâ. *Research in African Liter-
    ature* 31, no. 3 (Fall 2000): 1–17.
Austen, Ralph A., and Jonathan Derrick. *Middlemen of the Cameroons Rivers: The
    Duala and Their Hinterland, ca. 1600–ca. 1960.* Cambridge: Cambridge Univer-
    sity Press, 1999.
Avornyo, Raphael Quarshie. *Deutschland und Togo (1847–1987).* Frankfurt am
    Main: Peter Lang, 1989.
Ayandele, E. A. *The Educated Elite in the Nigerian Society.* Ibadan, Nigeria: Ibadan
    University Press, 1974.
Ballantyne, Tony. "Re-reading the Archive and Opening up the Nation-State:
    Colonial Knowledge in South Asia (and Beyond)." In *After the Imperial Turn:
    Thinking with and through the Nation,* edited by Antoinette Burton. Durham,
    N.C.: Duke University Press, 2003.
Barry, Boubacar. *Bokar Biro: Le dernier grand Almamy du Fouta Djallon.* Paris:
    ABC, 1976.
Barry, Ismaël. *Le Fuuta-Jaloo face á la colonization: Conquête et mise en place de
    l'administration en Guinée.* 2 vols. Paris: L'Harmattan, 1997.
Bathily, Abdoulaye. "Notices socio-historiques sur l'ancien royaume soninké
    du Gadiaga. D'après Ibrahima Diaman Bathily (1897–1947)." *Bulletin de
    l'IFAN* 41 (1969): 31–105.
Bayart, Jean-François. *L'État en Afrique: La politique du ventre.* Paris: Fayard,
    1989.
————. "The 'Social Capital' of the Felonious State or the Ruses of Political In-
    telligence." In *The Criminalization of the State in Africa,* edited by J.-F. Bayart,
    S. Ellis, and B. Hibou, 32–48. Oxford: James Currey, 1999.
Benjamin, Walter. "The Task of the Translator." In *Illuminations,* edited by

Hannah Arendt, translated by Harry Zohn, 70–82. New York: Schocken Books, 1968.

Benton, Lauren. *Law and Colonial Cultures: Legal Regimes in World History, 1400–1900.* New York: Cambridge University Press, 2000.

Berman, Bruce J. *Control and Crisis in Colonial Kenya: The Dialectic of Domination.* Athens: Ohio University Press, 1990.

——. "Ethnicity, Patronage and the African State: The Politics of Uncivil Nationalism." *African Affairs* 97, no. 388 (1998): 305–41.

——. "The Perils of Bula Matari: Constraint and Power in the Colonial State." *Canadian Journal of African Studies* 31 (1997): 556–70.

Berman, Bruce J., and John Lonsdale. "Coping with the Contradictions: The Development of the Colonial State in Kenya, 1895–1914." *Journal of African History* 20, no. 4 (1979): 487–505. Reprinted as chapter 4 in Berman and Lonsdale, *Unhappy Valley.*

——. *Unhappy Valley: Conflict in Kenya and Africa.* Athens: Ohio University Press, 1992.

Berry, Sara. *"Chiefs Know Their Boundaries": Essays on Property, Power, and the Past in Asante, 1896–1996.* Portsmouth, N.H.: Heinemann, 2001.

——. *No Condition Is Permanent: The Social Dynamics of Agrarian Change in Sub-Saharan Africa.* Madison: University of Wisconsin Press, 1993.

Beurdeley, E. *La justice indigène en Afrique Occidentale française: Mission d'études, 1913–1914.* Paris: Comité de l'Afrique française, 1916.

Bienen, Henry. *Tanzania: Party Transformation and Economic Development.* Princeton, N.J.: Princeton University Press, 1967.

Bloom, Harry. 1956. *Transvaal Episode.* London: Collins.

Boahen, Adu. *Ghana: Evolution and Change in the Nineteenth and Twentieth Centuries.* London: Longman, 1974.

Bouche, Denise. *L'enseignement dans les territoires français de l'Afrique occidentale, de 1817 à 1920: Mission civilisatrice ou formation d'une élite.* Paris: Librarie Honoré Champion, 1975.

——. *Historie de la colonisation française: Flux et reflux (1815–1962).* Vol. 2. Paris: Fayard, 1991.

Brennan, James R. "Nation, Race and Urbanization in Dar es Salaam, Tanzania, 1916–1976." PhD diss., Northwestern University, 2002.

Brenner, Louis. "Amadou Hampâté Bâ: Tijani francophone." In *La Tijaniyya: Une confrérie musulmane à la conquête de l'Afrique,* edited by Jean-Louis Triaud and David Robinson, 289–365.

——. "Becoming Muslim in Soudan français." In Robinson and Triaud, *Le temps des marabouts,* 467–92.

Brooks, George, Jr. *Eurafricans in Western Africa: Commerce, Social Status, Gender, and Religious Observance from the Sixteenth to the Eighteenth Century.* Athens: Ohio University Press, 2003.

——. "A Nhara of the Guinea-Bissau Region: Mãe Aurélia Correia." In

Women and Slavery in Africa, edited by Claire Robertson and Martin Klein, 295–319. Madison: University of Wisconsin Press, 1983.

———. "The *Signarés* of Saint Louis and Gorée: Women Entrepreneurs in Eighteenth-Century Senegal." In *Women in Africa: Studies in Social and Economic Change,* edited by Nancy J. Hafkin and Edna G. Bay, 19–44. Stanford, Calif.: Stanford University Press, 1976.

Brown, David. "Politics in the Kpandu Area of Ghana, 1925 to 1969: A Study of the Influence of Central Government and National Politics upon Local Factional Competition." PhD diss., University of Birmingham, U.K., 1977.

Brunschwig, Henri. *Noirs et Blancs dans l'Afrique noire française: Comment le colonisé devient colonisateur, 1870–1914.* Paris: Flammarion, 1983.

Cairns, J. C. *Bush and Boma.* London: John Murray, 1959.

Cary, Joyce. *The African Witch.* London: Michael Joseph, 1936.

———. *Mister Johnson.* London: Michael Joseph, 1939.

Cell, John W. "Colonial Rule." In *The Oxford History of the British Empire,* vol. 4, *The Twentieth Century,* edited by Judith M. Brown and Wm. Roger Louis, 233–54. Oxford: Oxford University Press, 1999.

Chagga Council and G. K. Whiltamsmith, eds. *Recent Trends in Chagga Political Development.* Moshi, Tanzania: Chagga Council, n.d.

Chanock, Martin. *Law, Custom, and Social Order: The Colonial Experience in Malawi and Zambia.* Cambridge: Cambridge University Press, 1985.

———. "Making Customary Law: Men, Women, and Courts in Colonial Northern Rhodesia." In Hay and Wright, *African Women and the Law,* 53–67.

Christelow, Allan. *Muslim Law Courts and the French Colonial State in Algeria.* Princeton, N.J.: Princeton University Press, 1985.

Cissé, Mouhamadou Lamine, and Mamadou Sèye, comps. *Répertoire de la sous-série 4Z2: "Archives notariées de Saint-Louis du Sénégal et Dépendances."* Dakar: Direction des Archives, 2001.

Cohen, David W. "'A Case for the Basoga': Lloyd Fallers and the Construction of an African Legal System." In Mann and Roberts, *Law in Colonial Africa,* 239–54.

Cohen, David W., and E. S. Atieno-Odhiambo. *Burying SM: The Politics of Knowledge and the Sociology of Power in Africa.* Portsmouth, N.H.: Heinemann, 1992.

Cohen, William. *Rulers of Empire: The French Colonial Service in Africa.* Stanford, Calif.: Hoover Institution Press, 1971.

Colonial Office. *Education Policy in British Tropical Africa.* London: HMSO, 1925.

Comaroff, Jean, and John Comaroff. *Christianity, Colonialism, and Consciousness in South Africa.* Vol. 1 of *Of Revelation and Revolution.* Chicago: University of Chicago Press, 1991.

———. *The Dialectics of Modernity on a South African Frontier.* Vol. 2 of *Of Revelation and Revolution.* Chicago: University of Chicago Press, 1997.

Conklin, Alice L. *A Mission to Civilize: The Republican Idea of Empire in France and West Africa, 1895–1930.* Stanford, Calif.: Stanford University Press, 1997.

Conrad, David C., and Barbara E. Frank, eds. *Status and Identity in West Africa: Nyamakalaw of Mande.* Bloomington: Indiana, 1985.

Cooper, Frederick. *Africa since 1940: The Past of the Present.* Cambridge: Cambridge University Press, 2002.

———. "Conflict and Connection: Rethinking Colonial African History." *American Historical Review* 99 (1994): 1516–45.

———. *Decolonization and African Society: The Labor Question in French and British Africa.* New York: Cambridge University Press, 1996.

———. "Modernizing Bureaucrats, Backward Africans, and the Development Concept." In *International Development and the Social Sciences: Essays on the History and Politics of Knowledge,* edited by Frederick Cooper and Randall Packard, 64–92. Berkeley: University of California Press, 1997.

Cory, G. E. *The Rise of South Africa.* London: Longmans, Green, 1910.

Cotran, Eugene. *Casebook on Kenya Customary Law.* Nairobi: Professional Books, 1987.

Coulson, N. J. *Succession in the Muslim Family.* Cambridge: Cambridge University Press, 1971.

Crafford, D. "Jan Tshatshu." In *Trail-Blazers of the Gospel: Black Pioneers in the Missionary History of Southern Africa,* edited by D. Crafford, 15–19. Pretoria: Institute for Missiological Research, 1991.

Crais, Clifton. *The Politics of Evil: Magic, State Power, and the Political Imagination in South Africa.* Cambridge: Cambridge University Press, 2002.

———. *White Supremacy and Black Resistance in Pre-industrial South Africa: The Making of the Colonial Order in the Eastern Cape, 1770–1865.* Cambridge: Cambridge University Press, 1992.

Créspin, M. "Alfa Yaya et M. Frézouls." *Revue indigène* 2 (February 1906): 45–46.

Crowder, Michael, and Obaro Ikime, eds. *West African Chiefs: Their Changing Status under Colonial Rule and Independence.* Ife, Nigeria: Ife University Press; New York: Africana Publishing, 1970.

Cudjoe, Robert. "Some Reminiscences of a Senior Interpreter." *The Nigerian Field* 18 (1953): 148–64.

Curtin, Philip D. *Cross-cultural Trade in World History.* New York: Cambridge University Press, 1984.

Davis, Natalie. *Fiction in the Archives: Pardon Tales and Their Tellers in Sixteenth-Century France.* Stanford, Calif.: Stanford University Press, 1987.

Debien, G. "Papiers Ernest Noirot." *Bulletin IFAN,* series B, 3–4 (1964): 676–93.

Delavignette, Robert. *Freedom and Authority in French West Africa.* London: Cass, 1968.

———. *Service africain.* Paris: Gallimard, 1946.

———. *Les vrais chefs de l'empire.* Paris: Gallimard, 1939.

Derrick, Jonathan. "The 'Native Clerk' in Colonial West Africa." *African Affairs* 82 (1983): 61–74.

Devey, Muriel. *Hampâté Bâ, l'homme de la tradition.* Senegal: Livre Sud, 1993.

Diallo, Thierno. *Alfa Yaya: Roi du Labé.* Paris: ABC, 1976.

Diop, Birago. *La plume raboutée.* 3 vols. Paris: Présence Africaine, 1978, 1982, 1985.

Echenberg, Myron. *Colonial Conscripts: The Tirailleurs Sénégalais in French West Africa, 1857–1960.* Portsmouth, N.H.: Heinemann, 1991.

Eckert, Andreas. *Herrschen und Verwalten: Afrikanische Bürokraten, staatliche Ordnung und Politik in Tanzania, 1920–1970.* Munich: Oldenbourg, 2006.

———. "Kulturelle Pendler: Zwei afrikanische Bürokraten im kolonialen Tanzania." In *Akteure des Wandels: Lebensläufe und Gruppenbilder an Schnittstellen von Kulturen,* edited by Petra Heidrich und Heike Liebau, 179–201. Berlin: Das Arabische Buch, 2001.

Elbourne, Elizabeth. *Blood Ground: Colonialism, Missions, and the Contest for Christianity in the Cape Colony and Britain, 1799–1853.* Montreal: McGill-Queen's University Press, 2002.

Elphick, Richard, and Robert Shell. "Intergroup Relations: Khoikhoi, Settlers, Slaves, and Free Blacks, 1652–1795." In *The Shaping of South African Society, 1652–1840,* edited by Richard Elphick and Hermann Giliomee, 184–239. Middletown, Conn.: Wesleyan, 1989.

Engels, Dagmar, and Shula Marks, eds. *Contesting Colonial Hegemony: State and Society in Africa and India.* London: German Historical Institute/British Academic Press, 1994.

Erbar, Ralph. *Ein Platz an der Sonne? Die Verwaltungs- und Wirtschaftsgeschichte der deutschen Kolonie Togo, 1884–1914.* Stuttgart: Franz Steiner Verlag, 1991.

Etherington, Norman. "The 'Shepstone System' in the Colony of Natal and beyond the Borders." In *Natal and Zululand from Earliest Times to 1910: A New History,* edited by A. Duminy and B. Guest, 170–92. Pietermaritzburg, South Africa: University of Natal Press, 1989.

Fabian, Johannes. *Language and Colonial Power: The Appropriation of Swahili in the Former Belgian Congo 1880–1938.* Cambridge: Cambridge University Press, 1986.

Fall, Babacar. *Le travail forcé en Afrique occidentale française: 1900–1946.* Paris: Karthala, 1993.

Fallers, Lloyd. *Law without Precedent: Legal Ideas in Action in the Courts of Busoga.* Chicago: University of Chicago Press, 1969.

Famechon, Lucien. *Notice sur la Guinée française: Exposition universelle internationale de 1900.* Paris: Alcan-Lévy, 1900.

Feierman, Steve. *Peasant Intellectuals: Anthropology and History in Tanzania.* Madison: University of Wisconsin Press, 1990.

Fields, Karen. "Political Contingencies of Witchcraft in Colonial Central Africa: Culture and the State in Marxist Theory." *Canadian Journal of African Studies* 16 (1982): 567–93.

———. *Revival and Rebellion in Colonial East Africa.* Princeton, N.J.: Princeton University Press, 1985.

Fillot, M. Henry. "Affaires de Guinée." *Revue indigène* 4 (April 1906): 84–88.

Fourchard, Laurent. "Propriétaires et commerçants Africains à Ougadougou et à Bobo-Dioulasso (Haute-Volta), fin 19ème siècle–1960." *Journal of African History* 44 (2003): 433–61.

Franco, J. "Culture-Specific Items in Translation." In Alvarez-Rodríguez and Vidal, *Translation, Power, Subversion*, 52–78.

Fuglestad, Finn. *A History of Niger.* Cambridge: Cambridge University Press, 1983.

Gaden, Henri. "Du régime des terres de la vallée du Sénégal au Fouta antérieurement à l'occupation française." *Bulletin du Comité d'études Historiques et Scientifiques de l'AOF* 18 (1935): 403–14.

Gavaghan, Terence. *Of Lions and Dung Beetles.* Elms Court, U.K.: Arthur H. Stockwell, 1999.

Gayibor, Nicoué L. "Agokoli et la dispersion de Notsé." In *Peuples du Golfe du Bénin (Aja-Ewé)*, edited by F. de Medeiros, 21–34. Paris: Karthala, 1984.

———. *Les Aja-Ewe.* Lomé: Les Presses de l'Université de Bénin, 1975.

Geider, Thomas. "Swahilisprachige Ethnographien (ca. 1890–heute): Produktionsbedingungen und Autoreninteressen." In *Afrikaner schreiben zurück: Texte und Bilder afrikanischer Ethnographen*, edited by Heike Behrendt and Thomas Geider. Cologne: Köppe, 1998.

Geschiere, Peter. *The Modernity of Witchcraft: Politics and the Occult in Postcolonial Africa.* Charlottesville: University Press of Virginia, 1997.

Getty, J. Arc, and Oleg V. Naumov. *The Road to Terror: Stalin and the Self-Destruction of the Bolsheviks, 1932–1939.* New Haven, Conn.: Yale University Press, 1999.

Ghai, Y. P., and Patrick McAuslan. *Public Law and Political Change in Kenya: A Study of the Legal Framework of Government from Colonial Times to the Present.* Nairobi: Oxford University Press, 1970.

Ginio, Ruth. "French Colonial Reading of Ethnographic Research: The Case of the 'Desertion' of the Abron King and Its Aftermath." *Cahiers d'Études Africaines* 42 (vol. 2), no. 166 (2002): 337–57.

Gluckman, Max. *Ideas and Procedures in African Customary Law.* Oxford: Oxford University Press, 1969.

Gocking, Roger. "A Chieftaincy Dispute and Ritual Murder in Elmina, Ghana, 1945–6." *Journal of African History* 41 (2000): 197–219.

———. "Creole Society and the Revival of Traditional Culture in Cape Coast during the Colonial Period." *International Journal of African Historical Studies* 17 (1984): 601–22.

Goerg, Odile. *Commerce et colonisation en Guinée, 1850–1913.* Paris: l'Harmattan, 1986.

———. *Pouvoir colonial, municipalités et espaces urbains: Conakry-Freetown des années 1880 à 1914.* 2 vols. Paris: l'Harmattan, 1997.

Gologo, Mamadou. *Le rescapé de l'ethylos.* Paris: Présence Africaine, 1963.

Gordon, Ruth. *Shepstone: The Role of the Family in the History of South Africa, 1820–1900.* Cape Town: A. A. Balkema, 1968.

Groff, David. "The Dynamics of Collaboration and the Rule of Law in French West Africa: The Case of Kwame Kangah of Assikasso (Côte d'Ivoire), 1898–1922." In Mann and Roberts, *Law in Colonial Africa,* 146–65.

Guy, Camille. "La langue française et les langues indigènes." *Bulletin mensuel du comité de l'Afrique française et du comité du Maroc.* January 1922.

Guy, Jeff. *The View across the River: Harriette Colenso and the Zulu Struggle against Imperialism.* Charlottesville: University Press of Virginia, 2002.

Hailey, William Malcolm. *An African Survey: A Study of Problems Arising in Africa South of the Sahara.* London: Oxford University Press, 1938.

Hamilton, Carolyn. *Terrific Majesty: The Powers of Shaka Zulu and the Limits of Historical Invention.* Cambridge, Mass.: Harvard University Press, 1998.

Hampâté Bâ, Amadou. *Amkoullel, l'enfant peul: Mémoires.* Arles: Babel, 1992. First published 1991 by Actes Sud.

———. *L'étrange destin de Wangrin; ou, Les roueries d'un interprète africain.* Paris: Union générale d'éditions, 1973.

———. *The Fortunes of Wangrin.* Translated by Aina Pagolini Taylor. Bloomington: Indiana University Press, 1999.

———. *Oui mon commandant!: Mémoires (II).* Arles: Actes Sud, 1994

Harms, Robert W. *The Diligent: A Voyage through the Worlds of the Slave Trade.* New York: Basic Books, 2002.

Hatch, John. *Two African Statesmen: Kaunda of Zambia and Nyerere of Tanzania.* London: Secker &Warburg, 1976.

Hawkins, Sean. *Writing and Colonialism in Northern Ghana: The Encounter between the LoDaaga and "the World on Paper."* Toronto: University of Toronto Press, 2002.

Hay, Margaret Jean, and Marcia Wright, eds. *African Women and the Law: Historical Perspectives.* Boston: Boston University African Studies Center, 1982.

Heckman, Hélène. "Annexe I: Genèse et authenticité des ouvrages *L'étrange destin de Wangrin* et la serie des *Mémoires.*" In Hampâté Bâ, *Oui mon commandant!,* 389–93.

Herbst, Jeffrey. *States and Power in Africa: Comparative Lessons in Authority and Control.* Princeton, N.J.: Princeton University Press, 2000.

Hodgson, Janet. *Ntsikana's Great Hymn: A Xhosa Expression of Christianity in the Early Nineteenth Century Eastern Cape.* Cape Town: Centre for African Studies, 1980.

———. "A Study of the Xhosa Prophet Nxele." *Religion in Southern Africa* 6 (1985): 11–36; 7 (1986): 3–23.

Hogendorn, Jan, and K. M. Scott. "Very Large-Scale Agricultural Projects: The Lessons of the East African Groundnut Scheme." In *Imperialism, Colonialism and Hunger: East and Central Africa,* edited by Robert I. Rotberg, 167–98. Lexington, Mass.: Lexington Books, 1983.

Holt, Basil. *Joseph Williams and the Pioneer Mission to the South-Eastern Bantu.* Lovedale, South Africa: Lovedale Press, 1954.

Hopkins, Anthony G. *An Economic History of West Africa.* London: Longman, 1973.

Howe, Stephen. *Anticolonialism in British Politics: The Left and the End of Empire, 1918–1964.* Oxford: Clarendon, 1993.

Hunt, Nancy Rose. *A Colonial Lexicon of Birth Ritual, Medicalization, and Mobility in the Congo.* Durham, N.C.: Duke University Press, 1999.

Hyam, Ronald. Introduction to *The Labour Government and the End of Empire, 1945–1951,* Vol. 1, edited by Ronald Hyam, xxii–lxxviii. London: HMSO, 1992.

Iliffe, John. *A Modern History of Tanganyika.* Cambridge: Cambridge University Press, 1979.

———. "The Spokesman: Martin Kayamba." In *Modern Tanzanians,* edited by John Iliffe, 66–94. Nairobi: East African Publishing House, 1973.

Isaacman, Allen. *Cotton Is the Mother of Poverty: Peasants, Work, and Rural Struggle in Colonial Mozambique, 1938–1961.* Portsmouth, N.H.: Heinemann, 1996.

———. *Mozambique: The Africanization of a European Institution, the Zambesi Prazos, 1750–1902.* Madison: University of Wisconsin Press, 1972.

Isaacman, Allen, and Barbara Isaacman. "Resistance and Collaboration in Southern and Central Africa, c. 1850–1920." *International Journal of African History Studies* 10 (1977): 31–62.

Jackson, Lynette. "'When in the White Man's Town': Zimbabwean Women Remember *Chibeura.*" In Allman, Geiger, and Musisi, *Women in African Colonial Histories,* 191–218.

Jeater, Diana. "Rethinking the 'African Voice': Language Interpretation in the Native Commissioner's and Magistrate's Courts, Melsetter District, Southern Rhodesia, 1896–1914." In *Rethinking African History,* edited by S. McGrath et al., 379–402. Edinburgh: University of Edinburgh Center for African Studies, 1997.

———. "Speaking like a Native: Vernacular Languages and the State in Southern Rhodesia, 1890–1935." *Journal of African History* 42 (2001): 449–68.

Jedrej, M. C. "Medicine, Fetish and Secret Society in a West African Culture." *Africa* 46 (1976): 247–57.

Jézéquel, Jean-Hervé. "Les 'mangeurs de craies': Socio-histoire d'une catégorie lettrée à l'époque coloniale. Les instituteurs diplômés de l'école normale William-Ponty (c. 1900–c.1960)." PhD diss., l'École des Hautes Études en Sciences Sociales, Paris, 2002.

———. "Maurice Delafosse et l'émergence d'une littérature africaine à vocation scientifique." In *Maurice Delafosse: Entre orientalisme et ethnographie:*

l'itinéraire d'un africaniste (1870–1926), edited by Jean-Loup Amselle and Emmanuelle Sibeud, 90–104. Paris: Maisonneuve & Larose, 1998.

———. "Le théâtre des instituteurs africains en A. O. F.: Pratique socio-culturelle et vecteur de cristallisation des nouvelles identities." In *Fêtes urbaines en Afrique noire*, edited by Odile Goerg, 181–200. Paris: l'Harmattan, 1999.

Johnson, G. Wesley. *The Emergence of Black Politics in Senegal: The Struggle for Power in the Four Communes, 1900–1920*. Stanford, Calif.: Stanford University Press, 1971.

Johnson, Samuel. *The History of the Yorubas from the Earliest Times to the Beginning of the British Protectorate*. London: Routledge, 1921.

Jonas, P. J. "Jan Tshatshu and the Eastern Cape Mission—A Contextual Analysis." *Missionalia* 18 (1990): 277–92.

Joset, P.-E. *Les sociétés secrètes: Des hommes-léopards en Afrique noire*. Paris: Payot, 1955.

Kalanda, Mabika. *Remise en question: Base de la décolonisation mentale*. Brussels: Éditions Remarques africaines, 1967.

Kamboi-Ferrand, Jeanne-Marie. "Souffre, gémis, mais marche! Regard d'une paysanne lobi sur sa vie au temps colonial." In *La Haute-Volta coloniale: Témoignages, recherches, regards*, edited by J. Gabriel Mass and Y. Georges Madiéga, 147–56. Paris: Karthala, 1995.

Kane, Abdoul Salam. "Coutume civile et pénale toucouleur (cercle de Matam)." In *Coutumes juridiques de l'AOF*, vol. 1, *Le Sénégal*, 55–115. Dakar: Publications du Gouvernement general de l'AOF, 1939.

———. "Du régime des terres chez les populations du Fouta sénégalais." *Bulletin du Comité d'Études Historiques et Scientifiques de l'AOF* 18 (1935): 449–62.

Kanya-Forstner, A. S. *The Conquest of the Western Sudan: A Study in French Military Imperialism*. Cambridge: Cambridge University Press, 1969.

Kaptue, Léon. *Travail et main-d'oeuvre au Cameroun sous régime français, 1916–1952*. Paris: L'Harmattan, 1986.

Kartunnen, Francis. *Between Worlds: Interpreters, Guides and Survivors*. New Brunswick, N.J.: Rutgers University Press, 1994.

Kayamba, Martin. *African Problems*. London: United Society for Christian Literature, 1948.

———. "The Story of Martin Kayamba." In *Ten Africans*, edited by M. Perham, 173–99. London: Faber & Faber, 1936.

Keegan, Timothy. *Colonial South Africa and the Origins of the Radical Order*. Charlottesville: University Press of Virginia, 1996.

Keïta, Awa. *Femme d'Afrique*. Paris: Présence Africaine, 1975.

Kirkby, Diane, and Catherine Coleborne, eds. *Law, History, Colonialism: The Reach of Empire*. Manchester: Manchester University Press, 2001.

Kirk-Greene, A. H. M. *Britain's Imperial Administrators, 1858–1966*. New York: St. Martin's Press, 2000.

———, ed. *Lugard and the Amalgamation of Nigeria: A Documentary Record*. London: Frank Cass, 1968.

———. *On Crown Service: A History of HM Colonial and Overseas Civil Services, 1837–1997*. London: I. B. Tauris, 1999.

———, ed. *The Principles of Native Administration in Nigeria: Selected Documents*. London: Oxford University Press, 1965.

———. "The Thin White Line: The Size of the British Colonial Service in Africa." *African Affairs* 79 (1980): 25–44.

Kjerland, Kirsten Alsaker. "Cattle Breed, Shillings Don't: The Belated Incorporation of the abaKuria into Modern Kenya." PhD diss., University of Bergen, 1995.

Klein, Martin. "Chiefship in Sine-Saloum, 1887–1914." In *Colonialism in Africa, 1870–1960*, vol. 3, *Profiles of Change: African Society and Colonial Rule*, edited by Victor Turner. Cambridge: Cambridge University Press, 1971.

———. *Islam and Imperialism: Sine-Saloum 1847–1914*. Stanford, Calif.: Stanford University Press, 1968.

———. "The Rule of Law and the Abuse of Power in Colonial French Guinea: The Hubert-Noirot Affair." Paper presented at the Law in Colonial Africa Conference, Stanford University, 1988.

———. *Slavery and Colonial Rule in French West Africa*. Cambridge: Cambridge University Press. 1998.

———. "Slavery and Emancipation in French West Africa." In *Breaking the Chains: Slavery, Bondage, and Emancipation in Modern Africa and Asia*, edited by Martin A. Klein, 170–96. Madison: University of Wisconsin Press, 1993.

Knoll, Arthur J. "Taxation in the Gold Coast Colony and in Togo: A Study in Early Administration, 1884–1914." In *Britain and Germany in Africa: Imperial Rivalry and Colonial Rule*, edited by Prosser Gifford and William Roger Louis, 417–53. New Haven, Conn.: Yale University Press, 1967.

———. *Togo under Imperial Germany, 1884–1914: A Case Study in Colonial Rule*. Stanford, Calif.: Hoover Institution Press, 1978.

Kourouma, Ahmadou. *Monnè, outrages et défis*. Paris: Editions du Seuil, 1990.

———. *Monnew*. Translated by Nidra Poller. San Francisco: Mercury House, 1993.

Kuoh Moukouri, Jacques. "Le Cameroun et ses références: l'âme du peuple Duala." Unpublished manuscript.

———. *Doigts noirs: "Je fus Ecrivain-Interprète au Cameroun."* Montreal: Les éditions à la page, 1963.

Lambert, John. *Betrayed Trust: Africans and the Colonial State in Natal*. Scottsville, South Africa: University of Natal Press, 1995.

Landau, Paul. *The Realm of the Word: Language, Gender and Christianity in a Southern African Kingdom*. Portsmouth, N.H.: Heinemann, 1995.

———. "'Religion' and Christian Conversion in African History: A New Model." *Journal of Religious History* 23 (1999): 8–30.

Lange, Marie-France. *L'école au Togo: Processus de scolarisaion et institution de l'école en Afrique.* Paris: Karthala, 1999.

Larson, Pier. *History and Memory in the Age of Enslavement: Becoming Merina in Highland Madagascar, 1770–1822.* Portsmouth, N.H.: Heinemann, 2000.

Launay, Robert, and Benjamin Soares. "The Formation of an 'Islamic Sphere' in French Colonial West Africa." *Economy and Society* 28, no. 4 (1999): 497–519.

Law, R. "Human Sacrifice in Pre-Colonial West Africa." *African Affairs* 84 (1985): 53–87.

Lawrance, Benjamin N. "Bankoe v. Dome: Traditions and Petitions in the Ho-Asogli Amalgamation, British Mandated Togoland, 1919–1939." *Journal of African History* 46 (2005): 243–67.

———. "Language between Powers, Power between Languages: Further Discussion of Education and Policy in Togoland under the French Mandate, 1919–1945." *Cahiers d'Études Africaines* 41 (vols. 3–4), nos. 163–164 (2001): 517–39.

———. "Most Obedient Servants: The Politics of Language in German Colonial Togo." *Cahiers d'Études Africaines* 40 (vol. 3), no. 157 (2000): 489–524.

———. "*La Révolte de Femmes:* Economic Upheaval and the Gender of Political Authority in Lomé, Togo, 1931–33." *African Studies Review* 46 (2003): 43–67.

Lentz, Carola, and Paul Nugent. *Ethnicity in Ghana: The Limits of Invention.* New York: Palgrave, 2000.

Lepore, Jill. "Historians Who Love Too Much: Reflections on Microhistory and Biography." *Journal of American History* 88 (2001): 129–44.

Leservoisier, Olivier. "L'évolution foncière de la rive droite du fleuve Sénégal sous la colonisation (Mauritanie)." *Cahiers d'Études Africaines* 34, nos. 133–135 (1994): 55–83.

Lester, Alan. *Imperial Networks: Creating Identities in Nineteenth-Century South Africa and Britain.* London: Routledge, 2001.

Lévi-Strauss, Claude. *La pensée sauvage.* Paris: Plon, 1960.

Levine, Roger S. "Sable Son of Africa: The Many Worlds of an African Cultural Intermediary on the Eastern Cape Frontier of South Africa, 1800–1848." PhD diss, Yale University, 2004.

Lindsay, Lisa, and Stephan Miescher, eds. *Men and Masculinities in Modern Africa.* Portsmouth, N.H.: Heinemann, 2003.

Lindskog, Birger. *African Leopard Men.* Studia Ethnographica Upsaliensia 7. Uppsala: Almquist & Wiksells Boktryckeri AB, 1954.

Lovejoy, Paul E., and David Richardson. "The Business of Slaving: Pawning in Western Africa, ca. 1600–1800." *Journal of African History* 42, no. 1 (2001): 67–89.

Lunn, Joseph. *Memoirs of the Maelstrom: A Senegalese Oral History of the First World War.* Postsmouth, N.H.: Heinemann, 1999.

Maddox, Gregory. "The Ironies of 'Historia, Mila na Desturi za Wagogo.'" In Mnyampala, *The Gogo,* 1–34.

Maier, Donna J. E. "Slave Labor and Wage Labor in German Togo, 1885–1914."

In *Germans in the Tropics: Essays in German Colonial History,* edited by A. J. Knoll and L. H. Gann, 73–92. Westport, Conn.: Greenwood Press, 1987.

Mamdani, Mahmood. *Citizen and Subject: Contemporary Africa and the Legacy of Late Colonialism.* Princeton, N.J.: Princeton University Press, 1996.

Manchuelle, François. *Willing Migrants: Soninke Labor Diasporas, 1848–1960.* Athens: Ohio University Press, 1997.

Mandela, Nelson. *Long Walk to Freedom: The Autobiography of Nelson Mandela.* Boston: Little, Brown, 1994.

Mang'enya, Erasto A. M. *Discipline and Tears: Reminiscences of an African Civil Servant on Colonial Tanganyika.* Dar es Salaam: Dar es Salaam University Press, 1984.

Mann, Kristin, and Richard Roberts, eds. *Law in Colonial Africa.* Portsmouth, N.H.: Heinemann, 1991.

Marchal, J. Y., ed. *Chroniques d'un cercle de l'A.O.F.: Recueil d'archives du poste de Ouahigouya (Haute Volta), 1908–1941.* Paris: ORSTOM, 1980.

Marguerat, Yves. "A chacun son 'Chez' . . . Histoire des practiques foncières urbaines à Lomé." In Marguerat, *Dynamique urbaine,* 61–108.

———, ed. *Dynamique urbaine, jeunesse et Histoire au Togo: Articles et documents, 1984–1993.* Lomé: Presses de l'Université du Bénin, 1999.

———. "Histoire et société urbaine: Les années anglaises de Lomé (1914–1920), une période méconnue et pourtant decisive." *Cahiers d'Études Africaines* 39 (vol. 2), no. 154 (1998): 409–32.

———. "La naissance d'une capitale africaine: Lomé." In Marguerat, *Dynamique urbaine,* 17–40.

Marks, Shula. *The Ambiguities of Dependence in South Africa: Class, Nationalism, and the State in Twentieth-Century Natal.* Baltimore: Johns Hopkins University Press, 1986.

Martin, Benjamin F. "The Courts, the Magistrature, and Promotions in Third Republic France, 1871–1914." *American Historical Review* 87, no. 4 (1982): 977–1009.

Martin, Robert. *Personal Freedom and the Law in Tanzania: A Study in Socialist State Administration.* Nairobi: Oxford University Press, 1974.

Mason, Michael. "The History of Mr. Johnson: Progress and Protest in Northern Nigeria, 1900–1921." *Canadian Journal of African Studies* 27, no. 2 (1993): 196–217.

Mayer, Phillip, and Iona Mayer. "Land Law in the Making." In *African Law: Adaptation and Development,* edited by Hilda Kuper and Leo Kuper, 51–78. Berkeley: University of California Press, 1965.

Mbaye, Saliou. "Cadis et interprètes de l'administration colonial au Sénégal, 1850–1911." Paper presented at the Law, Colonialism, and Intermediaries in Africa workshop, Stanford University, May 20, 2003.

Mboya, Paul. *Utawala na Maendeleo ya Local Government South Nyanza, 1926–1957.* Nairobi: East African Literature Bureau, 1959.

McCall, J. A. G. "Comment on the 'Leopard' Killings." *Africa* 56 (1986): 441–45.

McClendon, Thomas. "Coercion and Conversation: African Voices in the Making of Customary Law in Natal." In *The Culture of Power in Southern Africa: Essays on State Formation and the Political Imagination,* edited by Clifton Crais, 49–63. Portsmouth, N.H.: Heinemann, 2003.

———. "The Man Who Would Be *Inkosi:* Civilising Missions in Shepstone's Early Career." *Journal of Southern African Studies* 30 (2004): 251–70.

McClure, James. *Snake.* New York: Harper & Row, 1976.

McGowan, Patrick J., and Patrick Bolland. *The Political and Social Elite of Tanzania: An Analysis of Social Background Factors.* Syracuse, N.Y.: Syracuse University, Program of Eastern African Studies, 1971.

McGowan, Winston. "Fula Resistance to French Expansion into Futa Jallon, 1889–1896." *Journal of African History* 22 (1981): 245–61.

Merryman, J. H. *The Civil Law Tradition: An Introduction to the Legal Systems of Western Europe and Latin America.* Stanford, Calif.: Stanford University, 1969.

Mianda, Gertrude. "Colonialism, Education, and Gender Relations in the Belgian Congo: The *Evolué* Case." In Allman, Geiger, and Musisi, *Women in African Colonial Histories,* 144–63.

Mnyampala, Mathias E. *The Gogo: History, Customs, Traditions.* Edited, introduced, and translated by Gregory Maddox. Armonk, N.Y.: M. E. Sharpe, 1995.

Monson, Jaimie. "Claims to History and the Politics of Memory in Southern Tanzania, 1940–1960." *International Journal of African Historical Studies* 33 (2000): 543–65.

Moore, Donald, and Richard Roberts. "Listening for Silences." *History in Africa* 17 (1990): 319–25.

Moore, Sally Falk. "Individual Interests and Organizational Structures: Dispute Settlements as 'Events of Articulation.'" In *Social Anthropology and Law,* edited by Ian Hamnett, 159–88. London: Academic Press, 1977.

———. *Social Facts and Fabrications: "Customary" Law on Kilimanjaro, 1880–1980.* Cambridge: Cambridge University Press, 1986.

Morgenthau, Ruth S. *Political Parties in French-Speaking West Africa.* Oxford: Clarendon, 1964.

Morris, H. F., and James S. Read. *Indirect Rule and the Search for Justice: Essays in East African Legal History.* London: Oxford University Press, 1972.

Mostert, Noel. *Frontiers: The Epic of South Africa's Creation and the Tragedy of the Xhosa People.* London: Jonathan Cape, 1992.

Mueller, Susanne D. "The Historical Origins of Tanzania's Ruling Class." *Canadian Journal of African Historical Studies* 15 (1981): 459–97.

Mungeam, G. H. *Kenya: Select Historical Documents, 1884–1923.* Nairobi: East African Publishing House, 1978.

Murray, Corrin, and Peter Sanders. "Medicine Murder in Basutoland: Colonial Rule and Moral Crisis." *Africa* 70 (2000): 49–78.

Mutungi, O. *Legal Aspects of Witchcraft in East Africa.* Nairobi: East African Publishing House, 1977.

Naanen, B. B. B. "Economy within an Economy: The Manilla Currency, Exchange Rate Instability and Social Conditions in South-Eastern Nigeria, 1900–48." *Journal of African History* 34 (1993): 425–46.

Napo, Pierre Alì. "Le Togo à l'époque allemande (1884–1914)." PhD diss., Université de Paris–La Sorbonne, 1996.

Nasson, Bill. "What They Fought As: Black Citizens of the Cape Colony and the Experience of Imperial Wars, 1899–1918." Paper presented at the Mellon Sawyer Seminar on Settler Colonialism, Racial Formation, and Partial Sovereignty in North America, South Africa, and Israel/Palestine, Stanford University, March 2004.

Newbury, Colin. *Patrons, Clients, and Empire: Chieftaincy and Over-Rule in Asia, Africa, and the Pacific.* Oxford: Oxford University Press, 2003.

Niang, Boubacar. "La Politique coloniale de gestion des personnels indigènes de l'administration publique de la fin de la conquête à la veille de la deuxième guerre mondiale, 1890–1930: Le cas de la colonie du Sénégal." PhD diss., University of Dakar, 1999.

Nicolson, I. F. *The Administration of Nigeria, 1900–1960: Men, Methods, and Myths.* Oxford: Clarendon Press, 1969.

Niranjana, Tejaswini. *Siting Translation: History, Post-structuralism, and the Colonial Context.* Berkeley: University of California Press, 1992.

Noah, M. E. "The Ibibio Union, 1928–1966." *Canadian Journal of African Studies* 21 (1987): 38–53.

Noirot, Ernest. *À travers le Fouta-Diallon et le Bambouc (Soudan occidental), souvenirs de voyage.* Paris: M. Dreyfous, 1885.

Nussbaum, Manfred. *Togo—Eine Musterkolonie?* Berlin, GDR: 1962.

Nwaka, G. "The Ibibio Union and Colonial Change." *Nigeria Magazine* 146 (1983): 85–94.

——. "The 'Leopard' Killings of Southern Anang, Nigeria, 1943–48." *Africa* 56 (1986): 417–45.

Nye, Joseph S. *Pan-Africanism and East African Integration.* Cambridge, Mass.: Harvard University Press, 1965.

Okon, S. E. "The Man-Leopard Society in Annang/Ibibioland of Old Calabar Province, 1939–1948: An Anti-Colonial Movement." PhD diss., University of Calabar, 1982.

Okonkwo, Rina. "The Nigeria Civil Service Union, 1919–1922." *International Journal of African Historical Studies* 26 (1993): 613–15.

Olivier de Sardan, Jean-Pierre. *Les sociétés Songhai-Zarma (Niger-Mali): Chefs, guerriers, esclaves, paysans.* Paris: Karthala, 1984.

Osborn, Emily Lynn. "Circle of Iron: African Colonial Employees and the Interpretation of Colonial Rule in French West Africa." *Journal of African History* 44 (2003): 29–50.

——. "'Rubber Fever,' Commerce and French Colonial Rule in Upper Guinée, 1890–1913." *Journal of African History* 45, no. 3 (2004): 445–65.

Osei-Tutu, John Kwadwo. "Petitions and Other Forms of 'Peaceful' Protest between State and Society on the Gold Coast (Ghana), 1860–1920." Unpublished manuscript.

Oyono, Ferdinand. *Houseboy.* London: Heinemann, 1966.

Peel, J. D. Y. *Ijeshas and Nigerians: The Incorporation of a Yoruba Kingdom, 1880s–1970s.* African Studies Series 39. Cambridge: Cambridge University Press, 1983.

Peires, Jeffrey. *The Dead Will Arise: Nongqawuse and the Great Xhosa Cattle-Killing Movement of 1856–7.* Johannesburg: Ravan Press, 1989.

———. *The House of Phalo: A History of the Xhosa People in the Days in Their Independence.* Johannesburg: Ravan Press, 1989.

Perham, Margery, ed. *Ten Africans.* London: Faber & Faber, 1936.

Peterson, Derek R. *Creative Writing: Translation, Bookkeeping, and the Work of Imagination in Colonial Kenya.* Portsmouth, N.H.: Heinemann, 2004.

———. "Translating the Word: Dialogism and Debate in Two Gikuyu Dictionaries." *Journal of Religious History* 23 (1999): 31–50.

Peterson, Derek, and Jean Allman. "Introduction: New Directions in the History of Missions in Africa." *Journal of Religious History* 23 (1999): 1–7.

Peterson, Edward N. *The Limits of Hitler's Power.* Princeton, N.J.: Princeton University Press, 1969.

Phillips, Arthur. "The Future of Customary Law in Africa." In *The Future of Customary Law in Africa; L'avenir du droit coutumier en Afrique,* 88–101. Leiden: Universitaire Pers Leiden, 1956.

———. *Report on Native Tribunals.* Nairobi: Colony and Protectorate of Kenya, 1944.

Piault, Marc H. *La colonisation: Rupture ou parenthèse?* Paris: l'Harmattan, 1984.

Plaatje, Sol. *Native Life in South Africa: Before and since the European War and the Boer Rebellion.* London: P. S. King, 1916; New York: Negro University Press, 1969.

———. *Sechuana Proverbs with Literal Translations and Their European Equivalents = Diane tsa secoana le malel a sekgooa a a dumalanang naco.* Kimberley, South Africa: Sol. Plaatje Education Trust, 2002.

Pratt, Cranford. *The Critical Phase in Tanzania, 1945–1968: Nyerere and the Emergence of a Socialist Strategy.* Cambridge: Cambridge University Press, 1976.

Ranger, Terence. "The Invention of Tradition in Colonial Africa." In *The Invention of Tradition,* edited by Eric Hobsbawm and Terence Ranger, 211–61. Cambridge: Cambridge University Press, 1983.

———. "The Invention of Tradition Revisited: The Case of Colonial Africa." In *Legitimacy and the State in Twentieth-Century Africa,* edited by Terence Ranger and Olufemi Vaughan, 62–111. Oxford: Palgrave Macmillan, 1992.

Raphael, Vincente. *Contracting Colonialism: Translation and Christian Conversion in Tagalog Society under Early Spanish Rule.* Quezon City: Ateneo de Manila University Press, 1988; Durham, N.C.: Duke University Press, 1993.

Rapport annuel au Conseil de la Société des Nations sur l'administration sous mandat du territoire du Cameroun. Paris: Imprémerie général Lahare, 1923–39.

Rathbone, Richard. "The Gold Coast, the Closing of the Atlantic Slave Trade, and Africans of the Diaspora." In *Slave Cultures and the Cultures of Slavery*, edited by Stephan Palmie, 55–66. Knoxville: University of Tennessee Press, 1995.

———. *Murder and Politics in Colonial Ghana.* New Haven, Conn.: Yale University Press, 1993.

Report by His Majesty's Government to the Trusteeship Council of the United Nations on the Administration of Tanganyika Territory for the Year 1960. London: HMSO, 1961.

Report of the Commission on the Civil Services of the East African Territories and the East African High Commission, 1953–54. London: HMSO, 1954.

Rich, Jeremy. "Troubles at the Office: Clerks, State Authorities, and Social Conflict in Gabon, 1920–1945." *Canadian Journal of African Studies* 38 (2004): 58–87.

Richards, Thomas. *The Imperial Archive: Knowledge and Fantasy of Empire.* London: Verso, 1993.

Roberts, Richard L. "The Case of Fama Mademba Sy and the Ambiguities of Legal Jurisdiction in Early Colonial French Soudan." In Mann and Roberts, *Law in Colonial Africa*, 184–204.

———. "Representation, Structure and Agency: Divorce in the French Sudan during the Early 20th Century." *Journal of African History* 40 (1999): 389–410.

———. "Text and Testimony in the Tribunal de Première Instance, Dakar, during the Early Twentieth Century." *Journal of African History* 31 (1990): 447–63.

Roberts, Richard L., and Kristin Mann. "Law in Colonial Africa." In Mann and Roberts, *Law in Colonial Africa*, 3–60.

Robinson, David. *Chiefs and Clerics: The History of Abdul Bokar Kan and Futa Toro, 1853–1891.* Oxford: Oxford University Press, 1975.

———. "Ethnography and Customary Law in Senegal." *Cahiers d'Études Africaines* 32 (vol. 2), no. 126 (1992): 221–37.

———. *Paths of Accommodation: Muslim Societies and French Colonial Authority in Senegal and Mauritania, 1880–1920.* Athens: Ohio University Press, 2000.

Robinson, David, and Jean-Louis Triaud. *Le temps des marabouts: Itinéraires et stratégies islamiques en Afrique occidentale française v.1880–1960.* Paris: Karthala, 1997.

Robinson, Douglas. *Translation and Empire: Postcolonial Theories Explained.* Manchester: St. Jerome, 1996.

———. *What Is Translation? Centrifugal Theories, Critical Interventions.* Kent, Ohio: Kent State University Press, 1997.

Robinson, Ronald. "Non-European Foundations of European Imperialism: Sketch for a Theory of Collaboration." In *Studies in the Theory of Imperialism*, edited by Roger Owen and Bob Sutcliffe, 117–42. London: Longman, 1972.

Robinson, R. E. "The Administration of African Customary Law." *Journal of African Administration* 1 (1949): 158–76.

Rogers, Susan Geiger. "The Search for Political Focus on Kilimanjaro: A History of Chagga Politics, 1916–1952." PhD diss., University of Dar es Salaam, 1972.

Sabatier, Peggy Roark. "Educating a Colonial Elite: The William Ponty School and Its Graduates." PhD diss., University of Chicago, 1977.

Samoff, Joel. *Tanzania: Local Politics and the Structure of Power.* Madison: University of Wisconsin Press, 1974.

Sanankoua, Bintou. "Hampâté Bâ (v. 1900–1991)." In Robinson and Triaud, *Le temps des marabouts*, 395–411.

Sanneh, Lamin. *Translating the Message: The Missionary Impact on Culture.* Maryknoll, N.Y.: Orbis Books, 1989.

Sarr, Dominique. "La chamber spéciale d'homologation de la cour d'appel de l'AOF et les coutumes pénales de 1903 à 1920." *Annales Africaines* 1 (1974): 101–15.

Schmidt, Elizabeth. *Peasants, Traders, and Wives: Shona Women in the History of Zimbabwe, 1870–1939.* Portsmouth, N.H.: Heinemann, 1992.

Schmitz, Jean. "Cités noires: Les républiques villageoises du Fuuta Tooro (Vallée du fleuve Sénégal)." *Cahiers d'Études Africaines* 34, nos. 133–135 (1994): 419–60.

Schnapper, Bernard. "Les Tribunaux musulmans et la politique coloniale au Sénégal, 1830–1914." *Revue historique de droit français et étranger* 39 (1961): 90–128.

Schuerkens, Ulrike. *Du Togo allemande aux Togo et Ghana independents: Changement social sous régime colonial.* Paris: L'Harmattan, 2001.

Scott, James C. *Domination and the Arts of Resistance: Hidden Transcripts.* New Haven, Conn.: Yale University Press, 1990.

———. *Seeing like a State: How Certain Schemes to Improve the Human Condition Have Failed.* New Haven, Conn.: Yale University Press, 1998.

———. *Weapons of the Weak: Everyday Forms of Peasant Resistance.* New Haven, Conn.: Yale University Press, 1985.

Sebald, Peter. *Togo, 1884–1914: Eine Geschichte der deutschen "Musterkolonie" auf der Grundlage amtlicher Quellen.* Berlin: Akademie, 1987.

Shadle, Brett L. "Bridewealth and Female Consent: Marriage Disputes in African Courts, Gusiiland, Kenya." *Journal of African History* 44 (2003): 257–59.

———. "Changing Traditions to Meet Current Alerting Conditions: Customary Law, African Courts and the Rejection of Codification in Kenya, 1930–1960." *Journal of African History* 40 (1999): 411–31.

Shakespeare, William. *Dintshontso tsa bo-Juisue Kesara.* Translated by Sol. T. Plaatje. Kimberley, South Africa: Sol. Plaatje Education Trust, 2002.

Sharkey, Heather J. *Living with Colonialism: Nationalism and Culture in the Anglo-Egyptian Sudan.* Berkeley: California University Press, 2003.

Sibeud, Emmanuelle. "La naissance de l'ethnographie africaniste en France avant 1914." *Cahiers d'Études Africaines* 34, no. 136 (1994): 639–58.

———. *Une science impériale pour l'Afrique? La construction des saviors africanistes en France, 1878–1930.* Paris: Éd. de l'École des hautes études en sciences sociales, 2002.

Sidibé, Mamby. "Coutumier du cercle de Kita." *Bulletin du Comité d'études historiques et scientifiques de l'AOF,* 15 (1932): 72–177.

———. "Monographie régionale. Le Fada N'Gourma." *Bulletin de l'enseignement de l'Afrique Occidentale française* (June 1918): 111–30.

Sissoko, Fily Dabo. *La savane rouge.* Avignon: Presses universelles, 1962.

Smith, John. "The Relationship between the British Political Officer to His Chief in Northern Nigeria," in Crowder and Ikime, *West African Chiefs,* 14–22.

Soga, John Henderson. *The Ama-Xosa: Life and Customs.* Lovedale, South Africa: Lovedale Press, 1931.

Sow, Alpha Ibrahim. *Inventaire du fonds Amadou Hampâté Bâ.* Paris: Klincksieck, 1970.

Soyinka, Wole. *Isarà.* New York: Random House, 1989.

Spear, Thomas. "Neo-Traditionalism and the Limits of Invention in British Colonial Africa." *Journal of African History* 44 (2003): 3–27.

Spivak, Gayatri. "The Rani of Simur: An Essay in Reading the Archives." *History and Theory* 24 (1985).

Stahl, Kathleen. *Tanganyika: Sail in the Wilderness.* The Hague: Mouton, 1961.

Stam, Robert. *Subversive Pleasures: Bakhtin, Cultural Criticism, and Film.* Baltimore: Johns Hopkins University Press, 1989.

Stapleton, Timothy. *Maqoma: Xhosa Resistance to Colonial Advance, 1798–1873.* Johannesburg: Jonathan Ball, 1994.

Steinberg, Johnny. *Midlands.* Johannesburg: Jonathan Ball, 2002.

Stoecker, Helmuth. "The Position of Africans in the German Colonies." In *Germans in the Tropics: Essays in German Colonial History,* edited by Arthur J. Knoll and Lewis Gann, 119–29. New York: Greenwood Press, 1987.

Summers, Carol. *Colonial Lessons: Africans' Education in Southern Rhodesia, 1918–1940.* Portsmouth, N.H.: Heinemann, 2002.

Suret-Canale, Jean. "The Fouta-Djalon Chieftaincy." In Crowder and Ikime, *West African Chiefs,* 79–97.

———. *French Colonialism in Tropical Africa, 1900–1945.* Translated by Till Gotteiner. London: C. Hurst, 1971.

Theal, George McCall. *History of South Africa from 1795 to 1872.* London: George Allen & Unwin, 1902.

Thompson, Dorothy. *The Chartists.* London: Temple Smith, 1984.

Thompson, E. P. *Customs in Common.* London: Merlin, 1993.

———. *The Making of the English Working Class.* Harmondsworth, U.K.: Penguin, 1968.

Thornton, John K. *Kongolese Saint Anthony: Dona Beatriz Kimpa Vita and the Antonian Movement, 1684–1706.* Cambridge: Cambridge University Press, 1998.

Throup, David. "Crime, Politics and the Police in Colonial Kenya, 1939–63." In Anderson and Killingray, *Policing the Empire,* 127–57.

Tordoff, William. *Government and Politics in Tanzania.* Nairobi: East African Literature Bureau, 1967.

Trocki, Carl. "Political Structures in the Nineteenth and Early Twentieth Centuries." In *The Cambridge History of Southeast Asia*, edited by Nicholas Tarling, vol. 2, *The Nineteenth and Twentieth Centuries*, 79-130. Cambridge: Cambridge University Press, 1993.

Trotha, Trutz von. *Koloniale Herrschaft: Zur soziologischen Theorie der Staatsenstehung am Beispiel des "Schutzgebietes Togo."* Tübingen: Mohr, 1994.

Turrittin, Jane. "Colonial Midwives and Modernizing Childbirth in French West Africa." In Allman, Geiger, and Musisi, *Women in African Colonial Histories*, 71-94.

Udoma, U. *The Story of the Ibibio State Union.* Ibadan, Nigeria: Spectrum Books, 1987.

Vail, Leroy, ed. *The Creation of Tribalism in South Africa.* Berkeley: University of California Press, 1989.

Van Onselen, Charles. *The Seed Is Mine: The Life of Kas Maine, a South African Sharecropper, 1894-1985.* New York: Hill & Wang, 1996.

Van Hoven, Ed. "Representing Social Hierarchy: Administrators-Ethnographers in the French Sudan—Delafosse, Monteil, and Labouret." *Cahiers d'Études Africaines* 30, no. 118 (1990): 179-98.

Venuti, Lawrence. *The Scandals of Translation: Towards an Ethics of Difference.* New York: Routledge, 1998.

———. *The Translator's Invisibility: A History of Translation.* New York: Routledge, 1995.

Verdon, Michel. *The Abutia Ewe of West Africa: A Chiefdom That Never Was.* New York: Mouton, 1986.

Vidal, M. "Rapport sur l'étude des terres indigènes au Fouta." *Bulletin du Comité d'études Historiques et Scientifiques de l'AOF* 18 (1935): 415-48.

Weber, Max. *Wirtschaft und Gesellschaft.* 5th ed. Tübingen: Mohr, 1976.

Welsh, David. *The Roots of Segregation: Native Policy in Colonial Natal, 1845-1910.* Cape Town: Oxford University Press, 1971.

Westcott, Nicholas J. "An East African Radical: The Life of Erica Fiah." *Journal of African History* 22 (1981): 85-101.

———. "The Impact of the Second World War on Tanganyika, 1939-1949." PhD diss., Cambridge University, 1982.

Westermann, Diedrich, ed. *Autobiographies d'Africains: Onze autobiographies d'indigènes originaires de diverses régions de l'Afrique et représentant des métiers et des degrés de culture différents.* Paris, Payot, 1943. Originally published as *Afrikaner erzählen ihr Leben* in 1938.

White, Owen. *Children of the French Empire: Miscegenation and Colonial Society in French West Africa, 1895-1960.* Oxford: Clarendon Press, 1999.

Who's Who in East Africa, 1963-1964. Nairobi: Marco Surveys, 1964.

Willan, Brian. *Sol Plaatje, South African Nationalist, 1876-1932.* London: Heinemann, 1984.

Williams, Thora. *Gold Coast Diaries: Chronicles of Political Officers in West Africa, 1900–1919.* Edited by A. H. M. Kirk-Greene. New York: Radcliffe Press, 2000.

Willis, Justin. "The Administration of Bonde, 1920–1960: A Study in the Implementation of Indirect Rule in Tanganyika." *African Affairs* 92, no. 366 (1993): 53–67.

Wilson, Gordon. *Luo Customary Law and Marriage Law Customs.* Nairobi: Colony and Protectorate of Kenya, 1961.

Wilson, Monica. *The Interpreters.* Grahamstown, South Africa: 1820 Settlers' National Monument Foundation, 1972.

Wirz, Albert. "Körper, Raum und Zeit der Herrschaft." In *Alles unter Kontrolle: Disziplinierungsprozesse im kolonialen Tansania, 1850–1960,* edited by Albert Wirz, Andreas Eckert, and Katrin Bromber. Cologne: Köppe, 2003.

Worger, William. "Parsing God: Conversations about the Meaning of Words and Metaphors in Nineteenth-Century Southern Africa." *Journal of African History* 42 (2001): 417–47.

Young, Crawford. *The African Colonial State in Comparative Perspective.* New Haven, Conn.: Yale University Press, 1994.

Young, Ronald, and Henry Fosbrooke. *Land and Politics among the Luguru of Tanganyika.* London: Routledge & Kegan Paul, 1960.

Contributors

MAURICE NYAMANGA AMUTABI is the Deputy Vice-Chancellor (Academic Affairs) at Kisii University in Kenya. He was formerly a Fulbright Fellow in the Department of History, University of Illinois at Urbana–Champaign, where he completed his PhD. Dr. Amutabi has also taught at the Catholic University of Eastern Africa in Nairobi, Kenya, Central Washington University in the United States, and Moi University in Kenya. He has published essays in edited volumes and his articles have appeared in *African Studies Review, Canadian Journal of African Studies*, and *Jenda: A Journal of Culture and African Women Studies*. He is the coauthor (with E. M. Were) of *Nationalism and Democracy for People-Centered Development in Africa* (Moi University Press, 2000). His coedited volume *Regime Change and Succession Politics in Africa* was published by Routledge Press in 2013.

RALPH A. AUSTEN is professor emeritus of African history at the University of Chicago. His current research focuses on the political economy and cultural dimensions of European overseas expansion, including the comparative study of indigenous agents of colonial regimes in Africa and South Asia. His works include *In Search of Sunjata: The Mande Epic as History, Literature and Performance* (editor, Indiana University Press, 1998); *Middlemen of the Cameroons Rivers: The Duala and Their Hinterland, ca. 1600–ca. 1960* (coauthor, with Jonathan Derrick, Cambridge University Press, 1998); *Trans-Saharan Africa in World History* (Oxford University Press, 2010); and "Finding the Historical Wangrin or the Banality of Virtue," *Journal of West African History* (2015).

ANDREAS ECKERT is a professor of African history at Humboldt University Berlin and Director of the International Research Center "Work and Human Life Course in Global History." He has published numerous articles on nineteenth- and twentieth-century African history and historiography. He is the author of *Die Duala und die Kolonialmächte* (1991); *Grundbesitz, Landkonflikte und kolonialer Wandel: Douala 1880 bis 1960* (1999); *Kolonialismus* (2006); and *Herrschen und*

Verwalten: Afrikanische Bürokraten, staatliche Ordnung und Politik in Tanzania, 1920–1970 (2007).

RUTH GINIO is a senior lecturer in the Department of History at Ben Gurion University of the Negev. She is the author of *French Colonialism Unmasked: The Vichy Years in French West Africa* (University of Nebraska Press, 2006); the coeditor with Pal Ahluwalia and Louise Bethlehem of *Violence and Non-Violence in Africa* (Routledge, 2007); and the coeditor with Efrat Ben Zéev and Jay Winter of *Shadows of War: A History of Silence in the Twentieth Century* (Cambridge University Press, 2010). She is completing a book manuscript on the French armed forces, African soldiers, and decolonization in French West Africa.

JEAN-HERVÉ JÉZÉQUEL received his PhD at l'École des Hautes Études en Sciences Sociales, Paris, for his dissertation on West African school teachers who graduated from the École Normale William Ponty and who went on to play significant roles in shaping the colonial order. He has published widely on the production of knowledge during the colonial period in French West Africa. He is a Senior Analyst at International Crisis Group.

MARTIN KLEIN is a professor emeritus at the University of Toronto. He is a specialist on Francophone West Africa and has written on Islam, French colonial rule, and the history of slavery. He is the author of *Islam and Imperialism in Senegal: Sine Saloum 1847–1914* (Stanford University Press, 1968) and *Slavery and Colonial Rule in French West Africa* (Cambridge University Press, 1998). He is the editor of *Breaking the Chains: Slavery, Bondage and Emancipation in Modern Africa and Asia* (University of Wisconsin Press, 1993); *Women and Slavery in Africa* (University of Wisconsin Press, 1983), with Clare Robertson; and *African Voices on Slavery and the Slave Trade* (Cambridge University Press, 2013), with Sandra Greene and Alice Bellagamba.

BENJAMIN N. LAWRANCE is the Hon. Barber B. Conable, Jr. Endowed Chair in International Studies and a professor of history and anthropology at the Rochester Institute of Technology. His research interests include comparative and contemporary slavery, human trafficking, cuisine and globalization, human rights, refugee issues, and asylum policies. His nine books include *Amistad's Orphans: An Atlantic Story of Children, Slavery, and Smuggling* (Yale University Press, 2014); *Adjudicating Refugee and Asylum Status: The Role of Witness, Expertise, and Testimony* (Cambridge University Press, 2015), with Galya Ruffer; and *African Asylum at a Crossroads: Activism, Expert Testimony, and Refugee Rights* (Ohio University Press, 2015), with Iris Berger, Tricia Redeker Hepner, Joanna Tague, and Meredith Terretta.

ROGER S. LEVINE is an associate professor of history at Sewanee: The University of the South. His essay on the environmental history of colonial warfare in southern Africa appeared in *Natural Enemy, Natural Ally: Toward an Environmental History of War* (Oregon State University Press, 2004), and he has published articles on Jan Tzatzoe in *Kronos: Southern African Histories* and the *African Historical Review*. Yale University Press published his narrative history *A Living Man from Africa: Jan Tzatzoe, Xhosa Chief and Missionary, and the Making of Nineteenth-Century South Africa* in 2010. His current project is a study of race, gender, and popular culture in segregation-era South Africa.

SALIOU MBAYE is the director emeritus of the Senegalese National Archives and holds a PhD from the University of Chartres in archival science and history. He currently teaches at the Ecole des Bibliothécaires, Archivistes et Documentalistes (EBAD), Université Cheikh Anta Diop in Dakar. In addition to his many published archival guides, Mbaye has edited *AOF: Réalités et heritages: Sociétés ouest-africaines et order colonial, 1895–1960* (Dakar, 1997), with Charles Becker and Ibrahima Thioub; *Histoire des institutions coloniales françaises en Afrique de l'Ouest (1816–1960)* (Dakar, 1991); and *Histoire des institutions contemporaines du Sénégal (1956–2000)* (Dakar, 2012).

THOMAS MCCLENDON is a professor of history at Southwestern University in Texas. A specialist in the history of colonial and settler-state South Africa, he is the coeditor (with Clifton Crais) of *The South Africa Reader: History, Culture, Politics* (Duke University Press, 2014) and the author of *White Chief, Black Lords: Shepstone and the Colonial State in Natal, South Africa, 1845–1878* (University of Rochester Press, 2010) and *Genders and Generations Apart: Labor Tenants and Customary Law in Segregation-Era South Africa* (Heinemann, 2002).

EMILY LYNN OSBORN is an associate professor in the Department of History at the University of Chicago. She has published articles and book chapters on colonial intermediaries, French rule, colonial economies, and African labor history. Her first book, *Our New Husbands Are Here: Households, Gender, and Politics in a West African State from the Slave Trade to Colonial Rule*, was published by Ohio University Press in 2011. She is currently writing a book on the intertwined histories of artisanal aluminum production, technology, and energy use in West Africa.

DAVID PRATTEN is an associate professor at the African Studies Centre and Institute of Social and Cultural Anthropology, Oxford University, UK. He is the author of *The Man-Leopard Murders: History and Society in Colonial Nigeria* (Edinburgh University Press, 2007) and coedits *AFRICA: The Journal of the International African Institute*. His research focuses on youth, vigilantism, and masking.

RICHARD L. ROBERTS is the Frances and Charles Professor of History at Stanford University, where he also codirects the Center for African Studies. He has published widely on the social history of French West Africa, including

Slaves, Warriors, and Merchants: The State and the Economy in the Middle Niger Valley, 1700–1914 (Stanford University Press, 1987); *Two Worlds of Cotton: Colonialism and the Regional Economy of the French Soudan, 1800–1946* (Stanford University Press, 1996); and *African Disputes and Colonial Courts in the French Soudan, 1895–1912* (Heinemann, 2005). He has also coedited eight volumes, the most recent of which deal with domestic violence (with Emily Burrill and Benjamin Lawrance, 2010), Muslim family law in sub-Saharan Africa (with Shamil Jeppie and Ebrahim Moosa, 2010), trafficking in women and children (with Benjamin Lawrance, 2012), and forced marriage in Africa (with Anne Bunting and Benjamin Lawrance, forthcoming).

BRETT L. SHADLE is an associate professor of history at Virginia Tech. In addition to articles on various aspects of Kenyan history, he is the author of *"Girl Cases": Marriage and Colonialism in Gusiiland, Kenya, 1890–1970* (Heinemann, 2006) and *The Souls of White Folk: White Settlers in Kenya, 1900–1920s* (Manchester University Press, 2015). His current research deals with the history of refugees.

Index

Abak, 222–23, 225–27, 240, 245
Accra, Ghana, 101, 105, 110, 113
Achebe, Chinua, 56, 73, 277
Adewoye, Omoniyi, 99, 104–5, 109–10, 112–14
Adrar, 293
Afigbo, A. E., 14, 222
African Interior Church, 203, 210–13
African languages: administrators did not know local languages, 131, 278; Ewe, 100, 101, 102, 106, 109, 112; isi-Zulu, 18–19, 22, 77, 81, 85, 92; KiSwahili, 11, 14, 15, 23–24, 203, 206–8, 214–15, 218, 250, 260, 266; Lingala, 14, 23; Nguni, 92; Oluluyia, 213, 217; Wolof, 278; Xhosa, 17–18, 21, 79–80
African National Congress, 78
African soldiers, 15, 62, 130, 274
Akurang-Parry, K. O., 98
Alcock, Rauri, 77–78
Alexandre, Pierre, 57, 278
Alfaya, 58, 60
Alfa Yaya, 61, 67, 73, 75
Algeria, 119
Alimou, Baba, 60–62, 66, 70, 74
almamy, 58, 60–62, 68, 70
Amselle, Jean-Loup, 149
Ane (Ann), Hamat N'Diaye, 144, 292
Annang, 223–27, 231–32, 238–39, 242, 244, 246
anticorruption measures, 195. *See also* corruption

appeals, 96, 102, 104–8, 207, 212, 291; *chambre d'homologation*, 118, 119, 127, 133. *See also* courts
Apter, Emily, 204
Arabic, 14, 16, 23, 119, 122, 123, 290–94
Archinard, Louis, 143
Arochukwu, 227, 245
Asian employees, 254–57, 260
Asituywa, Caleb, 203, 208, 210, 213–15, 217, 219
assessors, 17, 115–21, 123–34. *See also* courts; customary law; customs; translation
Atieno-Odhiambo, E. S., 206
Atkins, C. Farquhar, 182, 186–87, 197
Atkins, Keletso, 11
Ayandele, E. A., 221

Bademba, Oumarou, 60, 68, 70, 73, 74, 76
Bafoulabé, 150
Bakel, 153
Ballantyne, Tony, 205
Bamako, 150, 157
Bamba, Ahmadou, 293
Bandiagara, 167, 169, 280
Banfora, 150
bargains of collaboration, 5–7, 10, 13, 15, 24, 57, 96–97, 111, 277, 283. *See also* strategies of accumulation and self promotion
Basoga, 29

Palmer, H. R., 11
parse, parsing, 12, 17, 21–22, 31. *See also* interpretation; translation
personnel files for employees, 289
Peterson, Derek, 40
petitions, petitioning, 98, 107, 108, 112, 254, 255
Phillips, Arthur, 182–83
Pine, Benjamin, 82, 88
Plaatje, Sol, 3, 78, 91
police, 82, 83, 216, 221, 267
polyglossia, 12
Ponty, Governor General William, 117, 122–23, 133, 294
production of knowledge about African societies, 4, 11, 85–87, 91, 140, 154, 162, 214, 265; linked codification, 139, 148, 153–55. *See also coutumiers;* ethnographic writing; invention of tradition
progressives, 181, 183–84, 187–88, 193, 196, 276. *See also* modernizers

qadi, 16, 119, 125, 290–93. *See also* courts
Qua Iboe River, 224–25
Quénum, Maximilien, 142, 149

Ranger, Terence, 15, 147
Rattray, R. S., 11
Rauch, 63–64, 74
resistance, 6, 7, 8, 97, 168, 250, 264. *See also* collaboration, collaborators
Rich, Jeremy, 280, 285
Richards, Audrey, 240
Roberts, Richard, 97–98, 105, 115, 204
Robinson, David, 16, 140, 291
Robinson, Ronald, 6–7, 131, 277
Roume, Governor General Ernest, 117, 126, 140

Saint-Louis, 12, 27, 32, 144, 150, 153, 289–94
Sakiliba, Niaka, 128, 129, 130
salaries, wages, 82, 84, 99, 104, 105, 108, 249, 253, 256–57, 262; cost of living, 254, 260, 266; fees, 95, 99, 104–5, 110; pensions, 254. *See also* bureaucracy

Salifou, Alioune, 70, 75–76
Sanja, Hudson, 188–90, 198–99
Sarakolle, 154
Sassandra, Cote d'Ivoire, 126, 134
Satourou, 27, 28, 68, 70
scandals, 5, 57, 71, 97, 102
Schmitz, Jean, 146
School for Chiefs' Sons and Interpreters, 12–13, 24, 150, 153, 275–76, 291
schools, 77, 149, 214; secondary, 256, 264, 276; universities, 78, 260, 264. *See also* education, colonial; education, mission
Scott, James, 8
Seck, Bou El Moghdad, 292, 293
segregation, 102, 254, 257. *See also* colonialism; white settlers
Séléty, 127
Selwyn-Clarke, Hilda, 262, 268
Senegal, 12, 16, 27, 57–59, 67, 71, 74, 76, 97, 105–6, 113, 141–45, 153–54, 275, 279, 281, 285, 289–92, 294–95
Senegal River, 143, 144
Sereer customary law, 125
Seventh Day Adventist Church, 183–85, 194
Shaka, 90
Shakespeare, William, 3, 263
Sharkey, Heather, 10
Shepstone, Theophilus, 11, 18–19, 22, 77, 79–93, 282
Sidibé, Mamby, 141–42, 148–55, 157–58, 281
Sidibé, Moro, 276, 279
Sierra Leone, 105
signarés, 27. *See also* women, African
Sine Saloum, 58, 73, 279
Sissoko, Fily Dabo, 141
Somerset, Governor, 43, 44
Soriya, 58, 60
South Africa, 3, 8, 17, 27, 30, 77–78, 92; Cape Colony, 78–79, 92; Eastern Cape, 78, 80–81, 88; KwaZulu-Natal, 77–82, 86–93; Transvaal, 89
southeastern Nigeria, 221, 222, 241, 243
South Kavirondo, 15, 181–84, 186, 193–94, 196–201

AFRICA AND THE DIASPORA
History, Politics, Culture

Nachituti's Gift: Economy, Society, and Environment in Central Africa
David M. Gordon

A Hill among a Thousand: Transformations and Ruptures in Rural Rwanda
Danielle de Lame

*Intermediaries, Interpreters, and Clerks: African Employees in the Making
   of Colonial Africa*
Edited by Benjamin N. Lawrance, Emily Lynn Osborn, and
   Richard L. Roberts

Antecedents to Modern Rwanda: The Nyiginya Kingdom
Jan Vansina

www.ingramcontent.com/pod-product-compliance
Lightning Source LLC
Chambersburg PA
CBHW071637270326
41928CB00010B/1956